# Children and Families
# in the Social Environment

# Children and Families in the Social Environment

## James Garbarino

*with:*

Robert H. Abramowitz

Joanne L. Benn

Mario Thomas Gaboury

Nancy L. Galambos

Anne C. Garbarino

Patricia A. Grandjean

Florence N. Long

Margaret C. Plantz

Aldine Publishing Company
New York

Consulting Editor: James K. Whittaker
Editor: Kyle Wallace
Project Editor: Barry Katzen
Managing Editor: Robin Solinger
Book Designer: Roberta Landi
Compositor: Maple-Vail
Printer and Binder: The Maple-Vail Book Manufacturing Group

First published 1982
Aldine Publishing Company
200 Saw Mill River Road
Hawthorne, New York 10532


ISBN 0-202-36029-6 cloth; 0-202-36030-X paper

Library of Congress Catalog Number 81-71342


Printed in the United States of America
10 9 8 7 6 5 4 3 2

To our families—past, present, and future

# Table of Contents

# Foreword

In *Children and Families in the Social Environment,* Garbarino and his colleagues have given us a gem of a book. It could become for the '80s and '90s what Erikson's classic, *Childhood and Society,* became for the '50s and '60s: a broadly gauged and integrative schema for understanding the developing child in his or her environmental settings, narrow or broad. It is evident that such a book is sorely needed when we consider that the rudderless direction of human behavior and human environment courses has been due to the interpretation of "human development theory" as "Freudian development theory" in social work and human services curricula. Those who find psychodynamic development constructs useful will not be disappointed by this present volume, which respects the notion of ego development while adding greatly to our knowledge of how the environment influences the developing child. Similarly, those who advocate a "systems approach" will appreciate how the authors have extended and deepened that perspective—in relation to biopsychosocial development—in ways that have countless implications for client practice. Make no mistake about it, this is a book about child development from the "outside in." As Erikson earlier shifted our focus from the intrapersonal to the interpersonal and the sociocultural, Garbarino and his associates paint an even broader landscape. They masterfully and convincingly demonstrate, through research and practice, how the smallest development contexts such as the family (here called "microsystems" following Bronfenbrenner's taxonomy) interact with and are influenced by such larger systems as the neighborhood, school, world of work, and general society. The authors go straight to the heart of the matter by examining how such cherished societal values as "independence" and "individualism" shape and direct the most basic and essential of the family's activities: the rearing of children. Through summarization of empirical research and by asking thoughtful questions, the authors provide a foundation for understanding human behavior in a social environment that is, at one and the same time, rigorous and relevant. In point of fact, this is a book with a definite point of view evidenced not simply in the final chapter on the "issue of human quality," but throughout the chapters as the authors draw from relevant research and practice examples to illustrate how the environment can support and enhance or, alternately, undermine good child development. Family advocates will not be disappointed either: this book is "pro-family" in the very best sense; that is, it talks about the kinds of supports and encouragements parents need to undertake that most difficult task in the real world of a highly mobile, highly technical society with all of its potential for "sociocultural risk."

Finally, this is a practical book for practical people. Garbarino, a developmental psychologist in the mold of his mentor, Urie Bronfenbrenner, writes in a straightforward, engaging style that will appeal to social work and other human services students and practitioners. Theory and empirical findings about children and families are always presented with an eye towards practical application. In fact, taken as a whole, this book is proof positive of Kurt Lewin's famous dictum that "there is nothing so practical as a good theory." The present authors have done much to translate and extend to the world of social work and human services the ecological perspective articulated by Lewin and elaborated by Bronfenbrenner. As "practical theorists" of their own day, Garbarino and his colleagues have succeeded in providing a benchmark volume in human behavior and social environment for all those whose professional calling involves the care, treatment, and nurture of children and their families.

James K. Whittaker
University of Washington
Seattle, Washington
August 1981

# Preface

"No man is an island" is a message that we need to hear repeated over and over again in this individualistic culture of ours. We Americans need to understand that our successes and our failures come to us as much by the efforts of others as they do by our own actions. The people close to us on a day-to-day basis play a large role in how well we channel our impulses into constructive activity, as well as in how we define our very self-concept. Likewise, people we may not know or even ever see exert significant influence over our lives through their institutional power and authority. This lesson on interdependence is vital to learn if we are to meet the environmental and political challenges of the 1980s.

Our success as *parents* depends in large measure upon the character and quality of the social environment in which we bear and raise our children. Likewise, as professional helpers we need to understand how the social environment works for children and families, and why it sometimes fails to work on their behalf. We need an appreciation for how the practitioner and the policymaker can cooperate with and enhance social support systems in the family's environment. This book sets out to relate basic knowledge about human development to the problems of social risk and opportunity in a manner that is accessible and useful to the professional helper or the student in training for a professional role.

To write this book, I assembled a group of talented professionals, all graduate students at The Pennsylvania State University. Each student shared special responsibility with me for at least one chapter, and all contributed to the overall writing of the book. Thus, this book reflects a collective orientation in form and process as well as content. The book is organic to the group, and its success is a credit to their collective wisdom and knowledge. As senior member of the group, I assume responsibility for its faults. No book can be all things and in every way complete, so I have taken responsibility for deciding what we would not say as well as much of what we would. Briefly, the individuals besides me involved in writing each chapter are as follows:

Chapter  1: Mario Thomas Gaboury
Chapter  2: Robert H. Abramowitz
Chapter  3: Robert H. Abramowitz
Chapter  4: Robert H. Abramowitz
Chapter  5: Patricia A. Grandjean and Robert H. Abramowitz
Chapter  6: Joanne L. Benn
Chapter  7: Nancy L. Galambos and Margaret C. Plantz
Chapter  8: Florence N. Long
Chapter  9: Mario Thomas Gaboury and Margaret C. Plantz
Chapter 10: Anne C. Garbarino

The Afterword is a very personal statement on my part.

We have tried to speak clearly, without jargon. As teachers all, we have sought to present ideas, principles, and human lessons first, and recite facts only second, as necessary to illustrate and validate our view of the issues. Each chapter contains research and practice capsules, questions for exploration, and annotated suggestions for further reading. We hope these will aid the student reader to make good use of the book.

They say an army travels on its stomach. It's fair to say that a book travels on its typing. We have been fortunate to be on the receiving end of some excellent help in preparing the successive drafts of this manuscript. We tip our hats to Alice Saxion and Kathie Hooven who made the whole project go. Thanks also to Joy Barger, Joanne Kempher, and Pamala Kennedy.

A number of people read the first draft of the manuscript and their comments and suggestions helped us to improve it. Our thanks to Susan Bates, Laura Dittmann, Eileen Furgeson, Marian Petroski, Stephen Smith, Karen Stierman, and Mary Ellen Yonushonis.

I also offer my thanks to Jim Whittaker, who "incited" this project and who has offered advice and counsel along the way.

James Garbarino
University Park, Pennsylvania
September 1981

# 1: An Introduction

## Beginning at the End, or Ending at the Beginning?

Where does one start in seeking an understanding of children and families in the social environment? With the processes of development that characterize the individual child as a biological organism? With the family as a social entity? With the environment as a network of social institutions and events? Where is the beginning of this chain of relationships that binds together child, parents, aunts, uncles, grandparents, friends, neighbors, communities, and professional helpers? And where is the end? It would be easy to cast aside the many interconnections and pretend that there is *just* the developing child, or *just* the family as a social unit, or *just* the community power structure, or *just* the professional delivering human services. It would be easy, but we believe it would not be enough. Rather, we seek to capture the whole tangled mass of relationships connecting child, family, and social environment.

Much of what makes us human beings is bound up in the social dimensions that shape and are shaped by our biology. As human beings we are social creatures: we need society and society needs each of us to function. The ancient Greek philosopher, Aristotle put it this way:

> He who is unable to live in society or who has no need because he is sufficient for himself, must be either a beast or a god.
>
> *(Politics)*

We are all neither beasts nor gods. Therefore, we must understand ourselves in a social context, in a society where we must sink or swim. In this book we consider how we swim, and why we sometimes sink.

1

## An Overview of Themes

The focal point of this book is the development of *competence*—the ability to succeed in specific social contexts. Of course, intelligence, or general "adaptivity" as psychologists often call it, plays a large part in determining whether or not one will handle situations competently. But there is more (McClelland, 1973). *Communication skills* are vitally important. One must be able to communicate accurately in word, look, or gesture. One must send and receive messages accurately. *Patience* is also important. Delaying one's response to a stimulus as long as it takes to respond effectively is a skill relevant to success in many situations. Likewise, it helps to have a reservoir of self-esteem and self-confidence to go along with social and intellectual abilities. We can call this generally positive orientation toward oneself and toward one's ability to master the world—*"ego development."*

Where does competence come from? How do people get it? By and large, they develop it in childhood, and their families play a large role in the process. Furthermore, within some general guidelines that we will consider as we go along, many different strategies and tactics lead to developing competence. Many alternate social arrangements are developmentally sound; they are different but genuinely equal. Therefore, we are led to a commitment to *pluralism,* to letting families utilize and pursue their different strategies and tactics for producing competent children within some common agreement on basic principles such as the need for love, affection, and acceptance. We respect diversity, but want to search for ways to ensure that where there really are general standards, all families can and do meet those standards. Pluralism implies diversity within some fundamental consensus or agreement on basic principles. Throughout this book we seek pluralist models of human development as a guide for professional helpers.

To do justice to our central themes—the development of competence and pluralism—we need to find some way to pull apart and then reassemble the complex interconnections among child, family, and social environment. We have found an intellectual tool for accomplishing this ambitious task. It is an ecological model of human development elaborated by human developmentalist Urie Bronfenbrenner. Bronfenbrenner's approach suits us well because:

1. It focuses on the developing child in the real world.
2. It pays a lot of attention to the social environment in its many diverse forms.

3. It recognizes the essentially active role of the individual—shaping as well as being shaped by social contexts.
4. It sees the social environment as a grand human experiment, and thus invites our efforts to improve it, to make it better, in short, to help.

## An Overview of Topics

With all this in mind, this book begins with a discussion of Bronfenbrenner's ecological model in Chapter 2. In Chapter 3 we expand upon the model to analyze the issue of social risk and opportunity for children. Chapter 4 looks at the family as the primary environment for children. In Chapters 5 and 6 we examine two fundamental topics: the child as a biological organism, and childbearing and child rearing. Chapter 7 explores the community and the neighborhood as environments for children. In Chapters 8 and 9 we outline how human services and social policy work with regard to children. Chapter 10 concludes the book by setting the issues of children, family, and social environment in the broader perspective of our society's history and future. Having reached the end, let's begin again with a more detailed introduction to these chapters.

### The Ecology of Human Development

Chapter 2 discusses several factors that influence developing individuals. Each of these can be tied to one or more situations or "contexts" within which people develop. *Contexts* of development are those regularly-occurring environmental settings that can affect development by presenting risks or opportunities. Some of the relevant developmental contexts are family, friendship groups, neighborhoods, schools, communities, states, and nations. We can arrange them on a scale from smallest (microsystems) to largest (macrosystems). Events that take place at each of these contextual levels have effects on children and their families.

Subsequent chapters concentrate on the various contexts more specifically. These more detailed analyses, however, should not detract from our explicit premise that the subsystems of the overall ecological system are inextricably interrelated, one with the other. We hope to demonstrate throughout this text the *interconnectedness* of the various actors and activities in the human ecology of the child. The degree of cooperation among these interconnected systems is a vital issue for those concerned with the quality or "habitability" of the social environment.

Contexts can be positive or negative influences on development. Depending upon the balance of the multiple factors (ranging from individual biological endowments to environmental forces), individuals or families are exposed to various types of developmental risk and opportunity. We introduce this notion of *sociocultural risk and opportunity* in Chapter 2. Later in Chapter 3, we elaborate on it in greater detail.

## Sociocultural Risk and Opportunity

Chapter 3 lays out more specifically the theme of sociocultural risk and opportunity. Disruption of the sociocultural systems that surround individual development results in the disruption of people's lives. This relationship is a basic equation in human development. Chapter 3 concentrates on relating the aspects of risk and opportunity to the social levels of the ecological system—from micro- to macro. For example, it considers the impact of smaller households in the United States, styles of raising children, emotional climates in the family, density of communities, local employment levels, conditions in the work place, national economic and political attitudes, and war, all as important contributors to or detractors from child and family development.

We undertake a discussion of pluralism in Chapter 3. Considered as a macrosystem issue, pluralism leads us to recognize that our culture is comprised of a diversity of traditions, each with its own strengths and weaknesses relative to any particular environmental condition. Our approach recognizes and respects the diversity of Americans. Pluralism stresses the importance of fostering the strengths in a people's special heritage. A pluralistic perspective helps us avoid imposing one cultural view upon another. It promotes tolerance and enhances the creative approaches available to human services workers and researchers. However, pluralism has its own set of challenges. Most important is gaining respect for diversity culture-wide, and divesting dominant groups of some decision-making power. Many of us tend to view "different" as meaning "less good," with the underlying danger that dominant beliefs, habits, and attitudes can be foisted unjustifiably on those with fewer numbers and less political clout.

## The Family as a Social System

The discussion of both risk and opportunity on the one hand and pluralism on the other leads us to the family. In Chapter 4 we move from bigger levels of analysis (cultures and societies) to inquire into a smaller level, the family—its various types and functions within our social system. Utilizing sociohistorical, cross-cultural, and family systems perspectives to understand the variety of views regarding families, we review some interesting patterns: First, we draw a distinction between the abstract notion of "family" (what families *should be* based on dominant views) versus the particular types of families that exist (the different ways families actually *are*). Crucial to an understanding of pluralism and environmental influences is appreciation of the conflicts that often result from the imposition of the abstract "ideal" family on specific "real" families.

Are families important? The simple fact that humans have created family units in various forms throughout history and across cultures suggests the answer to this question. Chapter 4 makes the case that families are the mediators between individuals and their society. The various forms families take are related to their adaptiveness to contextual constraints. As well, many changes in the sociocultural environment are responses to the collective force of families. Interplay between social systems is the key here.

We explore family systems in detail in this chapter, emphasizing models that consider relationships between families and their settings in terms of stages of family development. Families change both in size and structure. Therefore, it is inappropriate to view them as static entities. How do families work? This becomes a central question in light of the almost overwhelming and complicated array of pressures involved. Forces within families (e.g., family goals, and drives, and structure), and forces outside families (e.g., links to society, community/neighborhood make-up) are topics that we must consider.

## The Developing Child

In Chapter 5 we descend our analytical ladder still further to consider the developing organism—the child. Children have been viewed quite differently throughout history. Differing perceptions of children's abilities and developmental agendas have resulted in wholly different descriptions of and proscriptions for proper and healthy growth. Is the child basically innocent and to be taught, or inherently wicked and to be punished? Many questions like these pervade the history of childhood and contemporary issues such as child abuse.

At the individual level of analysis, the biological or physiological aspects of development assume a prominent position. The focus here is on the intricate interrelationship between individual make-up and environmental forces. Chapter 5 broadly reviews the stages of development from conception through prenatal—perinatal development, early-, middle-, and late-childhood. At each level, we discuss developmental landmarks (e.g., key changes and infant reactiveness, early language development, gender—identity, as well as in thinking ability and adolescent maturation). We introduce questions about the relative contribution of heredity and environment, and explore the relationships among biological, psychological, and social influences.

## Childbearing and Child Rearing

Individual development represents our basic unit of analysis. However, individual development is intertwined with the other, broader levels. Having suspended our primarily social concerns in Chapter 5, we return to them in Chapter 6. Chapter 6 begins our journey back up through the ecological system, with the eventual goal being a discussion of society in its largest sense. We revisit the family and investigate more specifically the most important family functions, the bearing and rearing of children.

In every culture, having a child is an important event celebrated in traditional folkways and institutionalized rituals. Also, the culturally defined correct manner of raising one's children is generally specified for parents and other caregivers. In this chapter, we are primarily concerned with the dynamics of parent-child relationships from childhood through adolescence. Chapter 5 supplied the child development foundation necessary for understanding parent–child interactions, and Chapter 6 relates this information about individual development to the child's first and primary context, the nuclear family.

Childbearing is the first topic we consider in this chapter. There are many influences on this miraculous event. Most births in the United States take place in a hospital, and this setting, with its related practices, exerts influence over the possibilities and probabilities of early experiences between parents and their children. However, not all hospitals are alike, and various forms of childbirth practices—some old, some new—are available. Each can have impact on the childbearing experience. This variety of possible practices involves changes in the physical setting (e.g., home-like hospital rooms and dimly lit delivery rooms), the psychological atmosphere (e.g., supportive versus insensitive) and the range of participants at each stage (e.g., dad's presence in the delivery room). The context of this birthing experience then is linked to early parent–child interaction, and to later parent–child relationships.

The child rearing section of this chapter picks up from the point of early experience to explore changes in parent–child interaction throughout the family's life-span. We discuss the emotional climate within a family, rearing styles, the roles of various participants, and other adult–child relationships in terms of their impact on the intellectual development and competencies of children and the various patterns of parent–child relationships that ensue. Again, we view the family as the basic unit of human experience embedded within a series of environmental contexts. We consider cultural and institutional constraints on the family to be quite important, and we recognize them as professional issues, for the family is the mediator of sociocultural risks and opportunities for children and parents.

## The Territory of Childhood

Chapters 5 and 6 offer a grounding in individual and interpersonal development, and thus provide a turning point in our analysis. We turn back to the task of understanding the social environment *around* families, having examined the social environment *within* families. Chapter 7 begins this process by focusing on the neighborhood and community levels of the ecology. Here we deal with the first wave of influence outside the family. As children are developing within families so families develop within neighborhoods and communities. Various attributes of these contexts affect the quality of a neighborhood as an environment for families. How densely populated is the area? What type of context for child development results from the design, amount, and level of maintenance of local housing? How active are family-supporting networks in the neighborhood?

American communities are not static in nature. They change, in response to their internal dynamics and in response to broader social forces. Changes have occurred in response to historical events like mass immigration and world wars. Local business and industry managers, politicians, and other "social influentials" make decisions that also result in changes. Communities respond to changing levels of ethnic influence, and many are experiencing increasing diversity and decreasing homogeneity. Communities are urban, suburban, and rural. They are old, new, and in between. Most of all, neighborhoods and communities are contexts within which families and children behave, grow, and develop. As we demonstrate, what goes on at this level of the social ecology has much to do with the positive or negative course that individual development takes.

## Developmental Issues in Human Services

Human service agencies and systems form an important link between families and neighborhoods, on the one hand, and state and national agendas for service delivery, on the other. Chapter 8 deals with many issues in the delivery of human services as they relate to the themes and concerns derived from our ecological analysis of developmental risk and opportunity. We delve into several issues in an effort to suggest some alternatives to conventional service practice. What is the proper role of the human service provider? What is the correct timing for intervention? What should be the scope of intervention? Where should a family's inalienable right to privacy begin, and is this threshold always the same? How are the costs of service delivery weighed against the benefits?

A brief historical background provides a perspective for discussing the present day politics of providing human services. These political, even philosophical, trends of thought have a great impact on the sort of practices and services that society and individual professionals see as legitimate. The nature of social supports, like many notions discussed in this book, is not a uniform and unchanging entity. Indeed, changes in attitudes result in changes in practices. Should we be "hands off" regarding our families, or rush in at the earliest sign of difficulty? What are the criteria for such decisions, and who is the proper decision-maker? What are the goals of the human services?

Families have the largest share of responsibility for producing competent members of society. Services provided to children and families by the state imply society's responsibility to compensate for forces in the family or beyond the family's control that by nature are detrimental to development. The interdependence issue arises again as we note the mutual obligations of family and state to improve and maintain healthy human development. We discuss new models for facilitating healthy development. Based in notions of shared responsibility, interdependence, and the strengths of people, we recommend a mix of formal and informal support and suggest various programmatic models.

## Social Policy, Children, and Their Families

Chapter 9 brings us to the point of discussing how the mechanics of human services and the conditions of risk and opportunity are rooted in social policy. Here we discuss the many problems of families and children as they relate to social policy at the broader levels of the social ecology and different institutions and agencies within it. New perspectives on contexts of development come into focus so that we include transportation authorities, big business, and government as actors in the family's life together. The decisions made in these contexts reverberate through communities, the workplace, and service agencies, eventually taking their toll on or providing support for children and their families.

After a description of the policy scene, we make some suggestions about how to influence policy makers. How does someone who has embraced an innovative approach go about encouraging its implementation? Although there is no single method to influencing policy, and, of course, nothing is guaranteed, there are some basic approaches. One is the systematic documentation of the problem. Following initial identification is the gathering of information about who is being affected, who makes the important decisions, and so on. The chapter concludes with a discussion of the most important aspect of policy intervention: personal commitment to improving the lives of children and their families.

## In Conclusion: The Issue Is Human Quality

Chapter 10 seeks to place our professional concern for the social environment of children and families in its broadest cultural and historical context. Where are we going as a society? Are we heading towards economic, political, and environmental disaster? Or, are we on the verge of cultural breakthroughs that will lead to a more humane, sane, and ecologically sustainable society? Is the current scene the precursor of an ugly future in which we turn our backs on children in favor of conspicuous materialistic consumption? Or, can we see the dawn of a brighter day? We think society's treatment of families will go a long way toward answering these questions. Chapter 10 explains our thinking.

## Afterword: What Does It Mean to Be Human?

Throughout this book we speak of human development. But what does it mean to be human? What is this humanness we are seeking to protect, to conserve, to nurture, and to enhance in our efforts as professionals? Although it takes us far beyond the day-to-day confines of social science and professional services, we cannot end without considering this biggest of questions. Therefore, we have included an afterword to briefly raise and discuss the question of humanness. We think the answer lies somewhere in our ability and obligation to wrestle with the issue of good and evil. We believe this discussion is a fitting conclusion to our book.


# Conclusion

Having mapped out our path through the complex tangle of human development in social context we are ready to begin our journey. The first step leads to our ecological perspective on human development in Chapter 2.

# Chapter 2

Was ist das Schwerste von allem?
Was dir das Leichste dunket,
    mit den Augen Zu sehen,
Was vor den Augen dir liegt.
                Goethe, *Xenien qus dem Nachlass* *#45*
(What is the most difficult of all?
That which seems to you the easiest,
To see with one's eyes
what is lying before them.)


What makes a person? This simple question lies before our eyes, but the answer is hard to see. Chapter 2 explores the ecology of human development, those forces in the person's environment that affect and influence development. This ecological approach includes not only the immediate family and home environment, but also the wider social and cultural world as it affects the child and family. Urie Bronfenbrenner's model of the human ecosystem guides our discussion, making connections between the child in the family and in the community and the larger society that surrounds him or her. The human ecosystem model is much like the study of the natural ecology, focusing on the interactions between subjects at various levels of the environment as they affect each other.

# The Ecology of
# Human Development

## Human Beings as Social Animals

By virtue of their helplessness in the first few years of life, human beings are dependent on others for their very survival. The developing infant's basic reality lies in the relationship he or she has to primary care givers—particularly the mother, in most families in most societies. It is impossible for individuals to exist independently of the influence of other people. Indeed, that which makes us human is our relatedness—linguistic, intellectual, economic, political, and religious. Aristotle correctly called us social animals.

We believe that any discussion of human development must consider the contexts or settings in which development occurs. Like the biologist who must study an animal in context by learning about the animal's habitat, sources of food, predators, and social practices, the complete study of people involves examining how people live and grow in the social wild. The term "environment" here includes everything outside the organism. The developing child's setting includes family, friends, neighborhood, and school, as well as less immediate forces such as laws, social attitudes, and institutions that directly or indirectly affect the child. The result of these forces acting on the individual is called "environmental press."

"Environmental press" is the combined influence of forces working in a setting to shape the behavior and development of people in that setting. Environmental press arises from the circumstances confronting and surrounding an individual that generate psychosocial momentum and tend to guide that individual in a particular direction. As we shall see, the child's environment has specific physical dimensions, but it has multiple facets and multiple levels and is a complex network of forces. Our orientation to context and the interaction between organism and environment defines an ecological perspective, and like all fields using an ecological framework, we look beyond the individual organism to the organism's environment for questions and explanations about the organism's behavior and development. We do so from a tradition exemplified by developmentalist Urie Bronfenbrenner.

## Experiments by Nature and Design

Bronfenbrenner represents a compelling "fourth force" for students of human development and social service practitioners (with the first three "forces" having behaviorist, psychodynamic, and humanistic perspectives).

Until recently, it could hardly be said that the experimental ecology of human development was a systematic theoretical conception. Indeed, it did not aspire to the status of a theory as we use the term in speaking of Freud's psychoanalytic theory, Rogers' humanistic theory, Piaget's cognitive theory, or Skinner's reinforcement theory. Rather, it was an emerging critique of conventional developmental psychology; a critique of what it studied and how it studied it. It then became an effort to define a field of inquiry, and its principal use has been as a framework for organizing knowledge, generating research questions and evaluating social policy (e.g., in the areas of child maltreatment, day care, and handicapped children). We will use it in this way throughout this text.

From efforts to understand issues of social policy and professional practice arose a set of propositions about the study of human development. These propositions and the rationale for them constitute the core of Bronfenbrenner's book *The Ecology of Human Development*. This view sees the process of development as one which enlarges the child's conception of the world and the child's ability to act upon that world. We need not go very far in summarizing this view here (but will do so later), except to say that it incorporates different levels of related social systems around the developing child in which what happens outside the immediate experiences of a child (i.e., outside a child's "microsystem") affects what goes on inside those experiences as much as if not more than do the internal forces of the child (biology and psychology). The infuriating thing about all this (and the source of its creative analytic power) is that almost everything in the content of development is variable, almost nothing is fixed, and the answer to most questions of the sort "Does X affect Y?" is "it depends."

What contributions has this perspective on the ecology of human development made? There are at least four that deserve attention.

a. Provoking a serious response from "conventional" developmental psychology.
b. Enhancing the common ground for collaboration and dialogue between European and American students of human development.
c. Providing a vehicle for serious interchange between sociologists and developmental psychologists.
d. Developing a model for defining issues, formulating questions, and approaching social policy problems.

The first contribution has been to provoke a response from more "conventional" or "establishment" developmental psychologists. The ecological critique, while vigorously resisted by some, has begun to permeate American developmental psychology. Major figures feel compelled to respond to the criticism with words if not always with deeds. And while this is only a necessary beginning to genuine reform, it is significant. For thought to proceed, an adequate conceptual language is imperative. One contribution of *The Ecology of Human Development* is to provide such a policy- and practice-oriented conceptual language with which to analyze the validity of research and theory in developmental psychology, and thus contribute to a dialogue on the progress of this "science" of ours.

A second contribution has been to increase the basis for European-American dialogue. The ecology of human development contains three themes that link it to characteristically European approaches to human development. First, it emphasizes the "critical mode." Second, it emphasizes the subjective side of experience (phenomenology), a major theme in European work. This is no coincidence since one of the formative influences of Bronfenbrenner's work was Kurt Lewin, a German psychologist of the first order. In seeking to integrate American interest in the "objective" with European concern for the "subjective," a more valid conception of "meaning" is emerging. Third, the ecology of human development stresses the role of political economy in shaping human development. This emphasis is undoubtedly strong (many would say too strong) in European work. It naturally leads to cross-cultural research, which allows for macrosystem variation.

In a similar vein, the ecology of human development has contributed to— and is in part a result of—serious dialogue between sociologists and developmental psychologists. In the United States such collaboration is rare, and rarely has it been as productive as Bronfenbrenner's association with Devereux, Brim, Kohn, Clausen, and Elder, for example. Indeed, some would say the ecology of human development is the result of a deliberate sociological "conspiracy" to coopt developmental psychology. The ecology of human development is more than sociology, however, for two reasons. First, it places the *developing* organism at center stage, as an *active* force shaping social experience. Second, it envisions experimentation at *all* levels of environmental systems and does not accept the static or deterministic thrust of sociology. The subtitle of Bronfenbrenner's book, "Experiments by nature and design," is significant and leads naturally to a concern for policy.

The final area in which a significant contribution has been made is in the development of a model or "paradigm." In this, the results of a positive conspiracy with sociologists are also evident. In addition to the theoretical propositions being developed, research is being generated. Moreover, researchers are being trained to have an appreciation for the ecology of human development. And now, students can have access to a text based on the model.

The experimental ecology of human development is *not* a theory as the term is used here. Rather, it is a point of view or definition of a field of inquiry that aids in question formulation. Its content is that of other disciplines. Indeed, each of the systems (and levels of systems) proposed in the scheme has its own attendant discipline or disciplines. Bronfenbrenner's ecology of human development is different from traditional human ecology (cf., Hawley, 1950) and ecological psychology (cf., Barker & Schoggen, 1973). One of these is a substantive discipline and the other a substantive theory. The experimental ecology of human development is not really either a discipline or a substantive theory. Its principal virtue is its potential for substantive eclecticism. In fact, it requires such an eclecticism—or "interdisciplinary focus"—because it focuses on intersystem relationships. This characteristic is a valuable one in the present intellectual epoch when narrow specialization (and *intra*system analysis) is so prevalent, and indeed is embedded in the dominant paradigms.

The experimental ecology of human development basically takes a critical stance. It is an "imagination machine": It generates questions (good questions) in response to the statement of policy issues, substantive interpretations of research findings, sociohistorical events, and intervention strategies. This is the sense in which we join Bronfenbrenner in embracing Kurt Lewin's maxim that "There is nothing so practical as a good theory." In this way the ecology of human development is "limited" in its scope and purpose to improving the *quality* of our knowledge (something the human service field so desperately needs). If we recognize that qualitative issues outweigh quantitative ones, the significance of this becomes even more apparent. But it goes further to embrace Dearborn's Dictum: "If you want to understand something, try to change it." Bronfenbrenner has tried this with his view of child development and its relation to social policy and practice. We can make good use of the progress that has been made.

## The Interaction Between Person and Environment

Within an ecological framework, the balance of environmental forces is not the sole determinant of outcomes for an organism. The character of the individual organism also figures significantly. Those who study people from an ecological perspective view individuals and their environments as mutually shaping systems, each changing over time, each adapting in response to changes in the other. Therefore, while environmental press is the environment's contribution to individual–environment transactions, the individual brings to the situation a unique arrangement of personal resources, a particular level of development, and other attributes. Different people thus react differently to the same environment (just as different environments react differently to the same person).

This *interaction* between individual and environment forms the basis of an ecological approach to human development. This view sees the process of development as the expansion of the child's conception of the world and the child's ability to act upon that world. An individual organism and the environment engage in reciprocal interaction: each influences the other in an ever-changing interplay of biology and society—with intelligence and emotion as the mediators.

The relationship between parent and child, for example, changes and becomes more complex over time as each continually learns from and responds to the other. Neither can be viewed as a constant causing the others to develop; rather *the relationship itself* is a cause of change in both parents and children. One of the reasons brothers and sisters often have different experiences with the same parents is that the process of rearing one child makes the parents treat a later child in a different fashion.

A major contribution of an ecological approach is the way it focuses our attention upon the relation of development to both the immediate and the more distant cultural environment. Parents raising a child respond to this cultural environment, which is a complex web of activities, beliefs, and values. The ecology of human development is really the study of how a whole society functions to raise the children who will eventually take their place within that society. Children are the bridge between past and future, and society is always in a state of "becoming."

All over the world societies have different value systems, norms of behavior, and forms of social relations. Yet some basic human needs are the same everywhere: food, shelter, affection, and continuity (Mead, 1966). In our society, as in most others, development varies greatly due to factors ranging from the different ways we go about meeting individual needs to the diversity of individuals themselves. The opportunities or risks for development that each individual faces depends on one's particular mental and physical make-up and the type of environment one inhabits. One's "ecological niche" is the joining of both.

By opportunities for development we mean a person–environment relation in which the developing child is offered material, emotional, and social encouragement compatible with the needs and capacities of the child at a given time. The best fit between child and environment must be worked out by experience for each child within some very broad guidelines. Chapter 3 considers some of these guidelines.

Risks to development can come from both direct threats and the absence of opportunities for development. Besides such obvious biological risks as malnutrition or injury, there are sociocultural risks that threaten development. Sociocultural risk refers to the impoverishment in the child's world of essential experiences and relationships. Chapter 3 considers these risks in detail.

We know that biology and society (or "nature" and "nurture" as we often refer to these forces) can work to enhance or impede development. Nature and nurture can work together or in opposition. The extent of risk and damage, opportunity and benefit experienced by a specific individual depends upon the interplay of these two forces. In extreme cases, facts of nature can all but overwhelm environmental differences. For example, severe genetic or prenatal deficits can bring about mental retardation; an exceptionally gifted organism can triumph over adversity. Likewise, environmental conditions can be so powerful as to override all but the most powerful and extreme conditions of biology. In the case of extremes of either nature or nurture, optimal conditions of the one can do much to ameliorate developmental risk or negative influences arising from the other. This is one of the keys to successful human services.

Understanding the interaction between nature and nurture in development is no easy matter. In fact, it is so difficult that most researchers do not even try to handle both parts of the equation at once. Rather, they tend to hold one side constant while letting the other side vary—as in studying genetically identical twins (nature constant) reared apart (nurture varied) to learn about the role of nature and nurture in intelligence, or as in seeing how different newborns (nature varied) respond to the same stimulus (nurture constant) such as a smiling face. Or, they systematically vary one while letting the other vary randomly— as in presenting .children of different ages in a school with three different teaching styles and seeing what the overall effect of each is. Thus, a researcher is rarely able to really look at the interplay of nature and nurture in development.

Because of this complexity, we rarely know what the real limits, potentials, and costs are in human development. Where risk is concerned, this is extremely unfortunate because the inevitable issues of policy making and service delivery *need* a science of the possibilities, along with the costs and benefits, of alternative experiences to the individual and to the society. In computing these costs and benefits, we have much to learn from the ways in which history fits into individual and cultural development. Understanding what has come before can illuminate the questions we ask today.

In a sense, our interest in development is really an interest in biography. We must discover how the lives of individuals and the lives of societies are interdependent. Events taking place at the level of nations—the big picture—often reverberate right down into the day-to-day life of the individual family—the little picture—such as when the actions of an oil-producing cartel lead to unemployment that affects family relationships. Conversely, millions of individual decisions can add up to major social changes, such as when millions of women individually decide to delay childbearing so that they can pursue careers. This interplay of biography and history is at the heart of our interest in human development. While easy enough to convey in generalities, this ecological conception of development is very difficult to apply in practice.

In using the word "ecological" here we mean to convey an interest in the way the organism and its immediate environment (the "ecological niche") respond to each other. It means that we cannot account for or understand the intimate relationships between the child and the parents without understanding how the conditions surrounding the family affect interaction between child and parent and define each family's particular experience.

The most important thing about this ecological perspective is that it reveals connections that might otherwise go unnoticed and helps us look beyond the immediate and the obvious to see where the most significant influences lie. Trying to understand many important developmental phenomena is like a shell game. You think you're sure where the pea is, only to find it's really somewhere else. Let's consider a specific example.

## The Great Depression as a Source of Risk

What was the effect of the Great Depression of the 1930s on families? This question is actually like the one that asks, "What is more important, nature or nurture?" The answer is, "it depends." Few events—even things like economic depressions that may seem obviously and totally bad—have a guaranteed, universal, and inevitable significance. Most derive their importance from the context in which they occur. In the case of the Great Depression, we have more than just speculation to go on.

Economic deprivation is generally recognized as the principal source of sociocultural risk to children. Within the space of two years (1976–1978), two major analyses of family life conducted by blue-ribbon panels of experts separately concluded that poverty remains the principal threat to family life. The National

Academy of Sciences (1976) and the Carnegie Foundation (Keniston, 1977b) both cited inadequate economic resources as the central villain in undermining the adequacy of families as contexts for child development. Inadequate income is not the only source of troubles for families, of course. Rich people have family troubles, too. But anyone who looks at the data on the connection between poverty and family life must agree with Sophie Tucker when she said, "I've been rich and I've been poor, and rich is better."

It is exciting, therefore, to see a good study of the consequences of economic deprivation on human development. Conducted by sociologist Glen Elder (1974; Elder and Rockwell, 1977), this study permits us to look at the impact of the Great Depression of the 1930s on the children of that era. Two longitudinal studies of child development had been launched by an earlier generation of investigators in the period of 1929–1932 in Northern California, one in Oakland, the other in Berkeley. The first dealt with children born 1920–1921, the second with children born 1928–1929. Both studies included middle-class and working-class families. A wide range of information was obtained about the children and their parents. The data were collected for more than forty years. When Elder came to the project in 1962, he saw a unique opportunity to explore the impact of the Great Depression on the life course of the children in these two studies. The data permitted him to look at how the Depression affected children as a function of the following:

1. Age: The Berkeley children were just entering school at the worst of the Depression, while the Oakland children were teenagers by that time.
2. Social class: Both middle-class and blue-collar families were included.
3. Level of economic deprivation: Some families were relatively unaffected, while others lost more than 35% of their income.
4. Sex: Both males and females were included.
5. Pre-Depression quality of family-life: Both strong and weak marriages had been identified.
6. Self-concept and subjective analysis of personal experience.

Would you expect that the Depression affected all these subgroups equally and in the same areas? Elder found a very complex pattern of results. These findings are worth noting here because they demonstrate just how complicated this matter of sociocultural risk really is and just why we need the ecological framework to make sense of the data.

In families where the husband lost his job or much of his income and the marital relationship was weak, the mother often led the way in blaming the father for "his" economic failure. When this happened, girls were encouraged by the dominant performance of their mothers and boys were disillusioned by their father's failure, with the result that girls had less personality and emotional problems than boys in this case. All these factors were intensified if the sons and daughters were young children when the economic deprivation occurred, because they were then more dependent upon their parents and were exposed to the new situation for a longer period of time in the home. On the other hand, a strong marital bond was strengthened under the pressures of economic loss as families banded together in crisis. The effects were greatest for middle-class families—the positive effects on teenagers from homes with strong marital bonds and the negative effects on young children from homes with a weak marital relationship. Perhaps blue-collar families are more accustomed to dealing with unemployment and income loss.

These findings all refer to the long-term effects of economic deprivation. The short-term effects were somewhat different. Some of the groups showing the worst long-term prognosis showed few short-term problems, and vice versa. We should note that all these findings come from families with a pre-Depression record of relative stability—parents were married and had an adequate work history. These were not the "hard-core" unemployed, nor were they single-parent households. For them, the experience of economic deprivation was an *event*, not a permanent condition. That is a significant part of the story and cautions against simple generalizations about other groups—such as the single-parent, chronic welfare case.

As if all this complexity were not enough, we must remember that the Great Depression was followed by the economic "boom" of World War II and the 1950s. Teenage male "victims" of that era were ready to benefit from that opportunity while the child "victims" were not. What is more, one response to events of the Depression itself was the creation and expansion of our whole social welfare system—unemployment insurance, Social Security, and the like. Ironically, many now consider this very system to be part of today's problems. Also, Depression families were much more likely to see their economic deprivation as being their own fault, as opposed to families today with our greater appreciation for the influence of impersonal economic forces in arbitrarily imposing financial hardship on individual workers (Terkel, 1963). All these things add to the already large number of variables that we must take into account.

To be a child during a time of economic or social disaster adds an element of potential risk that is not present in less troubled times. However, whether or not the impact of those troubled times will produce damage to a child depends upon how those forces are experienced by the child's family and community, and how they are transmitted to the child. Elder's study makes this clear. Families who were not directly hit with income loss did not show the effects that deprived families did; some occupations were more affected than were others; some communities suffered more than others.

What is more, we must keep in mind that the individual is not a passive participant. While Elder's account stresses the average effects of economic change and development, there was, of course, substantial individual variation. Some individuals were more affected than others; some capitalized upon opportunities while others did not. It is precisely the characteristics of each individual, in concert with social factors, that make the ecological approach a valid model of the real world. Rarely is risk absolute; nor is it static. The child's vulnerability changes. Risk can be overcome or "disarmed." This comes through in Elder's study. However, the more impoverished the child's world is to start with, the more likely the child is to fail when hurt by social, economic, or psychological stress.

## A Systems Approach to Sociocultural Risk

The framework proposed by Urie Bronfenbrenner (1979) provides a useful approach to the ecology of human development. It offers some tools to sort out the phenomena, highlight the issues, and formulate the questions we need to ask and answer about sociocultural risk. Like most frameworks, it relies on some special terms, and we need to define them before we can use them. We need them to proceed with the scientific study of how the individual develops interactively with the immediate social environment and how aspects of the larger social context affect what goes on in the individual's immediate settings.

The child plays an active role in an ever widening world. The newborn shapes the feeding behavior of its mother but is largely confined to a crib or a lap and has limited means of communicating its needs and wants. The ten-year-old, on the other hand, influences many adults and other children located in many different settings and has many ways of communicating. The adolescent's world is still larger and more diverse, as is his ability to influence it. The child and the environment negotiate their relationship over time through a process of reciprocity—neither is constant, *each* depends on the other. One cannot reliably predict the future of one without knowing something about the other. Does economic deprivation harm development? It depends on how old one is when it hits, what sex one is, what the future brings in the way of vocational opportunity, what the quality of family life was in the past, what one's economic expectations and assumptions are, and whether one looks at it in the short- or the long-term. In short, it depends.

Bronfenbrenner sees the individual's experience "as a set of nested structures, each inside the next, like a set of Russian dolls" (Bronfenbrenner, 1979, p. 22). In asking and answering questions about developmental risk and opportunity, we can and should always be ready to look at the next level "beyond" and "within" to find the questions and the answers. If we see husbands and wives in conflict over lost income, we need to look beyond to the economy that puts the husbands out of work and now may welcome the wives into the labor force, as well as to the culture that defines a person's personal worth in monetary terms and that blames the victims of economic dislocation for their own losses. But we must also look within to the parent–child relationships that are affected by the changing roles and status of the parents. In addition, we must also look "across" to see how the several systems involved (family, workplace, and economy) adjust to new conditions over time. These social forces are the keys to ecological analyses, namely interlocking social systems. Bronfenbrenner (1979) offers a language to express these concerns in a systematic way that permits scientific study.

## Microsystems

The level most immediate to the developing individual is the *"microsystem,"* the actual setting in which the individual experiences and creates day-to-day reality. For children, microsystems are the places they inhabit, the people who live there with them, and the things they do together. At first, for most children, the microsystem is quite small. It is the home, involving inter-action with only one or perhaps two people at a time ("dyadic or triadic interaction") doing relatively simple activities such as feeding, bathing, and cuddling. As the child develops, complexity normally increases: the child does more, with more people, in more places. Indeed, in Bronfenbrenner's view, the expanding capacity to do more is the very essence of development. Play figures prominently in this process from the early months of life, and eventually is joined by productive labor (work). Playing, working, and loving (what Freud called the essence of normal human existence) are the principal classes of activities that characterize the child's microsystem. However, how much one does of those activities and how complex they are differs from person to person.

One of the most important aspects of the microsystem as a force in development is the existence of relationships that go beyond simple dyads (two people). For a child, to be able to observe and learn from being exposed to other dyads (such as his mother and father), enhances development. Development is enhanced when the child is able to observe differences in his or her own dyadic experience because a third party is present. So long as increased numbers in a child's microsystem mean more enduring reciprocal relationships, larger and more complex microsystems as a function of the child's age mean enhanced development (Bronfenbrenner, 1979). We measure the social riches of a child by enduring, reciprocal, multifaceted relationships that emphasize playing, working, and loving. We will return to this idea later, in Chapter 3, when we look more directly at risk and opportunity in the microsystem. First, however, we should examine the next level of systems, what Bronfenbrenner calls "mesosystems."

## Mesosystems

*Mesosystems* are relationships between contexts or microsystems in which the developing person experiences reality. We measure the richness of mesosystems for the child by the number and quality of connections. Bronfenbrenner used the example of the child who goes to school on the first day unaccompanied. This means there is only a single link between home and school—the child's participation in both. Were this minimal "linkage" to persist it would place the child at risk, particularly if there is little agreement and overlap between home and school in terms of values, experiences, objects, and behavioral style. Homes that do not value schooling, do not have formally educated people or books, do not involve reading and other basic academic skills, and do not use the formal language used for instructional purposes put the child at a disadvantage in school. In contrast, where all these links are strong, the odds favor the development of academic competence (Garbarino, 1981b). Where the actual participation of people other than the child in both settings bolsters the similarity between the two settings, academic success is still more likely. Thus, it is an important start for the parents to visit the school, and even for teachers to visit the home.

The central principle here is that the stronger and more diverse the links between settings, the more powerful the resulting mesosystem will be as an influence on the child's development. A rich range of mesosystems is both a product and a cause of development. A well-connected child's competence increases, and increases her or his ability to form further connections. A poor set of mesosystems both derives from and produces impaired development—particularly when home and school are involved. What determines the quality of the child's mesosystems? The initiatives of the child and his or her parents play a role, of course. But it is events in those systems where the child does not participate—but where things happen that have a direct bearing on the parents and other adults who do interact with the child—that play the largest role. Bronfenbrenner calls these settings "exosystems."

## Exosystems

*Exosystems* are situations having a bearing on a child's development but in which the developing child does not actually play a direct role. The child's exosystems are those settings that have power over her or his life, yet in which the child does not participate. They include the workplace of the parents (for most children, since they are not participants there) and those centers of power (such as school boards and planning commissions) that make decisions affecting the child's day-to-day life.

In exosystem terms, risk comes about in two ways. The first is when the child's parents or other significant adults in the child's life suffer in a way that impoverishes their behavior in the child's microsystems: home, school, or peer group. For example, Melvin Kohn (1977) has found that when parents work in settings that demand conformity rather than self-direction, they reflect this orientation in their childrearing. Other examples include elements of the parent's working experience that result in an impoverishment of family life—such as long or inflexible hours, traveling, or stress.

The second way risk flows from the exosystem is when decisions made in those settings adversely affect the child or treat him or her unfairly. For example, when the school board suspends extracurricular programs in the child's school or the planning commission runs a highway through the child's neighborhood, they jeopardize the child's development. Thus, exosystem risk occurs when the child lacks effective advocates in decision-making bodies. Psychologist George Albee (1979) has gone so far as to identify powerlessness as *the* primary factor leading to impaired development and psychopathology. It certainly plays a large role in determining the fate of groups of children, and may even be very important when considering individual cases—such as whether or not a youth's parents have the "pull" to get him a "second chance" when he gets into trouble at school or with the police. Risk at the exosystem level is largely a political matter because "who gets what" is the basic political issue.

## Macrosystems

Meso- and exosystems are set within the broad ideological and institutional patterns of a particular culture or subculture. These are the *macrosystems.* Thus, macrosystems are the "blueprints" for the ecology of human development. These blueprints reflect a people's shared assumptions about "how things should be done." To identify a macrosystem is to do more than simply name a group— Israeli, Arab, Swiss, American or Latino, Black, Anglo, Indian—and is more like labeling a cultural system such as Judeo-Christian, Communist, or Democratic. We must compare these groups systematically on some common scales of measurement, such as "collective versus individual orientation" or "schooled versus unschooled." This analysis asks for variables rather than simple labels.

Macrosystem refers to the general organization of the world as it is *and as it might be.* The existence of historical change demonstrates that the "might be" is quite real, and occurs through evolution (many individual decisions guided by a common perception of reality) and through revolution introduced by a small cadre of decision makers. The suburbanization of America in the post-World War II era happened because of an intricate set of individual decisions, technological developments, and corporate and governmental initiatives. All together, they reshaped the experience of a great many children in families and schools (Wynne, 1977). The Iranian revolution of 1978–79 overturned a "modernizing" society and indicated a changed institutional and ideological landscape. We can assume that these changes have reverberated through the nation's schools and homes.

What are risk and opportunity when it comes to macrosystems? Risk is an ideology or cultural alignment that threatens to impoverish children's microsystems, mesosystems, and exosystem relations; opportunity promises to enrich development. It is a national economic policy that tolerates or even encourages economic dislocations and poverty for families with young children, versus one that gives special economic priority to families with young children. It is institutionalized support for high levels of geographic mobility that disrupt neighborhood and school connections, versus action to promote stability. It is a pattern of nonsupport for parents, tolerating or even condoning intense conflicts between the role of worker and parent, versus parent-oriented policies and practices. It is a pattern of racist or sexist values that demeans some parents and thus raises the level of stress for their children, versus a pluralistic ideology that welcomes diversity and increases self-worth. In general, macrosystem risk is any social pattern or societal event that impoverishes the ability and willingness of adults to care for children and children to learn from adults, while opportunity is a social pattern or event that encourages and supports parents and children. It is an essential aspect of the human ecology.

## An Ecological Map

In sum then, the ecological perspective on human development offers a kind of map for steering a course of study and intervention. With that in mind, examine the picture presented in Figure 2:1. It gives some visual approximation of Bronfenbrenner's framework.

Systems at each level have distinctive characteristics that are relevant to a child's development, and therefore different criteria are appropriate for assessing the impact of each level on the child. Furthermore, these effects may be either positive or negative—either opportunities or risks. And, while the family microsystem is usually the most important system for a child, the overall impact of the environment emerges from the dynamic balance among all influences over time. DeLone (1979) did a good job of expressing the importance of interactions among the various environmental systems.

> To the large developmental contexts of class and caste one must add more intimate ones of which school, neighborhood, and family are clearly among the most important. For young children, especially, it is through these intimate contexts that contact with the broader dimensions of class, race, and the social and economic order is made (deLone, 1979, pp. 158–159).

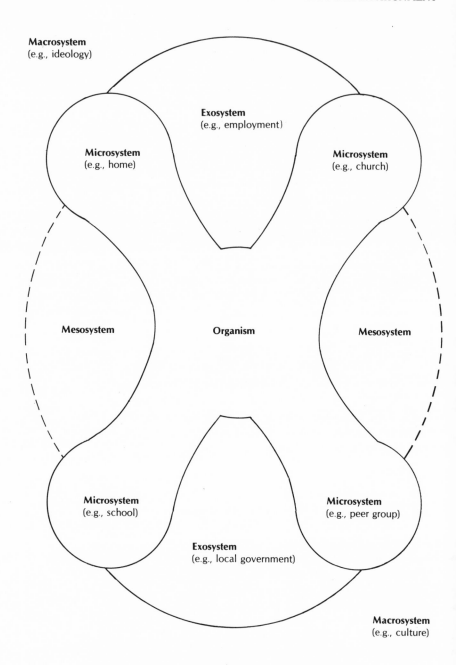

**Figure 2:1: The ecology of human development**

In the following chapter, we will take a closer look at specific examples of risk and opportunity at each of the four "levels" of the child's ecology. In so doing, we will be using the map presented in Figure 2:1 to help train our ability to see where the sociocultural threats to children are, to come up with some ideas on how to deal with those threats once we do recognize them, and to appreciate and encourage opportunities for development. In that way, we can fill in more detail in our picture of sociocultural risk and opportunity, making it an accurate picture that is both socially and scientifically useful, one that can help the human service professional operate successfully on behalf of children and families. Figure 2:2 summarizes the issues we will face.

## RESEARCH CAPSULE

Rubin, L. *Worlds of pain: Life in the working-class family.* New York: Basic Books, 1976.

The ecology of human development is an approach to human life emphasizing the interplay of person and social influences. The complexity of family, social, and cultural forces affecting individuals with their own unique strengths and weaknesses is awesome; the study of lives as they are experienced is left to the artist and the most sensitive of social scientists. One such scientist is Lillian Rubin.

*Worlds of Pain* is a depiction of working class life. The interviews she conducted with young adult men and women center on the problems and pride in their lives, painting a portrait of a certain type of American. Their distinctiveness is palpable; working class values and attitudes *make* them what they are. The

problems of making ends meet, raising children, coping with rigid sex roles, and striving for meaning, dignity, and control in their lives makes the experience of living in this type of life challenging. All four levels of the ecosystem can be seen as they come together to describe and delimit the voices of the subjects.

Research of this kind relies on long interviews, usually with just one person interviewed at a time. It is important to win the trust of subjects and to make them feel sufficiently at ease so that personal feelings and experiences may be shared. *Qualitative* research methods rely not on statistical analysis but on the richness and uniqueness of data gathered. Such data can lead to theories and hypotheses that may then be tested empirically. For this reason, qualitative research is important to contribute to our understanding of human development.

## PRACTICE CAPSULE

The Prenatal/Early Infancy Project (PEIP) in western New York State demonstrates ways that an ecological model of human development can be translated into the design of comprehensive intervention for infants and families. The project was designed with the premise that while regular health care is a requisite for optimal fetal and infant development, more

critical factors affecting early health and development are embedded in the environment in which the child is born and reared (Olds, 1977). Serving a population of mothers at risk for bearing and rearing children with developmental difficulties (e.g., the poor, adolescents, unwed mothers), the pilot project tests the effectiveness of providing various forms of

**Figure 2:2: A summary of the ecology of sociocultural risk and opportunity**

| Ecological Level | Definition | Examples | Issues Affecting Children |
|---|---|---|---|
| Microsystem | Situations in which the child has face to face contact with influential others | Family, school, peer group, church | Is the child regarded positively?<br><br>Is the child accepted?<br><br>Is the child reinforced for competent behavior?<br><br>Is the child exposed to enough diversity in roles and relationships?<br><br>Is the child given an active role in reciprocal relationships? |
| Mesosystem | Relationships between microsystems; the connections between situations | Home–school, home–church, school–neighborhood | Do settings respect each other?<br><br>Do settings present basic consistency in values? |
| Exosystem | Settings in which the child does not participate but in which significant decisions are made affecting the child or adults who do interact directly with the child. | Parent's place of employment, school board, local government, parents' peer group | Are decisions made with the interests of parents and children in mind?<br><br>How well do supports for families balance stresses for parents? |
| Macrosystem | "Blueprints" for defining and organizing the institutional life of the society | Ideology, social policy, shared assumptions about human nature, the "social contract" | Are some groups valued at the expense of others (e.g., sexism, racism)?<br><br>Is there an individualistic or a collectivistic orientation?<br><br>Is violence a norm? |

support to parents in both the home and community in order to create opportunities for the healthy growth of the child.

Participants in the project were randomly assigned to one of four treatment groups. Two of the groups received only early, periodic screening of infant development plus transportation for prenatal and well child care. In two other groups, the basic screening and transportation were supplemented with biweekly visits from a nurse–home visitor during pregnancy only or extending from the prenatal period through the first two postpartal years. The home visitation program was designed to prepare mothers for a healthy labor and delivery, to teach about infant growth and development, and to link the pregant woman to supportive friends and family as well as health and social services in the community.

Preliminary results from the project (Olds, et al., 1980) indicate that those mothers involved in the nurse visitation program were more likely to reduce smoking during pregnancy than those in the other treatment groups. Furthermore, a significantly greater percentage of those in the comprehensive treatment groups attended childbirth education and experienced labor and delivery in the presence of a familiar support figure. Finally, the visitation program heightened participants' awareness of formal community services available to them and their babies.

This project demonstrates the value of using a multimethod approach to early intervention. In particular, it suggests ways that a single program can be designed to meet the developmental needs of individuals and of the family as a unit.

# FOR FURTHER READING

Bronfenbrenner, U. *The ecology of human development: Experiments by nature and design.* Cambridge, MA: Harvard University Press, 1979, 330 pp.

This important book lays out Bronfenbrenner's framework of the human ecosystem. Bronfenbrenner argues that child development is best studied in the context in which it occurs; that is, within the layers of the ecosystem. As well, any attempt to intervene and enhance development must take into account the ongoing relations between organisms and environment. Bronfenbrenner in this book challenges the child development field to approach development in context; the questions and probabilities he raises cannot be ignored.

Elder, G. H. *Children of the great depression.* Chicago: University of Chicago Press, 1974, 400 pp.

This book, summarized in this chapter, is a classic in the sociology of the life course. It is one of the richest and most exciting examples of longitudinal studies attempting to understand the processes of human change over time. The concepts of cohort (people born in the same period who experience historical events at the same age), and linkage (the connections between social events in the macrosystem and personality development in microsystems) guide Elder's analysis. This is not an easy book, but one in which students at every level can find something of interest.

Kohn, M. L. *Class and conformity: A study in values* (2nd ed.). Chicago: University of Chicago Press, 1977, 315 pp.

Kohn here demonstrates the ecological approach to development with an important study which investigates the links between social class and family values that affect children. Kohn's study establishes that class as an exosystem affects children by the kind of goals parents set for their children. Working class parents who are subject to discipline and submissiveness instill the same in their children; middle-class occupations require flexibility and independence which is extended to middle-class children. It is an interestingly written study with a clear explanation of research methods and analysis.

Theodorson, G. A. *Studies in human ecology.* Evanston, IL: Harper and Row, 1961, 626 pp.

This edited volume contains many important works in the tradition of human ecology. Begun in the 1920s with Park & Burgess' *Human Ecology,* it was at first an attempt to view human communities in the same light in which natural ecosystems are understood. Concepts such as competition and symbiosis were seen as *biological,* applying to human as well as plant and animal ecology.

The field evolved in the 1950s to encompass human culture as an intervening variable between the physical environment and the human community. Thus, politics, values, and traditions play a part in determining the organization of human society in a more complex way than in the natural ecosystem.

The present state of human ecology has become increasingly more sophisticated. This volume chronicles the evolving field of human ecology from its inception as it laid the groundwork for contemporary thinking on the ecology of human development.

# QUESTIONS FOR THOUGHT

1. An extreme proponent of a "nature" or heredity stance on development would argue that biological factors overwhelm environmental factors in their effect on people, while an extreme "nurture" or environment position would take the opposite view. What are the implications for human services and social problems in general of an extreme "nature" or "nurture" position on human development? What are the practical benefits of a nurture vs. a nature position? What are the political implications?

2. Consider the concept of environmental press as it applies to differences between people, e.g., racial, social class, ethnic, age. Are *people* different? Is it their environment that is different? Or both? What are some examples of environmental press at all four levels of the human ecosystem? Consider your own life.

3. Elder's (1974) study of the Depression is one example of the interplay between history and personality development. What are some other historical events in your lifetime that have had major impact on the lives of children and families, and what were some of the effects?

4. Elder found that girls in the Depression were strengthened by their family's hard times. Do you think that similar patterns would be found in unemployed families today? Why or why not?

5. Review the four levels of the human ecosystem. Thinking of a child you know, or going back to your own childhood, what are some concrete examples of how each systemic level influences the boy or girl being considered?

6. Explain how the neighborhood can be involved with all four systemic levels. Give an example illustrating each level of the ecosystem. How does taking an ecological perspective enhance our understanding of the influences of neighborhoods on children and families? What are some other examples of social institutions that exist in multiple levels? How can these institutions influence the success of human service professionals?

7. The chapter talks about the ecological perspective as an "imagination machine." How could you use it to think about some particularly interesting questions about human development? Try it on some issue that fascinates you (Possible examples: teenage pregnancy, the "generation gap," Vietnam veterans' problems).

# Chapter 3

Who is on my side? Who?
II Kings, 9:32

Some children have everything going for them. Others face a hostile world alone. Under optimal conditions, the child grows up in a loving and supportive family and a stable, supporting community. Chapter 3 enlarges upon the human ecosystem framework set out in the previous chapter by presenting the risks and opportunities that affect development at each level of the human environment. We describe the benefits and dangers that can come to the child from family, community, political and economic decisions, and finally from the culture as a whole. Given our professional interests, we give special attention to recent patterns affecting children and families.

The ecological perspective not only seeks to describe and explain the effect of ecosystems on the individual, but also to help make the world a better place for children and families. Therefore, it takes a stand on the positive or negative impact of the social environment. This combination of moral and scientific elements is a powerful tool for the social scientist, service worker, or policymaker.

# Sociocultural Risk and Opportunity

## The Meaning of Risk: Case Studies

Sociocultural risk refers to the impoverishing of the child's world so that the child lacks the basic social and psychological necessities of life. Children who grow up wanting for food, for affection, for caring teachers, for good medical care, and for values consistent with intellectual progress and social competence grow up less well than those children who do not lack these things. Their absence places a child "at risk" for impaired development.

This simple truth is the beginning of our story: Children need loving care if they are to grow and develop normally. The sad fact is that some children are deprived of these basic necessities. They are starved physically and psychologically. Why? How do we make sense of a world that places children in jeopardy? It is not easy to understand the complicated chain of events that results in a child's basic needs not being met.

To see just how complicated this task is, let us take a look at some children at risk:

*Joey* is eighteen months old. He lives with his mother and father, both of whom are twenty years old. To put it bluntly, both parents feel Joey was a "mistake." Both parents feel resentful over being tied down. They can't afford to get out on weekends. Joey's father works long hours at a gas station and wants nothing more than to eat dinner and watch television when he comes home. He ignores Joey except to yell at him. Joey's mother feels trapped and depressed. She has no friends and sees little prospect of making any in the apartment building where they live. She blames Joey and his father. She belittles Joey when he "causes trouble" and ignores him the rest of the time.

*Sally's* family is large and a bit chaotic. At five, she has three sisters (two older) and two brothers (one younger). Her mother was married once before her present husband, who is not Sally's father. Both parents try their best: They both work (at low paying jobs) and they rent a little house in a run-down neighborhood. When her parents are at work, Sally is left at home on her own with her brothers and sisters. They have to stay inside the house because there are some "creepy" people on the street. Sally's family has lived in this house for seven months but still haven't really met the neighbors. Sally's mother is friendly, but she got such a cold reception when she spoke to the woman next door that she hasn't tried again since. There's a vacant house on the other side of the street that kids play in—breaking windows, writing on the walls, and so on.

*Annie* is twelve—the oldest of six kids. She hates to go to school because she doesn't fit in. She is having trouble learning to read and do arithmetic. Her favorite class is home economics, but she only has that two days a week, so she skips school as often as she can on the other days. At home she helps her mother, who came from Portugal when she was fifteen and now at twenty-nine speaks only broken English. No one in Annie's family reads except her father's sister, but even she would rather watch television. Annie's junior high school has 1500 students and she feels lost there. There are a couple of nice teachers— like the woman who teaches home economics—but they're all so busy keeping order and doing the daily assignments that there's not time for much personal attention. Annie figures she'll stop going to school altogether when she's sixteen so she can stay at home and help her mother take care of the other children.

Three-year-old *John's* life came crashing down this past year. Things were pretty good before that. His mother stayed home to take care of him and his older brother while his father worked on the assembly line at the truck factory in town. But eleven months ago, the plant laid off 300 employees because of declining sales, and John's father was one of the people who got a pink slip. His father couldn't find another job, became depressed, and started drinking heavily. His mother found a job as a waitress and insisted that John's father take over the household and child care. He refused, saying that was her job. They argued and fought until finally he left to go live with his brother in Kansas City. Now his mother has filed for divorce. John has started wetting the bed at night, and he doesn't talk much. He's a sad boy.

All of these children are at risk. Their normal growth and development is threatened. Each story has its distinctive elements, however. Joey is at risk because his parents reject him and, thereby, undermine his feelings of self-worth. Sally lives in a neighborhood that weakens her family's already marginal social existence. The unsupportive nature of her environment threatens her development. Annie needs all the help school can give her, but she gets lost in the shuffle at her large school. She needs a lot of personal attention and encouragement if she is going to make it, but most likely, she will not get it. John's life has been terribly disrupted by an economic and social catastrophe not of his making and which even his parents don't really understand. When his parents separated, John was overwhelmed.

All these children are at risk, but the source of the problem is different in each case. For Joey it lies in the poor quality of relationships within his family. He experiences rejection every day in every way. For Sally, the problem goes beyond her home to the neighborhood. Her family could make a go of it, and she would develop normally if the people nearby were a positive rather than a negative influence. Annie's problem is that she has trouble succeeding in one particular kind of situation, namely, school. She does fine at home, but her home life does little to prepare her for what is demanded of her at school. She could succeed in school if the school would encourage her, if she felt needed. But she doesn't, and that makes her give up trying. John's problem is related to the American economy. There is nothing really wrong with him, or even with his parents. The problem is that they live in a society undergoing economic disruption.

To deal with these children and their parents, we need to understand the sources of risk and opportunity in their social environments. We can profitably use the concepts of micro-, meso-, exo-, and macrosystems developed in Chapter 2.

## Risk and Opportunity in the Microsystem

The microsystem is the immediate setting in which the child develops. It includes people, objects, and events that occur directly to and with the child. Look around you, and see where the children are. They are at home, in play groups, and in schools. Each of these "places" implies the existence of a set of enduring roles and relationships—parents and children, leaders and followers, teachers and students. The shared experiences that occur in each setting provide a record of the microsystem and offer some clues to its future, because microsystems evolve and develop much as the children themselves do from forces within and without.

The setting "school" is very different in June than it was in September for the "same" children, who, of course, are themselves not "the same" as they were at the beginning of the school year. The setting of the family, as experienced by the first-born child, is different from that experienced by subsequent children. Naturally, children themselves change and develop as do others in the setting. We must remember that the microsystem has a life of its own—it develops, too.

It is also important to remember that Bronfenbrenner's definition speaks of the microsystem as a pattern experienced by the developing person. The child influences and is influenced by the microsystem. By his or her participation, the child has a say in the character of the microsystem, while at the same time the setting provides the child with ongoing norms, regularities, and experiences that come to be known as "normal" to the child. The cognitive maps we carry around in our heads are the reality we live by and act upon. Shakespeare said it well in *Hamlet* (II, ii, 259): "There is nothing good or bad, but thinking makes it so." Perhaps this idea was most clearly expressed by sociologist W. I. Thomas, who said: "If men define situations as real, they are real in their consequences" (Thomas & Thomas, 1928, p. 572). The individual child constructs the microsystem as much as he or she is shaped by it.

The child's microsystem becomes a source of developmental risk when it is socially impoverished. That is, the child's development suffers whenever the microsystem is stunted, be it because of too few participants, too little reciprocal interaction, psychologically destructive patterns of interaction, or some combination of the three.

A microsystem should be a gateway to the world, not a locked room. Bronfenbrenner recognizes this when he offers the following proposition about microsystems and individual development:

> The developmental status of the individual is reflected in the substantive variety and structural complexity of the . . . activities which he initiates and maintains in the absence of instigation or direction by others (1979, p. 55).

The "product" of a healthy microsystem is a child whose capacity for understanding and successfully dealing with ever wider spheres of reality increases. Such a child learns to have self-respect and self-confidence, to be socially and intellectually competent. Let us take a brief look at three types of socially impoverished microsystems—microsystems that are too small, too one-sided, and too negative—and how they work against competence and self-esteem.

## Small vs. Large

The U.S. Census Bureau has predicted that almost one out of every two children born in the United States in 1980 will spend at least some part of his or her first eighteen years in a single-parent household (U.S. Bureau of the Census, 1979). This represents the extension of a trend towards single-parent households that began after World War II and has gained momentum ever since. Add to this the fact that the proportion of single parents who maintain separate households—rather than incorporating with another, usually related household—has doubled in recent decades (Bronfenbrenner, 1975), and you can begin to see why we worry about these households producing family microsystems that are "too small" to meet the child's developmental needs.

As *individuals,* single parents may be excellent caregivers. But as *microsystems,* their households may be insufficient, unless they are augmented from the outside to produce a fuller, richer range of roles, activities, and relationships for the child to *use* in his or her development. In this respect, the single-parent household is part of a larger trend towards an "emptying" of the family microsystem. Mothers are more likely to be working outside the home in the labor force (more than half do), kin are less likely to be involved in the child's day-to-day life because of geographic mobility and a trend towards privatism, age segregation in housing has increased (with old and young going their separate ways), and the many distractions of "modern life" pull parents away from the home and result in less time being spent in the kind of purposeful, cooperative activities that nurture child development (Garbarino, 1981c). A recent replication of a survey of youth done originally some 50 years ago found that adolescents now wish their mothers would spend more time with them, where once they seemed to take for granted that she would (Bahr, 1978). (They still wish that of their fathers, testimony to our continuing problems with the paternal role.) It is reasonable for us to worry about this "emptying" of the family microsystem because the available data suggest that it is linked to a variety of developmental difficulties (Bronfenbrenner, 1975). It is, thus, an aspect of sociocultural risk.

Conversely, microsystems made up of large numbers of relatives, neighbors, and friends provide an opportunity for rich and stimulating experiences. Children who have the benefit of growing up amidst a diverse set of relationships that span age groups, generations, and backgrounds enjoy a special social opportunity, whatever other risks may attend upon their situation. Thus, social risk and opportunity can exist side by side in the same environment.

## Imbalanced vs. Balanced

One of the essential features of a healthy microsystem for the child is "reciprocity"—the give and take interaction that both respects and challenges the child, that stimulates and responds appropriately. When this essential reciprocity declines significantly, it jeopardizes the child's development. How does this happen?

It happens when the balance of power within the family microsystem breaks down. Typically, this means that the parent or parents seize complete control of the parent-child relationship and seek to dominate the child, thus thwarting his or her development. With an infant, this may mean taking a rigid stance with respect to feeding and other aspects of care giving. The "natural" and most developmentally enhancing way is for the infant to play an active role in shaping the parent's behavior, just as it is natural for the parent to influence the infant's behavior (Bell, 1968). This is a healthy family microsystem. When the parent *refuses* to be influenced by the infant's tempo, rhythms, cycles, and spontaneous verbal and facial gestures, the essential principle of reciprocity is violated.

For the older child, the issue of reciprocity is found in the child rearing "style" adopted by the parent(s). Baumrind's studies (1979) of child rearing styles and their consequences for development provide an insightful look at how important the principle of reciprocity is to the family microsystem. She found that where reciprocity was maintained in day-to-day interaction—what she called an "authoritative" orientation—the child enjoys the greatest number of opportunities to develop social competence. Where the principle of reciprocity was systematically violated, the child's development suffered. An "authoritarian" style violated the principle of reciprocity by lodging excessive power in the hands of the parent and, thus, placed the child in a passive role. A "permissive" style inappropriately gave *carte blanche* to the child and his or her unformed drives and, thus, placed the parent in a passive role. Neither does justice to the child's developmental needs because both undermine the social richness of the family microsystem.

Consider an incident in which a ten-year-old child shows up at 6 o'clock when dinner was scheduled for 5 o'clock. The authoritarian parent might respond with, "You're late. Go to your room. There will be no supper for you!" When the child responds with, "But I . . . ," the parent interrupts with, "No but's. Go to your room." In contrast, the permissive parent might respond with, "Welcome home, dear, I'll cook your supper now." The authoritarian parent has not permitted the child to offer a response; the potentially useful process of bargaining and negotiating is short-circuited. The permissive parent, on the other hand, has not set the child's behavior against a standard and in that way has done him a disservice. Albeit for different reasons, the permissive style joins the authoritarian style in shutting off the developmentally enhancing process of negotiation, a quintessentially reciprocal process.

In contrast, the authoritative style emphasizes negotiation. The parent greets the child with: "It's 6 o'clock, and dinner was scheduled for 5 o'clock. You're an hour late. What's the story here?" When the child responds with, "But I was playing and lost track of time, then I had to help the other kids find the ball . . . ," the parent responds with, "I can see how you could lose track of time, but having dinner together is pretty important, and besides it makes more work when you're late. I suggest you find a way to keep track of time better, or you'll have to come straight home from school. Let's work on that. For tonight, your dinner is in the oven. I'll expect you to clean up your own dishes when you're done." When the family microsystem is working this way, the balance of power between parent and child and standards and impulses is appropriate and developmentally enhancing. When it is too one-sided, it places the child at risk.

## Negative vs. Positive

The child's experiences in the microsystem color his or her whole view of the world. Children incorporate these experiences into their emerging concepts of themselves, the world, and their place in that world. The microsystem problems of "too small" and "too one-sided" are important, but probably the single most important microsystem issue is "affective tone"—the emotional climate. A negative tone can be expressed in the full range of microsystem behaviors, including what is said (or not said), what is done (or not done). A positive climate produces a kind of "social momentum" in the child, while a negative climate produces "social deadweight." Positive climate contributes to success in the world because it gives the child a reservoir of self-confidence or "ego strength" that is an important foundation for competence (McClelland, 1975). Negative climate makes the child vulnerable to being easily discouraged by everyday problems and turns the child away from full and satisfying participation in the world.

Coopersmith (1967) demonstrated that the microsystem plays an extremely important role in determining whether children experience their world and themselves in positive or negative terms. A nurturant, involved, and actively contributing parent tends to produce high self-eseeem while a passive, neglecting, and uninvolved parent produces low self-esteem. Much as the slogan "you are what you eat" conveys the notion that we become what is offered to us, so the statement "you are what you are shown about yourself by others" conveys the notion that children construct an image of themselves based on the feedback from significant others. This view of personality is in the classic tradition of George Herbert Mead (1934) and others who argue that by defining the role a person plays, we go far towards defining the person. To rob a child of positive self-regard, either by deliberately deprecating a child and his or her accomplishments or by conveying a sense of worthlessness by neglecting the child, is to place the child at developmental risk and may constitute emotional abuse (Garbarino, 1978a, 1980b).

To develop a positive sense of self, the child needs warm, responsive, and active "partners." The microsystem can fail the child in many ways, but the most serious threat comes from neglecting parents who starve the child of emotional sustenance. These parents are likely to exhibit what Polansky (1976) calls "the apathy–futility syndrome." The elements of this pattern are a kind of emotional deadness, an unwillingness to initiate or respond to actions of the child, a pervasive sense of ineffectiveness, and a general unresponsiveness to the initiative of the child. The developmental threat posed by adults who suffer from the apathy–futility syndrome is that they are unable or unwilling to provide the intense, responsive interaction necessary for the adequate development of competence and self-esteem in their children. Rather, these care givers project a world view of passivity, depression, and rejection. None of the active encouragement needed to develop a personal reservoir of self-esteem and positive regard exists.

Like all personality variables, the apathy-futility syndrome needs to be understood in terms of actual behaviors. Burgess and Conger (1978) provided such behavioral documentation. They observed families interacting in their homes, both in unstructured interaction and in pursuit of several tasks provided by the investigators. The principal conclusion of these studies was that parents who abuse and neglect their children characteristically ignore positive behavior in their children, have a low overall level of interaction, and emphasize negative behavior. This is certainly a "social engine" well-suited to the task of producing psychologically damaged human beings.

This starvation is bad for children. It is part and parcel of a broader risk: rejection. Children who are rejected are in trouble. This is the conclusion of Rohner's wide-ranging studies of the problem. Rohner (1975) examined rejection, its antecedents and consequences, in cultures all over the world. He found that across cultures, rejection is a kind of emotional malignancy, a psychologial cancer that eats away at the individual's capacity for self-esteem, social competence, and hope. Rohner concluded:

> . . . that parental rejection in children, as well as adults who were rejected as children, leads to: hostility, aggression, passive aggression, or problems with the management of hostility and aggression; dependency; probably emotional unresponsiveness and negative self-evaluation (negative self-esteem and negative self-adequacy); and probably, emotional instability as well as a negative world view (Rohner, 1975, p. 168).

In support of the ecological perspective, Rohner also found that rejection increased when a child's care givers were isolated from the nurturance and feedback of interested others—kith and kin. This is, of course, an issue that implicates the meso- and exosystems, and it is one we will consider shortly. At this point, suffice it to say that all three varieties of microsystem risk (too small, too imbalanced, and too negative) cannot be understood without looking at their antecedents and consequences in the meso-, exo-, and macrosystems. Just as parents guide and protect their children, the community is parent to all its families.

# Risk and Opportunity in the Mesosystem

Mesosystems are the relationships between two or more settings in which the child is an active participant, such as school and home. The social richness of a child's mesosystem derives from the number and quality of these connections. At one extreme we have the case where the child is the only connection; at the other, we have the case where there is total overlap between two or more settings. Mesosystem risk is defined first by the absence of connections and second by conflicts of values between one microsystem and another.

## Weak vs. Strong Connections

A mesosystem is established at the point where a child—or other developing person, to use the concept in its more general sense—first enters a new setting. This is what Bronfenbrenner calls an "ecological transition" (1979, p. 210). The two critical issues here are how this is done, and who is involved. If, for example, the ecological transition is defined as a very positive event by the child's parents, if the child is well prepared for the new setting, if the child is accompanied by the parents, and if the new setting receives the child with enthusiasm, the child is on his or her way to a strong and developmentally enhancing mesosystem. In such a positive case the whole (the mesosystem) will be greater than the sum of its parts (the microsystems).

## Negative vs. Positive Connections

The stronger, more positive, and more diverse the links between settings, the more powerful and beneficial the resulting mesosystem will be as an influence on the child's development. A rich range of mesosystems is a developmental opportunity; a poor set of mesosystems produces impaired development. When the microsystems work in concert—a strong mesosystem—the child benefits. When they work in isolation or in opposition, the child is at risk.

## The School-Home Relationship as an Example

All this is easiest to see when we look at the school-home mesosystem. For some children, this mesosystem is strongly positive: There are many connections, and there is mutual support between the two settings. The child's parents are interested and involved in the school. The home trains the child to be comfortable and competent in dealing with the school's basic activities: reading, writing, and arithmetic. The home conveys a positive regard for written materials and the use of language in formal, problem-solving, and systematic question and answer sessions, organized around the solution of problems involving objects, quantities, and relationships. Children raised with this pattern are more likely to work to the fullest of their potential at school. This pattern might be called the "academic culture" (Garbarino, 1981b), and it is composed of what J. W. Getzels (1974) calls "language codes" and "value codes."

> The language code gives the child the categories for structuring and communicating this experience. The value code tells him what in his experiences is important. For one child the codes learned in the family and those required by the school may be continuous; for another they may be discontinuous.

Some children come to school well equipped to be students, while others are aliens to the microsystem of the school and find its requirements alien to their own experience. In a world such as our own, where academic success is important, to be an alien to the academic culture is to be at developmental risk. Failure in school sets one up for a whole series of socially and personally "risky" experiences, e.g., conflicts over rules, economic penalties, threats to self-esteem, and further alienation from the mainstream of cultural and social experiences that the society has to offer. Trouble with school is a major contributor to juvenile delinquency (Gold, 1963).

Beyond this issue, there is the question of how well school and home work together to provide a healthy balance of objective and subjective responses to the child. Getzels (1974) has written persuasively that one measure of a healthy social environment is the balance between "universalism" and "particularism" in the child's experience. Universalism is based on treating everyone by the same standards, particularism looks at each person individually.

> In the particularistic relationship the important question is *who* is involved; in the universalistic relationship the important question is *what* is involved (p. 223).

While home and family tend to emphasize particularistic concerns, schools tend to emphasize universalistic ones. However, for a child to experience a healthy balance of particularistic and universalistic concerns, school and home must work in concert; they must complement each other. Neither should be so extreme as to place the role of the other in jeopardy. Also, some children may need the school to provide a compensatory "dose," either of particularistic or universalistic orientation, if the home is unable or unwilling to do so. This is clearly a mesosystem issue. Too much particularistic treatment will undermine the child's ability to deal with the abstract and the bureaucratic world. Too much universalistic treatment will impair the child's ability to deal with genuine intimacy. The implicit "danger" of the family is typically that it will go overboard on the particularistic end; the "danger" of the school is that it will overemphasize the universalistic. While there is no hard and fast rule to judge these matters, it does seem clear that large schools, because of their inherent tendency to overemphasize universalistic orientations, pose the danger of psychically starving students, particularly academically marginal students (Garbarino, 1980d). Like the small family, where there is a high ratio of adults to children (Lieberman, 1970), the small school provides more opportunities for the reciprocal interaction that enhances development (Barker & Gump, 1964).

The school–home mesosystem is one of the most important in the child's life. When it is strong and positive, it provides the child with the opportunity to develop intellectually and socially, to become a more complete human being. When it is weak and negative, it burdens the child with conflicts of values, style, and interest. So burdened, the child is held back from his fullest development. As schools have become more isolated from neighborhoods and other community institutions, the demands for academic success have increased, and the stresses on families magnified. The potential for developmental risk related to the school–home mesosystem seems to have increased (Garbarino, 1981b). However, studies of intervention programs aimed at strengthening this mesosystem have documented that this goal can be accomplished (Bronfenbrenner, 1975). Efforts to do so bring us naturally to the exosystem.

## Risk and Opportunity in the Exosystem

The exosystem is a setting in which the child does not participate, but which has an effect on the child through the meso- or microsystems. As we noted earlier, one source of exosystem risk is the world of work, such as when the child's parents are so stressed or discouraged by their jobs that they are unable to participate in a nurturant, responsive, and reciprocal manner in the family microsystem. A second is when people make decisions in their official capacities that adversely affect the child's day-to-day experience, as when the school board closes a small neighborhood school in favor of a large isolated school that requires a bus ride. Many of the most important exosystem risks to children fall within these two categories: a parent's diminished ability to participate productively in the child's microsystem, or people in institutional roles making decisions that adversely affect the child's microsystem. In both cases, the problem is likely to be one of social impoverishment.

One of the ground-breaking accomplishments of Bronfenbrenner's ecological approach is to highlight situations where the development of the child is significantly shaped by the actions of people with whom the child has no direct contact. Consider these two examples. First, because of fluctuations in the economy, a corporation board decides to shift operations from one plant to another, and hundreds of children are affected, either because their families are forced to move to a new location or because their parents lose their jobs. Second, parents who chronically abuse their children begin to attend Parents Anonymous group meetings and begin to be more nurturing to their children.

## Stresses and Supports for Parents

Exosystems enhance development when they make life easier for parents and undermine development when they make life harder for parents. Thus, exosystem opportunity lies in situations when there are forces at work outside the family on behalf of children and their parents. When child rearing "has friends in high places," the opportunities for children and parents increase.

At this point it is worth noting that the ecological perspective forces us to see risk beyond the narrow confines of individual personality and family dynamics (in the ecological approach, both are "causes" in the child's development and "reflections" of broader sociocultural causes). Perhaps the student is familiar with the saying "if the only tool you have is a hammer, you tend to treat every problem as if it were a nail." If we only think about children at risk in terms of personality and interpersonal dynamics, we will never see the many other avenues of influence that might be open to us as helpers or that might be topics of study for us as scientists.

## Anti-child vs. Pro-child Institutional Policies and Practices

Meso- and exosystem risk come together in contrasting the socially enriched with the socially impoverished neighborhood. It is fitting that we set the stage for our discussion of macrosystem risk by briefly examining how the multiple functions of neighborhoods—as microsystem, mesosystem, and exosystem—can exert a significant influence on children and their development. The neighborhood is the natural "ecological niche" of families, and it can serve as either a source of support or risk for the child.

Few concepts are so attractive and have so much feeling attached to them yet are so difficult to work with in a scientific way as is "neighborhood." The child acts as part of the neighborhood. It is a microsystem. However, the complementarity of neighborhood and family is a mesosystem issue. The neighborhood is also a setting in which the parent participates independently of the child, and the quality of the support, encouragement, and feedback given by the neighborhood to the parent has an effect upon the child's development. The neighborhood, thus, also functions as an exosystem influence upon development. A strong and healthy neighborhood enhances development by providing the kind of multiple connections and multiple situations for children that permit them to make the best use of their intellectual and social resources. Our point here is that the quality of the neighborhood depends in large part on how the community's economic and political institutions treat the neighborhood. Do they sustain it or undermine it?

All this has many important implications, two of which are worth noting here. First, it seems that many of the most important decisions people make that have an impact on child development are not *directly* about children. They are decisions about working, about residence, about budgets, about transportation, about housing, about the whole range of things that shape the actual content and process of a child's microsystem. Second, these decisions reflect basic, cultural "blueprints" that describe what people understand to be "human nature" and "the way things are done," and they are heavily influenced by social history: by government stability and disruption, war and peace, and prosperity and economic collapse. This leads us to the macrosystem.

## Risk and Opportunity in the Macrosystem

It should be clear by now that understanding the factors involved in producing sociocultural risk and in determining what its effects will be is no easy matter. It goes well beyond understanding individual personality, and even further than is implied in the notion of looking at the match of individual to situations. In fact, the issue of sociocultural risk goes directly to the heart of the culture and to the ideology of the society in which a given family, and therefore a child, is living.

Although we experience reality and construct it in the immediate settings in which interpersonal relationships take place (microsystems), and can extend our view to see the relevance of connections between settings (mesosystems) and the indirect influence of settings in which we do not ourselves participate (exosystems), many of the most important influences on our lives come from social, economic, and political changes that occur at the level of nations and whole societies. For example, World War I and World War II exerted profound effects on the day-to-day lives of nearly all Americans. General George Patton reportedly said, "War dwarfs all other forms of human activity into insignificance." While we may hate the truth of that statement, it does contain much truth. Patterns of migration brought Blacks out of the South and into the North in response to World War I. In both World War I and II, women entered the work force primarily in response to the needs of the war machine. Thousands of children experienced father absence, on a temporary or permanent basis. The economic face of the nation was permanently changed. Many men and women saw so many new worlds that they were motivated to reconstruct their own. (How *are* you going to keep them down on the farm after they've seen Paris?) These macro-events produced myriad technological changes that have diffused into day-to-day life. All these changes and many more are the result of macrosystem effects.

Bronfenbrenner thinks of macrosystems as cultural blueprints that underlie the organization of institutions, the assumptions people make about social relations, and the workings of the political and economic system. Two aspects of this definition are particularly important for our purposes.

The first is that this treatment of culture goes beyond simple description. That is, in specifying culture as the blueprint for society, the possibility that those blueprints may be "in error" is left open. Bronfenbrenner offers us the possibility of criticizing culture and society on the grounds that they impede human development. While this may seem self-evident, it does represent something of a departure from the way many social scientists think of culture. Using the term "cultural relativism," many social scientists argue that all cultures are equivalent, that one cannot and should not criticize cultures as being humanly wrong since all cultures arise as a specific adaptation to circumstances (cf., Tulkin, 1972). Translating culture into the concept of macrosystem, on the other hand, raises the possibility that such consistencies may not be in the best interests of children and their development. This, as we shall see, is an important point.

The second and related aspect of Bronfenbrenner's definition is found in his statement that macrosystem refers to consistencies "that *could* exist" (1979, p. 26). The ecological approach is intimately bound up with social policy, i.e., the decisions and principles guiding the behavior of public and private institutions. It necessitates a serious consideration of "social engineering" as a way of dealing with individual developmental problems. Naturally, this is of special relevance in the discussion of sociocultural risk, where the focus of attention is on problems in just those "consistencies in the form of lower-order systems" that do exist and have an adverse developmental effect on individuals. Thus, an ecological approach has a "moral imperative" attached to it; it both describes and prescribes. It tells us that to reduce risk at the most immediate level of the microsystem, we *should* consider changing things in the big picture. This means that the topic of sociocultural risk brings together the "helping" and "describing" traditions in human development. The meaning and implications of this moral and scientific approach to culture will emerge as we look at five examples of macrosystem issues implicated in understanding sociocultural risk.

## Pluralistic vs. Totalitarian Societies

At the very start, we can look at the sociopolitical organization of the society in our efforts to seek the roots of sociocultural risk. The development of children, particularly their moral development, depends on the "political" structure of their experiences (cf., Almond & Verba, 1965). Children need a world that combines stability and diversity, consensus on basic principles coupled with alternative and competing expressions of those principles. Very young children need to form powerful attachments that provide the basis for prosocial motivation to develop. Once they have developed that basic prosocial motivation (to obey, to attend to rules, and to develop the rudiments of conscience), they need more, however (Garbarino & Bronfenbrenner, 1976b). They need to be faced with moral dilemmas, but in a reasonably secure, nurturant, and supportive setting.

Two extremes, and therefore two dangers, are possible. On the one hand, there may be such a diversity of irreconcilable alternatives that the child cannot choose and at the same time avoid the hostility and alienation of those she chooses against. On an interpersonal level, Bateson (1972) has called such situations "double binds" ("damned if you do and damned if you don't") and linked them to schizophrenia. Children should be protected from these conflicts: They are unfair and developmentally threatening. On the other hand, where there is unanimity so complete that no choice is ever allowed and only a slavish obedience required, the child's moral development languishes.

One can imagine, for example, a society that irreconcilably pitted school and government against family. In such a situation, the child would be faced with an intense double bind. To remain loyal to the family would mean to estrange one's self from peers, from teachers, and in fact to place oneself in political jeopardy. To side with school and government would mean to make the intolerable choice of turning one's back on kin. Many totalitarian societies force this choice upon children as a matter of course; Nazi Germany for one (Shirer, 1960). Democratic societies do not do so as a matter of policy, although such dilemmas may occur when there are irreconcilable differences between family and state. The situation is familiar to Indians, Latinos, and Blacks in the United States.

In contrast to the society in which there is irreconcilable conflict between family and state, there stands the society in which all social agents are unified in single-minded devotion. Here the developmental problem is not one of double binds but rather that the lack of diversity will impede high order cognitive and moral development. For example, when church and state are under the same rulers (theocracy), such as in Iran under the Ayatollah Khomeini, there is unchecked absolutism, and moral sensibility languishes. Where there is no diversity, the child can too easily satisfy society's demands. This too stands in contrast to the democratic society in which a measure of social diversity necessarily exists, where there are competing allegiances that the youngster must sort out and in so doing learn to develop high order thinking and judgment (Garbarino, 1968). The child learns to live by principle in the democratic society.

The available data suggest that the greatest danger to children's moral development lies in the totalitarian society that commands total allegiance to the state. This is manifested in the authority of adults, such as teachers and youth group leaders. One study of these data (Garbarino & Bronfenbrenner, 1976b) looked at the moral judgments of youth (twelve years old) in countries with varying degrees of social and political diversity. At issue was the degree to which the youths' moral judgments reflected a balance of adult and peer influences as a function of whether the society was totalitarian or democratic. The study used the term "pluralistic" to refer to the middle ground between irreconcilably intense conflict on the one hand and the extreme absence of conflict on the other. In a pluralistic society, there are competing allegiances that operate within a common framework: a consensus on basic principles, agreement to the rules of the game, and appreciation for the need to spare individuals impossible choices as much as possible. The results of the study indicated that across both communist and noncommunist societies, the less pluralism a society manifested, the less balanced were the moral judgments of the youth. The issue is one of totalitarian versus pluralistic societies, not necessarily one of political East versus political West.

What does this have to do with sociocultural risk? It tells us that when looking at macrosystem matters we should attend to whether or not the political culture of a society forces children and parents into intolerable dilemmas. It tells us that there are developmental grounds for supporting the "pluralistic society." In fact, these developmental grounds have been illuminated in creative detail by White (1959). White speculated that there is an inherent drive to master the environment and a natural "incongruity mechanism." That is, the human being thrives on "optimal discrepancy," a balance of the familiar and the different, of the known and the novel. Environments that provide the organism with this kind of optimal discrepancy serve to stimulate and enhance development. They provide the kind of richness human beings need. Thus, classic, philosophical traditions of democracy stand on firm scientific grounds. A democratic society—a pluralistic society—is in fact a healthy environment for humans to grow in. It offers them the greatest exercise of those characteristics (evaluating, deciding, and comparing) that are innately and particularly human. To deprive people of such a pluralistic environment is to damage their growth and development. Therefore, a nondemocratic social system—a macrosystem dominated by totalitarian influence—presents a sociocultural risk for those who live within it.

## The Economic System: Triumph of the Marketplace?

The economic system is one of the most powerful aspects of the macrosystem. It connects work, goods and services, and the social, biological, and physical environments which more than anything else define the kind of life we lead. The type of economic system—for example, laissez-faire capitalism or state-run socialism—and a person's place in the economy—rich or poor, working or unemployed, superior or subordinate—have an enormous effect on one's relation to one's family, community, country, and oneself.

The American economy grew out of the free-market assumptions first advanced by Adam Smith, tempered by 20th century innovations of government intervention. Laws and regulations, taxes and government programs attempt to "fine tune" the economy so it works better and ensures the survival and minimum well-being of all Americans. How well is the economic system working to support our nation's children and families?

At the heart of this question stands one of the great political, economic, and social debates of our time. As we said earlier, human needs are constant and basic; societies much more "primitive" than ours have had long and happy histories with little of the "creature comforts" or technology so basic to our way of life. We can all easily cite the benefits of our economy: unprecedented material wealth for many, social and geographic mobility, rising health and educational standards, to name but a few. At the same time, we must ask about the costs of our system to people and to the environment. One way to consider this is in terms of the underlying assumptions that determine "how things are done" in the economy.

For example, our economy is based on the principle of permanent growth as a necessary condition for progress. Growth constantly requires new markets, resources, changing demands, and an emphasis on consumption. As a cultural blueprint, this idea seems obvious, even indisputable. Yet a small group of economists question the wisdom of continual growth (Daly, 1973). Starting from the idea that the Earth is a finite environment, they see the optimal economy as a steady-state system, with basically fixed levels of population and economic output. As technology advances, productivity and time, rather than increased production, would be gained. The economy would strive toward stable levels of consumption and economic activity and *maximum* durability and quality of goods, leaving people the means and freedom to fulfill their lives more independently of the economic system. One can imagine a combination of advanced technology and cottage industry, as people devote themselves to satisfying labor and minimize unpleasant work. Our ecological situation, of course, would be much improved by a system based on stability and the sustenance of all life, rather than constant growth and the exploitation that it requires.

Another aspect of the economic macrosystem is the use of the profit motive as a basis for economic decisions. Rather than directly considering basic human needs of consumption, satisfying labor, and human relatedness, our economy is based on the pursuit of profit. The distortions we suffer in unemployment, poverty, worker alienation, pollution, and stress, as well as the whole "malaise of affluence" (Lasch, 1978) are by-products of our economic status quo. While the riches we have accumulated may be unparalleled, so are the problems and dangers from which we suffer. We cannot take only the good; our economic tree bears poisons along with its fruits.

Finally, the economic notion of "efficiency" as a basis for making decisions is rarely examined. In a time of scarce energy and jobs, common sense would argue that a more labor-intensive approach to production would provide work for more people by using less non-human energy. Yet the trend throughout the economy is toward increasing mechanization and automation that puts people out of work and requires massive amounts of non-human energy. The agricultural sector, for example, has "released" 25 million people from the farms of the United States since 1940 by utilization of machinery (Berry, 1977). Yet, agriculture has never been in a more precarious state than it is now, as farmers are forced to farm larger acreage and go deeper and deeper into debt to afford land and machines, while the topsoil which must sustain us forever is being depleted at an alarming rate because of the necessity of "mining the soil" to reap short-term yields. Moreover, food production is in the hands of fewer and fewer people, unemployment is a permanent problem, especially for those at the bottom of the society who it need work most, and the quality of our food, if anything, is diminishing.

The fact that these basic assumptions are not questioned testifies to the extent to which they are ingrained. Market payoffs, rather than human concerns, dictate what is to be the structure of our economy. The point here is not the injustice or inefficiency per se. It is the fact that so much of what happens in the economic realm affects parents and children. It is precisely the way we *think* of our involvement in the economy as workers, consumers, investors, and taxpayers that keeps the problems from getting solved.

## Individualistic Competition vs. Interdependent Cooperation

One of the clearest ways to identify the operation of a macrosystem is to consider what people take for granted. Particularly when comparing macrosystems, one finds that what is taken for granted in one society is hotly disputed in another. American culture views independence and autonomy as a norm, as a positive goal towards which individuals should strive. It assumes that individual competition and independence are part of "human nature." This belief is so firmly fixed in our macrosystem that many of us would find it hard to consider an alternative. We see dependency as basically pathologic, or at least immature (Rotenberg, 1977). Our culture denigrates interdependency and sees it as a form of weakness. Just to present the issue this way is to raise the question: Is independence a self-evident good, or is it only good as defined within a particular culture, a culture subject to criticism on the grounds of its effect on development?

Few characteristics are without cost. We need to look at the social benefits and social risks of our culture. Our individualistic culture gives us a sense of personal responsibility, a rationale for achievement, and a justification for success. It provides a justification for our social system, differentiated as it is by economic and social levels. It provides justification for the winners (although it keeps a kind of Sword of Damocles of future failure always fixed above their heads). This narrowly individualistic culture of ours provides a kind of freedom, a fresh air of individuality that collective societies cannot match.

On the other hand, it clearly implies—and often makes painfully obvious— that if success is a matter of individual virtue, failure is a matter of individual deficiency. The other side of individualism is alienation, a sense of estrangement, of isolation, and of being perilously alone (Slater, 1970). Many social philosophers have argued that it is in the interdependencies and interconnections of one's social life that one finds enduring sources of what is meaningful. This basically philosophical position has received increasing scientific support as survey data and other investigations have shown that interpersonally well-connected people are the happiest and most satisfied with their day-to-day existence (Campbell, 1976).

The fact that social connectedness and enduring social relationships are what keeps us going in life suggests that our individualistic culture, and the competition and denigration of interdependency it implies, place us at sociocultural risk. Our culture tends to say "every man for himself" while our nature as human beings says "no man is an island." There is a real, enduring, and intense conflict here. This conflict has been identified repeatedly in social and historical analyses of our society. Sociologist David Riesman called it "the lonely crowd"; Philip Slater discussed it in his book, *The Pursuit of Loneliness;* James Webb, an historian, saw it throughout our history as "the parabola of individualism." It means that we value individual autonomy and privacy so much that we are always threatened with social isolation.

We seem to say that everyone should be on his own and free, without recognizing that the price for such independence is the risk of alienation, a pervasive sense of dissatisfaction, and a heightened vulnerability to depression. Who bears this burden most acutely? Children do. They pay the price because this network of values leading to social isolation and alienation undermines responsible parenthood. It is one of the central issues facing our society (Garbarino, 1981c). Altogether, our excessive and unrealistic valuing of independence sets us up for unhappiness and our children for impaired development. For example, depression among women often comes from social dislocation and produces neglectful childcare (Weissman & Paykel, 1974).

Just as is the case in moral development, where pluralism is the key, the matter of competition, individual responsibility, and interdependence requires a balanced, or middle road solution. Without a notion of individual responsibility and accountability, it is unlikely that one can develop sufficient "internal locus of control" (the belief that the individual himself rather than external forces determine the course of one's own life) to keep our kind of society going. Indeed the very cornerstone of our society is individual self-motivation and competition, with cooperation seen mainly as a means toward the goal of the individual's greater gain. On the other hand, without an appreciation for interdependence, and for the intrinsic worth of social connectedness, we are constantly in jeopardy of alienation and depression. Both of these are potentially serious social problems affecting parents, and therefore children. Dependency can make the individual unequipped to face the demands of our society, while extreme independence can make one unable to share life's joys and hardships with others.

That this is a macrosystem effect is demonstrated by the fact that it permeates all our institutional life. In schools we see it in the fact that individual competition—primarily for grades—is a corrosive force undermining the self-esteem and development of the majority of students who inevitably must be "losers" (Dreeben, 1968). On a broader scale, we see it in our virtual inability to restrain commercial exploitation of children and of their parents (Garbarino, 1981c), all of which goes forward under the banner of "individualism." Advertisers have an "individual right" to play to children, while parents have an "individual responsibility" to counteract this advertising blitz that emphasizes materialistic gratification. We saw it clearly when we once wrote to several airlines and government officials to complain that during a snow storm, parents with young children (one woman was stranded with a five year old and an 18 month old for 47 hours in the airport) were forced to "compete" on an equal basis with adults without children for available flights and accommodations. When we wrote, we were told, "We can't give special advantage to one group of our customers over another." Indeed!

An individualistic ideology tends to produce antichild, antifamily policies and practices. We see this ideology in policies that permit unrestrained development of shopping centers, even where it is evident to all parties—perhaps even the developers—that the net result will be fragmentation of the community and its neighborhoods.

There is very little notion of collective accomplishment in which individuals play diversified *and* complementary roles. All these things represent sociocultural risk because they expose the individual to values and experiences that undermine an important condition for healthy development, namely, social connectedness. One of the most bitter fruits of this "cultural poison" is domestic violence, our next macrosystem issue.

## Violence as a Norm

As we hope has become clear in this discussion of macrosystem issues, to speak of the macrosystem is to consider the meaning of "human nature." This is evident as well if we look at "normal" violence. Just as our culture sees individual competition as a fact of human nature, it tends to define violence as an inevitable and normal part of domestic relations (Gil, 1970). The use of violence and the approval of domestic violence is common in our society. The most recent and comprehensive study (Straus, Gelles, & Steinmetz, 1980) documents that among normal American families, domestic violence in some form is almost universal (involving at least some hitting in 90 percent of the families surveyed), and serious assault occurs in some 15 percent of our families.

The very fact that we define only the most damaging and extreme forms of physical punishment as "abuse" and permit the rest to be classified as only "normal discipline" is testimony to the status that violence has in our culture. This, too, is a macrosystem issue because violence figures prominently in the blueprint of our domestic and institutional life. It is, in fact, a normal part of our experience. Educators, clergymen, and police all approve of the use of physical force and corporal punishment in disciplining children and youth (Parke & Collmer, 1975). Few parents can conceive of—let alone implement—alternatives to the use of physical force in social control and discipline (Garbarino, 1977a). The incredulous or hostile response given to calls for domestic *nonviolence* is testimony to this. When Sweden's legislature reaffirmed and strengthened its opposition to the use of corporal punishment by parents with their children, the American press treated the action as a ludicrous bit of nonsense, much the way a racist responds to civil rights legislation. The parallel is illuminating. When psychologist John Valusek issued a booklet under the title "People Are Not for Hitting," he found that most readers "naturally" assumed that he didn't include children in that message. He had to add "And Children Are People, Too" before the message was clear to many readers. Violence in general, but particularly domestic violence, is deeply embedded in our macrosystem.

At the same time, there are grounds for believing that the use of physical force is not inevitable, that it is a reflection of social stress and that alternatives can and do exist. The same investigators who found such widespread support for and use of domestic violence found that the level of such violence rises in direct proportion to a host of predisposing social stress factors such as economic inadequacy, marital conflict, and personal inadequacy. Rather than being an inevitable expression of human nature, the use of violence is a culturally conditioned expression of distress. Desmond Morris made the following observation about domestic violence based on his look at nonhuman species:

> The viciousness with which children . . . are subjected to persecution is a measure of the weight of dominant pressures imposed on their persecutors (1970).

Cultural support for violence as a norm represents sociocultural risk because it presents and legitimatizes a dangerous outlet for stress. Some other cultures, mainly technologically primitive, tribal cultures, do not legitimize this outlet, and they have less domestic violence (Korbin, 1978). Some social stress is inevitable, and when we provide an outlet that can easily escalate into physically and psychically damaging behavior towards children, we place children in general at risk and the children of distressed families in special jeopardy. Where we condone the slapping of one child, we inevitably increase the likelihood that another will be punched. Where we accept physical abuse against wives on the grounds that it is a husband's right, we make it almost inevitable that children will be battered. The insidious thing about macrosystem effects is that they send ripples throughout the human experience. In supporting the "rightness" of violence, we set in motion a chain of events that inevitably places substantial numbers of children at risk. On the other hand, insofar as we are able to start a countermomentum of nonviolence, we may serve to protect children who find themselves in stressful circumstances. Domestic violence is one of the most poignant and pressing areas of sociocultural risk for our society to deal with.

## Sexism and Racism as Cultural Issues

One of the important principles guiding our efforts to enhance human development states that we should attempt to encourage the best possible match between individual characteristics and social settings. As we noted before, the ecological definition of development involves the idea that the more differentiated one's conception of reality and the greater one's skill in mastering reality, the greater the fulfillment of individual potential. This definition of development argues that ideologies or institutions which unnecessarily or unfairly limit the opportunities of individuals are a threat to development. Such factors unnecessarily and unduly restrict the experience, and hence the development, of those affected. Two such factors are sexism and racism because they oppose the goal of individual development and are not linked to *necessary* group identities. They narrow the range of *social* contexts to which *individual* characteristics must be matched.

As an ideology, sexism asserts that there are rigid, inherent, and inevitable differences between males and females that are and should be the basis for the differentiation of activities (Maccoby, 1966). In its best form, it is a "separate but equal" approach to development. In fact, according to research from a variety of sources, it contributes a "separate but unequal" macrosystem effect. It forces females into unduly and unnecessarily narrow choices of activity and exerts a depressing effect on their competence in all aspects. For example, research on occupational development has shown that whereas young males name a very wide range of potential occupations—ranging from the close-to-home (policeman, doctor, and mailman) to the far-flung (spaceman, baseball star, and president)—young females, as early as four years of age, will restrict virtually all their choices to teacher, nurse, and mother (O'Hara, 1962). Clearly, this does an injustice to the diversity of interests and abilities that exist among females. Therefore, there are developmental grounds for seeing sexism as a source of sociocultural risk.

Sexism also forces males and females into roles and personality styles that may be difficult for them to maintain. It means that males who are temperamentally inclined to nurturant roles may assume such roles only with decreased self-esteem and a sense of failure. It means that females who are temperamentally inclined to adopt aggressive, athletic roles, for example, must cope with the role incongruity this implies. All of this flies in the face of the principle of matching individual characteristics to situations and is therefore developmentally threatening. Whatever *group* differences there may be (and there *are* grounds for believing that such average differences between the sexes do exist, Hutt, 1972) do not justify values and institutions that run roughshod over quite significant *individual* differences (Rosenberg & Sutton-Smith, 1972).

In the same manner, racism is a direct threat to development. By postulating racial differences in intelligence, moral character, and general competence, racism undermines the development of the children it defines as inferior—and even impoverishes the development of those judged superior (Tulkin, 1972). It places the "inferior" children at risk by creating a negative reality with which they must contend at some almost inevitably serious cost. It has a demonstratively depressive effect on competence and contributes to a wide range of personality disturbances. Because it is a macrosystem effect, it permeates the institutional life of the society, and thus, forces its victims into extraordinary measures to cope.

Attributing characteristics to individuals within a group presents a threat to the development of those individuals—particularly if they are cast in a negative light. There is almost always overlap between groups, whether the differences are due to actual genetic differences (such as the height of Chinese vs. Bantu people) or discriminatory testing (such as when Jews, immigrating to the United States in the early 1900s, were judged to be intellectually inferior on the basis of IQ tests administered to them in English, which they did not all speak).

Human development proceeds *through individuals,* although aggregate differences can and do exist. "Isms" that limit and define the range of possibilities for groups have an inevitably adverse effect on the individual by disrupting the natural process by which individual and environment are matched to facilitate development. Science and ethics merge in rejecting sexism and racism. These ideologies are not consistent with the process of fullest human development.

## Reducing Sociocultural Risk: Support Systems

You may recall hearing or reading that when a team of aeronautical engineers set themselves to the task of writing up a set of blueprints for a bumblebee, they found that by all their best judgments, a bumblebee shouldn't be able to fly. Coming this far in our discussion of sociocultural risk may leave the student with a feeling that successful human development must be impossible, given the hostile forces aligned against the developing child. It might seem as though there is an overwhelming conspiracy at the micro, meso, exo, and macrolevels to undermine and impair development. For some children this is exactly the situation, of course. The chronicling of risks to development is not the whole story, however.

The human being is notable for intelligence and adaptability. Intelligence and adaptability have served us well in adjusting to an incredible range of environments. Adaptability is our strength. It means that humans may live, if not thrive, in many environments that are purely and simply hostile. Children grew up in the concentration camps run by the Nazis in World War II. Amid chaos and despair, children grew and learned. In their report on these children and efforts to work with them, Freud and Dann (1951) report that the children clearly adapted to concentration camp life, even though it was an inhuman and inhumane situation. Their adaptation, which meant their survival and mental progress, is a testament to the strength of the human species. However, as Freud and Dann point out, that adaptation was not without cost. The children exhibited a variety of clinical symptoms of disturbed, if not warped, development. This point must be understood in looking at and evaluating sociocultural risk. The fact that humans *can* survive in the face of these risks should not be enough to excuse or rationalize the threats that those risks present. In looking at children who survive socially and culturally risky situations, we must always ask, "What might they have been in a more nurturant and supportive environment?" and, "What of those who did not survive?" Also, we must recognize that there is great individual variation in the response to sociocultural risk.

We can reduce the risk posed by social and cultural factors that are inimical to optimal development; we have already done so in some areas. We can reduce risk by social action and by the individual characteristics of the child and those who care for the child. To understand how this happens and how to facilitate this process, we need to understand more about how families work and how children develop (Chapters 4–6). Once we have made progress in these basic areas, we can proceed to examine the social environment in which these basic structures and processes of life operate (Chapters 7–10). As a prelude to these discussions, however, we can examine two examples of sociocultural risk reduction.

There are at least two sources of sociocultural risk that run through the various micro-, meso-, exo-, and macrosystem problems discussed in this chapter.

The first of these is "social impoverishment." Social impoverishment is the denuding of the child's environment of significant social resources. The second source of risk is "cultural impoverishment." Cultural impoverishment is a set of values or view of the world that undermines the characteristics upon which competence is built. It may involve rationalizations for self-interest, values that benefit the individual at the expense of families, an ideology that is outdated and is no longer functional to meet the demands of a changed environment, a narrow and inaccurate view of child development, or values that otherwise seriously impair the child's ability to function in the required contexts of social life outside the family. Both these forms of impoverishment find their most significant expression in the day-to-day content and structure of formal and informal support systems in a family's environment.

A support system is a social arrangement that provides nurturance and feedback to individuals. One of the pioneering researchers and theorists in this field, Gerald Caplan, defines support system as:

> . . . continuing social aggregates that provide individuals with opportunities for feedback about themselves and for validations for their expectations about others, which may offset deficiencies in these communications within the larger community context. They tell him (the individual) what is expected of him and guide him in what to do. They watch what he does and judge his performance (Caplan, 1974, pp. 4–6).

Social and cultural impoverishment results when these support system functions are undermined, impaired, eroded, or destroyed. These destructive influences can come at the micro-, meso-, exo-, or macrosystem levels. They can come because of attitudes or beliefs that cause people to isolate themselves from support systems. They can come from institutional and social forces in the community that prevent these supportive relationships from forming and being maintained. They can come from a culture that poisons support systems by devaluing children and family life (Garbarino, 1981d). These support systems figure prominently, not simply in the day-to-day management of tasks and stress, but in the very creation of a meaningful existence. In his review of the data bearing on the meaningfulness of human experience, Campbell (1975) found over and over again that it is the *social* richness of individual experience that determines its meaningfulness—above and beyond material resources. Naturally, economic deprivation is a serious threat to the human being. But it is the *social* deprivation that accompanies economic poverty which is responsible for its truly devastating human consequences. Being poor is quite different from being impoverished. The former may exist along with social affluence, while the latter implies a total denuding of the environment of the human necessities of life.

To speak of sociocultural risk as it applies to children is to look at how the essential functions of the parent are supported, encouraged, and reviewed by people with a long-term investment in the welfare and well-being of the child. A truly poor child is one whose parents are left to their own devices, particularly when those devices are too limited for the difficult task of rearing a child. A poor child is one who is unprotected. A rich child is one whose life is full of diverse and enduring relationships and whose parents are similarly involved in an interlocking web of supportive, nurturant, and concerned relationships. The higher the personal risk of the child, the greater the importance of sociocultural resources. The principal task for the community is to know how socially well-fixed their families are and to proceed accordingly. The community needs to recognize positive forces where they exist naturally (and then leave them alone) and to learn how to generate and sustain them where they do not exist already. Community development is inseparable from reducing sociocultural risk in this sense. A prochild ideology is the foundation for a caring community.

The ecological approach used to organize our discussion clearly directs our attention to many points at which intervention is possible. If we think of the task as one of weaving a strong social fabric around the child and parent, the task becomes more comprehensible. The pressing need is to establish an effective partnership between formal and informal support systems so that each child is protected and nurtured by both, directly as in the case of the small school, and indirectly as through the child's parents and primary care givers. The principal implication of our discussion of sociocultural risk is that this wondrous human child can and will become a competent person, if we only give it the chance. Against the many hostile forces chronicled in this discussion of sociocultural risk stands the child's own innate drive to master and succeed in the world, the parents' love and commitment to aid the child, and the community's motivation to care for all its children. The constant challenge to professionals and lay people alike is to help the constructive forces overcome the destructive ones.

# RESEARCH CAPSULE

One clear and heartbreaking example of risk to development is child abuse and neglect. Scientists have looked at many different factors associated with child abuse in attempts to understand and prevent it, from the psychological attributes of the parents and child to the sociocultural home environment of the family.

One important study (Burgess, Anderson, & Schellenbach, 1980) examined the social inter-

action of abusive, neglectful, and control families. All families were drawn from similar social backgrounds: rural, poor, with parents averaging about ten years of education. By observing families performing simple tasks and engaging in discussions together, the researchers were able to score frequency of positive and negative communications and the types of sequences families engage in. The behaviors were scored by trained observers using a Datamyte 904 data collection system. This is a portable keyboard with number and four letter keys. Coded behaviors can be recorded and stored in computer format.

*Observational* research relies on accurate recording of phenomena as the basis of trying to understand it. Observations can be done in the laboratory or in naturalistic settings, and they can be done with or without the knowledge of the subject. The present study is an example of a structured naturalistic observation in which the researchers provided topics for interaction and then passively observed the families. The findings indicated that there is less interaction in abusive and neglectful families than in the control group. Both the abusive and neglectful families are less positive, more negative, and are more likely to recip-

rocate negative behavior than positive exchanges when compared to the control group.

The investigators also discuss demographic and family characteristics associated with patterns of abuse. Low socioeconomic status, single parenthood, large families, and particular child characteristics such as physical, intellectual, or behavior dysfunctions all are associated with high levels of abuse.

An intervention strategy aimed at increasing the positive interactions within abusive families is reported. The limited benefits suggest that while home-based skills training is possible, a more practical and effective strategy would involve the encouragement of natural helping networks to combat abuse and neglect among isolated, needy, and troubled families.

---

# PRACTICE CAPSULE

Preschool education has been proposed as an effective and practical method for enhancing the development of young children. Public-funded preschools attempt to provide less advantaged youngsters with opportunities which are available to middle-class children at private nursery schools. Often preschool programs try to involve parents in their child's activities, both by inviting parents to the preschool and by making home visits. This is in the hope of establishing a strong home–school mesosystem from the beginning, making parents more aware and disposed toward helping their children to learn.

Varying approaches to preschool education exist; a central problem is the evaluation of the effectiveness of these programs. An example of one preschool program which has been thoroughly evaluated is the Perry Preschool Project. Based in a Ypsilanti (Michigan) neighborhood, the study followed 123 children who were three years old in the early 1960s. All of the subjects were Blacks from low SES families who had scored below average on the Stanford–Binet Intelligence Test. Fifty-eight children attended preschool for two years, 65 did not. The two groups were matched on

personal, family, and demographic characteristics.

The curriculum at the Perry Preschool emphasized the child's cognitive development and the strength of the family–school mesosystem. The student–teacher ratio was 6 to 1, and there was a weekly home visit in which parents were encouraged to aid in their children's development. The students' progress in school was evaluated and compared annually. By the end of the eighth grade, the two groups differed significantly on academic achievement. The students who had attended the preschool scored over a full grade level above the non-preschool children in reading, language, and arithmetic on the California Achievement Test. In fact, 49 percent of the preschool group scored at or above the fifth-grade level, versus only 17 percent of the children without the preschool experience. In addition, the preschool children had a lower rate of repeating a grade and a lower arrest record than the control group. The investigators estimate that in 1979 dollars, the one-year program cost $5,984 for each child and saved the public $14,819 for each child in reduced remedial education and social interventions.

A study by Brown and Grotberg summarizing 700 studies of preschool programs done between 1969 and 1977 concludes: "The major findings are that preschool has brought about gains in intelligence and academic achievements, has had a positive effect on the health and social behavior of the children, and has benefitted their families."

---

# FOR FURTHER READING

Garbarino, J., & Gilliam, G. *Understanding abusive families*. Lexington, MA: Lexington Books, 1980, 263 pp.

This book examines child maltreatment as a developmental and ecological issue. It begins with a discussion of the nature and definition of abuse and the social context in which it is generally found. Family norms about childbirth and childrearing are then discussed with regard to risks and opportunities for bringing families closer together. Abuse is seen as an outgrowth of social isolation where parents lack the resources and support to effectively care for children. This book is an example of the applied work that can be done using the human ecosystem model.

Havighurst, R. J. *Growing up in River City*. New York: John Wiley & Sons, 1962, 189 pp.

An early classic in longitudinal studies of normal development, this book reports a nine-year study of adolescence and young adulthood. It was begun in 1951 when the subjects were in fifth grade and followed them until they were around 20 years old. The basic question the study asks is: What are the influences on these children's development, and how can we account for their success or failure as they embark on adult roles?

The children and their communities are studied together. The human ecosystem, from family to community agencies to social class difference are all considered together in their influence on the children. The book discusses the subjects' childhood, adolescence, and young adulthood, stressing the continuity of life patterns and the sociocultural influences on their development.

The book concludes with a review of the data and suggestions that this typical American town could enact to enhance the maturation of its children. These include more options and opportunities for the less successful and alienated students, increased possibilities for work experience, and preparation for the many girls who leave school for early marriage. *Growing Up in River City* is an easily readable and fascinating book, for its inside look at a time gone by and at the universal process of maturation in social context which produces human beings.

Sale, K. *Human scale*. New York: Coward, McCann, & Geoghegan, 1980, 558 pp.

A review of society, politics, economics, and community from the perspective of scale. Sale's thesis is that any institution, from school to families to government, will function best at an optimal size. Person-to-person interaction and understandable levels of complexity are important for the effective functioning of organizations, and this book argues that many current social and interpersonal problems share the common root cause of inflexible, oversized, and exploitative institutions which fail to address human needs. Numerous ideas are put forth describing various institutions designed "to the human scale," meeting the needs of children and families and of society as a whole.

---

# QUESTIONS FOR THOUGHT

1. In what ways can a family microsystem in which both parents work full-time be a risk to a child's development? In what ways an opportunity?

2. Negotiation is described in the chapter as a characteristic of authoritative parenting. Review how this differs from authoritarian and permissive styles of parenting and consider some risks to development in the latter two.

3. In this chapter we discovered the home-school relationship as one example of a mesosystem. What are some other important mesosystems for the child, and what are their risks and opportunities to development? What are some mesosystem problems that might arise? How might we avoid or prevent these problems?

4. What are some ways to counteract the risks of the exosystem? Can families better serve themselves individually or by banding together in the community in the face of exosystem risk?

5. The chapter discussed several examples of macrosystem risk. Think about some of their causes and the reasons they are so hard to overcome. What might be some ways of lessening their effect in our society?

6. Consider the concept "support system." Describe support systems at each level of the human ecosystem. What are some of the important systems for children? for parents?

# Chapter 4

Social historian Colin Geer points out five common views on the condition of "The American Family":

1. The family is decaying. In this view, the traditional family is falling apart, and the security of the national community is, as a result, in jeopardy.
2. The family is evolving. The adherents of this view say that the family, like any institution, must keep up with the times to do its job.
3. The family is not changing much at all. In this view, all the anxiety is misplaced—what is called the crisis of the family is simply a version of usual intergenerational conflict.
4. There are changes in the family, but there is no need to worry about them. From this point of view, the institutional structure of society is always changing and family changes are simply a reflection of that.
5. The family is in retreat, defending itself against the power of the human-potential movement. In this perspective, the family is an oppressive agent of an oppressive social system that is being beaten back by the positive, progressive forces freed in a postindustrial society undergoing liberation.

Any discussion about the human ecosystem must deal with the family. As the "headquarters for human development," families are the most basic and enduring of social institutions. At the same time, families are changing all the time in response to their members' needs and the pressures of the society around them.

This chapter looks at the family in two ways: as a small group of people sharing love, intimacy, and responsibility for children, and as a social institution that has different characteristics under different circumstances. All the richness and diversity of the human species are present in families. We view ethnic, cultural, historical, and personal variations as sources of strength, as adaptations to specific conditions that provide different answers to the age-old question of how to achieve personal closeness and share rights, responsibilities, and participation in the wider society. Finally, the chapter addresses current family weaknesses and points of stress with an eye toward ways that helpers and policymakers can build family strengths.

# The Family as a Social System

## What Is a Family?

Families are the thread that holds the human race together. Through our families we are connected to the past—the distant times and places of our ancestors—and to the future—the hope of our children's children. For most people, family means home, and home is where the heart is. In the words of Robert Frost: "Home is the place where/when you have to go there/they have to take you in" (from "The Death of the Hired Hand"). Of course a family is a psychological rather than a physical place.

How can we go about studying and trying to help families? Families are the central microsystem, the "headquarters" for human development. Therefore, we must know the kinds of experiences a family offers parents and children if we are to understand the ecology of human development. It is also possible to think of the family as a social institution and ask questions about family patterns throughout society. These viewpoints—individual families and "the" family—

will be the two main approaches to families we use in this chapter. We will also discuss how families can be understood and eventually strengthened and supported using the ecological approach to human development discussed in Chapters 2 and 3.

What is a family? Despite the fact that all over the world there are diverse cultures with widely differing family forms, three commonalities emerge in traditional analyses: marriage, childbearing, and kinship. According to Reiss, the universal essence of the family is "a small kinship-structured group with the key function of nurturant socialization" (Reiss, 1980, p. 29). "Kinship," however, is a matter of social definition, representing a consensus about the scope and limits of family membership. Generally it extends outward from the individual through linkages of blood and marriage. It can be based on genetic ties or social ties, and often implies economic rights and responsibilities. Within the family, parents contract with each other through marriage or at least through some enduring relationship to share the responsibilities of childrearing. Thus, the central elements of the family are kinship as seen by the family and others; marriage or its surrogate uniting parents; and dependent children cared for by family members. The family also serves a vital social function.

> The family means many things to many people, but in its essence it refers to those socially patterned ideals and practices concerned with biological and cultural survival of the species (Keller, 1971, p. 1).

Contemporary social forms, most particularly the single-parent household, challenge traditional formulations. We can hardly rule out these households from the definition of family, however. So perhaps we need to base our discussion on a less restrictive criterion, namely, "at least two people related by blood, marriage or adoption." Such a compromise seems better in tune with modern social realities. Our goal throughout this book is to respect diversity, and thus, we must adapt to changing norms without capitulating to the trends that produce them if we believe those trends to be harmful.

Individuals are born into a family—called the family of origin—and eventually may start a family of their own—the family of procreation. Children, parents, and the lifelong bonds of kinship make up the basic family concept. The family of origin precedes the child, because he or she does not choose his or her family. Children are almost completely dependent for the first few years of life, and this basic biological fact necessitates social patterns that protect, nurture, and teach children. Upon children depend both the future of the families and the society into which they are born. Childhood is the one time when life really does "owe us a living." In turn, children learn what they are expected to do to become members of society, what they must do to become a person. Adults must learn how to care for and socialize children. The family, thus, is a place for children to both love and learn, to be loved and to teach.

The family takes many different forms, both across nations and within societies. The norm for our culture is for a man and a woman to marry and then raise their children together. However, there are quite a few variations on that basic theme. Many children (18 percent at any one time) are raised by only one parent—almost half spend some time in a single parent household during their first eighteen years (U.S. Bureau of the Census, 1979). Not all couples have children—perhaps 20 percent do not (Blake, 1979). Yet, the marital institution is, in many ways, the center of the family in culture and in practice. Theoretically, at least, it is a voluntary tie, one which offers certain benefits and responsibilities to a couple, and which makes possible the nurturance of children. Considering the families of origin and procreation, most people spend much of their lives in family units, and virtually all of their lives as part of an active kin system of some sort. We fulfill our needs for identity, relatedness, intimacy, and growth—in short, our most deeply human qualities—through our lives in families. The family is the great humanizer. In the words of Margaret Mead:

> As in our bodies we share our humanity, so also through the family we have a common heritage . . . the task of each family is also the task of humanity. This is to cherish the living, remember those who have gone before, and prepare for those who are not yet born (Mead, 1965, p. 11).

## Families as Systems

Just as individuals develop within the family microsystem, families are situated within society. The relations between a family and the larger society are meso-, exo-, and macrosystem issues, as we defined these terms in Chapters 2 and 3. The mesosystems between families and such microsystems as schools, churches, and friendship networks are the most concrete expressions of the family–society relation. Exosystems of importance to the child include the parents' workplace and the local government. Finally, the overall cultural climate for families in society is an important influence on their well-being. This is a macrosystem concern, and we will consider it again in Chapter 6 and then again in Chapters 9 and 10.

The family mediates between individual and society (Lerner & Spanier, 1978). Most children are prepared for membership in society through family socialization in social relationships. In this way the family can be seen as "society in miniature," localizing and concretizing societal values and practices in every household to a greater or lesser degree. The match between what the family models and teaches and what society wants and needs is not perfect, however. The family is not a "rubber stamp," automatically producing model citizens.

The unique advantages and shortcomings of every family affect the future of our society in the form of our children, tomorrow's citizens. The macrosystem suggests blueprints, or models, for personal and social development; families respond based on their own inner workings, traditions, and values. The resulting dialogue between the individual, the family, and society is the stuff of history. Hagestad wrote: "It [the family] is an arena where lives are structured and interwoven, in which meanings are created in a blending of historical forces, family realities, and individual needs and resources" (Hagestad, 1981a, p. 11).

An excellent example of the kind of dynamics existing among individual, family, and society is Elder's (1974) study of the Great Depression summarized in Chapter 2. The intricate complexity of the connections may seem forbidding, but it does reflect the nature of these social realities. Family, individual, and society are inextricably intertwined; geneology, biography and history are wedded. Extricating the thread of family from the fabric of human experience is no easy task, as the following account demonstrates.

The balance of power among the individual, the family, and society seems to differ across time and culture. This variety has been the topic of much speculation. In the 1940s Carle Zimmerman analyzed civilizations through history in terms of the relations among individual, family, and social power (Zimmerman, 1947). He saw three main family forms, each associated with a different phase of historical development and each reflecting a particular constellation of social forces. His analysis tells us as much about him as it does about families, of course, and as much about his time and place as it does about the civilizations he studied.

In Zimmerman's view, the most primitive family type is the trustee family. Actually a clan or tribe, the trustee family tends to be the predominant force in "primitive" society. It is governed autocratically and parents rule by brute force. The individual is subservient, and there are few if any formal institutions apart from the clan. As Zimmerman saw it, the trustee family, based entirely on particularistic concerns, cannot exist outside of a primitive civilization. Of course, a more broadly based anthropological awareness tempers this view (Mead, 1935).

As Zimmerman saw it, the trustee family breaks down gradually. As individuals seek the freedom and diversity the clan does not offer, a more developed and elaborate community begins to evolve. A society emerges, with government, commerce, law, and literate culture. Individuals establish nuclear families ("the domestic family"), apart from the domination of the tribe, both as a cause and effect of socioeconomic development. An equilibrium is struck among the three levels (individual, family, and society), with each able to attain its goals. This phase of history, according to Zimmerman, constitutes a kind of Golden Age and has occurred in the prime of the Greek, Roman, and modern eras. Like most social commentators, however, Zimmerman saw his own era as a period of upheaval, and even dissolution, and "the decline of the family" was to blame. We must note that Zimmerman's era (the 1940s) is often cited by commentators in the 1980s as a Golden Era.

The "atomistic family" is the third of Zimmerman's (1947) family forms, and it represents an excessive swing away from the trustee family. The balance achieved under the domestic family is threatened as society begins to usurp powers and functions from the family. As the family weakens, individualism grows to become the predominant cultural force. Family and social allegiances are minimized. The atomistic family is held together only by a private agreement, with the sacred tradition and the social pressure to maintain family institutions weakened. Sociobiologists see this as an "unnatural" family form because it deviates so markedly from our evolutionary history as a species (vandenBerghe, 1979), and religious fundamentalists join them in this concern, albeit for quite different reasons. Zimmerman felt that the modern world was threatened with the fate suffered by the Greek and Roman eras, a downfall associated with the decline of the domestic family and the rise of atomism. Many contemporary Americans share this concern about their own society, our society. Certainly one of the issues before us throughout this book is the analysis of the status of the modern family. Like Zimmerman, we may be seduced by the idea that our times are the worst of times, the times of decline. Therefore, we must be careful lest we impose unfounded biases on the phenomena and treat as "decline" and "deterioration" what may actually be simply healthy adaptation to changed conditions. As the recent history of the term "cultural deficit" shows, this is a real and pressing danger for us (Tulkin, 1972). We are prone to see as deviation from necessary norms what may actually be quite legitimate, equivalent differences in style.

## Individual Families

As we said earlier, in some ways all families are alike, and in some ways each family is different. A family is a little society of its own, and in this sense every family has its own small-scale culture, government, language, foreign policy, and even its own myths. One way of understanding individual families is to describe the dimensions on which they vary.

Membership is the most basic dimension along which families vary. At a minimum, a family is two people related by blood or marriage, although such a small family is at one end of the membership continuum. These two can be a husband and wife, father and daughter, grandmother and grandson, or some other combination. An extended family, at the other extreme, is made up of a composite of nuclear families, with multigenerational ties. Cousins, aunts, and grandparents can join a couple and their young children to form a rich blend of ages and experiences.

A second important dimension along which families vary is their progress through various developmental stages. Several researchers have proposed models of these stages (e.g., Aldous & Hill, 1969). Duvall (1975) has advanced one model of family life that focuses on the expansion and shifting of roles, both of individual family members and the family as a whole. The eight-stage model begins with marriage and traces the family through the growth of children and parents. Even in these most basic aspects, there is variation among families, however. Some families begin without marriage. The 1980 U. S. Census showed a dramatic increase in the number of unmarried people cohabitating. These same data document a growing number of mothers starting families without a permanent father in the family picture. At the same time, more families are existing as married couples without children, only temporarily (for five to ten years) or permanently. Rather than jumping to the conclusion that these trends indicate social pathology, we ought to first consider how well such patterns work for their participants and for the rest of society. This will allow us to see the "model" as an empirical standard rather than a moralistic edict.

*Stage 1. Beginning Families:* when the couple is first married, before the birth of children. This represents creation of the microsystem. The principal ecological issue here is how macrostructural and other forces affect courtship and mating patterns. For example, wars tend to simultaneously speed up courtship and remove a major segment of the eligible bachelors. Both effects can influence who gets married and when.

*Stage 2. Childbearing Families:* when the first child is born until it is 30 months of age. Birth of a child radically alters the microsystem of the family. What is more, it makes relevant a whole new set of mesosystems (e.g., daycare-home) and exosystems (e.g., working conditions).

*Stage 3. Families with Preschool Children:* when the first child is between 2½ and 6 years old. Still additional mesosystems come into play (e.g., preschool-home), and the relevance of the neighborhood as a physical and social environment increases.

*Stage 4. Families with School Age Children:* first child between 6 and 13 years old. The school-home relationship is added to the list of relevant mesosystems, as is the relation between peer group and home.

*Stage 5. Families with Teenagers:* oldest child 13–20 years old. Again, the mesosystem potential (if not demand) increases, as does the influence of exosystems, as the child's world expands.

*Stage 6. Families as Launching Centers:* when the first child leaves until the last child leaves. Here the macrosystem becomes particularly important, because it has much to say about how ready the environment is to receive a specific youth.

*Stage 7. Families in the Middle Years:* from when all children are gone until breadwinner's retirement. Here the family depends upon the children to establish themselves so that the parents may find support from them. This is a mesosystem issue (home$_1$–home$_2$).

*Stage 8. Aging Families:* from retirement until the death of one spouse. Here the progress of the family depends very heavily on all levels of the human ecology—the health of the organism, the functionality of the marital relationship, the support from outside the home and the socioeconomic blueprints that affect pensions and the status of the elderly in society.

These eight stages are organized around typical or normative events and do not apply to all families equally. They provide, however, a general model that is useful for orienting ourselves to families and the relative importance of various social forces and institutions to them at different times. The differences we encounter across families, cultures, and communities are as important as the commonalities. The professional helper should be prepared to deal positively with these differences.

A third dimension of families is actually external to the family itself but exerts a powerful influence in determining a family's "personality." We refer to the cultural and historical context. Even within the United States, extensive variability exists among families, as we look across subcultures and over time. Family norms—commonly held ideas as to what should happen in families, and when—have a good deal of consistency *within* ethnic, religious, and socioeconomic subcultures (although even here there is substantial variability), at a given period of time, and a wide diversity *between* cultural and historical categories (although there are some generally common themes).

The most fruitful focal point for our discussion of family differences is ethnicity. Ethnic differences in family norms embrace nearly all aspects of definition, structure, process, and outcome. They derive from historical experience—e.g., an agrarian, peasant tradition versus an urban, commercial tradition—and perhaps even from the evolutionary history of gene pools (Freedman, 1974). They touch family form and membership—e.g., nuclear vs. extended. They figure as both causes and mediators of demographic trends—e.g., marriage, fertility, and divorce—and social status—e.g., occupational and vocational aspirations and achievement. They incorporate norms about sex roles—e.g., patriarchy vs. matriarchy—and intergenerational relations—e.g., the authority of grandparents. They affect critical aspects of parent-child relations—e.g., the use of corporal punishment and expectations about independence and maturity demands. While some ethnic differences have subsided in recent decades as the major pre-World War II immigrant groups have been acculturated, strong differences remain, even among these groups. What is more, the "Latinization" of much of the United States has meant a major upswing in concern for ethnic variations, as has the assertion of ethnic identity by American Indians, Blacks, and Orientals. Assessing the meaning, significance, and service implications of ethnic and cultural differences for family relations is a major unmet challenge (Garbarino & Ebata, 1981).

## How Do Families Work?

How does a family work? As a small group of individuals of different ages, sexes, and backgrounds, a family is a complicated, sometimes difficult, but harmonious blending of different voices. Some family researchers have found it useful to consider three types of systems (Kantor & Lehr, 1975): the family unit, the interpersonal subsystems, and the personal subsystems. These systems divide the family into sections of decreasing size. The family unit is the family as a whole, the interaction of all members of a family. The interpersonal subsystem is the collection of smaller relationships within the family. A family of five people, for example, can be thought of as containing ten different dyadic (two person) relationships. The personal subsystem is the total of individuals who come together to form a family and its interpersonal subsystems. Thus, a family of five members is five individuals in ten possible dyads making up one family unit; a family of three individuals contains three dyads; a family of four contains six. Each member is an individual, a family member related to other family members, and a part of the whole family group.

The three family subsystems are helpful in understanding how families function. Family process—the give-and-take of daily life—depends on individual members, interpersonal relations, and the whole family group being able to come together and apart as needed. We can consider some important issues common to all families to exemplify this point.

*Family boundaries* are the conceptual dividing line between individuals, the relationships between members, and between the family and the external world. Every family has its own ideas about where the rights and responsibilities of each member begin and leave off, vis-à-vis other members, the family as a whole, and the world at large. These ideas come mainly from the macrosystem's cultural blueprints, but may include idiosyncratic family traditions, personal histories, and ethnic aspects as well. Boundaries define how separate or connected the subsystems are, as well as the flexibility of movement between subsystems. Boundaries define who is a stranger. A stranger entering a home can be made to feel welcome or intruding, depending on the family's boundary to the external world. This can apply to a new baby, an adopted child, a step-child, a child returning from foster care, or a step-parent. Adolescence is a trying time for many families because of the pressure to change family boundaries as the youth recedes from family authority and protection and enters intimate relationships outside the family that she may try to import into the family.

*Internal organization* is the pattern of interaction within a family. Communications, decision making, and family activities are some of the areas of internal organization. Family interaction establishes expectations for how members are to act toward each other. These are important to understanding what is considered "right" or "normal" in a family. In general, the nature of family life seems to generate norms about intimacy, frequency of contact, and power assertion (Burgess, 1980).

*Family goals or themes* are the priorities, values, and commitments the family sets for itself and for its members. These may be explicit or implicit and can range from very specific goals for children—e.g., attending college—to very general hopes—e.g., that the family will remain close over the years. Family goals often span the generations, acting as a cultural or genealogical legacy from the past that fosters continuity. Family goals are a key to the emotions and possible conflicts within families. Often such conflict is a result of mutually exclusive individual and family goals that reach crisis proportions in the hothouse of family interaction, as when one member wants to pursue personal fulfillment at the expense of the family business.

Virginia Satir, a noted family therapist, cited four areas that often present problems in troubled families (Satir, 1972): self-worth, communication, rules, and the link to society. Doubts about self-worth, the first problem, afflict the personal subsystem. Families can help or hinder an individual's positive self-regard, and when people suffer from basic doubts about their own worth and esteem, the family as a whole suffers. Rohner's work on rejection discussed in Chapter 3 reinforces this view, and we will expand upon this in Chapter 6.

Communication problems are primarily problems of internal family organization. These can include a lack of dialogue, or a failure to get across each member's point of view. The classic complaint that teenagers and parents do not "speak the same language" is an example of this. Often more serious is the breakdown of communication between spouses. In their study of abusive and neglectful families, Burgess and Conger (1978) reported that dysfunctional families were characterized by a relatively low level of overall interaction, and by couples with a tendency to ignore positive behaviors and respond to negative behaviors.

Family rules can be an interaction problem, or a problem associated with disagreement about attaining goals. These rules are often implicit and unstated, but they determine the ways in which members conduct their interaction. The rules become problems when they are ineffective in controlling behavior, when they do not facilitate the meeting of goals, or when members are no longer satisfied with them. A lack of flexibility is often part of the problem about rules (Baumrind, 1980). In this case, a family is not able to adjust to the pressures of inner or external forces smoothly, and members resist the normal transitions of life that produce role changes—e.g., the onset of adolescence or the wife going to work.

We can think of the family's link to society as a boundary issue. Family-society relations (meso-, exo- and macrosystem issues) can be a problem when the walls are too high and rigid, as when a family is isolated from neighbors, institutions, and social supports. Social isolation is a correlate of many family problems, such as child abuse (Garbarino, 1977a,b). The other extreme can also be a problem. If the family has no demarcation apart from society and is defenseless against outside influences, it may not provide adequate identity, support, and guidance for its members.

As should be clear by now, scholars of the family are addicted to typologies, and the matter of boundaries is no exception. Kantor and Lehr (1975) have described three general types of contemporary families (not to be confused with Zimmerman's historical forms). Each has its own type of organization and method of attaining equilibrium among individuals, the family, and the outside world. Each views the family as a semipermeable system, with a constant stream of information and influence flowing in and through the family.

The first of Kantor and Lehr's family types is the "closed" family. Its limits are rigid, with clear and well-defined boundaries. Time is regular; the family functions on the basis of scheduled rhythms that supersede individual priorities or whim. Energy is steady, with family projects and concerns primary. The closed family is based on a "family comes first" philosophy, regulated by conformity to family goals, strict family events, family-defined reality, and an emphasis on stability. This family presents a challenge to us because it tends to resist the initiatives of human services and social policy, particularly when and if its members are having trouble. But there is usually strength and commitment to draw upon, if the professional can win over the family and gain its cooperation.

The second family type is "open." The open family is organized around flexibility. Its limits are variable, as members flow in and out of family realms easily. Scheduling of time is variable. Members try to accommodate family events and the family tries to accommodate its members' concerns. There are family events, but they are flexible, based on the shifting needs of the members. Energy is flexible, with members free to involve themselves in family and extrafamilial activities. Consensus is the usual operating procedure for decision-making in the family, and the family hangs together as the sum of individually and family-oriented members. It is strong, but inclined to be adaptive. It can make good use of external resources. It is the ideal form from the perspective of the human service provider and policy-maker. The danger, of course, is that the relative ease of serving this type of family will tend to make it the only family served.

The third family type is "random." The random family is marked by instability. Boundaries are unclear, shifting, and amorphous. Time is irregular, as each member follows his own individual schedule. Any family event is more a coincidence than a planned commitment. Energy is fluctuating; members seek involvements in or out of the family with no limits or ongoing pattern upheld. The family as such barely exists, and is rather a collection of individuals sharing a household and engaging in interaction only when it happens to suit them. The random family is often the bane of existence for the provider of human services. It is difficult to get any social leverage on individual or dyadic problems through such families. It is like boxing with jello. Unlike the closed family, it does not actively resist external forces, but often passively overcomes them. The challenge to the professional helper often seems overwhelming. One way to think about different types of families is in terms of family strengths, or the qualities that seem to make families "work."

## Building Strong Families

All families, as we have said, are unique. Just as clearly, some families work better than others. How does one recognize which families are more successful? How can we encourage family strengths?

The crucial property of families, and of systems in general, is that the whole and its parts must both be able to meet their goals for both to continue. A family "works" when its members feel good about the family, when their needs are being met, and development and relationships flow smoothly. The whole functions best when the subsystems, in Kantor and Lehr's (1975) terms, recognize their responsibilities toward the family as a whole (the family unit), and when the family unit is flexible enough to encompass all its members as they pursue their individual goals. It is a very complex "All for one and one for all," along with a dose of "Each man for himself."

Stinnett (1979) studied a group of families suggested by community contacts as "strong families." His interviews with them generated the following common characteristics:

*Appreciation:* The members regard each other warmly, positively, and give support to each other as individuals.

*Spending time together:* Strong families spend time together and enjoy it.

*Good communication patterns:* Family members were honest, open, and receptive towards each other.

*Commitment:* The family unit was important to its members, as were the interpersonal subsystems within the family. Much energy and time was directed inward toward the family rather than outward to other interests.

*High degree of religious orientation:* Strong families seem anchored in a sense of purpose that was often religiously based. A spiritual sense of life gave family members a common belief and promoted family values.

*Ability to deal with crises in a positive manner:* Strong families were able to deal with conflicts and banded together in mutual support when bad times arose.

Another study, conducted by a group of medical doctors and family specialists, investigated family characteristics associated with healthy families (Lewis et al., 1976). The study was based on urban Southern middle-class white intact families containing at least one adolescent child at home. Using rater observation scale, clinical interviews, and analysis of family communication, the investigators divided a small subsample of twelve families into six optimal and six adequately functioning families.

Based on six hours of clinical interview with each family, seven characteristics were found which distinguished the two groups and which correlated highly with the other two methods. The seven characteristics are:

1. An affiliative, as opposed to an oppositional, attitude about people.
2. A respect for the subjective world view of self and others.
3. Openness in communication, as opposed to confusing or distancing communication.
4. A firm and solid parental coalition in dealing with children, as opposed to parental competition.
5. Appreciation for complex human motivation, as opposed to a simple, controlling outlook.
6. Spontaneity, as opposed to a rigid or stereotyped approach to interaction.
7. The encouragement of unique and creative, as opposed to routine or bland, human characteristics and interests.

The individual members of the two groups also exhibited differences: Husbands from the optimal families were more interpersonally oriented, were supportive of their wives, and found vocational satisfaction important. Wives in the optimal group were more likely to have higher marital and family satisfaction than wives from the adequate group. Likewise, adequate wives more often suffered from symptoms of depression, psychopathology, and obesity. Of all family members, wives were the most vulnerable to family problems, being the first to show signs of distress. There were no striking differences among the children in the two groups.

The researchers also found family organization to be an important and distinctive characteristic. Similar to Kantor and Lehr's (1975) three family types, the most dysfunctional families were those with a chaotic, disorganized structure. Adequate families had a rigid, conforming orientation, while the optimal families tended to exhibit a flexible structure balanced between individual and family needs, similar to Kantor and Lehr's open family.

The characteristics found in the two studies cited can be interpreted as being either causes of, or as the results of, strong families. If it is the latter, it would not help to tell an unhappy, poorly functioning family to simply assume the characteristics of a strong family. But on the other hand, there are qualities associated with strong families that social service workers and all of society should recognize and respect as such. The welfare of each individual member and of the family as a whole is an important characteristic of strong families. Stressing one at the expense of the other can be an invitation to trouble.

Learning to think in "family" terms, as opposed to "individual" terms, has led many people toward the growing field of family therapy. Unlike individual therapy, which treats a person outside their social environment, family therapy focuses on the troubled family as the unit of analysis for treatment. Often the family may join the "identified patient" to therapy—a child afraid to go to school; a rebellious, self-destructive teenager; a feuding husband and wife—but it is the family that is seen as a primary cause of members' problems or dysfunctions.

There are a number of different approaches to and leading theoreticians in the family therapy movement, all attempting to help troubled individuals by intervening into patterns of family interaction. Some derive their approaches from psychoanalytic theory, others from behavioral modification theory, and still others from General Systems Theory. Family therapy holds out the hope of being an effective method of helping troubled families, as well as providing new insights into family process and dynamics.

## Whither *The* Family?

Although there is probably no such thing as a "typical" family, we are interested in what families are like on the whole and in how they change, particularly in how their structure and membership change. Demographic studies give us a sense of general family trends and allow us to speculate about the reasons for those trends. History is usually studied on a social level, but life is lived by individuals, and they are the real subject of attempts to understand the changing face of society. Rosa Luxemburg, the European Socialist of the early 20th century, said: "It is in the tiny domestic struggles of individual people, as they grope toward self-realization, that we can most truly discern the great movements of society." C. Wright Mills echoed this theme:

> We have come to see that the biographies of men and women, the kinds of individuals they have become, cannot be understood without reference to the historical structures in which the milieux of their everyday life are organized. Historical transformations carry meanings not only for individual ways of life, but for the very character—the limits and possibilities—of the human being (Mills, 1975).

Are Americans changing because American families are changing? The rate of divorce has more than doubled in the past twenty years (Reiss, 1980), so that now the Census Bureau estimates that between 40 percent and 50 percent of recent marriages will end in divorce (Spanier, 1980). Divorced parents are less likely than they were in the past to move in with a relative, and this separateness may produce both independence and vulnerability. One study reported that in 1900 one-half the households contained a nonparental adult (mainly boarders), while by 1970 less than 10 percent did (Bronfenbrenner, 1975). Demographers estimate that 45 percent of children born in the 1970s will spend some of their first eighteen years in single-parent homes (U.S. Bureau of the Census, 1979). Thus, the number of adults in our families has declined.

The number of children per family has also fallen, from an average of over three children per woman born in the 1930s to an estimated rate below two children per woman born in the 1950s (Cherlin, 1981). This may partially offset the declining number of adults in American households, but it may present other challenges to family dynamics. The age at first marriage seems to be rising, with the median age now 24.4 for men and 22.8 for women, up almost two years for both sexes since the 1950s (U.S. Bureau of the Census, 1980a). Women with children, whether the children are in school or preschool, are more than twice as likely to be working outside the home in 1979 as in 1950: 49 percent versus 12 percent for mothers of preschoolers, 59 percent versus 28 percent for those with older children (Cherlin, 1981). Finally, the 1980 census has reported that the average number of people per household has declined from 3.11 in 1970, to an average of 2.75. While there are increases in the percentage of single-parent and female-led households, the percentage of two-parent families has dropped from 81.2 percent of all households in 1970 to 74.9 percent of all households in 1978 (U.S. Bureau of the Census, 1980b). Table 4:1 presents a summary of family changes over the past decade.

One interpretation of these figures is that American families are becoming increasingly isolated. Because we are marrying later, divorcing more frequently, having fewer children, and living alone more often, the number of people living together is declining. What effect does this have on the family's social resources? When a child grows up in a household with "too few" people there is risk to development as discussed in Chapter 3. We naturally wonder whether parents, too, are increasingly deprived of intimacy and support, especially single parents who must raise children alone.

On the other hand, as Mary Jo Bane has shown in her book *Here to Stay* (1976) families are in no danger of extinction. The percentage of men and women who do marry eventually is quite high; by age thirty over ninety percent of men and women have been married at least once. Moreover, while many people delay childbearing, few forsake it completely. Though divorce is increasingly common, remarriage awaits 80 percent of currently divorced partners

Table 4:1: Summary of family changes, 1970 and 1980

| Nature of Change | 1970 | 1980 | % Change |
|---|---|---|---|
| Marriages Performed | 2,159,000 | 2,317,000 | + 7.3 |
| Divorces Granted | 708,000 | 1,170,000 | + 65.3 |
| Married Couples | 44,728,000 | 47,662,000 | + 6.6 |
| Unmarried (Cohabitating) Couples | 523,000 | 1,346,000 | +157.4 |
| People Living Alone | 10,851,000 | 17,202,000 | + 58.5 |
| Married Couples With Children | 25,541,000 | 24,625,000 | − 3.6 |
| Children Living With 2 Parents | 58,926,000 | 48,295,000 | − 18.0 |
| Children Living With 1 Parent | 8,230,000 | 11,528,000 | + 40.1 |
| Families With Both Husband and Wife Working | 20,327,000 | 24,253,000 | + 19.3 |

Source: U.S. Bureau of the Census.

(Reiss, 1980)—one-half within three years. Fewer children per family may actually improve the quality of parent–child relations by allowing more time for each child and by reducing the risk of unwanted or unaffordable children (Blake, 1979). Research also shows that within social classes, children in smaller families score higher on intelligence tests than children in larger families (Claussen, 1966; Zajonc & Markus, 1976). We can expect that smaller families make it easier to operate in the "authoritative" style described by Baumrind (1979).

How do people feel about their families? A study published in 1976 on the quality of life in America found marriage and family life to be highly important to people (Campbell, Converse, & Rodger, 1976). Seventeen domains of life including standard of living, religion, family, work, and friends were assessed for their contribution to life satisfaction and their importance to the respondents. Health, marriage, and family life were cited most often as being "extremely important" factors, and marriage and family life were the domains that best predicted overall life satisfaction. Fifty-six percent of the women and 60 percent of the men were completely happy with their marriage, and 44 percent of the women and 43 percent of the men were completely happy with their family life in general. Only 6 percent of the men and 8 percent of the women rated the family as less than neutral in satisfaction. Perhaps the increasing acceptance of divorce in unsatisfactory marriages means that the "still married" include more satisfactory spousal relationships. These survey results suggest that family life is a integral part of people's lives and does much toward determining their overall life satisfaction.

It is interesting to note that satisfaction with marriage (an individual life-cycle variable) varies systematically over the family life cycle. Studies show that the transition to parenthood brings about a reduction in marital satisfaction, with the low point being the time when the children are teenagers. Once the children leave the parents at the "empty nest" stage, marital satisfaction may actually increase, even returning to the levels found in newlyweds (Rollins & Feldman, 1970; Rollins & Cannon, 1974; Campbell et al. 1976).[1]

What can account for the current trends in family life and what can possibly help us understand the direction in which we are heading? One place to look is in the changes in fertility and mortality rates; the entrances and exits of individuals in families. The family is like a cross-country train. We may get on in Des Moines and get off in Denver, but the train started long ago in New York and will continue on without us until San Francisco. The actions of one generation have been influenced by the preceding generation and will have an effect on the next generations to come aboard. Hagestad writes:

> We have "ripple effects" because of the intimate interconnections of roles and lives. Marriage in one generation creates in-laws in another. Parenthood creates grandparenthood. Voluntary childlessness may create involuntary grandchildlessness. "Voluntary" divorce leaves children to be raised "involuntarily" in single-parent homes and creates "ex-relationships" (Hagestad, 1981a, p. 20).

Thus, the current trend toward small families will limit the possibility of large extended families in later years. An only child's daughter will have no aunts or uncles from that parent. The increase in the life span will mean that potential intergenerational relations will increase. There will be more grandparents and great-grandparents, and they will be alive, if not around, for more of the lives of their decendents. For the same reasons, people are spending proportionately fewer years of their lives with children at home, but they may paradoxically be financially responsible for them longer because of increased involvement in higher education (Garbarino, 1981b). The time spent in the "empty nest" stage of marriage may increase. Widowhood, too, is more probable because of the increasing gap in the life expectancy of men and women (Hagestad, 1981a). A family, then, changes along with the life patterns of its individual members.

## Families and Social Change

Social, cultural, and technological change has also had a profound effect on families. In the midst of rapid technological and economic change, we expect social institutions and relations, especially the family, to continue in an

---

[1] Interestingly, this may be due in part to the most dissatisfied couples divorcing, leaving the more satisfied couples overrepresented in later years. A longitudinal design may be required to assess changes in marital satisfaction over time (Spanier, Lewis, & Cole, 1975).

unchanging, eternal pattern. Any change is generally considered to be a loss, a decline (Bane, 1976). "The good old days" is the often heard refrain regarding the family of yesterday. Yet the very nature of the ecology of human development tells us that family and society are connected. Families respond to rapid and significant changes felt in every aspect of contemporary public life. We must always examine our view of family life for projections of our own fears and hopes about the phenomena. Thus, we must be careful of defining change as "decline" or "deterioration," unless we can actually evaluate the direction of the change as negative. Much of what we see as change is actually continuity; some of what we define as decline is actually healthy adaptation. And, even when we do observe real change, it may have no effect on children.

How have changes in society affected the family? The view of the family as a semipermeable system discussed earlier suggests an exchange between domestic and social forces, each influencing the other. Some say, however, that it is the family that has reacted to social change in this century, rather than the other way around. W. F. Ogburn, a sociologist writing in the early 20th century, concluded "that the nuclear family was inappropriate and unstable in an urban industrial society" (Ogburn, 1922). The problem he saw and emphasized was the loss of family functions. On the farm or in a small family business all family members worked together. Modern society stripped the family of its productive and educational responsibilities. The family became an emotional and developmental center, rather than an economic entity. Women, especially, were limited by the nuclear family because it provided them neither personal outlet nor opportunity for contribution to the family's material needs. Other scholars (e.g., Aries, 1962) emphasize that even these changes do not affect the nuclear family so much as the addition of functions previously handled by kin, elders, and church, or never performed in the first place.

The nuclear family may have rached a distinctive phase in the 1950s. Families in earlier generations were frequently broken up by death, in later decades by divorce. The 1950s were an oasis of stability (Hagestad, 1981a). Cherlin (1981) points out that long-term trends were suddenly reversed after World War II: More people married; they married earlier and more permanently, had more children, had children earlier, and lived more in nuclear families than did people before or after that time. Thus, what we often see as the deviant 1960s and 1970s may actually represent a return to a long-term trend, while it is the 1950s that may have been deviant.

Parsons and Bales' (1955) influential work on role specialization provided a theoretical perspective on nuclear families that was empirically well-suited to the 1950s. They found that small groups in laboratory studies contained "instrumental" and "expressive" leaders; the former were necessary to accomplish group goals, the latter, to keep the group's morale and feelings positive. Parsons and Bales saw men in the instrumental role, women in the expressive, despite the abundant evidence that both sexes perform both functions in different settings to varying degrees. This traditional ideology sees men as naturally extending their activities to instrumental spheres beyond the family (e.g., work), while women are primarily suited to the home or to limited involvements of an expressive nature beyond the home (e.g., nursing, teaching, volunteer work) (Parsons, 1949; Parson, Bales, & Shils, 1955).

The theoretical serenity of the 1950s was not permanent, however. Family role differentiation theories were assailed as being both simplistic and inaccurate. Critics charged that men and women display both expressive and instrumental qualities in family life (Slater, 1961; Udry, 1974). Women, who were questioning the justice of being confined in rigid roles and denied choice while their husbands had only to bring home a paycheck as fulfillment of familial responsibilities, were being heard publicly and in print in greater numbers.

Bernard (1981) calls this change the fall of the male "good provider" role. Men under the growing market economy had become identified and judged on the basis of their ability to provide for their families financially. Emotional and domestic responsibilities were secondary. The cooperation between men and women in providing for their families became a differentiated split. Separate? Surely. But equal? Each sex was identified in opposition to the other, unable to share in common tasks or concerns. Bernard describes the consequences of this role arrangement and conveys the hostility and resentment some feel:

> As the pampered wife in an affluent household came often to be an economic parasite, so also the good provider was often, in a way, a kind of emotional parasite (Bernard, 1981, p. 10).

The male provider role flourished as women were relegated to the home exclusively. Women have always been primarily responsible for childrearing, but only in the 19th and 20th centuries has mothering been the full-time job for most women (Degler, 1980). The homemaker role only makes sense when there are many children for whom to care. It declines when fertility declines. The good provider role only makes sense in a family in which women are to be provided for. Bernard (1981) foresees this role diminishing as, with increasing frequency, women both join the labor force and raise children alone. Some commentators now see the consequences of arbitrary sex roles, with men working and women home with children, as destructive to men, women, and their children (Slater, 1970; Chodorow, 1978).

More egalitarian sex roles will require deep changes in our institutions and in our relationships. Children, work inside and outside the home, and the options men and women can choose from in general will have to be reexamined in order to accommodate and support families who want to decide for themselves how to balance the activities and responsibilities of their lives. The changing role of women is, thus, a challenge and an opportunity for families. Can families continue to provide for the needs of their members, while at the same time allowing them to become all they would like to be?

Alternative roles and careers for women make new and different demands on the men in their lives, as well as on the women themselves. Successful adaptation to those changes will depend on adaptations both within and beyond the family as all of society learns to cope with new family forms. Such innovations in business and industry as in-house day care, flexible work hours, part-time and split-time positions, maternal and paternal leaves, and a rethinking about just what is women's and men's work will help. However, available research shows that we have a long way to go in making these adjustments (Bronfenbrenner & Crouter, 1981).

Work as an exosystem has traditionally been more an opponent than an ally of family relations. But as working mothers become the rule rather than the exception, and as more fathers seek increasing involvement with their growing children, business and industry is adapting to workers' needs as parents. Job satisfaction and stability can be enhanced by creating a working atmosphere where workers do not feel cut off from their personal lives all day. A better integration of work and family responsibilities will, no doubt, improve the quality and satisfaction of both adult microsystems.

Bruno Bettelheim, a child psychologist, singles out two other social innovations that have deeply affected the modern Western family: the rise in the standard of living and the availability of birth control (Bettelheim, 1980). The increased wealth made possible to the general public in modern society has tended to free the nuclear family from dependence on other families and family members. There is more mobility, both within and between families, as the economy expands. Young adults are able to move away from their parents, and older people are more likely to be able to support themselves. Wealth has facilitated and been accompanied by increased distance between family members. The questions is, Will that distance be experienced mainly as freedom or as isolation (Garbarino, 1977b)?

Advances in contraception have made childbearing less the destiny and more the choice of women. Clearly, sexual behavior, size of families, women in the labor force, and the role of women in general are all intimately affected by the ability to control pregnancy. Both affluence and birth control make the family an institution created and maintained more by choice and less by biological or economic necessity. The family of today faces challenges precisely because the family is more voluntary. What exactly are the challenges today's families face, and how can families be strengthened to stand a better chance of meeting them?

Families suffer from an ideological debate that has politicized issues perhaps better left to personal choice. On one side stand adherents of "traditional families," who view innovation as an enemy and personal fulfillment (especially women and children's) as a threat to the family. On the other side, many assail the family as repressive and stultifying, a domestic straitjacket of conventional morality and guilt. The middle road between these two extreme positions sees an appreciation for individual development and changing needs over the span of life, as well as for lifelong unconditional closeness and trust of family ties, with "family" defined loosely enough to encompass more than just the traditional form. Is not the ideal for people to have room to develop to their fullest, in the context of the support and feedback or caring kin?

Families are on their own. Family privacy, economic prosperity, and mobility patterns all separate parents and children from traditional sources of support and feedback, e.g., the church, elders, kin, and neighbors. Isolation is contagious; we become estranged from each other, and all families lose the social support of close and caring loved ones. It is increasingly difficult for family values to compete with the garish materialism and freedom of commercial society, and the ethic of individualism works against the cooperation and mutual sacrifices of stable families.

Our level of expectation is very high. A kind of social inflation, born of a rising tide of expectations, has made us acutely vulnerable to frustration and stress. The inevitable disappointments of life are magnified by what are often unrealistic standards for self-fulfillment. On the economic scene, our expectation that everyone can and should live in a single-family house, in the suburbs if possible, has led many families to become financially overcommitted. The result is a high level of stress and disruption of family life. We experience well-being because of social rather than material conditions, as discussed earlier (Campbell et al., 1976). A biblical passage speaks to this point: "What profiteth it a man that he should gain the world if he should lose his soul?" The same goes for families.

A family is in a constant state of becoming. Parents meet and marry, children are born and grow and move on, possibly to start families of their own. At this time, we still know little about the strain placed on individuals and families at each of these normative life changes. Looking back to Duvall's (1975) family life cycle, every stage involves adjustments by members to changes in their own and other members' lives. More understanding and attention, aimed at helping families deal with change, would go a long way to strengthen families and prevent further and more serious problems.

There is and there will continue to be an increasing flexibility and innovation in human relations. Traditional family forms will not be replaced, but will instead exist alongside less long-lasting unions, single parents, groups of adults (related and unrelated) living together and raising children, a breakdown of gender roles in family and society, and possibly even professional childraisers (Toffler, 1970). As customs and institutions, formerly required for economic survival, give way to more chosen and voluntary ties, we face an opportunity and a challenge to better meet people's needs for intimacy, love, and meaning, and to build social institutions that support these goals. The family will exist as long as people recognize and respond to members' needs for close lifelong bonds.

We have begun to see how important family life is to human development through the entire span of life. The family cannot stand up against the forces of society, the needs of individuals, and the crisis of confidence through which we have suffered without support from every level of the human ecosystem. We need a sense of toleration to new and different family forms along with a commitment to the need of children and parents. The community, our institutions, and all of society must move carefully and respectfully around families, so as not to disturb the fragile and terribly important process going on within them—the building and sustenance of human beings.

## RESEARCH CAPSULE

Of all the methods available in the study of families, none is more challenging or promising than naturalistic observation of families. Proponents of this method contend that family process can be best studied in the family's natural environment, where each family's unique dynamics are manifested.

The problems of naturalistic observation include the discomfort and anxiety of the families being observed and the great amount of time required to get a full and varied sampling of family life. Virtually any observational method will be faced with the problem of reactivity, of people acting differently because they are being observed. The advantage of natural observation as compared to laboratory or clinical studies is the fact that, in the home, the family is in their element and the subject of interaction will be the family's own concerns.

Two important examples of natural observation of families are Kantor and Lehr's *Inside*
*the Family* (1975) and Jules Henry's *Pathways to Madness* (1973). Kantor and Lehr's work is described in the chapter and was used primarily to advance theoretical systems of family dynamics. Henry's work is essentially anthropological; each family is entered as if it were a foreign culture. He entered and spent a week (approximately 100 hours) in five different families, each containing a psychotic institutionalized member. During the week he lived with the family, participating as a guest or visiting relative might have. His account of his observations is a fascinating and rich description of the personalities and family dynamics of each of the families observed. Naturalistic observations can uncover family norms and patterns, the "social reality" of each family, and in the case of these families, their destructive nature. Such research offers an experiential base from which theory and understanding can readily spring.

## PRACTICE CAPSULE

The idea of Family Impact Analysis arose in the late 1970s as a way of providing an evaluation of government policy on families.
In some ways analogous to environmental impact studies routinely done on the presumed effect of development on the local ecosystem,

family impact analysis would determine how government programs and policies would affect the nation's families, and advice would be given accordingly. As government is increasingly an influential factor in the lives of millions of Americans, the need to understand the effects of policies becomes more pronounced.

Currently, the idea is in the planning stage at George Washington University's Institute for Education Leadership. Headed by Sidney Johnson, the Family Impact Seminar is composed of 22 leading family researchers and policymakers. The goals of the seminar are to develop a "tool" for evaluating the effects of social programs on families.

The values of the group are based on supporting families in their role of supporting their members. When an institution reacts with a family, the family should maintain some degree of power in determining the course of action. Policies should provide families with options, recognizing the great diversity among families. A special concern is expressed, giving priority to the least privileged families in our society.

Three pilot family impact studies, in the areas of government as employer, foster care, and teenage pregnancy, are underway. The idea of family impact studies would provide input to virtually all aspects of the meso-, exo-, and macrosystems and virtually every government function, such as employment policies, urban development, taxation and social security, welfare, the military, and education.

# FOR FURTHER READING

Parker, B. *A mingled yarn*. New Haven: Yale University Press, 1972, 333 pp.

This account of a woman's family history, written by a psychologist, traces the forces which led to the dissolution of her family and one member's insanity. It reads like a good novel with a psychoanalytic flavor and offers a rare insight into a family's workings. Recommended for readers interested in the intergenerational transmission of values and problems.

Reiss, I. R. *Family systems in America* (3rd ed.). New York: Holt, Rinehart & Winston, 1980, 538 pp.

A leading text on the family, covering such topics as courtship, mate selection, marriage and childbearing, and cross-cultural and ethnic perspectives on the family. Reiss has a special interest in sexuality, and the book is particularly strong in that area. The section on family research methods is a welcome addition.

Satir, V. *People making*. Pala Alto, CA: Science and Behavior Books, 1972, 304 pp.

A wonderful book for and about families. It discusses common family problems and concerns in lay terms. There are many exercises and projects that families or groups can work on to facilitate communication, empathy, and family bonds. It is a very "up-beat" book with anecdotes and a "fun for all ages" appeal.

Stinnett, N., Chesser, B., & DeFrain, J. (Eds.). *Building family strengths: Blueprints for action*. Lincoln, NE: University of Nebraska Press, 1979, 449 pp.

This book is the first of a series coming out of an annual National Symposium on Building Family Strengths. Held at the University of Nebraska, this symposium is devoted to the advancement of "positive family life models." The volume contains articles on family strengths, approaches to family enrichment and counseling, effective parenting, children with special needs, and the family in later life. This book and the series which follows have proved successful in contributing to the growing literature on the strengthening and support of families.

# QUESTIONS FOR THOUGHT

1. Discuss the many types of families that occur in our society and around the world. Do they share any commonalities? How are they different?

2. What are some of the risks and opportunities families face in times of rapid social change? Think about such factors as mobility, changes in the labor force, sex roles, and generation gaps.

3. How are ethnic differences important for the person who works with children and families?

4. Duvall (1975) described eight developmental stages of families. Discuss some of the different challenges and problems families face at each stage of the family life cycle. What examples of families can you think of that do not fit this general pattern? What implications do those differences have for the development of these families? Are the same supports available to them as to families that are "typical?"

5. Satir (1972) regards self-worth, rules, communication, and links to society as four key areas with a potential for problems for the family. Review and discuss how each can become a source of family problems, and make suggestions on how to improve conditions for families with such problems.

6. What are problems you would expect to be typically associated with each of Kantor and Lehr's (1975) three family types?

7. Many families are currently adopting more egalitarian sex roles in child rearing, housework, decision making and work outside the home. What implications does this change in roles have for adults in the family? for children?

8. Considering the evidence of recent demographic trends, would you conclude that the family is in trouble, or merely adapting? Consider some of the family typologies described in the chapter (e.g., Zimmerman, Kantor & Lehr) to defend your point of view. Are new family functions replacing old ones no longer performed by the family?

# Chapter 5

When I was in my mother's body
she ate a lot of watermelons
An army of watermelon seeds came into the land
inside her body.
That's why I have so many freckles.
I'll get into my mother's body again
and let her eat a lot of lemons this time.
Then I'll be fair-skinned
and smelling good without any perfume.

Staats & Staats, *Looking up: A child's view of the adult world* (1978), p. 104.

From a child's struggle to understand what makes him or her the "way" he or she is, our attention is drawn to what makes childhood itself unique. It is difficult to fully conceptualize the relationship of the child to his environment without examining the child as an organism. This chapter raises these questions: What is the child? What is the developmental path the child follows? What influences this developmental path? The fact underlying these themes is that the child is an organism with a developmental agenda.

This chapter thus presumes to present the "child alone"—an organism with his or her own developmental agenda. We discuss the developmental process from the prenatal period through the adolescent years. Considered in this context are the changing historical definitions of childhood and how these historical perceptions have percolated down to the general public of today. External factors that influence the developmental process are also put into perspective. The developmental process is defined by the course of physical, cognitive, and socioemotional changes in the individual. If this chapter serves its purpose, it will give the reader a stronger grasp of the question, "What is a child?"

# The Developing Child

## What Is a Child?

What is a child? A thinking, feeling entity? An organism shaped by parental constrictions? A possession of his or her family, of the government, or of him or herself? A being in transit to adulthood? We see children as all of these, and more. We see children and their developmental needs as the fundamental building blocks of a human society. A society that does well by its children—and their parents—is basically sound (Bronfenbrenner, 1970). This theme runs through all our discussions. Our goal in this chapter is to outline some of the basic processes and events in child development. We will follow this in Chapter 6 with a discussion of parent–child relationships. In this chapter, however, we are most directly concerned with the child's own developmental agenda, albeit with a constant eye toward issues of social context. As ever, we are bringing to bear our ecological perspective.

Our theme in this chapter is the child as a developing, thinking, acting organism able to take initiatives to meet the challenges of the environment. We see children as resourceful and flexible, and we believe that challenge, *within limits,* is growth inducing. We will try in this chapter to outline some of these limits so that we will be in a better position to discuss how children use their resources in parent—child relations to meet developmentally appropriate challenges in their environments. This in turn will help us see how human services and social policy can and should work on behalf of children and families (Chapters 8 and 9).

The way the child's society defines the child influences contemporary policy and practice, and this macrosystem effect has existed since the ancient geniuses Plato and Aristotle began their efforts to develop a systematic conceptualization of human development. Their concern was to define the child in relation to family and society. Plato believed that most parents, imbued with the moral decadence of contemporary Athenian society, were unfit to raise their own children. Even parents who gave every appearance of being capable were still not up to the challenge of creating the caretakers of some future ideal state, because parenting techniques differed so widely that their separate influences would create a "medley of incongruities" in the character of the citizens. Therefore, all children were to be separated from their parents early in life, allowing the state to control child rearing and education. Plato struggled with the eternal issues of child rearing, most particularly with how to establish self-control in the child without destroying individuality and initiative. In any case, this notion of the state as arbiter of the child's well-being and best interests has obviously stayed with us and remains in contemporary child custody and child abuse laws (Biehler, 1981). We will return to these legal implications later, in Chapters 8 and 9.

Aristotle was also devoted to the concept of the "ideal society." However, he opposed state control of child rearing because he believed it denied most citizens the right to essential individual liberties and denied the family the right to provide personal and social stability for the child. He judged that different parents using different child rearing techniques would not provide undesirable "incongruities," but rather positive individuality. Aristotle proposed a transfer of power from the state to the parent. Rather than being a possession of the state, the child would be a possession of his parents. Unfortunately, to the present day, the child often finds himself either at the mercy of one force or another; always a possession, rarely a trust. An abused child, if not taken under the wing of the state, is left to contend unaided with the abusive parent. The imbalance of power is too great. Nowhere is this more clearly seen than in the case of incest, where the child cannot give truly informed consent because the child is asked to make a judgment inappropriate for her or his age and is forced to do so in a coercive climate where all the power lies outside her or his real control (Finkelhor, 1979). This is, of course, even true in those *rare* instances where incest occurs in a climate of love and respect.

The Platonic and Aristotelian conceptions of childhood have influenced successive generations by focusing on the question: "Who owns the child?" Aries (1962) proposed that during the Middle Ages, this issue was resolved by downplaying the notion of childhood as a separate period of life. Thus, children were not thought to be qualitatively different from adults, only smaller. Artistic depiction of children represented them as little adults. The children one sees in the paintings of the time do not have the characteristic "look" of modern children. Children who survived the critical period of early childhood immediately became "adults" in the eyes of society and were treated as such—with its positive and negative implications. Working, playing, and loving were shared with the young. Given the conditions of life, this was understandable. Life expectancy was short; most work was simple.

The advent of the Renaissance and the Reformation, followed by the eighteenth century revolutions in America and France, brought about important economic, political, and social changes. The influence of the Church diminished, as did social stratification, and economic opportunities grew. Families increasingly saw children as investments in the future. Childhood became a separate part of life, and more people began to recognize that children have their own inner lives. Whereas earlier the hardiest children had been sent to work or had been apprenticed, it became more and more common for children to go to school and prepare for careers (Gardner, 1978).

One of the attitudes toward children that underwent a most profound change was the shift from believing children to be wicked to viewing them as being innocent. "Expert opinion" believed children to be inherently sinful during the Middle Ages, and parents were advised to punish them often. Starting in the eighteenth century, however, a shift in attitude occurred. New religious forms stressed salvation and innocence. Baptism was believed to purify the soul. Child rearing began to be portrayed as a safeguard of the child's innocence. Debates as to the requirements of child education and child rearing became common as Western culture experienced significant liberalization.

The philosophers John Locke and Jean Jacques Rousseau placed particular emphasis on the importance of early child rearing and child learning. Locke developed what has been identified and handed down as the "environmental learning" view of child development. He envisioned the child's mind at birth as a "white paper" or blank slate ("tabula rasa") that provides form, but not content to the child as an individual. The knowledge that a child attains is learned through contact with the environment. Locke saw experience and observation as the sources of all ideas, yet he believed that children have personalities at birth that guide their responses. He also believed that parents should encourage the child's natural curiosity. He advocated the use of reinforcement rather than punishment in rearing and educating the child, techniques that have found their way into the theories of most contemporary psychologists, but still are resisted by some parents (Gardner, 1978).

Jean Jacques Rousseau believed in the inherent goodness of the young, but he believed this goodness was corrupted by the influences of society. His general message was that parents and teachers should fit education to the child, not force the child to learn what was beyond his or her natural grasp. If adults shield children from the negative aspects of society, their "natural goodness" would ensure that they make the right choices. Rousseau did not believe in the "perfectability" of human beings, as Locke did, but he suggested that education could "enhance" a child's desire to learn and develop. These ideas, too, have their contemporary counterparts (Biehler, 1981), although their philosophical character is foreign to much of contemporary scientific child development.

Certainly one of the environmental factors contributing to the past legal and cultural status of children was their relative physical vulnerability, given the poor sanitation and the inadequate health care characteristic of earlier eras. Children were not a good investment for the future, given their short life expectancy. As late as 1900, 55 percent of the children born in London's slums died before the age of five (Gardner, 1978), and even the rich had to contend with substantial infant mortality. After the Industrial Revolution, industrial managers came to see children as the least expensive source of labor, and their instrumental value increased. Concern for children began to increase in the early nineteenth century, as the standard of living began to rise and as epidemics became more subject to control. A few medical practitioners began to specialize in childhood diseases.

Along with the growing interest in the child and the questions raised about how best to train and educate children, the 1800s saw the growth of the discipline of biology, which became concerned with the study of the development of organisms. It was natural to study the "child-as-organism." Early studies of child development were initiated by Charles Darwin in the form of "baby biographies," daily diaries that reported happenings in a child's physical, mental, and emotional life.

The first person to conduct empirical research with children was G. Stanley Hall. Through the use of questionnaire data, he was able to develop an initial picture of how children viewed the world. Hall believed that human development proceeded in regular, ordered stages, one following the other, largely on the basis of internal cues. This approach was soon displaced, however, only to return to a position of prominence decades later.

Hall's theories, however, were based on environmental or mechanical learning theories of development. Learning theory emphasizes environmental influences, is skeptical about a natural course of development, and believes in drill and training. Environmental learning theory sees development as proceeding continuously rather than in stages. This theory values concrete, behavioral measures designed to avoid factors that defy careful definition and measurement. How has the notion of "environmental learning" come down to us in the present day?

The "environmental learning" concept was used first as the rationale for John

Watson's work in child behavior and development. Watson was inspired by the work of Pavlov in establishing a conditioned reflex in dogs. Combining Locke's ideas with Pavlov's techniques, he described a method whereby parents might shape the behavior of their children. As Watson developed his early views on behaviorism, he applied these views to controlled observations of newborn infants. His studies concentrated on the physical stimulation of babies and investigation of their reactions. He also was able to demonstrate classical conditioning (learned pairing of a previously unconnected set of events or objects) in infants.

The case of Albert and the white rat is now a legend. Albert was a small child whom Watson introduced to a white rat in a laboratory setting. Albert enjoyed playing with this rat until Watson introduced the stimulus of hitting a steel bar with a hammer just as Albert reached for the rat. Soon, the presentation of anything white and fuzzy to Albert caused fear, even without the loud sound. The process was later reversed to "cure" the child of his phobia. Watson's success in this endeavor led him to claim that if he had "a dozen healthy infants" to bring up in a prescribed environment, he could mold their lives totally. This claim was undermined by the demonstration that conditioned learning applied only to essentially involuntary reflex actions, and that attempts to build sequences of conditioned responses were rarely successful. But the idea that one can make children into whatever one wants through managing stimuli and reinforcements persists (Biehler, 1981).

Watson's work has been expanded by B. F. Skinner, who argues that every personality is the product of environmental experiences. He worked to condition voluntary responses, known as *operant conditioning*. Through control of voluntary responses, he proposed to shape sequences of behavior. In his fictional utopia *Walden Two,* Skinner envisioned placing children in the hands of child-rearing specialists who condition undesirable traits out of the children's behavior and desirable traits into it. Skinner recognizes that for behavior control to be effective in real life, we all must dispose of the notion of free will, the idea that there is some mysterious factor beyond behavior and reinforcement. To Skinner, "What a man does is the result of specifiable conditions, and once these conditions have been discovered, we can anticipate and determine his actions" (Biehler, 1981).

Albert Bandura is another proponent of environmental conditioning of human behavior. However, he has modified the environmental learning viewpoint. To Bandura, reinforcement does not influence behavior without the conscious involvement of the individual. Humans interpret stimuli and do not simply respond. From Bandura's perspective, human beings are capable of choosing how they will respond behaviorally to many situations—a phenomenon that he refers to as anticipatory control (Biehler, 1981). We can presume that this ability increases as the infant becomes the child, the adolescent, and then the adult. The concept of development presented in Chapters 1–3 sees this as standing at the heart of human experience.

Bandura provides a bridge from the strict environmental-learning approaches to those that emphasize the role of cognitive structures in human development. Two of the major pioneers in cognitive structural theories of development were Arnold Gesell and Abraham Maslow. Having observed that infants follow a uniform sequence of development, even in different environmental backgrounds, Gesell concluded that development was controlled by innate tendencies and that children mature according to a built-in timetable that controls much of their behavior. Children, therefore, are self-directed organisms that cannot be molded in the unlimited fashion envisioned by Watson and Skinner.

Maslow took the notion of cognitive structuralism and turned it into "self-determination." He concluded that each individual possesses an inner nature that determines behavior. Maslow believed that parents do not have the responsibility of *shaping* the behavior and growth of their child, but that they can make it possible for the child to follow an optimal course of development by optimizing the environment. To Maslow, optimization of the environment means trusting the child and being supportive rather than interfering. Maslow believed that given freedom, the growing child will choose the best path. He argued that only when children feel comfortable, safe, loved, and accepted *do* they choose the best path.

Is a child a self-directed or an environmental-directed organism? The preceding discussion indicates that both internal and external forces are important in child development, although exactly how these forces interact has not been definitely determined by science. As we will see, the controversy over what the child is and what controls the child's development provides a backdrop for policy issues (such as custody) and for other major theories we will discuss later in relation to processes of child development. If the history of childhood as a philosophical issue is important, the history of each human organism is miraculous.

## How Does a Child Come About?

A child is a miracle. From a microscopic speck containing the genetic equipment of the species comes an organism complete with individual variety. Before we move beyond the womb, we must understand the amazing drama that goes on within the womb (during the prenatal period), during birth and in the first few days afterward (the perinatal period), and in the months that follow (the postnatal period). The fine details of development during these and evolving periods are presented in Table 5:1. A brief overview is in order here.

An important question to keep in mind when reading this section is: When does life begin? This is a burning political and ethical issue that has divided scientists, theologians, and philosophers for centuries. Many answers are plausible on multiple grounds; conception and birth are not the only possible answers. This becomes clear as we proceed with our review of prenatal development.

Table 5:1: Developmental events timetable

| Period | Ages | Developmental Events |
|--------|------|----------------------|
| Prenatal & perinatal | 8–10 weeks | *Physical:* Cell differentiation into those that will be bones, nerves, or other cells. |
| | 2 months | *Physical:* Weight, ⅔ oz.; Length, 1½–2 inches. All organs present; leg buds and external genitalia just appearing. |
| | 3–4 months | *Physical:* Weight, ⅞–4 ozs.; Length, 3–6 inches. If aborted, will make primitive breathing movements and suck; bones forming; differentiation of organs. |
| | 5 months | *Physical:* Weight, 11 oz.; Length, 10 inches. Increased fetal movement. |
| | 6–7 months | *Physical:* Weight, 20–40 ozs.; Length, 12–15 inches. Heartbeat clearly discernable; eyelids present. |
| | 8–10 months | *Physical:* Weight, 4–7 lbs.; Length, 16–20 inches. All major changes have now occurred, development is matter of increasing weight and length. |
| Postnatal | 0–2 years | *Physical/Perceptual:* Development of prehension, early development of coordination and walking, rapid height and weight gain. Vision proceeds from focusing of eyes to interpretation of what is seen. Patterns differentiated, depth perception develops. |
| | | *Cognitive/Language:* Language proceeds from crying, cooing, and babbling to first words and meanings. **Sensorimotor period:** circular reactions, assimilation and accommodation, formation of the object concept, exploration, and beginnings of thought. |
| | | *Social/Emotional:* Responses to fear, anger, and love develop over time; smiling develops as a social response; expanding social contacts. |
| | 2–5 years | *Physical/Perceptual/Motor:* Slowdown in height and weight gain; recession and redistribution of "baby fat." Relationship develops between coordination/perception and cognition; walking improves; stabilization of equilibrium; hopping, skipping, running, climbing stairs added to repertoire; child can copy (draw) figures, button clothes, tie shoes. |
| | | *Cognitive/Language:* In language, two-word utterances become communications with applica- |

| Period | Ages | Developmental Events |
|---|---|---|
| | | tion of schemes; gradual perfecting of grammar; development of egocentric speech and thought. **Preoperational thought patterns:** "one-track" thinking, conservation, improved memory, relationship between thought and communication begins; beginning of intuitive thought; beginnings of play, creativity, and fantasy. |
| | | *Socio-Emotional:* Continued interaction with parents; early socialization with peers; early moral development; acquisition of sex roles; prosocial and antisocial behaviors develop. |
| | 6–12 years | *Physical/Motor:* Gains in weight and height; increased bone and muscle development; appearance and growth of sex characteristics. Increase in fine motor control; increased locomotor skills; agililty, coordination, and physical strength. |
| | | *Cognitive:* **Concrete operations:** Conservation, seriation, classification of objects, number concept. Development of measurable intelligence; growth of language and refinement of usage; refinement of creativity and expression. |
| | | *Social/Emotional:* Intensification of peer-group ties; growth in cooperation; strengthening of moral development and reasoning; ability to assume roles to empathize. |

## Prenatal Events

The prenatal period is divided into three parts: the germinal phase, the embryonic stage, and the fetal period. The germinal phase begins at conception and continues through subsequent cell divisions until the 2nd or 3rd week of pregnancy, but the gender and genetic heredity of the organism are determined at the moment of joining. The cell cluster formed by the union attaches itself to the wall of the mother's uterus. Is this the beginning of human life? Some say yes, others are not so sure. The amnion, a fluid-filled sac in which the developing organism floats, begins to form at this time. This sac protects and cushions the embryo and then later the fetus through its prenatal development. Thus, it is a vital aspect of the embryo's environment. During the third week after conception, the placenta and umbilical cord form. The *placenta* is a fleshy membrane that acts as a "way station" between mother and infant, supplying nutrition and removing wastes through the *umbilical cord,* which emanates from the placenta and connects with the infant at the navel. These physical structures create an intimately interdependent relationship between fetus and mother.

Three weeks after conception, the embryo's heart begins to beat. Most of the organs of the body appear during the following month and nervous system development also occurs during this period. By the end of the first month, the embryo is only a fraction of an inch long and weighs less than an ounce. By the end of the second month, the embryo is about one and one-half to two inches long and weighs about two-thirds of an ounce. All of the organs have appeared, and the embryo is clearly recognizable as human. Arms and limbs have begun their development, as have external genitalia, although it is still impossible to determine the sex of the infant by its external appearance. Is this the beginning of human life?

The eighth week marks the beginning of the fetal stage of development. This stage lasts until birth and is a period of growth and elaboration for the whole organism. The young fetus still weighs less than an ounce and is barely three inches long. The head of the fetus is far out of proportion to the total body length, perhaps as much as one third as long. Although the head will gradually become more proportional to the body, it will still be disproportionate in size at birth when compared to the average size of the adult head.

During the third month, the fetus is sufficiently developed so that, if aborted, it may make breathing and sucking movements, as well as demonstrate the Babinski reflex (fanning of toes) if stimulated. The fetus will have no chance of survival outside the womb at this stage. Is *this* the beginning of human life?

During the fourth month of pregnancy, the fetus grows to a length of six inches and weighs four ounces. Bones have begun to form, all organs are clearly differentiated, and there may be some evidence of intrauterine movement called "quickening." The mother feels the baby alive inside her and may report a feeling of real parenthood for the first time. Is *this* then the beginning of human life?

During the fifth month, a downy covering called lanugo begins to grow over most of the child's body. The fetus' weight jumps to eleven ounces, and the heartbeat is clearly discernable. The eyelids of the fetus are separated. It is about a foot long and soon weighs twenty ounces. The fetus might survive if born at this time, particularly if it receives modern medical care in an intensive care unit. Is *this* the beginning of human life?

During the last three months of its development, the fetus makes dramatic gains in size and weight. Brain development proceeds rapidly. The fetus grows from fifteen inches in the seventh month to sixteen inches in the eighth to twenty in the ninth. In the same time period, weight increases from approximately 2½ pounds to an average of about seven pounds at delivery (LeFrancois, 1980).

The fetus becomes more and more independently viable, i.e., it can live on its own if separated from the mother. Certainly this seems evidence that human life is achieved, does it not? However, there have been cultures in the world that do not accept an infant as achieving full human status until one year after it is born. This may seem strange and even inhuman to some of us. It should help us see, however, that *any* conclusion about when *human* life begins is just that, a conclusion. Our society has become embroiled in a controversy over when and why parents may legally and ethically terminate pregnancies. Some argue that efforts to prevent pregnancy are immoral. Others designate the period immediately after conception (as in the case of the IUD or the day-after pill). Others stop at the end of the germinal phase, and still others at the end of the embryo stage. Some accept the idea of termination in the early fetal period, and some will even go so far as the late fetal period. When does human life begin?

## Genetics and Issues of Heritability

Inherent in the process of pregnancy and birth is the process of genetic transmission. All cells that go into forming the embryo and the fetus, with the exception of the sperm and egg, contain 46 chromosomes—23 from the father and 23 from the mother. Chromosomes are particles in the cell nucleus containing the genes. Genes are the units of hereditary transmission that determine the traits that make each individual unique. Within each cell, there is a pair of chromosomes that determines the sex of the child. Women carry only X (or female) chromosomes. In males, the pair of chromosomes contains one X and one Y (male). If a sperm with an X chromosome fertilizes the egg, the child will be a girl. If a sperm with a Y chromosome fertilizes the egg, the child will be a boy. Therefore, the father's sperm determines the gender of the child.

What happens when the genetic transmission process goes awry? Genetic conditions can result from defects in genetic or chromosomal structure. One such disorder is phenylketonuria, or PKU, an inherited metabolic disorder that causes mental retardation unless the condition is detected at birth and the child is placed on a special diet. Down's Syndrome results from a faulty, missing, or extra chromosome #21 and is characterized by several distinctive physical traits and by mental retardation. It most frequently occurs in the offspring of older mothers because aging results in greater risk of chromosomal dislocation or damage in the eggs. Other genetic and chromosomal abnormalities are discussed in Table 5:2. Most of these are best viewed as a special kind of environmental challenge.

Group differences in genetic material exist. Thus, some groups are more prone to some genetic abnormalities because their common history has pooled some

**Table 5:2: Genetic, congenital, and situational threats to prenatal and perinatal development**

| Category | Problem | Cause | Result | Treatment |
|---|---|---|---|---|
| Genetic (Chromosomal) | Sex-linked recessive traits | Imperfect matching of X & Y chromosomes | Color blindness, hemophilia | |
| | Phenylketonuria (PKU) | Metabolic disorder | Mental retardation, neurological abnormalities, emotional disturbances | Special diet immediately following birth |
| | Down's Syndrome | Chromosomal abnormalities | Mental retardation, physiological defects | Counseling, special education, institutionalization |
| | Missing or extra sex chromosomes | Abnormalities in sperm and/or egg | Klinefelter's syndrome, (sterility, hormonal deficiencies, retardation in men) | Therapy with testosterone |
| | | | Turner's syndrome (blockage of breast development and menstruation in women) | Injection of estrogen prior to puberty |
| | | | XYY genetic structure (males overly tall, excessively violent, low intelligence) | |
| Congenital Problems | Musculo-skeletal malformations | Improper replication of genetic message | Club foot, cleft palate | Surgical correction (by choice) |
| | Central nervous system malformation | Mutant genes; drugs; chemical agents | Lesion/separation of vertebral elements | Genetic counseling; surgical repair |

| | | | |
|---|---|---|---|
| Spina bifida | X rays, viruses | Open spinal canal, hydrocephalus, paralysis, lack of muscle control, lack of sensation, retardation | Remedial physical therapy |
| Other | | | |
| Premature birth (low birth weight born after 30-week gestation) | Maternal health, nutritional status, maternal age, height and weight, weight gain, smoking, use of drugs, uterine problems, lack of prenatal care | Psychological and physiological stresses | Nutrient control, body temperature control, monitoring of acute problems of fetus |
| Small for date infants (full term) | Retardation of interuterine growth, inadequate nutrition, genetic or chromosomal anoma, mother's heart disease, toxemia, kidney disease, smoking, use of drugs, viruses, ethnicity, nutrition, infections, placental placement | Anoxia, asphyxia, hypoglycemia, pulmonary hemorrhage, brain insult, long-term effects on intelligence | Same as for premature birth |

characteristics. The concentration of these characteristics depends upon the exclusiveness of their mating (within the group) and particular evolutionary history. Thus, for example, people descended from areas of the world with serious malaria problems (e.g., Central Africa and the northern coasts of the Mediterranean Sea) are more likely to suffer from sickle cell anemia because the genes involved offer some protection against malaria. The gene pool gains a net advantage in such areas because the deaths attributable to the anemia problem are counterbalanced by the higher survival rate in response to malaria. Tay Sachs Disease illustrates the case where a damaging "deleterious" genetic trait remains strong in a population because of in-breeding within the group. Jews from Eastern Europe are particularly prone to this condition, which produces mental and physical deterioration.

Techniques of genetic analysis have become refined in recent years. It is now possible to predict the likelihood of any couple producing a child with one of several genetic defects. One of the most common forms of estimation is amniocentesis: a process whereby a long needle is inserted in the mother's abdomen to draw off some of the amniotic fluid. The fluid contains cast off skin cells of the fetus. The chromosomes of these cells are then examined for any abnormalities. The technique also reveals the child's gender, as the X and Y chromosomes are visible. Indeed, one of the more controversial aspects of amniocentesis is determining what information is appropriate to use in decision making by parents. Is gender an appropriate basis for terminating pregnancy? Is a "low-level" dysfunction? Is a serious dysfunction, for which there is a standard treatment, grounds enough? In recent years, the number of prenatal tests has increased significantly, e.g., to include both sickle cell anemia and Tay Sachs Disease. Thus, the issues continue to multiply, and the whole task of prenatal decision making and professional ethics becomes more difficult.

More and more people are becoming candidates for genetic counseling. Counseling centers are usually visited by potential parents who have genetic disease in their family backgrounds. These centers draw up family histories and do chromosomal analyses. They can make prediction on the odds involved concerning the occurrence of a defect. Thus far, the main result of new prenatal assessment technologies has been to *increase* the number of healthy pregnancies carried to term and decrease the number of damaged infants, rather than to produce large increases in abortion. Prenatal assessment sometimes even allows the correction of the defect *in utero* through nutritional treatment or other types of intervention.

Other prenatal factors beyond genetics influence the growth of the fetus. These are presented in Table 5:3. Nutrition is one factor, although evidence of the effects of the mother's nutrition on the fetus is unclear. However, we do know that malnutrition may retard the growth and intellectual capacity of the fetus. Many of the recommendations made regarding parental nutrition are

**Table 5:3: Influences of the maternal environment on prenatal and perinatal development**

| Influence (from mother) | Consequence (in infant) |
| --- | --- |
| Advanced Maternal Age | Down's syndrome, retardation, miscarriage, still births |
| Maternal Health (rubella, venereal disease, poliomyelitis, thyroid malfunction) | Mental deficiency, microencephaly, blindness, deafness, miscarriage, cretinism |
| Maternal Malnutrition | Fetal death, retardation, rickets, epilepsy, cerebral palsy neurological and emotional troubles, brain development, low birth weight |
| Maternal Emotions (tension, anxiety, chemical imbalance) | Increases in fetal activity, irritability, hyperactivity, feeding problems |
| Drugs (LSD & heroin, narcotics, aspirin & barbituates, quineal, pain killers, anesthesia, thalidomide, nicotine, tranquilizers, marijuana) | Morphological changes, congenital deafness, depression of fetal respiration/decreased responsiveness, increase in fetal heart rate, fetal hyperactivity, premature birth, fetal addiction and withdrawal, hyperirritability, genetic damage, abnormalities in sexual development |
| Alcohol | Fetal alcohol syndrome: low birth weight, retarded motor development, heart defects, physical abnormalities (joints and facial characteristics), retardation of intellectual development, withdrawal symptoms at birth |
| Poverty | Premature birth, infant death, mental retardation |
| Rh Incompatibility | Fetal erythroblastosis (anemia in newborn due to incompatibility of blood types between mother and infant) |
| Radiation | Brain, skull, eye formation |

preventive in nature: maintenance of an adequate diet throughout the childbearing years, monitoring by a health care professional, and a weight gain of no more than 25 pounds during pregnancy.

Certain infectious diseases may also lead to birth defects, particularly if contracted while the organism is still in the embryonic stage. German measles is the best known such cause of birth defects. Immunization of females, particularly married females, has done much to control it. However, syphillis, gonorrhea, polio, influenza, and mumps in the mother have also been associated with birth defects. In general, any effort to upgrade the basic health of the community reduces the incidence of birth defects. The health of the child *in utero* is thus an exo- and macrosystem issue.

The potential negative impact of drugs on fetal development is now widely recognized because of the thalidomide controversy of the 1960s. Thalidomide was a drug placed on the market for women to use in alleviating morning sickness. Use of the drug caused a significant increase in the number of children born with serious physical deformities affecting arms and legs. The damage occurred mainly in Europe, however, because the drug was not approved for widespread distribution in the United States. Despite pressure from drug manufacturers and criticism from colleagues for dragging her feet, a Food and Drug Administration physician stuck to her guns in requesting data on possible side effects. The data finally came—in the form of thousands of damaged children in the countries where the drug was dispensed. This physician's efforts spared many American children, but this is not to imply that the United States has not had tragedies of its own. A compound called DES (diethyl silbestrol) was introduced in the 1940s and early 1950s to pregnant mothers as a measure to prevent miscarriage. Approximately 25 years later, researchers reported that those mothers who might have taken the drug to *have* children may have passed on to these very offspring a tendency towards development of cancer at a very early age. Much research has focused on DES daughters, and the problems they face include not only cancer of the vagina but other reproductive difficulties. DES sons exist also, although their problems have been less publicized. Some of the problems seen to date have included underdeveloped testes and microphallus. The former causes a predisposition to cancer of the testes, and the latter is an uncorrectable malformation. Part of the responsibility for this tragedy must be assigned to a study conducted at the University of Chicago in the 1950s. In this study, DES was administered to a group of pregnant mothers to measure the effects it had on preventing miscarriages when compared to a placebo taken by members of a control group. The effectiveness of DES was deemed indifferent. But, this did not quell an existing enthusiasm for DES. The mothers who took part in the experiment were never informed what drug they were taking—a mistake the University is still, literally, paying for via lawsuits (Norwood, 1980). Where economic interest is strong, children need staunch allies and advocates. The thalidomide tragedies stimulated the Food and Drug Administration to look at other medications. Some evidence suggests that women who take aspirin during the last three months of pregnancy may have more prolonged labor in childbirth. It has also been suggested that certain tranquilizers may cause cleft palate and other defects if taken early in pregnancy. In general, it seems that pregnant women should avoid drugs of all sorts, as much as they can.

What about other substances the pregnant mother may ingest? Alcohol has joined the list of dangerous substances, and informed opinion discourages even small, "normal" amounts. Chronic alcoholics are more likely to bear children with a variety of physical and mental defects, some permanent. Alcohol may be the indirect cause or effect of other difficulties as well. The alcoholic mother may not be eating well and thus malnourishes the fetus. Alcoholism may also be the result of tension that is also transmitted to the fetus. There are certain facial defects that are characteristic of the child who is a victim of what is called "Fetal Alcohol Syndrome": small head circumference, mongoloid features of the eyes, thin upper lip, and short nose. Other effects include mental retardation, irritability, poor coordination, and hyperactivity in childhood. In this respect, the child of the alcoholic is a victim, just as the child of the heroin addict.

It seems that the pregnant woman is generally more sensitive to the effects of drugs and that she passes this vulnerability to the fetus. This extends to a very common "drug", tobacco. Smoking appears to retard the rate of fetal growth and to increase the chances of fetal death and spontaneous abortion. Experts believe that the children of smoking mothers often experience retarded physical, intellectual, and emotional development. These "personalized pollutants" do not exist alone, of course. Institutionalized pollutants are also a major and growing menace. Air, water, and soil have all been polluted with the by-products of industrial society—petrochemical residues, pesticides, radioactive materials, etc. The magnitude of these effects is unknown.

The mother affects the prenatal environment of the child in other ways. The age of the mother is a factor that affects the physical quality of the child. The optimal age for the birth of a healthy child is usually 20 to 29, as the social and biological conditions for the mother are usually best during this period. This is significant, as we have witnessed *both* more teenage births and more women who postpone childbearing into their 30s. The economic status of the mother is also related to the health of the fetus. Premature birth is the greatest correlate of infant death and infant retardation, and the phenomenon of low income is linked to premature birth. Continued anxiety or unhappiness in the mother is another threat to a successful pregnancy. Stress produces glandular changes that may alter the blood chemistry and blood pressure of the mother, causing developmental defects in the fetus, especially in early stages of development. The conditions of poverty also set in motion a host of negative influences on the unborn child.

Radiation also has an influence on pregnancy. Pregnant women exposed to the atomic bombs dropped on Japan at the end of World War II gave birth to babies with malformed eyes and brains. Incidents such as the breakdown at the Three Mile Island atomic power plant raise concern about both low-level radiation and the threat of catastrophes. The routine use of X-rays has received criticism for contributing to the background problem. However, in spite of all the prenatal threats and challenges we have outlined, most pregnancies are successful and produce a viable infant.

Following the nine months of pregnancy comes the process of childbirth. Hormonal changes and the reaction of a uterus that has been stretched to a maximum point trigger labor, the process whereby the fetus, placenta, and umbilical cord are separated and expelled from the woman's body. The onset of labor is gradual. The first stage begins with light contractions that gradually increase in frequency and intensity. The cervix dilates to allow passage of the baby through the birth canal. The second stage of labor involves the birth of the child. The third stage (afterbirth) involves the expulsion of the placenta and other membranes.

Although it is subject to a variety of medical complications, childbirth is a normal human function. As we shall see in Chapter 6, the social conditions of childbirth can play a significant role in influencing the infant's relationship with his or her family. A physically normal birth need not imply medical supervision or intervention, despite our customary hospital-oriented approach. By viewing birth as a natural process in Chapter 6, we will address its role in forming parent-child relations. First, however, we need to return to our account of the child's development.

## The First Two Years of Childhood

After birth, the child continues the sequence of development begun in the womb, and a child born prematurely is, thus, initially delayed in contrast to a full-term infant. From birth to the age of one month, the baby is called a neonate. The neonate is a developing but competent organism whose abilities have traditionally gone unrecognized and unappreciated. At birth it is already a very capable being; able to see, hear, and feel. What is more, all its senses seem to be primed for social interaction, for parent-child relationships.

Vision in the infant appears very early. Sensitivity to patterns and contours occurs at birth. Sensitivity to light intensity and the ability to follow moving objects are also early developments. Color vision is well developed by the age of two to four months. The human face is an ideal visual target for the neonate, and infants seem to have an innate preference for faces over other objects. The human being *is* the social animal.

The newborn is also highly sensitive to a wide range of sounds and can detect the location of sound. Sounds of different frequencies inspire individual responses—lower sounds are calming, higher pitched sounds, irritating. Human voices, and particularly female voices, are particularly attractive. Another well-developed sense in the newborn is olfaction, the sense of smell. At only five days, breast-fed neonates can discriminate the smell of their mother's breast milk from others (MacFarlane, 1977).

The newborn has many reflexes. Knowing what they are can help the professional understand and interpret infant behavior. For example, the rooting reflex causes the infant to turn its head towards any stimulation of the cheek. This becomes vital knowledge when seeking to initiate breast feeding. If the baby's head is turned toward the breast by pushing, the baby may instinctively turn its head away from the breast, toward the hand touching its cheek. To the uninformed, this can appear as "rejecting the breast" and can unnecessarily discourage the mother.

The mental world of the infant is a world of the here and now, devoid of memories and expectations. Rather than thinking, the infant behaves and does so largely in response to reflexes and very simply learned responses. Behavior influences and reflects the growth of the mind and acts as a stimulus to cognition at this early stage of development. Thus, the infant's mind emerges from its patterns of behavior (Piaget, 1953).

Infants exhibit three principal social behaviors: smiling, crying, and cuddling. Cuddling exists at birth but varies in intensity from baby to baby. Neonates smile in the first few weeks of life, but not as a social response. Social smiles do not appear until after the third week of life, and they are usually elicited by the sound of a human voice. By the fourth week, the neonate can establish genuine eye contact with a social stimulus, and thus, visual cues can elicit smiles. Smiling is the currency of early social relationships, while crying is the principal aversive (negative) stimulus that infants use to influence their social environments.

Crying takes several forms. There is the rhythmical cry, which follows a regulated pattern. The angry cry is also rhythmic but more energetic. The pain cry consists of an extended shriek followed by a pause (for the baby to catch its breath). The cry then takes on a more regular tone and is accompanied by frenzied activity. As early as the third week, the neonate develops a "deliberate cry," consisting of a low moan that may be used to attract attention. One of the major items on the parent–child agenda in the early weeks of life together is learning what the various cries mean and how to respond differentially to them.

Smiling and crying are considered early forms of communication for the neonate. Social smiles are more likely to be aroused by the human voice or face than by any nonhuman stimuli. Similarly, the various forms of crying and cooing may be the infant's earliest attempts at communicating feelings to others. The fact that mothers tend to respond to cries of pain more consistently than any other form of cry attests to this communicative power. Indeed, the course of emotional development is characterized by differentiation and elaboration of gross reactions (pain, pleasure, and interest) into the full range of human emotions (Ricciuti, 1973). The normal parent–infant relationship facilitates this development, but disrupted or abusive relationships may thwart it (Garbarino, 1980a).

Perceptual development also goes through some dramatic changes in the first two years. By the end of two months, eye-brain coordination allows infants to differentiate between distinctive features of a pattern and to translate these perceptions into simple coordinated behavior. Between two and five months, distinctions can be made between increasingly complicated patterns and more elaborately coordinated behaviors undertaken. By five months, infants show a preference for three-dimensional objects over two-dimensional pictures or pho-tographs. In the course of two years, the child progresses from focusing on patterns to interpreting and analyzing what he or she sees. Infants after two months may also become *habituated* to a particular pattern—they "memorize" it. Transfer of interest from an old to a new stimulus—which piques interests anew, for a time—is called dishabituation. This makes clear why the infant thrives in a stable but changing environment where things are constant enough to be learned but changeable enough to be interesting.

How does language develop during the first two years? As infants mature, they are increasingly able to make fine discriminations among sounds, which may lead the way to the ability to speak. The infant progresses in verbal development from crying to cooing and babbling. Babbling includes many of the sounds found in human language but soon becomes confined to sounds present in the language the infant hears spoken. By the end of the first year, children are producing only sounds that they hear. Language behavior is shaped by adult models and therefore loses some of the versatility it had at six months. Eventually, the first word emerges, and the child engages in *holophrasic speech*—using a single word, through inflection, to communicate a variety of meanings. For example, "mama?" or "mama." or "mama!" can mean, respectively, "Where is Mom?" or "Mom, I recognize you." or "HELP!" This is followed by the development of *telegraphic speech*—two word utterances that resemble telegrams in which nonessential words have been left out. "Daddy go?" is an example. More complex language follows naturally, given an environment that models spoken language.

How can one characterize the cognitive development of the child during this period? Jean Piaget, who pioneered a stage theory of cognitive development sees two basic human tendencies: organization (the tendency to combine processes into coherent systems) and adaptation (the tendency to adjust to the environment). Adaptation is the result of the processes of assimilation (making experiences fit one's world view) and accommodation (changing one's world view to meet experience). These processes lead to the development of schemes, or patterns of thought and action. Each stage builds upon the previous and involves more sophisticated thought and action in which abstraction plays an ever larger role (Ginsberg & Opper, 1972). Social development parallels these cognitive shifts, e.g., as the child becomes attached to the parents and begins to learn rules of conduct.

## Childhood: From Two to Twelve

By the end of two years, the child has become adept at picking up objects (prehension), and putting things together and rearranging them (relationships). Physical development enhances the progress from nearly total dependence to greater independence. During the preschool period, the child makes progress and refinement in motor development. The child gains equilibrium (balance in sitting and walking) and feet, arms, and legs are brought into alignment. As locomotion and coordination improve, the child can do more. From six to about twelve years of age, the child's motor development focuses on the shift from control of large muscle groups to control of the smaller muscles. By the end of this period, control of gross motor movements has improved greatly. Agility and strength increase, with males usually outdistancing females in these features. The link between physical competence and social independence is a logical and natural one—in childhood and throughout life.

Language development and communication undergo a revolution during this period as well. There appear to be three challenges in language development. The child hears a stream of language from another person and is able to break it into the units of which his or her language is composed—called phonemes. The child must also learn syntax—the way that words are put together to form phrases, clauses, and sentences. Finally, the child has to relate sounds to objects and events in the world—semantics. From here, the child advances beyond one- and two-word utterances to simple sentences. These sentences are generally declarative in nature and uncertain grammatically. The child then moves on to the mastery of morphemes—small units of meaning that are recognized words or embellishments to words (suffixes, prefixes). The child develops the ability to structure questions.

Much of children's language is unintentionally poetic, but language becomes ever more a means of precise and complex communication. Children just beginning school tend to use language to direct their personal behavior. In middle childhood and preadolescence, children are still developing some of the rudiments of language and mastering grammatical constructions, but they are also developing what is called a *metalinguistic ability*—the capacity to think of language as an object, and to reflect about words and meanings. A sensitivity to metaphor, logic, and the most distinctly human forms of intellectual activity arise (Vygotsky, 1965).

Language development has its parallel in cognitive development. Once children have passed through the stages of the early period of cognitive development, they enter a phase in which they are able to identify and classify objects in the world according to features. They know what makes a man a man, as opposed to a dog. They cannot distinguish individuals within a classification, however. Often preschoolers who see ten different department store Santa Clauses believe that they are seeing the same person repeatedly. Children at this point in their development are still prone to gross overgeneralization and oversimplistically leap to conclusions. Therefore, they are easily misled about social events, and adults must help them avoid drawing false emotional conclusions. Divorce, for example, may exceed the young child's analytic ability and produce a wide range of incorrect conclusions unless parents and others are careful, patient, and thorough in helping the child understand.

Intuitive thinking is based on immediate comprehension rather than logical and rational processes of thought. Problems tend to be solved on the basis of insight rather than logic. Intuitive thinking is characterized by a limited ability to classify, by an egocentric perspective, and by a marked over-reliance on physical appearances. This reliance on perception is seen in the phenomenon that Piaget refers to as conservation. When water is poured from a short, wide beaker into a tall thin one, the young child will generally focus on relative water levels and assume the tall beaker has more water, even if he saw the transference take place. This is different from the adolescent and the adult, who will rely on thought and logic to inform them that the quantity of water remains the same. These limits to children's understanding of the physical world extend to the social world as well, as the example of divorce reveals.

By middle childhood, the child proceeds to what Piaget calls the concrete operational stage. The concrete operational child is able to recognize that simply because an object changes shape or form does not mean that its mass has also changed. There is an increased reliance on logic in dealing with objects. The child also learns to deal with classes of objects. He understands what makes an object a member of a certain class and not of another, e.g., dogs vs. cats. The child also understands the concept of *serial ordering*—lining up objects in a hierarchy due to size, age, number, or shape. A third concept the child masters is that of number, in terms of the number's ordinal sequence and its quantitative properties. All of these intellectual improvements contribute to the social competence of the child as well.

How does the personality of the child develop from the ages of two through twelve? Personality is generally defined as a unique combination of characteristics that determine how individuals respond to experiences, how they get along with others, and how they get along with themselves. There are a number of factors that shape personality. *Constitutional* factors are inherited characteristics and predispositions. *Group membership* factors include general cultural influences on personality formation. *Role* factors include the person's self-concept and the role assumed in different situations. *Situational determinants* are the experiences of the individual that contribute to personality development. Researchers and others argue over the importance of one factor versus another. We will not discuss these arguments here. It is clear that both adults and peers, through their interaction with the individual child, contribute to personality development. We will discuss the influence of parent socialization on personality formation in Chapter 6. Peers also contribute a great deal to the child's development as models and reinforcers. If anything, the importance of peers as role models increases as the child grows older. Just as physical maturation permits a wider field of exploration, social maturation permits a wider circle of interpersonal influences.

Personality development is linked in part to the development of the capacity for play. In their play relationships, children reveal several types of play: unoccupied behavior (aimless and solitary play); solitary play (involving no interaction with other children, but more concerted interaction with objects); spectator play (watching others but not interacting); parallel play (playing in proximity to each other, but not *together*); associative play (playing together, but with no real direction); and cooperative play (organized play with others). Play involves social and cognitive functions and is an important arena for development. Some theorists believe it performs an essential function in facilitating creative thinking. All work and no play *does* make Jack a dull boy, and that goes for Jill as well.

For all its importance, play is not enough. Moral development—learning social norms for responsible behavior—is vital. Several theoreticians and researchers have proposed models for understanding moral development. Some emphasize modeling. Others emphasize the intellectual process of making judgments based on conclusions about one's self and one's relation to the world. All agree that children need to encounter a moral social reality in order to learn to think and act morally. Children are certainly preprogrammed to develop values and a conscience, but they won't do so in a social vacuum. As we shall see in Chapter 6, parent–child relations have a lot to do with how well children will learn the moral lessons they need to learn to be a positive influence on the people with whom they interact. Moral development begins with attachment (usually to the parents) and proceeds to ever more complex referents and ever more general and abstract principles (Garbarino & Bronfenbrenner, 1976b). The balance between general ethical principles and orientation to specific people, feelings, and relationships varies from culture to culture and perhaps is even generally different for males and females. Gilligan's research (1980) suggests that females tend to place the value of "not hurting people" in a central position.

Becoming female and male (feminine/masculine) is certainly one of the central issues on the developing child's agenda. The development of gender identity is a controversial issue in many circles, of course. We know that it is controlled jointly by biological forces (e.g., hormones) and social–psychological forces (e.g., modelling and reinforcement). We will discuss this further in Chapter 6, but here we simply need note that most gender-related differences are neither so fixed nor so big as many people seem to think. Most characteristics are quite modifiable, and most individuals contain a repertory of behaviors that includes both traditionally masculine and traditionally feminine characteristics (e.g., physical aggression and nurturance). Male hormones (androgens) seem to have the effect of predisposing the organism (whatever its sex) to rough and tumble activity and perhaps even to physical aggression (Maccoby & Jacklin, 1974). But, boys and girls are first and foremost children. To a large extent we make of them what we will.

By the end of the eleventh year of life, children have established themselves in the world. They have made their first peace with the world. They are boys or girls; they have values and conscience; they control their bodies and their minds; they have character. Then, just when things are relatively well established for them, along comes adolescence, and the pace of change and demands for adaptation increase rapidly, to the point where many of the issues faced in infancy must be dealt with again and reworked.

## What Is Adolescence in Biology and Culture?

Adolescence marks the end of childhood and the onset of the transition to adulthood. The changes adolescents undergo in their bodies, minds, and social relations are as profound as any that the human faces across the entire life span. Just prior to adolescence, the bodies of children have not developed sexual characteristics, and there is not much to physically distinguish boys from girls. In school, lessons are still mainly concerned with basic reading, writing, and arithmetic skills; preadolescents are not yet ready to reason abstractly. On their own among their peers, preteens are usually just beginning to notice the opposite sex and awkwardly participate in mixed-sex activities. Most are still very involved with and influenced by their parents on a day-to-day basis. By the end of adolescence a few short years later, young adults are mature physically, mentally, and socially. They may be starting to work, off at school, in the military, married, and may even be parents. Clearly the teenage years are a time of deep and dramatic changes.

Adolescence is stereotypically seen as a time of turbulence and intensity. Most of us who care to recall our own teenage years probably remember it as both better and worse than it actually was. Perhaps no time in life has been as alternately romanticized and feared. Stereotyped exaggerations and overgeneralizations abound. These plague those who would serve youth because they must always deal with the negative image of adolescence presented by the mass media, indeed in the culture as a whole.

The experience of adolescence can be likened to passing over a narrow and shaky bridge; the security of childhood is forever behind, the stability of adulthood looms far ahead. There is no way to go except forward. While on the bridge it seems an immeasurable distance, and falling off is a constant threat, though relatively few actually do. What are the changes occurring along the way? How can we make the passage safer? These are some of the questions we will attempt to answer in this section.

The very existence of adolescence illustrates the nature of human development. There are certain specific biological events occurring in the teenage years to both boys and girls. Yet the *meaning* and *importance* of these physical changes vary from culture to culture and over historical periods. In many cultures, and indeed, in our own culture until the present century, there was no period of life recognized as adolescence. Children simply matured and became adults as soon as they were able to take on adult roles. Adolescence as we know it today emerged as teenagers were consigned to a kind of social limbo (in school and out of the workforce). Thus, we must consider adolescence in historical and cultural context, as well as in terms of the biological, mental, and social dimensions of young people's experiences.

The biological start of adolescence is the growth spurt that signals the beginning of puberty (sexual maturity). From birth onward, the rate at which children grow each year slows. The growth spurt reverses this trend, and for about two years, the rate of growth approximately doubles. American boys currently begin their growth spurt between the ages of ten-and-a-half and sixteen, girls between eight and eleven-and-a-half. This difference alone causes some of the social static in peer relations, as short boys and tall girls maneuver for position in junior high school.

The growth spurt is followed by the maturation of the sexual organs (ovaries in girls, testicles and penises in boys), and later by secondary sex characteristics (facial hair and lowering of the voice in boys, breast development and broadening of the pelvis in girls, and the appearance of pigmented and axillary hair in both sexes). All this growth is stimulated and accompanied by hormonal changes that may precipitate mood swings. As if teenagers didn't have enough to contend with they have to face up to the ups and downs of feelings that often leave them—and the adults who care for them—confused.

The typical adolescent tends to be self-conscious about these changes, especially if they are early or late, i.e., if their physical maturation is "out of sync" with that of their peers. It seems that early-maturing girls and late-maturing boys have more trouble adjusting in adolescence than their friends who developed along with the majority (Weatherly, 1963). However, as adults they may have developed compensatory characteristics, e.g., humor, insight, and flexibility (Jones, 1965). There really is no perfect time to mature sexually nor perfect physical development, and most teens suffer anxiety over real or imagined physical flaws. One classic study found that 61 percent of the boys and 72 percent of the girls in the tenth grade desired some change in their physical selves: in their complexion, proportion, weight, hair, and so on (Franzier & Lisonbee, 1950). No doubt, all people feel some dissatisfaction with their appearance, but the rapid changes and new social involvements in the early teenage years intensify physical self-consciousness.

Menarche (the onset of menstruation) for girls and nocturnal emissions for boys are tangible proof that one is growing up. Together with the fact that the youngster looks different, puberty profoundly affects the self-image, and indeed the image others see of the adolescent. Depending on the context in which they occur, these sure signs of maturation can themselves generate either apprehension or pride or both in teenagers and their parents. For example, parental reaction is thought to be one of the primary determinants of the psychological impact of menarche (Konopka, 1966). Parents are often surprised by and uncomfortable with the emerging sexuality of their offspring, particularly their daughters, perhaps because they fear that sexuality will become a vehicle by which the adolescent challenges adult authority and power. No professional helper should ignore the power of teenage sexuality as an issue in the adolescent's psychology or in the family's dynamic interactions.

At the same time that puberty is occurring, equally drastic changes take place in the thinking of many adolescents. Abstract reasoning, the ability to develop theories and think hypothetically ("what if . . . ?"), typically begins around the age of twelve (Piaget, 1967). Piaget called this stage formal operations, and it is the ultimate stage of cognitive development. Adolescents are now capable of the same kind of logical and intellectual processes as adults. Formal operations extend to self-reflection as well. Bruner describes this cognitive development thus: "The child now can conjure up systematically the full range of possibilities that could exist at any given time" (Bruner, 1960). The individual personality begins to arise out of the ability to imagine one's own "life plan" and to exert discipline over the self in trying to realize one's goals (Piaget, 1967).

The basic mental and physical changes of early adolescence set the stage for the personal and social involvements that develop through the teenage years. It is important to understand the links between the mental, physical, and social aspects of the adolescent's life. As teenagers begin to look and feel more like adults, they consequently develop changing conceptions of themselves that reflect their new appearance. Changing appearance and new interests lead to new social contacts, contacts that can upset the stability of childhood. Altogether, the adolescent is thrown into a challenging, perhaps even overwhelming, situation—

a situation that we will now examine more closely.

## Psychosocial Development

Identity formation is an important issue in adolescence. By identity we mean the person's sense of self, the individual's way of thinking about his or her relation to the rest of the world. Erik Erikson, a Freudian psychologist and one of the leading theorists in this area, conceptualized adolescent identity as "a conscious sense of individual uniqueness . . . an unconscious striving for a continuity of experience, and . . . as a solidarity with a group's ideals" (Erikson, 1968, p. 208).

According to Erikson (1968), identity formation is the most important developmental task of adolescence. The newly acquired capacity to self-reflect and to consider possible courses of action allows, or even impels, the adolescent to reassess the past and begin to work toward a future. Social expectations to make commitments to love and work are challenges to identity—questions that demand answers: What do I want? What should I do? Who am I? These are the important and difficult concerns of identity formation facing the adolescent. They provide the backdrop for relations with adults and peers.

The journey from childhood to adulthood is a process of shifting and slowly coalescing self-definition. Offer (1969) describes three stages in this process: discovery, experimentation, and mastery. At first the young adolescent begins to think reflectively. New roles, relationships, ideas, and behaviors are tried in midadolescence, and by late adolescence, the youngster has begun to master feelings and to establish some sort of personal and social self-definition. The adolescent's environment—family, friends, school, neighborhood—will have a profound effect on identity formation. It is *through* interaction with others that the adolescent defines him or herself, and the support or resistance he or she gets from others will play a large role in the kind of adult the adolescent becomes.

The adolescent's most important social relations are generally with family and peers. As the scope and power of the peer group increases, the family may diminish as a source of day-to-day direction for the teenager. Issues of independence, responsibility, and freedom are contested in the family as the gradual process of disengagement by the teenager takes place. The teenager's changed physical status seems to stimulate efforts to change his or her social status within the family as well, and the teenager becomes more assertive in family interaction (Steinberg & Hill, 1978).

The adolescent's concern with identity and his place in the world is understood and supported by age-mates going through this process at the same time. The peer group emerges as a context for fostering adolescent independence from the family and reinforcing social ties among adolescents. It functions as a "reference group," defining values, behavior, and rules by which the individuals can measure and orient themselves (Sherif & Sherif, 1964). Winch (1965) goes so far as to describe the peer group as "an interim kin group between the family of origin and the family of procreation" (p. 522).

But the dominance of the peer group is relatively short-lived. As adolescents gain self-confidence and autonomy, they become less dependent on the group and more concerned with heterosexual relations and individual interests (Douvan & Adelson, 1966). Thus, patience is one of the primary virtues for adults charged with the responsibility of caring for adolescents.

## The Transition to Adulthood

If we think of adolescence as beginning with puberty and the prospect of formal operations, what marks the end of adolescence and the beginning of adulthood? There are no clear biological transitions, for the adolescent is already a functional adult, physiologically speaking. Adulthood is a *social* concept, and leaving adolescence is accomplished by taking on adult roles. At the heart of adulthood lies responsibility. Adults assume responsibility for their own behavior and well-being, for the well-being of their families and the development of children and youth.

How do adolescents become adults? They need to prepare for the work, social, and personal roles of adulthood. We can look at the roles adolescents engage in to see how well they prepare youth for adult roles. School, of course, is the teenager's primary responsibility. More children are receiving more education than ever before, partly because our technological society requires a more educated work force (Coleman et al., 1974). School dominates the human ecology of our adolescents (Garbarino, 1981b).

What is the effect of the increasing importance of education on young people? For one thing, school provides a kind of education that is intellectual, abstract, and individualistic. Many have criticized the isolation of schools from the larger community, even from people of other ages (Bronfenbrenner, 1975). For another thing, the deck is stacked against those who are not academically superior. As blue-collar jobs become a smaller part of the economy, there is increasing pressure to succeed in school and increasing hardship for those youths who do not. Anyone concerned with adolescents must be concerned with helping them make their peace with schools and schooling.

The increased emphasis on education in recent years has led researchers to wonder whether adolescence has extended into the early or even mid-twenties. Kenneth Keniston (1972), for example, has written of a new stage in the life cycle he calls "youth." These "post-adolescents" are young people of advanced education and moral development marked by their ambivalent relationship to society. Whether "youth" is a permanent part of the social landscape or a passing curiosity of the turbulent 60's remains to be seen. In either case, the possibility for further evolution or expansion of adolescence because of changes in the social environment remains clear.

The transition from being a child in a family to starting a family of one's own is another developmental issue that marks the advent of adulthood. For many adolescents, marriage is the most important step to adulthood. Indeed, sexuality is probably the only aspect of life in which adolescents can unilaterally declare themselves to be adults. Marriage can be a way out of school, family, or work, but adolescent marriages in our society tend to be most unstable (Bane, 1976). This instability is derived from the strain of premarital pregnancy and the pressure of premature parenthood or the poverty and dependence in which young people starting out find themselves. Studies indicate that adolescents who marry may suffer from a lack of self-confidence, compared to their age-mates who do not marry (Duvall, 1975). Patience is a virtue for adolescents, as much as for the adults who care for them.

Both work and family transitions can be eased by understanding the difficulty of passing from dependency and a lack of opportunities for meaningful activity, to responsible independence and autonomy. Settings that prepare adolescents for the future, that integrate them into (rather than segregate them out of) the larger community, and that foster the development and maturation of the complete adult person are at a premium. Our institutions, from the family and school to industry and government, can make the journey from childhood to adulthood smoother and more pleasant by arranging themselves to allow children to gradually take on the roles they must assume to become full-fledged adults (Benedict, 1938). Just as society created "the adolescent," society can change and ease the difficulty facing the adolescent as he or she passes through this most exciting and trying period of life. Adolescence provides enough intrinsic challenges. Our task is to encourage a social environment that allows youth an opportunity to safely take advantage of it.

---

# RESEARCH CAPSULE

According to Newman et al. (1979), the history of cross-cultural research is not noteworthy for its contributions to the research on child development. While researchers have been able to use different cultures as settings for research into important issues of child development, cross-cultural research has, by and large, failed in its ambition to "increase the generality of psychological laws." In other words, researchers are often unable to successfully investigate a particular developmental concept across cultures. What are the reasons for this failure? It may be that cross-cultural research is simply an untrustworthy method for unraveling the knot of variables affecting growth of the individual. The average researcher might like to be able to investigate the manifestation of one factor, such as cognitive development, across cultures, but he or she should realize that this does not exist in a vacuum. Any variable under examination is affected by a pooling of social, cognitive, physical, and cultural factors. This is a fact that has escaped some researchers.

Cross-cultural research offers a great promise as well: We can simply learn more about child development and cultural differences by using a cross-cultural design as the mode for investigation of a particular child development issue. Perhaps it is useful to look at one such study as an application of the strengths and weaknesses inherent in this type of study.

Furby (1978) sought to answer the following questions: What are the bases across cultures of childrens' decisions about *sharing?* With whom do they share their personal possessions and why? What is the relationship of the developmental course to the sharing of one's possessions?

The researcher took two samples: a "developmental" sample and a "cross-cultural" sample. The developmental sample consisted of 30 American subjects at each of five age levels: 5–6 years, 7–8 years, 10–11 years, 16–17 years, and adults. The cross-cultural sample was introduced to investigate "the degree of variability that might be found in Western, industrialized societies with respect to the use of sharing of personal possessions." The comparison groups were American children at both the ages of 5–6 and 10–11 years, compared with groups of Israeli city dwellers and Israeli kibbutz dwellers at the same ages. The comparison envisioned was that of the industrialized, individualistic society (American) vs. the collective society (kibbutz residents) vs. a hybrid of the two (Israeli city dwellers) which might contribute to an understanding of the differences between the two groups at "extreme" ends of the spectrum. For each group, 30 subjects were chosen at each of the two age levels. In all groups, there was equal participation by both sexes.

Subjects were interviewed as to the issue of sharing of personal possessions. They were asked questions about the "morality" of sharing

as well as other reasons for sharing. Each subject was interviewed in his or her own language. These interviews were then analyzed for their content.

In the developmental sample, it was found that 5–7-year-olds shared largely with their own family or with those they thought friendly. They believed "sharing is good"—a belief shared by older children. They feared damage and destruction of their possessions, and this was also a consideration for older children. Seven- to eight-year-old children implied that they would not share with those who would not share with them. Ten- to eleven-year-olds believed the evaluation of the person to be shared with was important. They also shared to foster well-being in the other person—to allow them to experience some activity or have something they did not already own. Sixteen- to seventeen-year-olds shared with those they believed honest and responsible. They also assessed their own need for the object and the use made of it by the borrower. Adults based sharing on the trustworthiness of the other and the happiness it gave them to share.

In the cross-cultural sample, the 5–6-year-olds in the American and nonkibbutz Israeli samples used their families as the basis of evaluation for sharing. In the kibbutz, children are surrounded by a family of their peers. Therefore, it is with respect to their peers that they receive the greatest pressures to share. Decisions about sharing tend to be based on the standard of "If you won't share with me, I won't share with you." This rationale became equally as important for American children at the ages 10–11, since by then they were spending much of their time in school.

Determination was also made about the morality surrounding sharing. In the developmental sample, younger children tended to believe that to share was inherently good, while older children and adolescents saw sharing as a way of "helping thy neighbor." Adults tended to feel that sharing "inspired positive interpersonal interactions." In the cross-cultural sample, younger children of American culture and the Israeli kibbutz saw sharing as inherently good, but Israeli children also deemed that the owner has the right *not* to share.

Older children across all groups were more concerned with doing a favor for another.

This study presents a sizeable amount of information as to the bases of decision making about sharing across two cultures and across a large age range. What are the strengths of this study? It clearly provides information on the subjective notion of sharing, particularly in childhood and adolescence, and presents how these notions change and stay the same across ages and cultures. But several shortcomings can also be noted.

The study, as such, is cumbersome due to the fact that it separates age from other factors on one level (the developmental sample), and then combines age and culture effects on the other (cross-cultural sample). It might have made more sense to combine these factors in one population or to totally separate them. The age samples and culture samples are arbitrarily selected—it is not clear why Israel was considered as a comparison site rather than England, France, or Russia. There is, likewise, no rationale given for the age grouping.

Caution must also be taken in how the findings are interpreted. This is *not* a study of sharing *behaviors*, but a study of subjective *beliefs* about sharing. One cannot determine from this study how actual *patterns* of sharing change across ages or cultures.

Most importantly, this study again falls prey to the pitfall that Newman and his colleagues (1979) talk about: It is an attempt to isolate the effects of two variables upon sharing without an acknowledgment of other influences. Furby does not consider what the influence of socioeconomic status or intelligence upon beliefs surrounding sharing may be, but they *are* part of the overall picture. To be fair, to consider the effects that all possible factors have on one belief or behavior may be beyond the grasp of the average researcher. It is still important for the reader to carefully scrutinize the message any study tries to support.

# PRACTICE CAPSULE

Health professionals are still learning how to improve the health and well-being of children. In the case of fetal development, they are particularly concerned about the possible effects of *teratogenic substances*, e.g., those substances that enter the mother's system (alcohol, drugs, etc.) and contribute to the creation of a less-than-optimum environment for the formation of the infant. One special problem that has arisen as the result of alcohol consumption during pregnancy is Fetal Alcohol Syndrome (FAS).

When a pregnant woman drinks, she increases the risk of birth defects for her baby (Iber, 1980). The ingestion of alcoholic beverages interferes with pregnancy, and the effects on the fetus may be permanent. The strength of these effects is a result of the susceptibility to alcohol of both the mother and the fetus. It is clear, however, that alcohol consumption is the most prevalent single cause of mental impairment in infants in the Western world.

Fetal Alcohol Syndrome was first noted and described by Dr. David W. Smith at the University of Washington. He determined that drinking any amount of alcohol, in excess of the level at which the body will detoxify it, will put the fetus at risk. The mother who takes as little as one drink per day may be causing the risk of learning impairments in her child. Those who take two or three drinks a day may run the risk of spontaneous abortion.

Severe defects may result in those children whose mothers consume five or more drinks daily. The effects can be modified by good nutrition on the part of the mother and the natural resistance of the fetus to adverse influences. The most severe injuries include: brain damage, deficiency in intellectual and neurological growth, low birth weight and size, small head size, abnormal facial features, nearsightedness, undersized teeth, cleft palate, and heart defects. None of these effects is reversible.

Twenty-three to 29 percent of children born to heavy drinkers demonstrate full-blown syndrome effects while 33 percent have minor congenital abnormalities. Two cases are reported for every 1,000 live births. This does not tell the whole story. A large number of cases still go undiagnosed, as not all doctors recognize the signs and symptoms of the syndrome as yet.

As much as reliable diagnosis techniques are needed, prevention campaigns aimed at reducing the occurrence of FAS are even more necessary. It is up to the health professional to recommend that the woman contemplating pregnancy avoid all alcohol from the time of conception until the child is born. If total avoidance of alcohol cannot be achieved, then at least vigilance and caution in alcohol intake should be insisted upon. The woman should be educated to know the effects of alcohol on her own system and to monitor these. There are existing education/prevention programs in this area for mothers-to-be as well as movements to label the hazard on the bottles of alcoholic beverages themselves. In the final analysis, the responsibility for the safety of the fetus lays in the hands of the mother herself and her primary health care giver.

# FOR FURTHER READING

Aries, P. *Centuries of childhood.* London: Jonathan Cape, 1962, 447 pp.

A pithy history of the Western family as an idea rather than as a reality. The major thesis explores how the ideas entertained about family relations have changed over historical time. The author asks the questions: How did we come from the ignorance of childhood in the tenth century to the centering of the family around the child in the nineteenth century? How far does this evaluation correspond to a parallel evolution of the concept people have of the family, the feelings they entertain towards the value they attribute to it? The book is worthwhile for its thoughtfulness and its unique approach to an underexamined area.

Coleman, J. *Youth: Transition to adulthood.* Chicago: University of Chicago Press, 1974, 193 pp.

This study grew out of one President's Science Advisory Committee and represents the combined work of social scientists and educators concerned about the process of becoming an adult in today's society. The group examined the environments that adolescents inhabit, especially school and work, with regard to the developmental needs of youth. The education system is faulted for segregating youth from the rest of society and for not providing more of a range of experiences important to maturation. The conclusion of the book is a thoughtful and dramatic collection of suggestions for social and institutional innovations offering youth varied opportunities in addition to, or instead of, traditional educational programs.

Hetherington, E. M., and Parke, R. D. *Child psychology: A contemporary viewpoint* (2nd ed.). New York: McGraw-Hill Book Company, 1979, 680 pp.

A standard text on child development that is up-to-date and comprehensive. The book is oriented around such topics as cognitive development, intelligence, language, early experience, genetics, sex typing, and moral development. It succeeds in presenting multiple theoretical viewpoints guiding research. The relationship between research knowledge and applied practice in understanding child development is emphasized.

Norwood, C. *At highest risk: Environmental hazards to young and unborn children.* New York: McGraw-Hill Book Company, 1979, 280 pp.

This book deals with new scientific research concerning *environmental* factors contributing to developmental risk in the fetus and young child. The relationships between the child and carcinogenic (cancer-causing), mutagenic (causing possible change over generations), and teratogenic agents (causing defective form or structure in the fetus) are examined. The book boasts particularly good discussions of the DES controversy and hyperactivity in the child.

Sameroff, A. J., and Chandler, M. J. Reproductive Risk and the Continuum of Care-Taking Casualty. In F. D. Horowitz (Ed.), *Review of Child Development Research,* 1979, pp. 187–244.

This chapter is also a review of the literature concerning reproductive risk, particularly on the identification of variables that increase the "risk" that a child will have a poor developmental outcome. The conclusion is that most research has focused on discovering the links between defects and causes of these defects. The authors feel that a transactional model is necessary to understand the range of developmental outcomes described in the literature. To the extent that the child elicits or is provided with nurturance from the environment, positive outcomes will be a consequence.

# QUESTIONS FOR THOUGHT

1.  When asked what made a child different from a grown-up, the children in *Looking Up* had a variety of responses: "Kids like winter and grown-ups don't," "Grown-ups can't hang by their knees." These are perceptions about the qualitative difference between adulthood and childhood. Can science say anything more? Using what is known about the developmental process, support one of the following positions: adulthood is qualitatively different (different in nature) from childhood, adulthood is quantitatively different (different in degree) from childhood, childhood is both qualitatively and quantitatively different from adulthood.

2.  Think of a novel you have read with a child or adolescent as the principal character (e.g., *To Kill a Mockingbird, Great Expectations, Catcher in the Rye, Ordinary People*). Do you think the author adequately captures the childhood/adolescent experience? Why or why not?

3.  Describe some of the infant's developmental needs. What are the important developmental issues that arise? How are they different/the same as those of an adolescent? What changes take place as the child grows? How are these needs answered?

4.  What role does each level of the ecosystem play in supporting individual development prenatally? In infancy? Childhood? Adolescence?

5.  Is it fair to say that modern society "invented" adolescence? Was adolescence formerly only the province of the rich?

6.  Some people charge that reformers are making too much fuss about the environmental hazards facing pregnant women. They charge that worrying about alcohol, tobacco, sugar, salt and the like is more of a threat than drinking, smoking, and eating. Is that a fair charge?

7.  As technology improves our ability for intrauterine diagnosis, will we simply be adding another psychological burden to pregnancy and risking a growing imperative to abort less-than-physiologically perfect fetuses? Is this result inevitable?

8.  What advice would you give to parents facing the puberty of their first child? What would your rationale be, based on the evidence presented in the chapter?

# Chapter 6

There are two lasting bequests
we can give our children—
one is roots, the other wings.
Anonymous

    The decision to accept the responsibilities of parenthood is a bold confrontation between dreams and doubts, between past and future. This chapter adopts an ecological perspective to examine the social and psychological aspects of becoming and sustaining a healthy family. Beginning with childbirth as a critical life event, we argue for active parent participation in decisions affecting child development and family life. Important variations in childbirth practices across cultural and historical contexts are considered. A detailed look at beginning the family is followed by a discussion of the basic issues in parent–child relationships from childhood through adolescence. Throughout the chapter, we place particular emphasis on the importance of transactions between developing individuals. Parents and others concerned with optimizing the potential of our youngest generation are urged to consider the monumental task of providing the delicate balance of supports and challenges which give children both roots and wings.

# The Ecology of Childbearing and Child Rearing

## Childbearing: Birth of the Parent–Child Relationship

After months of parental anticipation, a baby emerges from the protection of the mother's womb into a new environment. Without the buffering influence provided by the prenatal home, the newborn must adjust to bombardment by the sensations of light, sound, and temperature change. At the same time, the baby's parents, too, are encountering profound changes. For the mother, the final stages of labor and delivery mark the culmination of more than nine months of bodily changes to accommodate the growing fetus. For both parents, the delivery is another important phase in the psychological and social preparation for becoming a parent. The parents and their infant are experiencing important life changes that Bronfenbrenner (1979) calls ecological transitions.

Defined as alterations in an individual's position in the environment resulting from a change in role or setting, ecological transitions are numerous during the period of physical stress and heightened emotion surrounding the labor and delivery. Examples of transitional events experienced by most parents during the perinatal period include entering the setting where birth will take place, the first opportunities to see and touch the newborn, and taking the neonate home for the first time. Together, this cluster of activities and associated role changes defines and gives meaning to the birth experience as a critical life event that can profoundly affect both the newborn and the new parents for the remainder of their lives.

During the last decade, clinicians and researchers have paid considerable attention to the role of parents during a small segment of the transition to parenthood. In attempts to generalize from studies demonstrating a sensitive period for the development of mothering behavior among some animals, Marshall Klaus, John Kennell, and their associates have investigated the effects of opportunities for extended skin-to-skin contact with the newborn on the mother's tendency to "bond" or form strong attachments with her baby. In a much-cited study, the researchers compared the behaviors of two groups of mothers: one, experiencing the modest amount of contact with their newborns dictated by conventional hospital routine, the other, given opportunities for sixteen hours of additional contact beginning at the time of delivery and continuing for extended visitations throughout the hospital stay (Klaus et al., 1972). The researchers found that when presented with her nude baby, a mother in the extended contact group often displayed an "orderly progression of behavior," massaging and examining the infant's body and engaging in *en face,* or face-to-face, interaction with the baby. When observed during a feeding situation with their infants one month later, this group of mothers showed significantly more soothing, fondling, and *en face* exchanges than the controls. At one year, mothers in the treatment group were still rated higher than the controls on two measures of maternal responsiveness: proximity to the infant during a physical examination and tendency to soothe their babies when they cried (Kennell et al., 1974).

By providing a touching portrait of mother and child within a single time frame, this body of research has played a crucial role in heightening our awareness of the psychological components of the immediate postpartum period. In particular, it has expanded parental knowledge of infant capabilities and catalyzed research on the importance of early contact for individual and family development. In addition, it has led medical professionals to reconsider the advisability of routine separation of mother and infant following delivery (cf., AMA Recommendations on Parent and Newborn Interaction, 1977).

Unfortunately, the immediate and emotional response to initial investigations of bonding also may have obscured the fact that a number of important questions remain unanswered: What are the specific elements of early contact that translate into heightened maternal responsiveness? Might observed differences in the extended contact group be attributed to effects of the research team or hospital staff (so-called "Hawthorne effects")? How do race, parity, age, or socioeconomic status relate to parental responsiveness (Seashore, 1981)? What are the links between early bonding of parent to child and later evidence of specific attachments of the infant to a caregiver (Matas, Arend, & Sroufe, 1978)? Most importantly, what are the contributions of the infant, the father, and other family members to the bonding process, and how do their effects vary across social context and historical time?

Moreover, the inherent appeal of an opportunity to solve many problems associated with early parent–child relationships by merely providing for a few extra hours of mother–infant contact may have clouded our vision of important practice and policy issues. For example, if close contact during the immediate postpartum period enhances infant development, will the lack of contact necessarily have deletrious effects? How can we account for the generations of parent and offspring who successfully "made up for lost time," forming close, sensitive relationships despite the lack of early contact? Will the popular emphasis on bonding actually undermine the early parent–child relationship by increasing parental anxiety or producing feelings of guilt among those who don't experience bonding (Hersh & Levin, 1978)? Clearly, relationships between developing individuals across the life span are more complex than the literature on bonding reveals. While early contact within a supportive environment might serve as a rewarding component of early intervention, we still lack sufficient evidence that opportunities to bond, per se, can account for appreciable long-term differences in family outcomes.

To narrow one's perspective to the single act of bonding is to confine the conception of the perinatal period to a restricted number of actors and a limited time interval, or "sensitive period" (Hales et al., 1977). Specifically, it neglects the impact of a wide range of events and experiences on individual development and on the development of the family as a unit (Howells, 1972). Furthermore, viewing early family relationships through the bonding lens may well blind us to the far-reaching influences of sociocultural factors in shaping the developmentally formative events surrounding childbirth and the transition to parenthood.

As earlier discussions of the ecological approach have demonstrated, human development is not a single still photograph; it is an epic motion picture with a "cast of thousands" spanning numerous scenes and settings. Therefore, in order to understand the complexities of the period including delivery and the early weeks thereafter, we need to view childbirth as a social event in which the roles and status of family members influence their behavior and the outcomes—i.e. the child's healthy development and the quality of parent–child relations (Garbarino, 1980a; MacIntyre, 1977; Oakley, 1979). Use of the ecological approach helps us present childbearing in broader scope, as a period in which there are multiple sources of variation on each "side" of the equation.

## Beyond Psychological Approaches: Examining the Microsystem

Unlike the limited psychological, or bonding, approach that focuses on the feelings of one individual (the mother) toward another (the infant), an ecological perspective encourages us to study the transactions *between* the members of the dyad. Furthermore, because this approach recognizes the dyad as the essential building block of the microsystem (Bronfenbrenner, 1979), it provides us with a framework for viewing the multiple dyadic relationships that come into play during the perinatal period and the interconnections between those relationships.

Naturally, we direct much of our concern with the ecology of childbearing toward the roles, relationships, and activities of the microsystem of the delivery room. Ironically, while the parents are the two individuals most responsible for the birth of the infant, their roles and status have the greatest variability across delivery settings. In a delivery using anesthesia, for example, the mother may be unconscious or relegated to the role of passive observer. Often, the father is excluded from the setting. In that case, the principal dyadic relationships within the microsystem are those of doctor–nurse, doctor–infant, and nurse–infant. In contrast, unmedicated delivery replaces the passive observer with an alert and active mother. The father, or a familiar support figure selected by the mother, is on hand to "coach" the delivery, share the experience with the mother, and "greet" the newborn. Here, then, the number of potential dyads increases tremendously to include mother–father, mother–infant, mother– or father–doctor, mother– or father–nurse, and father–infant. The focus has clearly shifted to include the parents as important participants in the labor and delivery and to increase the number of connections within the setting.

A number of recent innovations in delivery and newborn care offer examples of ways that changes in the meso-, exo-, and macrosystems can affect every element of the microsystem of childbirth. First, let us consider a number of alternative delivery procedures. Prepared childbirth, sometimes called Lamaze delivery, or natural childbirth, is based on the use of physical and psychological exercises to help manage labor and delivery with little or no medication. A series of prenatal childbirth preparation classes offered to the pregnant woman and a selected support figure (usually the father) often include visits to the maternity ward, lectures on breastfeeding, and training in infant development. At some delivery sites, prepared childbirth is offered in conjunction with components of the "gentle birth" advocated by Frederick Leboyer (1975). Leboyer deliveries, conducted in a quiet, dimly lit setting, involve the newborn in a skin-to-skin massage on the mother's abdomen, delayed clamping of the umbilical cord, and a relaxing warm water bath administered to the newborn by the father or the delivery staff. In contrast, delivery by cesarean section, a surgical procedure removing the infant directly from the womb, necessarily lessens the degree of parental control offered in deliveries that are both prepared and unmedicated. Recently, however, parents' rights organizations such as Cesarean-Support, Education, and Concern (C-SEC) have made important advances in bolstering the role of parents during a cesarean delivery, e.g., gaining admission for fathers to the delivery room to support their wives and hold the baby soon after birth. Together, these alternative delivery practices suggest ways that parental roles and activities can be expanded during a crucial period in the transition to parenthood.

Still other variations in the microsystem of delivery accompany differences in the physical features of the setting. For example, a growing number of couples have reacted to the stark atmosphere and emphasis on illness pervading most hospital settings by opting for delivery at home. Attended by a nurse–midwife, a physician, or a lay support person, home births match familiarity of suroundings with high levels of parental control. Unlike traditional delivery settings that may separate mothers from familiar support figures, the setting for the home birth often includes friends, relatives, and even siblings (Lang, 1972). When medical risk or personal preferences make home birth an unacceptable option, couples may select an alternative birth setting located in a hospital or maternity center. Designed to offer the couple a comfortable, homelike setting, these "birthing rooms" often serve as a combined facility for labor, delivery, and aftercare. A third variation in the physical environment of the perinatal period is offered by the practice of "rooming in." Rather than confining infants to a newborn nursery for all but scheduled feeding periods, rooming-in offers an opportunity for neonates to remain in their mother's rooms for all or part of the hospital stay. Not only does rooming-in allow extended periods for mother–father–infant contact, it also provides opportunities for parents to gradually gain confidence in the role of caregiver prior to hospital discharge (Greenberg, Rosenberg, & Lind, 1973).

Each of these alternatives provides an illustration of ways that we can expand the microsystem of childbirth to accommodate the psychological and social needs of the family. Whether childbirth actually is a family-centered event and whether parents actually are actively involved across settings and activities, however, are issues grounded in the wider social and historical context.

## The Family in the Medical Setting: The Mesosystem

The most obvious and pressing mesosystem issue surrounding childbirth is, of course, congruence between home and hospital. How well do roles assigned to parents in hospitals approximate their roles in the home and family? Are the same people involved in both? Is the child the only link? One of the chief criticisms of hospital-based delivery has been that while parents have a high-status, active role in the home, they often assume a low-status, passive role in the hospital. Following an in-depth study of thirteen couples and the medical personnel they encountered from early pregnancy through delivery, sociologist Sandra Danziger (1979a,b) concluded that asymmetrical relationships were a key feature in the situation (1979b). Danziger found that the fathers' roles were particularly ill-defined. Overwhelmingly preoccupied with minimizing their perceived intrusion in the medical setting, many fathers assumed the role of passive observer. Those who took a more active stance, especially those who questioned medical procedures, were met with hostility. Capitalizing on their role as experts, doctors wielded control in determining the course of interactions with a patient. Patients, in turn, usually deferred to members of the medical staff, acting "like guests in someone else's home."

Danziger's findings are supported by another account of a particularly frustrating hospital delivery:

> I was truly well-behaved; I wasn't causing any trouble or crying out. I didn't feel as though I could ask the nurses any questions when they came in. . . . They wheeled me into the delivery room and strapped my arms down. I asked, "Do you have to do that" and (a nurse) said "yes." You're supposed to have your arms free in natural childbirth. But I was never one to protest, and in that vulnerable position I could never cross anybody on anything. Because you feel totally helpless and I just wouldn't want to make anybody mad at me in that situation (Harvey, 1977, p. 10).

Role discrepancies, such as those described, may work to the disadvantage of the parent–child relationship, particularly when that relationship is jeopardized by other risk factors. The deficit is especially striking when the high physical vulnerability of a premature infant is compounded by environmental factors undermining the parent's abilities to provide contact and care (Leidermann & Seashore, 1975; Solnit & Provence, 1979). As Seashore (1981) notes, the mother of the hospitalized newborn "is prevented from fulfilling her expected role as mother. It is a nurse, not she, who is caring for her infant's physical and emotional needs—feeding, soothing, and showing affection to the newborn" (1981, p. 76).

If the maternal role is thwarted within many medical settings, the role of father is often ignored altogether. For example, as recently as 1970, a meager 34 percent of the premature nurseries in a large national sample allowed mothers to visit and handle their infants in the nursery. Of that limited number, only 60 percent allowed similar access for fathers (Grobstein, 1974).

Often, hospital practices that undermine parental roles can have serious consequences for the family unit. Segal and Yahraes (1978) provide an example in their moving account of the events surrounding the death of a three-month-old baby who had spent his entire life in the hospital:

At no time had we considered the feelings of the parents who had visited every single day, standing at the observation window. When the baby died, the mother asked to hold him. Crying, she rocked him and explained this was the first time she had ever touched him (1978, p. 82).

While the couple in this example continued their vigil throughout the period that their child was in the intensive care unit, others respond to long-term separation by psychological abandonment. Prolonged separation of mothers and their premature infants has been linked to both maternal detachment and an inability to engage in close, reciprocal exchanges with the infant (Klaus & Kennell, 1976; Seashore, 1981). Indeed, in their follow-up study of 146 infants who had been placed in neonatal intensive care, Kennell, Voos, and Klaus (1976) found that 23 percent of those babies receiving less than three visits over a two week period, compared to only 2 percent of those visited more frequently, subsequently experienced serious problems in the early parent–child relationship including abuse, abandonment, or failure-to-thrive. As these findings attest, one of the strongest cases made for the developmental wisdom of family-centered childbirth may be its potential for diminishing family dysfunction associated with child maltreatment (Garbarino, 1980a; Gray et al., 1977; Gurry, 1977).

Obviously, mothers play an essential biological role during pregnancy, labor, and delivery. During the postpartum period, hormone levels and milk production help maintain a physiological link to nurturance of the newborn. Fathers, by contrast, have no direct physiological involvement after conception. Therefore, when obstetrical personnel view childbirth as merely a physiological, somewhat pathological event (Haire, 1973) father involvement may be dismissed as an unnecessary hindrance. However, when conceptions of the childbearing experience are expanded to include crucial social and psychological factors, the father becomes an integral part of the childbirth team (El Sherif, McGrath, & Smyrski, 1979).

Within the last decade, a number of studies have begun to demonstrate the importance of active participation by fathers for the way that both men and women experience the transition to parenthood. For example, two studies by Block and her colleagues (Block & Block, 1975; Block et al., 1981) have demonstrated the father's role in determining a couple's successful use of prepared childbirth techniques. Prenatally, the likelihood that either of the marital partners would attend Lamaze childbirth preparation classes was determined largely by the husband's willingness to participate and his ability to coordinate class attendance with other time commitments. Men retained their "gatekeeping" roles throughout labor; active assistance from the husband was linked to a woman's ability to manage pain during contractions and her subsequent evaluation of the labor experience. Similarly, interviews conducted by Fein (1976) revealed the importance of husband presence during delivery in determining the evaluation of that experience by their wives. In addition, active participation in labor and delivery has been shown to have direct effects on early father attachment to the newborn (Gearing, 1978; Greenberg & Morris, 1974; Peterson, Mehl, & Leiderman, 1979) and on the ease of entrance to the paternal role (Fein, 1976).

An additional way to consider the mesosystem of childbirth is to look beyond the congruence of parental role and status across home and hospital to consider ways of strengthening the family's relation to both formal and informal support systems. Many observers have remarked that the receptivity of some new parents to social connections while still in the microsystem of the hospital stands in stark contrast to their lack of receptivity to sources of support when they are back at home (e.g., Gray et al., 1977). This supposed "susceptibility," or openness of parents, at the time when a child, particularly the first child, is born (Klaus & Kennell, 1976) raises the possibility of interventions aimed at strengthening the family's ties to social support systems. Linking a representative of a supportive service with the family during pregnancy or while the family is still in the hospital can help establish a strong home–health services mesosystem. Thus, for example, a visiting nurse, a midwife, or a parent educator can begin a relationship with a family that extends from the early prenatal period, through childbirth, into infancy.

Recently, Olds (1980) created a project that involves a systematic design attempting to explore the relative power of various combinations of prenatal, perinatal, and postnatal support systems. One aspect of this program is its attempt to inject a helpful outsider—a home visitor—into the prospective family microsystem in the prenatal period as a basis for gaining access to the family during the perinatal period and building on that relationship by serving the family and protecting the child in the first years of life.

In many cases, participation in the project has helped increase family awareness of available community services. In addition, the home visitors encourage families to identify valuable resources within their informal support networks and to seek out others with similar concerns and interests. As in the case of childbirth preparation classes, families brought together during the prenatal period to learn about labor and delivery techniques often form strong support networks with activities ranging from reunions to child care cooperatives, support groups, and parent education classes.

The specific intervention technique may be inconsequential, provided that efforts are made to support parents in their roles across home and hospital settings. As pediatrician and family advocate T. Berry Brazelton explains:

> In a violated system such as the one we provide presently around labor, delivery, and being in a hospital with a new baby, the effects of *any* positive intervention are magnified. Any experience that can be interpreted by the patient as positive

or reinforcing for their feeling of self-value or importance to their new infant, becomes of enormous symbolic meaning as they search hungrily for support in such a non-reinforcing system in our present lying-in hospitals. To go on treating deliveries as if they were corrective surgery and patients as if they were ill, insensitive, or both, is patently destructive. Hence, any (prosocial) intervention . . . will be likely to produce surprisingly significant results in the light of the mother's (and father's) wish to feel individual, important, and adequate to that baby (Brazelton, 1981, p. 121).

As Brazelton's message reveals, decisions about the way a family adds a new member are often bound up in practices and policies established outside the family. The support necessary to institute programs that can bridge settings often resides in exosystem issues.

## The Institutional Context of Childbearing: Exosystem Issues

In the present case, the principal exosystem phenomena lie in the institutional policies and practices of the hospitals and medical establishments that have a bearing on the nature and construction of the microsystem of childbirth. As such, they also play a crucial role in shaping the mesosystem issues resulting from the relationships between settings. As in other areas of child and family development, action often results from scripts being written in administrative offices without input from the principal actors—the family members.

Over the span of several decades, the medical community has radically altered the character of the microsystems of labor and delivery. During the Colonial period, childbirth was characterized by a comprehensive social orientation (Wertz & Wertz, 1977). Pregnant women rarely became involved with a health care delivery system. Rather, infants were delivered at home with the assistance of midwives and family members; mother and newborn had ready access to family and community supports. During the nineteenth century, the Industrial Revolution was accompanied by urban crowding and menacing health problems. Many women died in childbirth; those infants who survived delivery were likely to succumb to sepsis or infant diarrhea. That era was also a period of great advances in medicine, public health, and education.

The medical approach to childbirth was a by-product of these parallel developments (cf., Clark, 1979; Klaus & Kennell, 1976). Early hospital deliveries were accompanied by a number of institutionalized practices, including moving patients from labor room to delivery room, issuing standing orders for anesthesia, delivery in the lethomony, or flat-on-back position, routine episiotomies, and separation of parents and newborn following delivery. With improvements in medical technology, these procedures, which had been designed for difficult or problem deliveries, soon became standard practice.

In recent years, hospital practices have expanded to include more elaborate forms of medical intervention in the delivery process. For example, expensive and often cumbersome fetal monitoring equipment is used to accurately measure changes in the fetal heart rate during uterine contractions. External monitoring, which uses a belt strapped around the mother's abdomen, necessitates confinement to bed during the time that monitoring is in progress. Significantly more invasive, internal monitoring uses a spiral electrode inserted into the vagina and attached to the presenting part of the fetus (usually the scalp). The use of sensitive monitoring equipment has been heralded by many obstetricians as an important advance in the diagnosis of fetal distress, a condition often tied to mental retardation (cf., Zuspan et al., 1979). Others, however, maintain that overzealous and improper use of fetal monitoring has led to an increase in unnecessary surgical intervention and skyrocketing delivery costs (Norwood, 1980; Rosen, 1980).

A second form of intervention, induction, involves artificial stimulation of labor by the injection of synthetic hormones. The use of therapeutic inductions can greatly benefit both mother and fetus when the pregnancy is placed at risk by maternal hypertension or diabetes or in cases of placental insufficiency, postmaturity, or premature rupture of the membranes (Butnarescu, Tillotson, & Villarreal, 1980). Increasingly, however, induction has been used as an elective procedure, with the delivery scheduled to meet the social schedules of doctors or parents. Norwood (1980) has estimated that by the mid-1970s, many hospitals in England and the United States were inducing labor in 20 to 30 percent of their private patients despite growing evidence of multiple risks, including unusually strong and frequent contractions necessitating the use of anesthesia, increased use of forceps or surgical delivery, prematurity, and respiratory distress of the newborn.

Both fetal monitoring and elective inductions have been tied to a third form of intervention, delivery by cesarean section. Accompanying trends toward defensive medicine, financial incentives, and greater specialization in obstetrics, the rate of cesarean delivery in this country increased nearly threefold, from 5.5 percent in 1970 to 15.2 percent in 1978, the sharpest national increase in the world (Rosen, 1980).

While many have heralded recent technological refinements in the delivery process, others argue that the original intention (intervention in high-risk pregnancies) has given way to the establishment of policies and practices designed for the convenience, legal protection, or economic benefit of medical personnel. Critics point out that despite the routine use of obstetrical technology—and perhaps because of the often unnecessary intrusions into the natural course of labor and delivery—the United States leads all developed countries in the rate of infant deaths associated with birth injury and respiratory distress. Of the fourteen countries with lower infant mortality rates, those with the lowest—

Sweden, the Netherlands, Finland, and Japan—are more likely to use "natural" or family-centered childbirth techniques and are less likely to use any form of obstetrical intervention. Furthermore, critics contend that invasive delivery practices not only contribute to medical risks but may also undermine important social aspects of the perinatal period.

Indeed, a growing body of data has begun to demonstrate that decisions about childbirth must be viewed within a field of possible alternatives and a complex package of likely consequences. For example, maternal fears and tension during the last trimester of pregnancy have been linked to increased discomfort during labor (Yang, 1981). The administration of larger doses of pain relieving drugs to reduce the discomfort is associated with longer first-stage labor as well as with drug effects on the newborn that extend through the important first weeks of postpartum life (Brackbill, 1979). Conversely, adequate preparation for childbirth has been related to decreases in the use of chemical and surgical intervention, lower rates of fetal distress and postpartum infection (Hughey et al., 1978), and strong positive reactions to the baby and the birth experience (Doering & Entwisle, 1975). It is also important to note that childbirth practices are sometimes associated with both mixed and unintended results. For example, two recent studies of families with infants delivered by cesarean section found that while the delivery mode was associated with negative evaluations of the birth experience and constrained parent-infant interactions for mothers, it also resulted in heightened paternal concern for the infants and a greater caregiving role for fathers (Grossman, Winickoff, & Eichler, 1980; Pedersen et al., 1980).

Perhaps one of the most dramatic examples of exosystem effects is associated with teenage parenthood. Despite the commonly accepted assumption that a teenage pregnancy is inevitably and intrinsically a high-risk pregnancy, increasing evidence suggest that most adolescent pregnancies need be no more risky than others, *if* adequately supported by parents, peers, teachers, and medical personnel (Shelton & Gladstone, 1979). Because of its perceived social deviancy in our society, however, teenage pregnancy and parenthood often lack appropriate or sufficient social support. The risks associated with teenage parenthood are most pronounced when the mother is poor and unwed.

Finally, in order to understand the exosystem issues associated with child-bearing, it is important to recognize the policies instituted by hospitals, schools, and governmental bodies that can affect infants and their families both during the immediate postpartal period and beyond. Examples of such far-reaching measures include the availability of educational opportunities for adolescent parents and the access to free or low-cost social and medical services for rural families. The prominent role of the exosystem is also reflected in the following policy questions: Should public schools offer information on family planning or provide early training for parenting? Can businesses create policies to bolster the parenting roles of their workers? Should a physician who blocks active parent participation in childbirth decisions be charged with malpractice? Will the federal government enact and enforce legislation regarding the assurance of both maternity and paternity leaves for American workers or the establishment of comprehensive child-care regulations? The diversity of opinions on these topics helps underscore the interplay between the exosystem and the wider contextual sphere, the macrosystem.

## The Macrosystem of Childbirth

Activities associated with the birth of a child vary widely with cultural setting and historical period. The macrosystem prescribes the context in which specific patterns of behavior take place and influences important social dimensions of the perinatal period. It defines what is normal for one time and place.

Often, childbirth practices within a subculture stand as a direct reflection of other life activities. Bing (1975), for example, has demonstrated the ways that the home-based activities of the Amish are particularly compatible with family-centered approaches to childbirth. Among other groups, such as the Navajo of North America and the Cuna of Panama, music is such an integral part of daily life that it is considered a requisite part of labor (Newton, 1979). Similarly, Mead (1955) reported that members of African tribes and certain groups of native Americans rejected modern hospital deliveries that would separate them from stimulating conversation during labor and from immediate postnatal support and care provided by family and friends.

Activity surrounding the addition of a new member to a group also reveals the tradition-bound values and beliefs of a culture. In Sixteenth-century Europe, for example, the only men allowed at the site of a delivery were astrologers summoned to cast a precise horoscope. While the midwives attending the event lacked any medical training, they were licensed by the bishop of the church to provide impromptu baptismal services for failing neonates (Tucker, 1974). The ceremonial nature of childbirth is also reflected in the practices of several traditional African cultures, where the pregnant woman observes local dietary taboos, dons ceremonial garb, and spends the period of confinement at the home of a culturally mandated family member. Her husband, in turn, might observe the custom of *couvade,* a rite of paternal passage. Prenatally, he may indulge in a wide range of pregnancy symptoms. During the delivery and subsequent lying-in period he engages in a kind of ceremonial childbirth, including seclusion and abstention from normal work activities (Munroe & Munroe, 1975).

As these examples reveal, many cultures regard childbirth and the transition to parenthood as an important social event. In contrast, critics have argued that our own country has instituted childbirth practices that limit the vital physiological, psychological, and social roles played by parents. Haire (1973) has implicated these practices in what she calls "the cultural warping of childbirth."

Furthermore, Rossi (1968) argues that the abruptness of the transition to parenthood, coupled with inadequate preparation for the responsibilities of the role, has been accompanied by a severe weakening of the web of supportive relationships available to new parents. Together, these factors undermine the ideological underpinnings of American parenthood.

Is it possible to change the macrosystem—to alter ideas and ideals woven into the very fabric of the culture? The best answer to that question is probably a qualified "yes." While certain beliefs and values are deeply ingrained, others have evolved in form or substance to accommodate the social and demographic characteristics of the times. As recently as thirty years ago, for example, the childbirth experience of most American couples was characterized by meager preparation. Most women were heavily medicated during labor and unconscious during delivery. Denied access to labor and delivery rooms, their husbands were usually left to pace in the hospital lounge.

> Parents approached the entire process of childbearing—pregnancy, childbirth and postpartum—unaware. . . . The mother did not question the use of obstetrical medication, did not know the value of breastfeeding, did not know that she might play an active role, have rights in, and assume responsibility in the birth of her baby (Otto, 1978).

During that period, at the peak of the postwar Baby Boom, a "sellers market" existed in the field of obstetrics. Flooded by requests for services, doctors had no reason to change their practices. Within the last decade, however, consumer action and the women's rights movement have made inroads into a number of institutional settings, including hospital maternity wards. Today, the birth rate has slowed; though fewer children are born, they are more likely to be planned. A "buyer's market" exists, as hospitals with empty beds are forced to compete for services. With increases in the perceived value of parents as consumers in the medical marketplace, medical personnel are likely to be more receptive to the needs and demands of their patients (Garbarino, 1980a).

There is growing evidence of a move toward family-centered perinatal practices, particularly among more affluent and better educated parents. In all likelihood, a significant shift toward the institutionalization of comprehensive family-centered childbirth for the majority of obstetrical patients will depend on alterations in attitudes about children and families in general and the social dimensions of childbearing in particular.

The ecological approach tells us that to understand the significance of changes in the microsystem of childbirth we must look to the mesosystem (the congruence between home and hospital), the exosystem (how decisions are made about childbirth in bureaucratic administrative and medical offices), and the macrosystem (how the broad social history of parenthood may increase the importance of

family-centered childbirth as a way of compe
support systems for families). The ecological fra
that to understand childbirth we must see the
alternative arrangements of the social events
individual development of child and paren
development of the family. As the remainder
perspective can also provide valuable clues to
complexities of child rearing.

## Child Rearing: Continuation of the Parent–Child Relationship

What do we know about childrearing, about the nature of parent–child relations?
Even the most cursory reading shows that there is an enormous number of
studies on the topic and, literally, thousands of "findings." Our task here is to
outline and summarize what we know in a manner that best meets the needs
of those who seek to understand and serve children and families in social context.
For our purposes, three general topics stand out: the basic issues and pitfalls in
parent–child relations, the way the immediate social context of the family affects
what happens between children and their parents, and how the broader society
affects the content and meaning of parent–child relationships. Let us begin by
examining the earliest phases of the parent–child relationship:

Prenatally, parents engage in a special psychological acquaintance process with
the fetus (Colman & Colman, 1971). Particularly after quickening occurs,
expectant parents are likely to nickname the unborn child or make predictions
about the infant's temperament or appearance from the amount of fetal activity
or the mother's symptomology. As studies of early postpartum contact reveal,
birth accelerates the acquaintance process. Parents anxiously explore the physical
and temperamental features of the newborn using a kind of mental checklist:
Which family members does the infant resemble? Are there any features that
are distinctively the infant's own? How does the infant compare to prenatal
expectations? Is everything all right?

As parents discover the capabilities and distinctive characteristics of their
babies, we can assume that these early, emotion-charged encounters begin to
teach infants important lessons about the social environment. For example, in
healthy social settings, infants learn that when they make social overtures and
signal their need for caregiving, they will get a response from special others.
They begin to trust themselves and those around them (Erikson, 1963). In
time, they will use the relationship with specific attachment figures, usually the
parents, as a secure base from which to discover the expanding horizons of the
physical and social environment (Ainsworth, 1973). Throughout this period of
active learning, the infant is also an effective teacher, communicating interests,

nd needs. As Susan Goldberg's (1979) work with preterm infants
Fraiberg's (1968, 1973) studies of the attachment behaviors of blind
make abundantly clear, one of the most important tasks of new parents
learn to understand, or decode, infant communications and respond
propriately. It is an essential fact of development that starting from the very
earliest social exchanges, socialization is a reciprocal process (Bell, 1968, 1974).

The mutuality of parent–child influences has been demonstrated by descriptions
of the patterns of interactional behaviors used in the early social exchanges of
mothers and infants. Examining videotapes of mother-infant social play, Stern
(1971, 1973) described maneuvers used by mothers to capture and retain infant
attention (i.e., high-pitch, sing-song speech, exaggerated facial expressions, and
close-range body placement). Infants, in turn, use gazes, smiles, and changes in
head and body position to initiate, respond to, or discontinue social exchanges.
Stern found that a baby's attention seems to cycle toward and away from the
mother. A related study by Brazelton, Koslowski, and Main (1974) complements
Stern's research by showing that the most positive mother–infant interactions
occur when the partners read each other's cues, negotiating synchronized cycles
of attention and nonattention.

Over time, the content of the exchanges between parents and children will
vary with the developmental needs of the individual actors (Newson & Newson,
1972; Richardson, 1981). Reciprocity and mutual socialization remain central
features of the parent–child relationship, however. Although we tend to think
of a family relationship as something that ends when a young adult leaves home,
perhaps to start a new generation, it does not. The parent–child relationship
continues to affect one's life long after one leaves home and may even endure
after the death of one of the members of the dyad (Hagestad, 1981b). Whatever
else a developing individual becomes in life, that individual is always the child
of his or her parents. Research on child abuse, for example, shows that the
memory of one's parents lives on in one's own child rearing style, particularly
when that style was harsh and punitive (Kempe & Kempe, 1978).

Just as the nature of the parent–child relationship shows variations with the
capabilities and ages of the individual actors, a growing body of research suggests
that still other variations may be associated with parents' gender-related roles.
Especially during the periods of infancy and early childhood, mothers tend to
assume the primary responsibility for child care. While the quantity of time
devoted to father–child interaction usually increases with the age of the child
(Lewis & Weinraub, 1976), the amount of time fathers spend in direct contact
with infants has been estimated to be less than an hour per day (Pedersen &
Robson, 1969; Rebelsky & Hanks, 1971). Of greater importance than the
*quantity* of father–infant interaction, however, is the father's contribution to the
*quality* of interactions within the family unit. Ross Parke (Parke, 1979; Parke
& O'Leary, 1975; Parke & Sawin, 1976; Sawin & Parke, 1979), for example,

conducted a series of observational studies during the perinatal period that show high levels of paternal interest and sensitivity to infant cues. Similarly, Michael Lamb (1976, 1977a, b, 1978) has demonstrated that while fathers provide less care giving and initiate fewer conventional games than mothers, they are more likely to engage infants in unique kinds of physically stimulating play.

Recently, studies have shown that fathers also exert powerful indirect influences on the quality of a child's experiences. In the interest shown to the infant and the support given to his spouse as a mother and a wife, the father is able to mediate mothering behavior toward the infant (Lamb, 1978; Sawin & Parke, 1979). These influences, which Bronfenbrenner (1979) calls second-order effects, underscore the value of studying the parent–child relationship within the context of the family system (Feiring & Lewis, 1978).

Without question, parent–child relations present us with some real intellectual, policy, and practice puzzles. On the one hand, we know that what parents do with their children makes a difference. As we saw in earlier chapters, virtually all social events are mediated by parents; very few touch children directly. The nature of a specific parent–child relationship is the single most important social factor in one's biography. And yet, we know—and research shows—that while differences in style and orientation make some difference, overall, most parents tend to do reasonably well by most children, most of the time. Despite the widespread assumption that each and every childhood event carries with it life-long consequences, we are learning that for each constancy there is a variable, that development is a continuing process in which contemporary events play a large role in shaping what we are (Brim & Kagan, 1980). We all know families where the parents' best laid plans for their children have gone awry or even have been actively thwarted by those same children. The authors recall a cartoon that appeared in the *New Yorker* magazine some years ago. It pictured two denim-clad, bead-laden hippies lamenting the "failure" of their parenting efforts—a boy dressed in suit and tie carrying a briefcase. It is clear that parents rarely are able to prescribe or orchestrate the details of their offspring's lives. Temperament, out-of-home experiences, and unintentional parental effects play a large role.

## The Basic Tools of Healthy Development

What we need is some specification of the psychological basic necessities that parents must help children receive and experience. Perhaps the single most important psychological necessity is "positive self-regard." Children can and do grow up to be adequate adults within a wide variety of disciplinary styles, intellectual climates, and levels of social interaction. But, when all is said and done, it appears that very few children can grow up adequately on a psychological diet of rejection (Rohner, 1975; Rohner & Neilson, 1978). Acceptance, then, seems to be a prerequisite for adequate human development. Perhaps the Beatles were nearly right when they sang, "All you need is love."

Chapter 3 posed rejection as the underlying danger of sociocultural risk, the most surely deadly poison that can contaminate parent–child relations. Rejection is a general term, of course, but we can identify some of its more specific behavioral expressions as the child moves from infancy to adolescence.

In infancy, the dangers are twofold: First, we must be concerned about the rejection of positive, natural behaviors such as smiling, mobility, exploration, vocalization, and manipulation of objects. Research from a variety of contexts demonstrates that caregiver behavior can have a direct impact on the performance of these basic human skills (cf., Brackbill, 1958; Foss, 1965). There is an inherent drive for mastery or effectance (Goldberg, 1977; White, 1959). To punish or ignore this drive and its accompanying behaviors is a decided threat to the child's development of competence.

The second danger comes from parents thwarting the attachment relationship between themselves and the child. As we saw earlier in this chapter, caregiver–infant bonding and later attachment have emerged as important issues in child development (Klaus & Kennell, 1976). Disruptions of attachment have been linked to physical abuse (Kennell, Voos, & Klaus, 1976), failure to thrive (Spitz, 1945), and a variety of competence deficits (Bronfenbrenner, 1970). Child rearing styles that consistently undermine attachment, therefore, pose a direct threat to adequate development.

Once the infant advances into childhood, the rejection issue—like the child—changes as a function of development and maturation. While attachment is no longer so simply and directly at stake, its natural product—a sense of self worth—is. Self-esteem, one of the engines driving adequate development, is the positive valuing of one's characteristics, a positive identity. It rises and falls in response to the behavior of others, and it is linked to a variety of prosocial characteristics (Coopersmith, 1967). The unloved of any age must always suspect that they are unlovable. To discourage self-esteem is to attack a fundamental component of competent development. To reject developing children is to jeopardize their very view of their place in the world.

What else do children need from their parents beyond a measure of acceptance? A child needs the experience of learning how to regulate impulses. Thus, matters of discipline and control emerge repeatedly in studies of parent–child relations to complement the fundamental issue of acceptance–rejection. This discipline–control issue has found expression in many studies, under many names. Put in broad terms, however, the key is that parents should be flexible in providing enough in the way of limits and controls to offer adequate protection *for a particular child* and to model the necessary process of self-control. While many theorists use different terms for this essential process, the underlying issue is the same: children need moral structure to their lives.

Of course, as Aristotle tells us from across the centuries, "In all things, moderation." Both too much and too little control threaten the optimal development of children. Of course, the optimal level varies from child to child and from one developmental phase to the next, but either extreme is dangerous for most children. How does one decide the proper mix of freedom and control? The research suggests that most successful families accomplish a good balance by negotiating among members with both respect and dignity (Baumrind, 1980). Successful parents avoid the extreme of too little control ("I'm his mother, so I should do whatever he wants.") and too much control ("He's my child, so he should do whatever I want him to do."). Baumrind called this middle road the "authoritative" approach (in contrast to permissive and authoritarian styles), and concluded that it achieves an appropriate balance of high levels of control, maturity demands, clear communication, and nurturance (Baumrind & Block, 1967). In short, parents who were most successful in facilitating the development of socially competent and happy children were those who did not shortchange any of the child's basic psychological needs for protection and reality testing, for encouragement to achieve and become competent, for rich verbal interaction, and for positive regard, openly expressed.

An essential feature of one's sense of self is gender identity. Everyone must achieve some sense of gender identity or risk severe psychological disruption. Biology, or genetic endowment, sets the stage for maleness and femaleness. Examples are provided by the generally greater verbal facility of girls and the generally greater visual-spatial and mathematical ability of boys (Maccoby & Jacklin, 1974). Of course, these average differences should not obscure the substantial overlap in the characteristics of boys and girls. In fact, overall, the two sexes are far more alike than they are different (Maccoby & Jacklin, 1980).

The crucial role played by socialization in shaping an individual's gender identity has been underscored by the work of John Money and his colleagues at Johns Hopkins University. The researchers followed the development of several children who, because of ambiguous genitalia at birth, were given a gender label that contradicted their chromosomal blueprint for maleness or femaleness. Following the mistake of gender assignment, they were exposed to the sexual tradition-bound socialization, or canalization, for the "wrong" sex. The researchers found that the child's core gender identity, or the definition of self as male or female, was so firmly established during the second year of life that it defied change. By puberty, when secondary-sex characteristics began to appear, it was easier to perform a sex change operation in order to bring the body into accordance with the gender identity than to attempt to change the psychological sense of being male or female. It was concluded that most of the stereotyped distinctions between the sexes are derived from the interaction of biologically based average trends and differences with culturally reinforced differences in roles (Money & Ehrhardt, 1972). In short, while biology determines basic physiological differences between the sexes, the combined effects of such powerful influences as parents, peers, schools, and the media determine just how traditionally feminine or masculine a child will be.

Clearly, the process of socialization for both children and their parents involves influences outside the individual and family contexts.

## Parents and Children and the Wider Social Context

How do parents know how to provide all a child needs, on an on-going basis, in a way that is appropriate for a specific child? Of course, it takes the motivation to give. Fortunately, nearly all parents have that motivation because of their personal investment in the child's character and well-being (Barash, 1977; Garbarino, 1981a). In part, parents' efforts come as a natural by-product of being socially competent and happy adults.

Parental incentives also come from being part of a parent-child relationship that is embedded in a network of social resources that provide feedback and nurturance (Caplan, 1974). Valuable information from the support network consists of both regular feedback on parent–child relations and general knowledge of appropriate norms, expectations, and techniques concerning child rearing. It is derived from regular day-to-day observation and discussion of parent–child relations, informal folk wisdom based on extensive historically validated first-hand experience, and formal, professional expertise.

The need for information is a direct function of situational demands that are both internal and external to the parent–child relationship. The family that is adapting to separation or divorce provides a prime example. With more than one fourth of our children expected to spend some part of their first eighteen years in a household where parental divorce or separation has occurred, parent–child relationships must often progress in a changing variety of family forms. Most children can and do cope with having only one parent, having divorcing or divorced parents, and having stepparents. For the most part, children can meet these challenges if their basic psychological necessities continue to be met—if they still receive nurturance, appropriate maturity demands, sufficient control, and clear communication. Too often, however, family disruption and changes in form and composition of the family unit *tend* to undermine delivery of these basic psychological necessities. When family members are separated, for example, the noncustodial parent's role is often ambiguous and his or her involvement in the family's life is reduced to the point where the child feels abandoned and the custodial parent (the one in whose household the child is living) feels overwhelmed by responsibilities. Moreover, the child-care and housekeeping responsibilities of the divorced woman are frequently compounded by economic stresses. Less than half of all divorced women receive alimony or child support. When they seek employment, they generally receive lower salaries than their male counterparts. As demands on the family increase, so do the parents' needs for information.

Formal institutions can become effective sources of information when they are actively linked to the family's social network—either directly through the parent or indirectly through relationships with others who, in turn, link the parent with formal institutions. Social isolation can be a serious threat to adequacy in the parent—child relationship because those indirect links to resources are lacking. Like their parents, children need the skills, support, and opportunities necessary to participate in the social environment.

While the process of child rearing begins as a dyad or triad with one child, it soon comes to include other children. If there are other children in the family, parents must consider how siblings affect child rearing and serve as an adjunct to their child rearing efforts. Eventually, the child's nonfamily peers come into the picture. The child may go to a baby-sitting group or a nursery school or begin to have contact with neighborhood children.

Peer-group relations are an important influence in development, particularly in their contribution to the socialization of both aggressive and prosocial behavior (Hartup, 1978). Throughout childhood, more and more peers in wider and wider circles become part of the child's life. At each step of the way, the parent's influence may remain strong—even prominent—in matters of basic values and in the acquisition of intimate behaviors. In matters of fashion, taste, and custom, however, the parent must be increasingly ready and able to recognize the existence of their child's peer reference group in family discussions. The four-year-old wants a Superman T-Shirt because the other kids in his or her preschool have them. The seven-year-old must watch the latest "in" show on television. The thirteen-year-old will "die" if her or his haircut is the wrong one. The seventeen-year-old cannot come home before midnight because "no one is leaving that early!" The point is that every age responds to peer influences, but the central role of the parent—child relationship remains.

When parents reject the child's efforts to make a place in the world beyond the family, they deprive the child of one of the basic psychosocial necessities of life, and create what has been called the "World of Abnormal Rearing" (Helfer, 1980). To create such a world and force the child to live in it is one of the principal threats to adequate child development.

Punishing interpersonal skills necessary for adequate performance in nonfamilial contexts, such as schools and peer groups, is another form of rejection with which we must be concerned. Burgess and Conger (1978) observe that abusive and neglectful parents do not provide positive reinforcement for key interpersonal behaviors. Others have noted that abusive parents typically discourage normal social relations among their children—e.g., the formation of friendships outside the home (cf., Friedman, 1976; Garbarino, 1977a,b; Parke & Collmer, 1975).

Few parent—child relationships will go seriously awry and stay that way if both parents and children are well-connected or if they are part of a social network that has psychological investment in the welfare and progress of that relationship. The social character of family relationships is a central aspect of the health and vitality of the child's life. Just as we can join with John Donne in asserting that "no man is an island," we know that no family can always stand alone. A positive orientation toward relationships beyond the family (beyond even the larger kinship network) is necessary to complement or even counteract the particularism of family patterns, of one kinship network's "information" about children and child rearing.

This principle is underscored by examples provided by three prominent agents of socialization—supplemental caregivers, the schools, and television.

## Child Care

Almost all cultures have developed arrangements which enable mothers to provide for basic child care while maintaining other duties that are instrumental to family well-being. Among hunter–gatherer societies, for example, mothers carry their nursing infants in slings when they go on gathering expeditions. As the children grow older, they spend most of their time playing with a large group of age-mates under the watchful eyes of the entire social group (Konner, 1976). In contrast, Weisner and Gallimore (1977) have demonstrated that in many traditional sedentary societies as the mother engages in work away from the home, her youngest children are left in the care of a designated sibling.

Most child-care arrangements may be seen as solutions offered for the support of the parents and the well-being of the child. As demonstrated by the examples of the child-care centers of the Israeli kibbutzim, the Soviet Union, and China, however, supplemental child care can also be an instrument used to help a society meet its goals. In those systems, day care centers are viewed as a key to providing for full participation of adults in the political and economic life of the society, as well as for the socialization of children in a manner appropriate to societal goals (Robinson et al., 1979).

In our own country, supports provided to parents in the provision of quality care for children lag far behind that of other industrial countries. Traditionally, child care in the United States has been viewed as the sole domain of the parents. Supplemental care, when necessary, was to be provided by close friends and relatives. Today, an estimated 87 percent of day-care-age children of working mothers are still looked after by relatives or baby-sitters. Too often, by school age, even that care is removed, and they join the growing cadre of "latchkey" children (Garbarino, 1980c). The government-mandated extended maternity and paternity leaves of the Scandinavian countries and the social insurance which gives parents in Poland, Sweden, and West Germany funds to cover the salary lost while caring for a sick youngster are largely unheard of in this country.

Neither are our children offered the choice of state-supported preschool education and care found in France, Belgium, and the Soviet Union.

While the growing number of dual-career families necessitates the need for a variety of supplements to parental care, day care still lacks widespread public and governmental support. Sibbison (1972), for example, found that of the mothers she surveyed, 29 percent rejected the use of day-care services for other people's children under most conditions, while 44 percent rejected that option for their own children. Moreover, in a survey conducted by Rodes and Moore (1975), one in five of the respondents felt that working women neglect their children. Nowhere is our country's anti-day care sentiment more prevalent, however, than in the failure of the federal government to legislate and enforce guidelines assuring quality comprehensive care.

Just as much of the research on day care in the United States has failed to demonstrate appreciable long-term gains from supplemental care, detractors of day care also have not been successful in showing that adequate out-of-home care has any serious negative effects on young children (Peters, 1980). Quality day care can supplement the direct child rearing functions of the family by serving as a source of nurturance, affection, instruction, and socialization (Peters & Benn, 1980). While children's ties to their parents remain primary, the day care setting can offer rich opportunities for children to interact and form close relationships with other caregivers and their peers (Ricciuti, 1974, 1977). In addition, when parents and day-care providers establish a partnership of care, a number of indirect functions can also be achieved (e.g., economic, self-actualization, and advocacy).

> . . . the relationships among the day-care provider, the natural parent(s) and the children are seen as dynamic, multidimensional and developmental ones that have the potential of serving many of the functions formerly provided by the extended family. In this sense, they represent a social support for, rather than a replacement for, the responsibilities of the nuclear family in whatever form it is currently found (Peters & Benn, 1980).

## The Family and the Schools

In a modern society, school success is an important precursor to life success (Garbarino, 1981b). Thus, one of the major tasks in parent–child relations is to facilitate academic achievement. After many years of research and efforts at intervention, we know that two aspects of the parent–child relationship stand out on this score. First, we know that parent–child relationships vary in their manifestation of the "academic culture." To the extent that parents adopt a style of interaction that emphasizes the use of conceptual language in solving problems, manipulation of symbols, and a hypothesis-oriented style of personal inquiry (Garbarino, 1981b), they teach their children skills that are adaptive in academic settings.

A second aspect of the parent–child relationship relevant to school success is whether or not the parent communicates a positive regard for schooling. Two primary indicators are a positive orientation toward written materials (e.g., reading and having books in the home) and efforts to support and encourage the school's activities (e.g., by attending meetings or checking homework). These are keys to academic development (Bronfenbrenner, 1974).

Of course, the parents' willingness and ability to convey positive attitudes about schools and the educational process is predicted by their own academic histories. Joy and triumph or bitterness and defeat from early school experiences are bound to color the way that parents perceive later educational opportunities for themselves and their children. Those early feelings may also be magnified by the attitudes of teachers and the policies of the schools. Does the school system recognize and support the value of ethnic and racial diversity in its classrooms? Are the family and the community acknowledged as rich sources of information? Do teachers and parents recognize learning as a life-long process that is enhanced by cooperation and sharing? As evidence from our nation's experiments with Head Start reveals, a key factor in building a strong home-school mesosystem is the degree to which parents are welcomed into the educational arena and recognized as the primary educators of their children.

## Television

At least one television set resides in more than ninety-seven percent of all American homes. Parents and children alike are drawn to its appeal as a mesmerizing entertainer and "babysitter." In fact, today, most American children devote more time to watching television than to any other waking activity (Kaye, 1974). The overwhelming popularity of this electronic family member has been demonstrated by startling data from a study conducted in Southern Virginia. When asked to state a preference, 44 percent of a group of four- to six-year-olds said that they liked television better than their fathers! Certainly any socializing agent that is that popular must also serve as a powerful educator. Given the pervasiveness of television violence (Liebert, Neal, and Davidson 1973) and the media's presentation of stereotypic and often degrading portrayals of gender roles, ethnic characteristics, and age-related differences, television challenges many of the essential values of parents. To turn on the television set for a child is a parental agreement to share part of the child-rearing responsibilities with powerful outside forces—forces that usually have a commercial motive.

Whatever else it is, television is big business. Researchers estimate that the average American child will watch 22,000 hours of television advertising before reaching age eighteen. The advertising budgets aimed at children are enormous and raise many questions about how society views its obligations to protect children from exploitation (Action for Children's Television News, 1976). By and large, the institutions of our society have adopted an attitude of tolerance toward the economic exploitation of children and have simply exhorted parents to monitor and resist these commercial onslaughts. Perhaps our society's inability or unwillingness to prevent or even seriously limit child pornography is but an extreme form of this tolerance for the "use" of children to serve adult commercial interests.

It seems we generally expect parents to go it alone in meeting their responsibilities as parents while contending with the institutional life of the society. This brings us to another general issue in parent–child relations, one so fundamental it deserves a special category: the economic and ideological value of parenthood.

## The Political and Economic Value of Parenthood

Are we a child-centered society? Do we really want to be? When W. C. Fields said, "A man who hates children and dogs can't be all bad," he struck a responsive chord, one that resonates with some fundamental aspects of our culture. These feelings need close scrutiny, for as Edward Zigler (first Director of the federal government's Office for Child Development) has remarked: "The greatest single impediment to our improving the lives of America's children is the myth that we are a child-oriented society already doing all that needs to be done" (Zigler, 1976).

How can this be? Don't we give and give and then give some more so that our children can live well? Don't we work overtime so our kids will be well provided for? Don't we put our children first? We do all these things and yet Zigler's claim is well-founded. In fact, the very nature of our *personal* sacrifices on behalf of *our* children is ironic testimony to the validity of Zigler's analysis. It is because our society is not child-centered that we must struggle so much in our personal lives to give children their due. We are swimming against the institutional and cultural tide, and that is what makes it so hard to do well by our children.

What do we say when children respond to the existence of Father's Day and Mother's Day with the perfectly plausible question, "When is Kid's Day?" We reply, with more or less annoyance depending upon our mood, "Every day is Kid's Day!" Is it really? In one sense, every day (or nearly every day) *is* Kid's Day. Contemporary adults are preoccupied with their relationships with children—whether or not to have them, how many to have, how much time to spend with them, what will become of them. Indeed, one's relation to children has become a topic of intense speculation. It is a key social and personal issue. Elective parenthood has turned an assumption (one's relation to children) into a question. Adding to the issue raised by the biology of elective conception is the whole cultural paraphernalia of integrating the often discrepant roles of worker and parent.

The fact that the roles of worker and parent are so often at odds and that government does so little to help is one of the principal challenges faced by individuals and institutions in the final quarter of the twentieth century. Resolution of this issue will force us to put our money where our mouths are in relation to children and will test our cultural mettle. We see evidence of this all around us.

In a press release announcing his decision not to seek reelection, John Cavanaugh, a successful young Midwestern congressman remarked:

> While I consider participation in our political process a noble goal and the sacred duty of each citizen. . . . I am removing myself from consideration for further public service. . . . In order to serve the people I have asked my wife, Kate, to make more personal sacrifices than either the bonds of marriage or the boundless generosities of life entitle me. She has made them cheerfully, and we have greatly enjoyed our ten years together. But now I have other considerations as well. Four children under the age of seven years have a rightful claim to the attention and affection of their father. I have concluded that to continue to defer those claims "until after the next election" is an endless road traveled sadly by too many men too deeply captivated by public life. Simply stated, I want to pursue the opportunity of spending more time with my wife and children.

How many successful men and women would or do make this choice? How many could "afford" to do so? There's a genuine cultural conflict here. On one side stand children, hearth, and home; on the other stand adulthood, achievement, and personal autonomy. Men are increasingly troubled by the home side of the equation, while increasing numbers of women are now contending with the career side. Can one be a success and still follow the baby's progress on the potty? Is it possible to pursue an idea, a career, or any wordly goal and yet still take the numerous times off to stay home with a sick child, go to parent-teacher meetings, and give birthday parties? These issues are permanent features of human experience—at least in modern historical times. What makes them different for us now is the changed historical context. Now, both parts of the questions and issues apply to women and men alike.

The real test for our society, the measure of its child-centeredness, will come in how well we do in responding to the circumstances. A host of cultural currents indicates that the matter is far from resolved, and the issue remains in doubt. As they arrange for substitute child care, many modern couples find themselves saying, "We wish we had a wife." Many child-service workers ironically are pulled away from *their* children to care for the children of *other* people. If Aristotle once posed the question, "Who guards the guardians?" We now ask, "Who cares for the caregiver's children?" It's an issue we all face as professionals serving children and families.

Clearly, the decision to bear and raise a child is a complex one with lifelong implications. Once one begins a child, one remains a parent. It seems too many people don't seem to realize that choosing to become the parent of a cute baby also implies becoming the parent of a teenager in the next decade. In this chapter, we have tried to show how the human ecology can help or impede parents gaining positive psychological momentum with their children. In the next chapter, we will examine how the community and the neighborhood work on that psychological momentum, how they support and nurture families, and why they sometimes do not.

---

# RESEARCH CAPSULE

While divorce is a legal arrangement between the individuals in a marital dyad, E. Mavis Hetherington and her colleagues (Hetherington, Cox, & Cox, 1978) also define divorce as "a critical life event that affects the entire family system and the functioning and interactions of members within that system (1978, p. 149)."

To study the impact of divorce on family functioning and child development, the researchers completed a longitudinal study of 48 middle-class families during the two-year period following divorce. Each of the families had at least one nursery school-age child placed in the custody of the mother. The divorced families were matched with intact families having a preschooler of the same sex, age, and birth order as the target child from the divorced family. Measures included personality scales, interviews, and diary records from the parents, observations of child behavior and parent–child interaction at home and in the nursery school, and peer and teacher ratings along with tests of sex-role typing, cognitive performance, and social development for each target child.

Individual adjustment, exchanges between the former spouses, and the nature of parent–child interactions changed drastically over the two-year period. The two months following the divorce were a time of particularly intense emotions, coupled with often unsuccessful attempts to redefine family relationships. Ex-

changes between the former spouses were characterized by sustained attachment, ambivalence, and resentment. Sixty-six percent of all interactions between divorced couples involved conflict, including disagreements over finances, intimate relations with others, and child-rearing. Showing an immediate reaction to separation from their children, divorced fathers maintained high levels of contact with their children. Indeed, one-fourth of the divorced fathers had more face-to-face contact with their children during this initial adjustment period than before the divorce. While divorced fathers were extremely permissive and indulgent with their children, the child-rearing strategies of divorced women often included futile attempts to control children with greater restrictiveness and commands.

A peak period of family disorganization and conflict was reached one year following divorce. During that time, the formerly married were distinguished from those in intact relationships by higher levels of anxiety, depression, anger, and rejection. Feelings of competence plummeted; the divorced subjects felt that they had failed as parents and spouses and expressed doubts about their abilities to be successful in any future marriages. The stress was reflected in household disorganization, with divorced families reporting problems coping with routine household management and in maintaining family routines. This period was marked by maximum levels of negative behavior for children in divorced families and by troubled parent–child relations, particularly for mothers and sons.

Two years after divorce, families appeared to be engaged in a period of reduced conflict and reorganization. Divorced parents and their children seemed to develop new and better organized life patterns. Contact with fathers in divorced families had dropped significantly, with only nineteen of the fathers having contact with their children once a week or more. While some parent–child interactions remained troubled, especially between divorced parents and sons, one-fourth of the fathers and one-half of the mothers reported that the relationship with their children had actually improved over those prior to divorce.

Overall, a key to successful family adaptation to divorce was support from friends and relatives and from those within the nuclear family unit. In particular, family disruption was less extreme and restabilization was achieved earlier in those families where former spouses could establish a positive, mutually supportive relationship including continued father involvement and agreement about child discipline. The researchers conclude that while divorce is often accompanied by family distress and disrupted behavior, it can also be a positive solution to destructive family functioning. They call for additional research and applied programs oriented toward the identification and promotion of constructive parenting and family coping following divorce.

This study underscores the dramatic effects of individual actions on the entire family system. The use of a multimethod approach provides a rich body of data on the effects of divorce on several areas of family functioning. The longitudinal design allows for the study of the family as a complex group of developing individuals rather than as a static entity. By studying families over a two-year period, this research documented severe reactions to the stresses of divorce as well as the process of adaptation and reorganization that could result.

## PRACTICE CAPSULE

Teenage pregnancy is an event with far-reaching consequences. The mounting "epidemic" of adolescent pregnancies presents considerable burdens on the capacities of both these young women and their families. Furthermore, it has been estimated that the 600,000 births to American teenagers each year may cost federal, state, and local governments as much as $8.3 billion dollars per year in welfare and medical services alone.

In 1978, George Washington University's Family Impact Seminar devoted a year's time and the efforts of 50 participants from a variety of disciplines to an analysis of policies directed toward pregnant teens and their families. The seminar, which was built on the findings of nine commissioned reports and the testimony from a two-day conference, was scheduled to coincide with the development and passage of PL 95-626, originally introduced as the Adolescent Health, Services, Pregnancy Prevention and Care Act of 1978.

Preliminary work by the seminar focused on the basic requirements of any analysis—the operationalization of terms, the identification of specific family impact questions, and the statement of specific value assumptions underlying the analysis. Next, the seminar members used that basic framework, together with empirical findings and discussion of the commissioned papers, to derive the principles that would guide their assessment of policies affecting pregnant teenagers. The seven guiding principles are listed below:

1. Policy needs to recognize that the causes and consequences of adolescent pregnancy are multiple and complex.
2. Policy should not regard teenage pregnancy as an issue solely of female concern, but should strive to encourage male responsibility and involvement when appropriate.
3. Policy should seek to help *families* help their teenagers avoid too early pregnancy and childbearing.

4. Policy should seek to help *families* help their teenagers cope with pregnancy, early childbearing, and its consequences.

5. Policy should identify and support the different needs of teenagers from different family backgrounds and contexts.

6. Policy needs to more openly recognize the transitional status of adolescents. Teenagers, especially school-age teenagers, are not yet fully adult, in spite of their sexual maturity, nor are they capable of handling major adult responsibilities.

7. Policy needs to be particularly aware of those adolescents who are seriously alienated from their families or who have no families and develop programs to meet their special and more comprehensive needs.

These principles were used to develop specific suggestions regarding the translation of general guidelines into specific practices for pregnant teenagers and their families. Finally, this comprehensive package of tools was used to analyze the federal legislation directed at pregnant adolescents and to make recommendations regarding its implementation. Specifically, the group called for strong family emphasis in service delivery, coordination between cooperating agencies and the public and private sectors, the collection of data related to the characteristics and needs of teenagers and their families and the evaluation of any intervention efforts. In sum, the Family Impact Seminar concluded that most adults are avoiding their responsibilities to adolescents. They advocated:

a vigorous nationwide effort . . . which would raise community awareness about the extent and complexity of the problems of teenage pregnancy, and mobilize all segments of society to find ways to help teenagers and their families avoid the occurrence and consequences of teenage pregnancies (Ooms, 1979, p. 43).

This example of a specific social service practice—the analysis of a policy and the development of recommendations for implementation—demonstrates the need for close coordination of service providers, policymakers, and researchers in meeting the needs of children and their families. In doing so, it underscores a basic tenet of the ecological approach: "If you want to understand something, try to change it" (Bronfenbrenner, 1974).

# FOR FURTHER READING

Lerner, R. M., & Spanier, G. B. (Eds.), *Child influences on marital and family interaction.* New York: Academic Press, 1978, 360 pp.

   The editors have assembled 12 high quality chapters that help demonstrate the value of a dynamic interactionist, or dialectical, approach to studying children and families. Particular attention is focused on the contribution of specific characteristics of the child (e.g., developmental level or handicapping condition) to both parent–child and spousal relationships. The book's life-span perspective, following the parent–offspring relationship from the child's infancy into adulthood, makes this an important resource for those interested in the developmental issues confronting individuals and families.

Lewis, M., & Rosenblum, L. A. (Eds.) *The child and its family.* New York: Plenum Press, 1979, 304 pp.

   The third volume in a series on the Genesis of Behavior, this collection of articles focuses on children's development within the context of their social networks. Social relationships with parents, siblings, peers, and even toys are examined. Chapters on family reciprocity, paternal influences during infancy, and maternal employment are particularly relevant supplements to this text.

Macfarlane, A. *The psychology of childbirth.* Cambridge, MA: Harvard University Press, 1977, 143 pp.

   This brief, easy-to-read book follows the activities of mother and child from the prenatal period to early infancy. Materials including historical and cross-cultural accounts of delivery techniques, dialogues recorded during deliveries, and nontechnical discussion of current research are skillfully combined.

Osofsky, J. D. (Ed.) *Handbook of infant development.* New York: John Wiley & Sons, 1979, 954 pp.

An expansive collection of 28 chapters, this volume includes valuable information about prenatal influences, early assessment, the parent–infant relationship, and patterns of infant development. A section on clinical issues is necessary reading for those who provide intervention services to infants and their families.

Stevens, J. H., & Matthews, M. (Eds.) *Mother/child, father/child relationships,* Washington, D.C.: National Association for the Education of Young Children, 1978, 258 pp.

The roles of both mothers and fathers in the development of infants and young children are highlighted in this important collection of articles. Reviews of current literature on early parent–child relationships are complemented by research reports on parent-infant bonding, divorce, and alternative family styles. A concluding chapter focuses on the important issues of research and practice.

---

# QUESTIONS FOR THOUGHT

1. Using materials from Chapters 4, 5, and 6, list several ways that the father, siblings, and other family members might be involved during pregnancy, labor and delivery, and the early postpartal period.

2. Consider the childbirth alternatives discussed in the chapter. Formulate and justify your own personal preferences.

3. Discuss the relative contributions of family members, the peer group, television, and the schools to individual development from infancy through adolescence. Use examples from your own childhood.

4. Parenthood is one of the most important roles we can assume in life. Often, however, individuals enter the role without the preparation necessary to meet its demands and responsibilities. What are the greatest challenges facing American parents? Discuss ways that child rearing practices and school curricula can be modified to help prepare children for later parenting roles. Suggest a number of different ways that both formal and informal support systems can provide promotive services to parents.

5. What changes in parent's lives are presented by their child's passage from infancy to childhood and on to adolescence and young adulthood? How must lifestyles be altered to meet the changing needs of both the parents and the child?

6. Imagine that you have been asked to talk to a group of teachers, caseworkers, or judges about helping families adapt to divorce. What recommendations will you make regarding child rearing by divorced parents and the maintenance of strong parent–child relationships?

7. This chapter mentions that although Americans celebrate Mother's Day and Father's Day, there is no official Children's Day. Japan, however, does have such a holiday. Consider the significance of a day set aside to observe the value of children.

# Chapter 7

In building a neighbourhood that meets human needs, we start with the needs of infants. These give us the groundwork on which we can build for contact with other human beings, with the physical environment, with the living world, and with the experiences through which the individual's full humanity can be realized. For every culture, the criteria must be modified. We cannot set our sights too low, but we can aim at any height, for we have as yet scarcely begun to explore human potentialities. How these are developed will depend on the learning experiences we can provide for children through the human habitat in which they live.

Margaret Mead, "Neighbourhoods and Human Needs," 1966, pp. 106–107.

We have moved from an introduction to the ecology of human development through the examination of issues that bear directly on the parent–child relationship and the family as a whole. All throughout history, human beings have collected together and shared their energies in order to survive. Families have fought their environment, shaped it, and loved it. It is to the geographic side of the environmental context of families that we now turn. We begin with an exploration of the modern-day community and will examine the neighborhood as a major influence in the lives of families. Our ecological perspective leads us to look at the various settings in which families interact and grow. We then focus on various social problems as expressions of the physical and social environment. Our goal is to gain a better understanding of the dynamics between families and their contexts, an understanding that will lead to implications for improving the welfare of families.

# The Territory of Childhood

## A Child's Turf

The territory of childhood—the neighborhood and community—plays an important role in molding the child's experiences and in determining how well the child adapts to many individuals and situations. The child's first turf is the neighborhood. It is the child's to explore, become a part of, and use. The neighborhood in which a child lives is an early and major arena for exploration and social interaction, and serves as a setting for the physical and emotional development of the child. It plays an important part in determining with whom a child will come in contact and how safe the child will be in those contacts. At first the child's turf hardly extends beyond the front door, but it expands gradually as the child roams farther from home. Later, in adolescence, it may range over the entire community, particularly if the child has access to mass transit or an automobile. But the characteristics of that larger community territory and the decisions of the community power structure significantly affect the resources and experiences available to the child of any age.

The territory of childhood also influences adults, particularly as they function in their roles as parents. Neighborhood safety, recreational facilities, health and social services, schools, economic conditions, and opportunities to develop supportive relationships are all factors that affect the lives of families. In a reciprocal manner, the community responds to—and is shaped by—the needs and demands of individuals and families within it. Their choices about staying or moving, participating or not participating, and seeking change or accepting existing conditions affect many aspects of the community as it is and can become.

In this chapter we explore the geography of family life and child development, beginning with the community as the joint expression of the social and physical environment. Of particular interest to us is the nature of social support for families. As noted in Chapter 3, social support systems are networks of individuals that nurture and care for people and serve as resources in times of physical and emotional need. We consider both formal support systems (organizations structured for the purpose of giving care, such as social service agencies, day-care centers, and community mental health centers), and informal support systems (nonprofessional care giving, such as neighbors, family, and friends). As we shall see, communities vary in the amount of formal and informal social support that they provide, thereby affecting the extent to which families can rely on others for help.

## The Community and Human Ecology

The term "community" has taken on a fuzzy warm glow in loose public and professional usage, as in the amorphous way people use "sense of community" to convey a feeling of fellowship. The term does have a core meaning for many students of human development, however. Although one can speak of a community that is not linked to a geographical setting, such as "the academic community" (Toennies, 1957), our concern with families directs our attention to territory-based "place" communities (Anderson & Carter, 1978).

Hillery's (1955) classic distillation of the common elements of community endures: "Community consists of persons in social interaction within a geographic area and having one or more additional common ties" (p. 111). More recently, R. Warren (1973) characterized a community as a collection of social systems that performs the locality-relevant functions of social control, social participation, socialization, mutual support, and economic production, distribution, and consumption. A community, thus, has both social and economic components. The characteristics of a specific community are shaped in part by its own history and geography, in part by decisions of the local power structure and community residents, and in part by trends and influences that originate outside the community.

The characteristics of a community, in turn, exert powerful influences on the quality of life for the families that live within it. These influences are of many types, and our ecological perspective reminds us to consider both direct and indirect effects at all levels of a family's environment. This perspective directs our attention to how the community affects the internal dynamics of family microsystems. For example, it leads us to be concerned with how disruptions of the community's primary economy (e.g., the closing of major industrial plants) affect rates of domestic violence (cf., Steinberg, Catalano & Dooley, 1981); Straus, Gelles & Steinmetz, 1980). It reminds us, too, to consider the impact of communities on other microsystems such as schools and neighborhoods. Furthermore, an ecological perspective leads us to explore ways in which the community affects relationships *between* families and other contexts. These intersystem relationships—mesosystems—play an important part in defining the day-to-day lives of families, as in the way school and home relate in the education of children. An ecological approach also causes us to inquire about the way families are treated by the institutions of the community, a matter of exosystems. Are employers sympathetic to the needs of parents for child care (Garbarino, 1980c)? Does local government seek to serve family interests in zoning and tax decisions (Garbarino & Plantz, 1980)? In addition, we can also view the community as an important force in carrying out the ideologies and beliefs of the larger macrosystem. For example, tacit societal acceptance of domestic violence filters down through communities to families. If a community ethic against violence existed, abuse in families would probably decrease (Garbarino, 1977a). All of these issues deepen our appreciation of the ways in which various characteristics of the community affect the lives of its members.

## Community-Level Effects on Children and Families

One of the issues facing researchers interested in community effects on families is the issue of just what *is* a "community" effect. Many studies simply aggregate or group together the data on individuals in the community and call that aggregate a "community effect." However, if we know that inadequate income is associated with child maltreatment at an individual level, then calling the relationship between average income in a community and overall community rate of child maltreatment a "community effect" is using the term in its simplest sense. We can observe a more theoretically interesting and significant community effect in situations in which community factors override individual characteristics in producing an effect on families. While there are many community effects of this type, we are particularly interested in four: the economy of the community; its character as an urban, suburban, or rural setting; the social density of the family's environment; and the stability of that environment.

## Community Economy

Economic factors play a central role in shaping the day-to-day life of families. Although the overall economy of the nation influences every community in the United States, there are wide variations *among* communities in the composition and vitality of their primary economies. As one of our colleagues (Rockwell, 1978) is fond of reminding us, "No one lives in America. People live in Boise, in Newark, in Chadron, in Atlanta, in Los Angeles or in Waco." While this somewhat overstates the point, it is basically correct. The effects of the national economy are certainly mediated by community differences. Local economic systems vary depending upon the jobs, goods, and services provided by businesses and industries in that community. The substantial intercommunity variation in unemployment rates indicates the magnitude of economic differences in communities. We note that in late 1979, the unemployment rate varied from a high of more than ten percent (13.0 percent in Union City, New Jersey, and 10.3 percent in Detroit, Michigan) to a low of less than four percent (2.8 percent in Cheyenne City, Wyoming, and 3.1 percent in Raleigh, North Carolina) according to the U.S. Bureau of Labor Statistics (1980).

The 1980 census revealed community effects in population change. For example, Florida experienced a 40 percent increase in population, while Rhode Island's population actually declined. Although most communities within these states show trends that match overall state data, some communities show reversals (U.S. Bureau of the Census, 1981). In Florida, for example, some cities grew less than 10 percent in population (e.g., Jacksonville's 7.3 percent) while others grew more than 50 percent (e.g., Coral Gables' extraordinary 90+ percent). The shifts in political power that follow these economic and demographic changes have important effects on families. As reported in *The New York Times* on January 4, 1981, the President's Commission for a National Agenda for the Eighties tacitly recognized this "community effect" when it urged the federal government to cease its efforts to maintain artificially the primary economies of "Snow Belt" cities of the Northeast and Midwest and instead to facilitate the natural expansion of "Sun Belt" cities in the Southeast, Southwest, and West. Such a policy is derived from the premise that the population and vitality of a community depend upon the nature of its primary economy, and federal efforts to override this dynamic are ineffective at best.

Shifts in the work force are an important community-level economic event with family-level effects. For example, Elder (1974) reported that severe income loss during the Great Depression of the 1930s was largely a community-level effect, independent of the characteristics of individual workers. That is, a downturn in a community's primary economy produced unemployment randomly or nearly so among workers in the community, as opposed to being systematically based on worker performance. Some communities, and thus some occupations and individual workers, were spared. In other efforts to identify community characteristics that affect families regardless of their individual attributes, Steinberg, Catalano, and Dooley (1981) demonstrated a negative relationship between the number of jobs in a community and its rate of child maltreatment.

Community-level effects also could be demonstrated by findings that the relationship between income and child maltreatment is different for different communities, or that the degree of economic homogeneity versus heterogeneity affects the rate of maltreatment uniformly among communities. Unfortunately, there is little research that addresses this sort of community effect. Much community research has methodological limitations such that one mistakenly infers individual-level effects from aggregate data analysis. Where the units of analysis are relatively small (e.g., census tracts) and the effects large, however, we can draw some conclusions about what individuals are doing, based on what the community is doing (Bogue & Bogue, 1976).

## Urban, Suburban, and Rural Settings

The economy of a community clearly is an important determinant of the quality of life for its families. Another major community-level effect derives from a community's status as an urban, suburban, or rural setting. The traditional urban-rural dichotomy for classifying communities has become increasingly obsolete in the period following World War II (VanEs & Brown, 1974; Photiadis, 1970). The rise of the automotive society gave birth to new residential forms that have altered the foundations of both urban and rural life. The automobile and the cheap-energy economy it represented made possible new and attractive suburban, rural, and urban patterns that by their very existence undermined the older forms (cf., Kowinski, 1980; Wynne, 1977). With the new mobility, members of families have become increasingly separated from each other, an occurrence that has probably increased their reliance on community- and neighborhood-based support systems (Bronfenbrenner, 1975).

The automotive era appears to have had its clearest and most profound effects on the evolving patterns of suburban life. Wynne (1977) distinguished between "old" and "new" suburbs, concepts that seem to apply most readily to older cities, particularly in the Northeast and Midwest. "Old" suburbs were formerly small towns on the periphery of a city, having railroad stations for commuting as focal points. "New" suburbs are bedroom communities without a primary economy that are dependent upon automobile-based commuting. In 1956 about 80 percent of America's suburbs were of the old type, whereas the figure for

1980 was about 45 percent (Wynne, 1977). Wynne speculated that new suburbs may be less supportive of families because they overemphasize peer group relations, and because they lack sufficient formal and informal activities (e.g., Chamber of Commerce, service clubs, etc.) to offer children a socially rich and varied existence. Thus, they place greater demands on parents to act as socializing agents.

The automotive era's main effects on cities have been movement of the population away from the core of old cities to new cities and suburbs, and increased noise and accident hazards (Michelson & Roberts, 1979). Both of these may have adverse effects on young children (Aiello, in press). Furthermore, erosion of the urban tax base and increasing concentration of high-risk populations have jeopardized schools, governments, businesses, and neighborhoods—in short, the essential infrastructure of community (Jacobs, 1961). The effect of this sort of breakdown on families is of undetermined magnitude, although we presume that its direction is negative. We assume that these problems affect some families more than others and are of greatest concern for families with young children otherwise at social risk. Of course, increased mobility has allowed many families to leave socially stressed environments and move to areas that are more conducive to a healthy family life. They may, for example, leave poor urban areas and relocate to small communities or suburbs with better schools for their children, leaving those with the least resources to fend for themselves in the center city areas.

Although industrialization has led to a shift in families from rural areas to suburban and urban environments, some regions of the United States can still be considered "rural America." Southern Appalachia, for example, has maintained a relatively isolated and semi-autonomous existence. Photiadis (1970) reported, however, that values from the larger society have infiltrated the traditional social system, thereby creating changes in the social equilibrium. The desire for economic achievement that produced migration to cities has increased stress on the family and has increased the need for reorganization of the social system. Schwarzweller (1970) emphasized that the family has withstood the social change. In support of this observation, Heller and Quesada (1977) found that families in rural southeastern United States are characterized by strong ties and close geographic location to members of the extended family, little support for geographic mobility, and more participation in kinship rather than in community activities. Rural society in the western United States, on the other hand, is composed of strong nuclear families, dependence on the community for activities and support, and more geographic mobility. Heller and Quesada (1977) concluded that the two distinct forms of rural families evolved as a result of different ecological conditions. That is, greater numbers of kin in eastern settlements and fewer numbers in the west because of their recent migration.

## Social Density

One of the most intriguing community effects seems to be on the "social density" of the family environment (Garbarino, in press). By social density we mean the degree to which an environment contains a diversity of roles for children to learn from and for parents to draw upon. The density of roles— that is, their relative homogeneity versus heterogeneity in the setting—is an important issue. A heterogeneous setting is one in which multiple roles exist, while in a homogeneous setting few roles predominate. In this and many other respects, homogeneity tends to be developmentally stultifying, while pluralism is invigorating (Garbarino & Bronfenbrenner, 1976b).

Within the family microsystem, for example, the same two adults represent a more homogeneous setting if both are in the same role (e.g., both in an instrumental "provider" role) than if they are in different roles (e.g., one in an economic provider role and the other in a homemaker role). In this sense, the latter is a denser setting. Similarly, multigeneration households or neighborhoods offer greater social density than those in which children encounter only one generation of adults. People, of course, ideally play multiple roles (e.g., homemaker, provider, and organization officer). The presence in a child's environment of adults who fill several roles contributes to the social richness of the child's experiences.

The spectrum of roles in the immediate social environment of the child contributes to development. Most students of human development seem to be in agreement that children do best when they are set within a community environment that offers stable opportunities to observe and practice basic human roles (Aldrich, 1979). A dense setting with respect to roles may be developmentally enhancing, as when the neighborhood contains shopkeepers, retired persons, and a variety of kinship and friendship relations. As we shall see, the fragments of data available to us suggest that it is typically small towns or neighborhoods nested within communities that are the best vehicles for providing these experiences. Aldrich (1979) speculated that "a complete community of around 5,000 people allows a child to get a rather good idea of what community relations are all about" (p. 87).

A socially dense environment also may provide social resources that parents can draw upon. One necessary resource is the availability of adults who are "free from drain." Adults who are "free from drain" are those whose energies are not totally consumed by day-to-day responsibilities, and who, therefore, can devote time and energy to serving in the informal helping networks that support families in need (Collins & Pancoast, 1976; Gottlieb, 1980; Pancoast, 1980; Tietjen, 1980). Thus, the social density of the community has an effect on the amount of support that families receive.

Investigators have reported that children in a small town have more knowledge of people and roles than do urban children living in an area without a well-developed neighborhood, while those in a well-functioning urban neighborhood stand somewhere between the town and city in this respect (Gump & Adelberg, 1978). The small town tends to be underpeopled in that it has a low ratio of people to roles needing to be filled. As a community, it has the full range of community activities to maintain and, thus, is very "dense" or heterogeneous with respect to roles and mesosystems. The less well-developed urban neighborhood is not a complete community; it must rely on the larger city for many functions, including the provision of jobs. We speculate that because adults are drawn away from such a neighborhood, children see less of life's basic social functions in it. It is less socially dense. The well-developed urban neighborhood, while not a complete community, may approximate the small town in its social density. The socially undeveloped urban neighborhood may have so little going on that it impoverishes the social experience and knowledge of its children. Even further, what *is* going on may not enrich their lives.

## Environmental Stability

Just as the community context of the family's immediate setting is important in determining the richness of the child's and parent's social experience, so is the stability of that setting and context. We know from informal observation that neighborhoods are hard to transplant because relocation disrupts the "natural" social systems of the area (Jacobs, 1961). These informal networks are important community characteristics that can compensate for, and override the effects of, individual situations.

Decisions of the community power structure often affect the vitality of these personal support systems. When natural disaster strikes a community (e.g., a flood or tornado), the biggest problem is how to recreate not the physical, but the *social* landscape (Nuttal, 1980; cf., Erikson, 1976). When the "disaster" results from social policy, such as industrial, highway, or dam development that requires relocating residents, we face the same issues. Rebuilding social networks often is more difficult than physical reconstruction. Warren (1968), for instance, reported that when a small town was relocated because of a dam project, only one quarter of the town's accustomed settings for social interaction survived the move. In 1981, the case of Hamtramck, a Polish-settled neighborhood in Detroit, received national attention as the municipal administration exercised eminent domain to tear down the 1500 private homes, schools, businesses, and churches in the neighborhood and sell the land to the General Motors Corporation to build a massive industrial plant. Whatever its economically salubrious effects on the rest of the community, the decision meant social annihilation for the neighborhood, relocation of 3400 people (one-half of whom were elderly), and confrontations between neighborhood members and the corporation (Kelly, 1981). Its longer-term effects on families are as yet undetermined.

Community effects resulting from a lack of stability can also occur in less drastic situations. The closing of schools, decisions to bus children to different neighborhoods, and shutdown of businesses and industries can affect the social interactions within and among individuals in the community. As Devereux (1977) demonstrated in his critique of ecological psychology, community changes are probably the principal forces affecting the quantity and quality of settings in which social behavior occurs. While we have some research documenting such community changes, we have virtually nothing linking these changes to effects on families.

## Family–Community Interface

There are several aspects of the family–community relationship that affect children and parents in the community. Local government practices, the parent's place of work, the relationship between home and school, and community response to the need for day-care services determine the nature of the environment's support for families. While it is the combined interactions within and among these systems that comprise the family–community interface, we will present each aspect separately in order to examine some important issues.

### Family–Local Government

Local government exerts an important influence on families. Through their zoning and planning agencies, local governments do much to shape the community context of families. They are involved, for instance, in balancing the desires and needs of adult-only and adult-plus-children households. Local government policies may permit or even encourage landlords to exclude children from rental housing. There are areas in the United States where adults may reside only if they have no children at home. By limiting their options, this discrimination puts psychological, and perhaps even financial, stress on families. It also increases age segregation and reduces the adult-to-child ratio in residential areas.

Local governments also play central roles in decisions that disrupt existing neighborhoods. A neighborhood is vulnerable to external assault in a variety of ways. Urban renewal and highway projects, like natural disasters, can seriously disrupt the ability of a community's neighborhoods to serve as family support systems. We find that one of the important current aspects of the government-family interface is the extent to which local governments are protective and restorative in their efforts to control the residential environments of families

(Michelson & Roberts, 1979). The protective function of a local government was exemplified by the successful fight against developers who wished to build a large jetport in a small community in western New York. Citizens in the community were upset and concerned that the noise and pollution would disrupt their lives. The battle between local citizens and outside officials continued for a few years until the local government, aided by community support, succeeded in preventing construction of the jetport. If the local government had placed a higher priority on the financial reasons for supporting the jetport than on the comfort of local families, the result might have been much different.

We see that the restorative function of local government varies in policies that promote renovating or restoring old buildings, homes, or areas. The government that razes impossibly deteriorated buildings, constructs new housing, and restores run-down homes is improving the quality of the community. Some communities are attempting to improve residential life through a policy that allows families to rent or purchase, at very low prices, old homes that need renovation. Families move into these homes with an agreement that their responsibility is to restore the homes. Through such policies, government and families work cooperatively to enhance neighborhoods. On the other hand, a government that allows the continual decay of buildings within a community is potentially harming the community. Children may be injured by playing in dangerous areas, businesses may not be attracted to the area, and the community may become a breeding ground for crime. These effects will diminish the financial and aesthetic value of the community. Clearly, the local government has a large effect on families in a variety of ways.

## Family–Work

The family–work interface is a critical feature in any review of family life and its effects on child development (Bronfenbrenner & Crouter, 1981). Here, as elsewhere, community factors mediate the relationship. Because work and work-related factors are near or at the top of the list of day-to-day stresses for parents, anything a community does to provide work-related support and reduce work-related stress is important. House (1981) emphasized the need to build work-related supports into organizations and made several recommendations, such as sensitizing supervisors to employee problems. As we noted at the outset of our discussion, community differences in primary economy account for significant variations in unemployment—in many ways the ultimate work-related stress. Naturally, the nature of the community's primary economy also affects the types of available jobs—blue versus white versus pink collar (i.e., jobs such as waitressing that are traditionally taken by women). The wage levels associated with these variations produce different socioeconomic and ethnic mixes. The impact of this variation on families is undertermined, but we can assume that the child exposed to very homogeneous populations of working individuals will have different experiences from the child whose parents have contact with a number of people from different backgrounds.

The very centrality of the work–family relationship means that many community policies and decisions relevant to working conditions, such as those affecting mass transit and zoning, have direct effects on the family. We mentioned previously the effects of opening or closing industries and businesses. In communities that already have mass transportation systems, the effects of strikes by transit workers are great on both the community and individuals within the community.

## Home–School

The home–school interface is perhaps the most widely recognized aspect of the family–community relationship. However, for all the professional, political, and public attention it receives, it is not adequately understood. We know that the congruence between home and school can have a large and significant effect upon child development—particularly upon academic success. Where this mesosystem is strong, the child benefits. A strong home–school mesosystem is a set of multiple and mutually respectful relationships between families and school officials. Naturally, the nature and strength of the home–school relationship are variable from community to community.

Community factors impinge upon the home–school mesosystem in several ways. First, the community partially defines the degree to which schools are neighborhood-based. Many studies document the importance of a school's catchment area (i.e., the area served by a school) in shaping its success as an academic socializer (Jencks, 1972). However, the strength of this relationship appears to be greater in some settings than in others (Coleman, 1966): the more socioeconomically deprived the community, the greater the difference that the school's efforts produce (Garbarino, 1981b). The size of the community's schools can also have important effects on families. As a result of decreases in the number of dropouts, urban and suburban concentrations of students, and academic and economic policies that favor consolidation of smaller schools into larger ones, most secondary schools (grades 9–12) have more than 500 students. This imposes psychological and social costs on the community and its young people. Large schools have their worst and strongest effects on academically and socially marginal students. These youth tend to become alienated, unappreciated, and unsuccessful (Garbarino, 1980d).

Community factors can also affect the congruence of school and home. Policies concerning bilingual education, for example, may affect the degree of respect for the home's culture, a factor more relevant in communities such as Miami or Los Angeles that have large concentrations of non-English-speaking families.

The federal government's 1981 decision to discontinue national efforts to promote bilingualism and leave the matter to local discretion will presumably increase the differences among communities in this and other cultural matters, such as the use of physical force as punishment and the provision of sex education in schools.

The community affects the home—school relationship by encouraging or discouraging academic success in children of low-income families. The Children's Defense Fund (1974) reported that most of the school-age children out of school on a regular basis were in effect excluded from school—often because of economically related requirements such as paying for books or transportation. They reported substantial variation among communities on this score. On the other hand, community efforts to promote school success (e.g., by special enrichment programs) for low-income children can significantly modify the mesosystem mismatch that often occurs between low-income families and middle-class oriented schools (Garbarino, 1981b). Head Start, a national program for young children of low-income families, was designed to overcome the academic impoverishment that these children experienced. The object was to give them the skills and experiences they needed in order to succeed in America's schools, or in other words, to improve the school—home mesosystem.

The issue of desegregation also shows how families affect and are affected by the school, community, and local government. The decision about whether or not to bus students to schools that are outside of their neighborhood is often made after considerable debate. Many residents do not want their children bused, while community leaders often desire integration of racial groups. It is obvious that community decisions affect interactions within the home—school mesosystem that, in turn, have direct effects upon children and their parents.

## Day Care

One indicator of the quality and quantity of community support for families is the provision of day care. Indeed, international studies of community development often use provision of child care as a social indicator. We know that there is a substantial need for day care, given the dramatic increase in the number of mothers working outside the home who have young children. We also know that the predominant providers of day care are the informal (friends, relatives, and neighbors) rather than the formal (nursery schools and day-care centers) support systems of the community. The National Childcare Consumer Study (Unco, 1975) indicated that for children under six, in-home baby-sitter care is most common (26 percent), followed by care in someone else's home (16 percent), followed by nursery school (8 percent), with care in day-care centers trailing far behind (3 percent). With these figures in mind, it should come as no surprise that the richness of the informal support systems surrounding home-based day care is one of the most important dimensions of the community—family interface (Collins & Watson, 1976; Unger & Powell, 1980). Social networks and neighborhood interaction serve a vital function in making this link work well.

Although there is less evidence to document its importance, the formal support system represented by the "day-care council" may also be an important aspect of this interface, since this agency typically provides important services to home-based day-care providers, as well as referrals for parents. All communities do not have a day-care council, and many local citizens have to rely more on informal support systems or the more technical day-care centers and nursery schools.

One of the newest aspects of the community—family interface is the provision of after-school care for children in the six- to 13-year-old age range (Levine, 1976). A report by the U.S. Bureau of the Census (1976) indicated that in 1974 roughly 13 percent of the children aged seven to 13 whose mothers were employed cared for themselves after school. This means that at least two million school-age children were possible candidates for after-school care, an estimate that probably holds true today given the recently reported increase in the number of mothers who are employed (U.S. Department of Commerce, 1979). Unsupervised children were twice as likely to come from single- rather than two-parent families (U.S. Bureau of the Census, 1976). If a community is poor and has many single parents, there will be a widespread need for informal and formal child-care systems that are affordable and easily accessible. Communities with a concentration of older or nonparental young adults may not view the establishment of day-care centers and nursery schools as a priority. Parents of school-age children in such communities have to depend on more informal systems of support. Certainly there are community differences in both the likelihood that a school-age child needs care and that formal or informal services exist to provide that care.

## The Neighborhood and Support Systems

In order to examine the relationship between social support systems and families, it is helpful to focus on the neighborhood. As we said in Chapters 2 and 3, the neighborhood is the place in which parents interact with their children and also interact with others, independently of the children. The children are participants in the neighborhood, too, and are often given the freedom to socialize without the presence of the parents. The quality of the support, encouragement, and feedback given by the neighborhood to the family has an effect upon the child's development. What are neighborhood characteristics that influence families?

Keller (1968) identified functions of a neighborhood as those fulfilled by members within it. A neighbor is characterized as "the helper in times of need, who is expected to step in when other resources fail" (p. 29). The occasions of sickness, death, and emergencies, as well as weddings and other festivities, call neighbors together. Therefore, neighboring is a socially defined relationship that involves the duties of exchanging resources, information, and help. Neighbors form an informal support system that a family can look to in times of need. Another function of the neighborhood is to maintain social control and standards. Neighbors provide feedback to one another about moral conduct, the appearance of the home, and child care.

A good neighborhood in Kromkowski's (1976) terms enhances development by providing the kind of multiple connections and multiple situations that permit children to make the best use of their intellectual and social equipment. It also gives them a sense of familiarity and belonging, a territorial base. What Bronfenbrenner calls "cross-contextual dyads" (relationships that exist in more than one situation) flourish in a healthy, well-developed neighborhood. Likewise, a strong neighborhood offers a sense of security and peace of mind for the parent, feelings that translate into a more relaxed and positive stance toward the task of child rearing and toward the child in particular.

Neighborhoods differ in how strong and healthy they are. We can attribute these variations in part to conventional economic influences. Within equivalent economic levels, however, neighborhoods can vary quite substantially. Developed and underdeveloped neighborhoods are found among both the rich and the poor (Warren & Warren, 1977). However, the importance of the neighborhood as a factor in family life and in child development is probably greater among the poor (Smith, 1976). While the rich can use their material resources to purchase other avenues of support, encouragement, and guidance, the less affluent are more likely to be dependent upon whatever informal support systems are available to them in the neighborhood. A high-risk neighborhood is one that weakens rather than strengthens families by virtue of the character of the neighborhood. This leads us to consider community ecology and family social pathology.

## Community Ecology and Family Social Pathology

Families are subject to a variety of social pathologies. Social pathologies are problems or dysfunctions that are related to the quality of the social environment. Research has shown that there is a relationship between social pathology, stress, and support (Cooper & Gath, 1977). "Where the environment is supportive, creative adaptation and growth occur. Where the environment is nonprotective or depriving, stress is created, and adaptive functioning may be impeded" (Germain, 1978, p. 522).

Both the availability of effective supports for families and the level of environmental stress they face derive in part from community factors—characteristics of the community as well as decisions made within it. Individual neighborhoods add their own mix of pressures and protection. We should expect, then, that the qualities of a family's neighborhood and community, its community ecology, are important forces in the patterns of family social pathologies. We should expect that areas with high concentrations of pathology will be areas where the balance of environmental stresses and supports tips against families. Conversely, if we can identify communities and neighborhoods with characteristics that make them high-risk places for families, then we can predict that rates of social pathology among their families will be high.

A geographic approach to family social pathology is new ground for many, if not most, students of child development. The value of epidemiological methods that map the incidence and distribution of disease is well illustrated by an instance of epidemiological sleuthing from New York State. During the 1960s, a high proportion of cases of cleft palate in various counties in upstate New York came to the attention of the U.S. Public Health Service. As was the accustomed procedure of public health physicians, the local director of the Public Health Service placed a pin for each case of cleft palate and all other congenital malformations on a map of New York, denoting the location of each case. The resulting pattern corresponded to the pattern of igneous rock formations in New York, revealing the probable source of the health problems. Igneous rock emits natural radiation and had been associated with deformities present at birth, such as cleft palate (Bronfenbrenner and Mahoney, 1975). The mapping technique, in this case, lead to the root of the physical problems. The usefulness of a geographic orientation goes beyond physical disability and illness. It extends to psychological and social dysfunction as well, to mapping *social* radiation if you will.

Some of the impediments to the general use of a community approach to family social pathology are technical, while others are conceptual. The technical problems include the fact that data are often difficult to obtain in a form that permits efficient geographic mapping. It seems that our individualistic conception of pathology and the necessity of protecting confidentiality lead to data that are detached from their geographic location. One technological innovation has been the development of computer programs to perform "geocoding" of family data by translating addresses into mapped data points. The investigator, thus, can plot data to correspond with other data sets that describe census-tract or neighborhood-level indices of economic or demographic stress and support. The investigator can then determine the relationship between these data sets. Geocoding can become a vital resource for social workers, health planners, students, and others seeking to obtain more knowledge of communities (Kromkowski, 1976).

A second technical innovation that can aid in analyzing community effects is "social area analysis." Pioneered by Shevky and Bell (1955), and refined and expanded in the last twenty years by many researchers (Janson, 1980), social area analysis promises a systematic way of classifying and categorizing the sources of socioeconomic and demographic stress and support. The technique gives specific criteria for judging when a particular pattern of data is abnormal or deviant. It relies upon routinely available data and does not require the special surveys and field study demanded by other approaches to neighborhood analysis (e.g., Warren & Warren, 1977). The major limitation is the quality and quantity of the data base. The approach depends upon contemporary accuracy of data that often must come from census reports. These data rapidly become outdated for unstable communities and changing neighborhoods—precisely those areas that are often of greatest interest and concern in matters of family social pathology.

There have been other efforts to relate community factors to family social pathology using existing data and techniques. These efforts view the extent of various family social pathologies as indicators of the social habitability or quality of life in communities (Brim, 1975). Kogan, Smith, and Jenkins (1977), for example, created a multivariable index of stress indicators. Its acronym is DIPOV, and it includes a mix of measures that tap health and socioeconomic deprivation: *D*ependency (proportion of children under 18 in families receiving AFDC—Aid to Families with Dependent Children); *I*ncomplete Families (proportion of children under 18 not living with both parents); *P*remature Births (rate of infants with birth weight under 2,501 grams per 1,000 live births); *O*ut-of-Wedlock births (as a proportion of all live births); and *V*enereal Disease, Juvenile (rate of reported cases of primary or secondary syphilis or gonorrhea among persons under age 20 per 100,000 population under age 20). The investigators calculated DIPOV indices at county, census-unit, and neighborhood levels.

The researchers then sought to verify DIPOV by conducting an interview survey of families in areas with different scores on the index. Their analyses showed that the DIPOV Index performed progressively better as a predictor of difficulties of children (e.g., antisocial behavior) and parents (e.g., punitiveness) as the level of analysis moved from the larger (county) to the smaller (neighborhood) unit. Thus, preliminary use of DIPOV suggests it does have some validity as a correlate of family social pathology.

Four of the more significant social pathologies involving families are obstetric and pediatric illness, child maltreatment and domestic violence, juvenile delinquency, and teenage pregnancy. Each reflects the nature of transactions between the family and the social environment and demonstrates the nature of social stress and support in that environment. It is likely that community factors affect the prevalence of these pathologies. However, few community studies of these or other family social pathologies employ the DIPOV index, social area analysis, or any alternative social indicator approach. Greater use of such approaches is part of a more general need for empirical studies exploring the nature and power of relationships between communities and families. This need is reflected in, and supported by, the following brief review of these four types of family social pathology.

## Infant Mortality and Morbidity

Infant mortality (death in the first year of life) and morbidity (illness) are two of the traditional indices of social pathology (Kessner et al., 1973). Community effects are common. We can begin with the "natural" variation evidenced in standard descriptive statistics. Metropolitan versus nonmetropolitan differences within states are reflected in data from Mississippi, with 11.6 deaths per thousand for metropolitan communities versus 19.7 per thousand for nonmetropolitan communities; in Louisiana, 18.2 versus 17.6; in Maine, 6.2 versus 10.3; and in Arkansas, 16.9 versus 14.6 (U. S. National Center for Health Statistics, 1980). Note that in some states, the metropolitan area rates are higher than the nonmetropolitan rates, while in others, the difference reverses.

These gross differences are difficult to interpret and evaluate. They certainly reflect, at least in part, ecological correlations between low income and infant mortality and morbidity (Keniston, 1977a,b; National Academy of Sciences, 1976). We have reason to believe that they indicate more than these aggregate community effects, however. The demonstrated effects of prenatal health care, coupled with community-level variation in provision of such care, testify to a genuine community effect (Kessner et al., 1973). In 14 communities where maternal- and infant-care projects were sponsored by the Department of Health, Education, and Welfare for low income neighborhoods in the mid 1960s, significant decreases in infant mortality were observed: from 34.2 deaths per 1,000 live births in 1964 to 21.5 in 1969 in Denver; from 33.4 to 13.4 in Omaha; and from 25.4 to 14.3 in Birmingham. More recently, efforts to enhance the supportiveness of the prenatal and perinatal experience of young, high-risk mothers have resulted in decreased infant morbidity (O'Connor et al., 1977; Olds, 1980). Such results are appropriately considered community effects because the changes in policies, practices, and priorities they represent result from shifts in the direction of institutions, such as hospitals, that reflect community power structures and values. The whole movement toward family-centered childbirth has advanced community by community across the country (Garbarino, 1980a). These effects are equally apparent for teenage pregnancy.

## Teenage Pregnancy

As a form of family social pathology, teenage pregnancy has received significant public and professional attention, but little systematic, quantitative analysis has addressed it as a community problem. We know that socioeconomic and ethnic factors seem to influence the rates of teenage pregnancy: low-income blacks have the highest rates (Baldwin, 1976; Bolton, 1980). One source of apparent community effects is the level and quality of support and guidance given to the teenager involved in a first pregnancy (Shelton & Gladstone, 1979). The response of schools, operating under community mandate, can influence the subsequent educational, occupational, and thus, of course, family prospects of the adolescent parent (Furstenberg, 1976). Community support for an active family-planning effort can prevent or delay second pregnancies among teenagers (Bolton, 1980; Furstenberg, 1976). The principal community effect in this aspect of family social pathology is, thus, to moderate the effects of teenage pregnancies—on children, on parents, indeed on the very creation and maintenance of parent–child relationships. Indeed, some observers (Shelton & Gladstone, 1979) note that much of the medical and social pathology associated with teenage pregnancy derives from the community's response. As evidence, they cite both a decrease in adverse consequences—as society has become more supportive and less punitive with respect to teenage pregnancy—and the fact that among well-supported groups, the level of medical pathology and social disadvantage is minimal. Of course, these are measures of maternal and child health at birth and do not address consequences to the child of growing up in a teenage-parented, often, single-parented household, so we should not overgeneralize the significance of these findings.

## Juvenile Delinquency

Juvenile delinquency was one of the earliest interests of human ecologists working at the University of Chicago in the 1920s and 1930s (Hawley, 1950; Lander, 1954; Shaw and McKay, 1942; Shaw et al., 1929). Extensive data exist documenting community differences in the reported incidence of juvenile delinquency. Typically, these data involve comparisons based on community size and the urban–rural dimension. For example, the proportion of criminal arrests accounted for by juveniles (under age 18) varies substantially. Among very small cities (population under 10,000) this figure was 32.8 percent in 1977; among medium-sized cities (population between 100,000 and 250,000) it was 27.9 percent; among large cities (population greater than 250,000), 22.2 percent (Federal Bureau of Investigation, 1978). The corresponding figures for rural and suburban communities were 20.2 percent and 31.9 percent. More broadly, in 1979, juveniles accounted for different proportions of violent crimes versus property crimes across the broad urban-suburban-rural continuum: 21.9 percent of arrests for property crimes versus 44.5 percent of arrests for violent crimes for urban areas; 20 percent versus 46.3 percent for suburban areas; 8.3 percent versus 33.4 percent for rural areas (Federal Bureau of Investigation, 1980). In addition, studies such as the Nebraska Social Indicators Study report a correlation between community size and "fear of walking alone at night near one's home" (a good measure of social climate). Using these data, Eells (1981) reported that as community size increases, so does the percentage of residents expressing this fear: rural, 9 percent; towns under 2,500 population, 16 percent; small cities, 24 percent; cities 10,000–50,000, 32 percent; city of 100,000, 41 percent; city of 300,000, 49 percent.

The rich community case study literature (e.g., McKay, cited by Short, 1966) suggests that local decisions regarding zoning, law enforcement strategies, schooling, youth employment, curfews, recreation, and the like all can have the effect of mediating the family dynamics, peer relationships, personality shifts, and behavioral contingencies that generate or suppress juvenile delinquency. Neighborhood-oriented research of this sort reports that stability is associated with lower delinquency, while disruption is associated with increased delinquency (McKay, cited by Short, 1966). Social cohesion appears to be a precondition for social control, but it is the effective power of prosocial forces within the neighborhood or community that tells the story (Short, 1966). More specifically, investigators have found that juvenile delinquency rates differ between neighborhoods that are socioeconomically and demographically comparable if the neighborhoods differ in how capable they are of exerting social control, with the critical dimension being degree of social cohesion on behalf of prosocial goals among residents (Maccoby, Johnson, and Church, 1958). Research on child maltreatment has taken this finding and moved towards a more comprehensive conception of how community and neighborhood influence family social pathology.

## Child Maltreatment

Following upon earlier neighborhood-oriented work (Sattin & Miller, 1971), Garbarino and his colleagues (Garbarino, 1976; Garbarino and Crouter, 1978; Garbarino and Sherman, 1980) undertook research designed to illustrate the use of child maltreatment report data as a social indicator of the quality of life for families. This research addressed the feedback function of family support systems, and linked maltreatment to the overall balance of stresses and supports in the neighborhood context of families. The first study provided county-level correlations relating socioeconomic and demographic stress on mothers to rates of child maltreatment (Garbarino, 1976).

Further study focused on the reported incidence of child abuse and neglect in 93 neighborhood areas in a single metropolitan county. The statistical technique of multiple regression analysis was used to develop equations to predict abuse and neglect rates from socioeconomic, demographic, and attitudinal data (Garbarino & Crouter, 1978). For the 93 neighborhoods, 52 percent of the difference in reported rates was accounted for by five variables—two measuring family income, one assessing the presence of single parent households, one indexing transience, and one indicating the presence of mothers, working outside the house who have young children. This study extended and validated the earlier research reporting similar results using counties as the units of analysis (Garbarino, 1976) and formed the basis for a more in-depth neighborhood-focused study (Garbarino & Sherman, 1980).

The multiple regression analyses identified two low-income neighborhoods that, although matched in socioeconomic level and demographic character, differed significantly in the rates of child maltreatment. One neighborhood with a child maltreatment rate greatly exceeding what was predicted by its socioeconomic and demographic profile was termed high-risk, while another neighborhood in which the actual rate was much less than the predicted rate was termed low-risk. Both neighborhoods had 72 percent of their families in the low-income category, but the first had a rate of child maltreatment eight times that of the second: 130 per 1,000 versus 16 per 1,000 families (Garbarino & Sherman, 1980). Interviews with expert informants, ranging from elementary school

Table 7:1: Illustrative data comparing families in two neighborhoods
(after Garbarino and Sherman, 1980)

| | Low-Risk Neighborhood (21 families) | High-Risk Neighborhood (20 families) |
|---|---|---|
| 1. Percent of school-age children cared for by parents in after-school hours. | 86% | 25% |
| 2. Percent of those interviewed who never engage in neighborhood exchanges. | 8% | 32% |
| 3. Percent of children for whom neighborhood children regularly serve as playmates. | 86% | 40% |
| 4. Average number of people mothers name as taking an interest in their child's welfare. | 5.3 | 4.1 |
| 5. Mean score on Holmes-Rahe Social Readjustment Scale (200+ indicates moderate or major crisis). | 166 | 258 |
| 6. Average rating by mothers of neighborhood as a place to raise children (−4 to +4). | 1.66 | .09 |

Note: All differences are significant at $p$ less than .05

principals to mail carriers, were used to develop profiles of the two neighborhoods. Samples of families were drawn from each neighborhood and interviews were conducted to identify stresses and supports, with special emphasis on sources of help, social networks, evaluation of the neighborhood, and use of formal family support systems. Table 7:1 presents some of the results.

As shown in the table, families in the high-risk neighborhood, though socioeconomically similar to families in the low-risk neighborhood, reported less positive evaluations of the neighborhood as a context for child and family development. Furthermore, they revealed a general pattern of "social impoverishment" in comparison with families in the low-risk neighborhood. These findings lend support to the assertion that there are neighborhood effects related to child maltreatment.

The approach used in these neighborhood studies represents, along with geocoding, social area analysis, and the DIPOV Index, an additional method of analyzing community effects on families and children. These and other ecologically oriented research techniques will enable us to document in greater detail the relationships between various community characteristics and the well-being of residents. With enhanced understanding of these connections, we can identify community attributes that are most closely related to the quality of life for families and spot areas that may be high-risk places for children. This will enable us to act more effectively in minimizing the risks and maximizing the opportunities presented to the developing child by the territory of childhood. This leads us to consider the nature and structure of human services, and that is the topic of our next chapter.

# RESEARCH CAPSULE

The importance of the environmental context and its effects on family functioning have been explored in this book. One of the aspects of the environment that deserves mention is density. Density usually refers to the number of individuals per unit of space. However, various indices of density also include the number of rooms per house, the number of houses per acre, and so on. Galle, Gove, and McPherson (1972) found that of the above indices, the number of persons per room best predicted rates of social pathology. As the number of persons increased, so did mortality, juvenile delinquency, and public assistance rates. Lower cognitive development is also associated with a large number of persons per room (Wachs,

Uzgiris, & Hunt, 1971). In a review of residential density and child development, van Vliet (in press) concluded that there appears to be a relationship between crowded households, on the one hand, and behavior problems and maladjustment in children, on the other. The environmental impact of density on the child seems to be such that too much social stimulation may be harmful to adequate development.

Wohlwill (in press) noted that the existing research on density points to a greater effect of density on children than adults. He hypothesized that adults have learned to adapt to adverse living conditions, but children have not had the experience or opportunity to know how best to fit in with their surroundings. One of the variables that may affect the family's adjustment to dense households is housing preference (Booth, in press). For those families who prefer to live in close quarters, there may not be any stress associated with that situation. In those cases where families would prefer to live in a less crowded household but have little choice in the matter, stress in the family and in the parent–child relationship may be experienced. Poor families may be most at risk, as they do not have the economic resources to be able to make a choice in housing. Research on density needs to examine more fully the relationship between poverty, density, and adjustment to density levels.

Density is clearly an important issue that needs further research. It has implications for policies concerning housing, land use, and population distribution (Booth, in press). Planners can use information on density to guide their decisions in ways that improve the social environment of children through their physical environment. Social welfare agencies, schools, and other human services can also benefit from research on density, as all are involved in serving the needs of families.

# PRACTICE CAPSULE

Pancoast (1980) and Collins (1980) have developed a community-based preventive program aimed at strengthening support systems in neighborhoods to reduce the risk of child maltreatment. They call their approach "the neighborhood consulting model," so termed because of the importance of consultation to central figures or adults who are "free from drain" in the natural helping network of a community. Generally, a community agency supports a consultant whose role it is to become knowledgeable about the supportive networks within a given community, gather information about the central figures in the network (those members of the neighborhood who serve as informal helpers through their frequent contact with families, e.g., school personnel, merchants, the local busybody, etc.), establish rapport with the central figures, and serve as a consultant to the central figures through listening, empathizing, and giving support, information, and advice.

From the initial attempt to identify a neighborhood that has a high risk of child maltreatment to identifying those people who are central figures and to finally establishing trust-ing relationships with central figures, the process takes many months. After achieving these goals, the consultant regularly meets with each central figure and listens to his or her concerns about families in the neighborhood. The consultant, through contact with the central figure, is able to influence families at risk. Reporting neglect and abuse cases can be encouraged, particularly when children are in dangerous situations. Information about healthy child rearing attitudes and practices can filter down to the parents, suggestions for referrals to local human service agencies can occur, and strategies for involving isolated families in a social network can emerge. The consultant's precise goals will vary from neighborhood to neighborhood, across different informal helping networks and involved families.

The strengths of this consultation model are that it takes advantage of the support systems that already do exist, it minimizes professional interference into family lives, and reaches families in a cost-efficient manner. While the model is relatively recent in the realm of treatment for abusive families, it has exciting possibilities.

# FOR FURTHER READING

Fandetti, D. V. Ethnicity and neighborhood services. In D. Thursz & J. L. Vigilante. *Reaching people: The structure of neighborhood services.* Beverly Hills: Sage, 1978, 15 pp.

Stressing the pluralism of our communities, Fandetti explores the relationships between ethnicity, social class, and the emotional significance ascribed to one's neighborhood. Discussing implications for service delivery strategies, he suggests that programs can build on neighborhood attachment by affiliating with local places and institutions and by strengthening traditional mechanisms of assistance, such as families and churches.

Jacobs, J. *The death and life of great American cities.* New York: Vintage, 1961, 458 pp.

Jacobs presents a lively analysis of the workings of city neighborhoods from the perspective of their residents, including their youngest residents, the children. She disputes much "common wisdom" about what makes successful neighborhoods. The importance of an active sidewalk life is a recurring theme. Implications for city planning are presented.

Keller, S. *The urban neighborhood: A sociological perspective.* New York: Random House, 1968, 201 pp.

Neighborhoods, neighbors, and neighboring in the urban setting are addressed as distinct, but related, phenomena in this readable classic. Keller charts many of the changes occurring in these phenomena as cities, families, and the general social order change over time. She finds that increased heterogeneity in urban neighborhoods, less dependence of families on their environments, and more impersonal forms of social control lessen the traditional importance of neighborhoods.

Michelson, W., Levine, S. V., & Michelson, E. (Eds.) *The child in the city: Today and Tomorrow.* Toronto: University of Toronto Press, 1979, 272 pp.

The situation of the child in the metropolis is discussed in chapters by scholars representing history, law, social welfare, medicine, developmental psychology, and sociology. The companion volume by W. Michelson, S. V. Levine, and A. R. Spina, *The child in the city: Changes and challenges* (520 pages), contains discussions of specific urban-child issues such as community services, the adolescent in the city, and ethnic diversity and children.

Stack, C. *All our kin: Strategies for survival in a black community.* New York: Harper and Row, 1974, 175 pp.

This is a white participant-observer's vivid account of the resilient support networks operating in a poverty-stricken black neighborhood and the elaborate rules and protocols governing network functioning. She shows how the effects of severe economic impoverishment are mitigated by active social networks that provide some reasonable assurance of survival.

Warren, R. L. The community's vertical pattern: Ties to the larger society and culture (and) The community's horizontal pattern: The relation of local units to each other. In R. L. Warren, *The community in America* (2nd ed.). Chicago: Rand McNally, 1973, 65 pp.

In these two chapters, Warren presents the concepts of the vertical and horizontal ties of a community and discusses different types of ties and their influences on communities. A useful perspective on closed versus open communities and local versus extra-local demands and standards that can help to explain how and why some communities are more responsive to their residents' needs than others.

Wynne, E. *Growing up suburban.* Austin: University of Texas Press, 1977, 236 pp.

Wynne clearly and concisely addresses issues associated with suburban children and parents, and focuses on the school and community as settings that can facilitate the child's development. The fundamental assumption is that life in suburbia may not be ideal for the development of the child. Suggestions for improvement include fostering better community–school relations, selecting teachers with affective skills, and increasing the diversity and residential stability of the community.

# QUESTIONS FOR THOUGHT

1. We have presented evidence that communities differ in their effects on families. Unemployment rates, local economy, and social density are but a few of the factors that affect family functioning. What other factors can you think of that could have effects on families as a result of different communities?

2. The chapter suggested that social density (the variety and number of roles in a community) affects the development and experiences of children. Are children better off in a large city with people of all ages, professions, and nationalities or in a small town where there are a limited number of roles to be observed? Be sure to take into account other aspects of a community that affect child development (e.g., number of people, amount of social contact).

3. Imagine yourself as a member of a local government that is receiving pressure from the state to allow a major highway to be built through a section of town. The highway, if approved, will disrupt a close-knit neighborhood consisting of many families with small children. If you vote for the highway, what policy would you adopt toward relocation of those families? If you vote against it, explain the reasons for your choice.

4. The lack of availability of day care for children while parents are working presents difficulties to parents. Suppose that you are the president of a large factory and have the power to make decisions regarding the implementation of on-site day-care facilities and/or support for parents who wish to use community day-care facilities. Draw up reasonable plans of action that would allow parents the comfort of working without having to worry about the safety and care of their children.

5. In examining the influence of informal support systems on the welfare of families, we have found that neighbors serve several important functions. Describe five stressful situations that families might encounter and give examples of ways in which neighbors could help.

6. We have looked at infant mortality, juvenile delinquency, teenage pregnancy, and child maltreatment as indices of social pathology in a community. What other indices can you think of that might be useful in pointing out community variation in social pathology? After you have identified other indices, describe what you could do to improve situations in a community that does indicate high levels of such social pathology.

7. The importance of the home–school relationship cannot be overemphasized. Think about ways in which parents could be convinced to become more a part of the school and community. Describe the effects that such involvement might have on parents and their children.

# Chapter 8

Margaret W. is a divorced parent with 3 children, ages 10, 5, and 2. The 5-year-old was born prematurely and has speech and hearing defects. His kindergarten teacher told Margaret that he is a slow learner; speech therapy and a hearing aid would help him. Margaret's ex-husband has moved to another state. His alimony payments are often late, if they arrive at all. There is no money available for a hearing aid right now.

Margaret works from 10:00 A.M. to 4:00 P.M. in a school cafeteria. She leaves the 2-year-old and the kindergartner with a neighbor who goes to work at 2:30. By then, the 10-year-old is home to care for the younger children, but the neighbor reports that several times in the past month, Susan, the 10-year-old, has not been home when the neighbor has had to leave for work. Susan says she started talking with friends and forgot about the time. Susan complains that it's not fair that she has to stay home with her brothers while her friends can play after school.

Margaret's father had a mild stroke several weeks ago. She would like him to live with her. He could watch after the kids, and he wouldn't have to live alone. But she doesn't have room in her apartment; Medicaid would pay for him to go into a nursing home, but it won't pay the rent for a larger apartment.

Margaret W. represents a common situation in the U.S. today—families who are scraping by on their own in less than optimal conditions. Her family could benefit from many social services: day care, therapeutic services for the 5-year-old, housing assistance, legal assistance to secure alimony. Perhaps Margaret W. lives in a community where these services are available, but she is not aware of them or not eligible because her marginal income disqualifies her.

In this chapter, we examine dimensions of the human services that influence how services are delivered. We will explore the historical roots of social services in the U.S. with consideration of the ideological bases for these services. We will discuss some of the issues involved in delivering services that meet the developmental needs of children and families. Finally, we will present examples of human services that we feel are meeting these needs.

# Developmental Issues in the Human Services

## Concepts of Helping

The term "human services" encompasses a broad range of activities, programs, and agencies designed to meet the physical, intellectual, and social-emotional needs of individuals and families. These services are encountered primarily in microsystems (e.g., dyadic counseling) or mesosystems (e.g., referral or liaison between agencies). Community services, on the other hand, are those that directly address larger social forces—for example, controlling pollution or building sanitation facilities. They are thus mainly found in exosystems with respect to children. Many services fall somewhere between the extremes of direct service to individuals and indirect service through management of the physical and social environment. Both human and community services can deal with a wide range of life's domains: education, mental and physical health, safety and sanitation, religion, transportation, housing, employment, legal services, and recreation (Urban & Vondracek, 1977). Not all of us do, or will ever, require some of these services: mental health services, unemployment benefits, or the medical care of a coronary resuscitation unit. But all of us use some of them, at one time or another.

We can classify human services on the following dimensions:

1. *Timing:* do they aim to prevent a problem from occurring or to repair it after it occurs?
2. *Goals:* do they seek to minimize negative factors or to optimize positive factors; are they oriented to reducing risks or increasing opportunities?
3. *Scope:* are they single-purpose or comprehensive?

Beyond these three dimensions, there are others. Human services can be offered directly (e.g., education) or indirectly (e.g., guarantees for banks to offer mortgages for restoring delapidated homes). They are public (e.g., Aid to Families with Dependent Children), private nonprofit (e.g., the March of Dimes), or private for-profit (e.g., a day-care center run as a profit-making business). The human services can also be formal and bureaucratically created or informal and spontaneously occurring. The formal services include all those offered by federal, state, and local government agencies as well as programs, voluntary organizations, and private groups and institutions officially recognized as providers of support to children and families. By "informal" we mean the activities of those systems that we discussed in Chapters 2, 4, and 7—families, friends, neighborhoods, and other social connections. These informal connections or support systems provide both tangible and intangible services: child care exchanges between neighbors (Unger & Powell, 1980), for instance, or emotional support after the loss of a family member (Caine, 1974). Most of us turn for help to our informal support systems far more quickly and more frequently than we look to the formal helping services (Gottlieb, 1980). For many of us, the informal support systems are a natural part of our daily lives, and therefore, we do not often consider their role as "human services." We take them for granted, whether we give or receive them. But for others of us, these supports are lacking. The lives of these individuals may be less successful and satisfying because of the absence of support. Our lives would be significantly less satisfying without the feedback, nurturance, and guidance we receive from our support systems. Earlier chapters suggested some ways to meet this need. Later in this chapter, we will develop further the notion of informal support systems as helping services.

Social services can be described on several dimensions that relate to the goals of intervention. In this discussion, we describe the end points of these dimensions, recognizing that actual service delivery often falls between the extremes. The first dimension concerns whether one seeks to *minimize* negative outcomes or *optimize* positive ones. Minimizing interventions start with an individual or family who is perceived as malfunctioning or functioning inadequately. Thus, the client must step over an invisible line of failure or inadequacy before service begins. Even then, the intervention offers only those services necessary to bring the individual or family back across the threshold to an acceptable level of functioning. For instance, families receive financial support from most public assistance programs when their incomes fall below a prespecified criterion set at the lower end of the continuum of economic adequacy. Once they reach the defined level of adequacy, the program disengages from them (often abruptly, we might add). We find a particularly graphic example of this in the Special Supplemental Food Program for Women, Infants and Children (WIC), which offers food supplements for pregnant women and children up to five years of age. Need is determined jointly by income and by the child's nutritional status and placement outside an acceptable range on a growth curve (measuring height and weight by age). When children enter the acceptable growth range, they are dropped from the program. The subsequent loss of food supplements may mean that the family will have difficulty continuing to provide fully nutritious meals to the child. Thus, a minimal approach to the delivery of social services may leave many families functioning marginally, just over the threshold of need, or may result in families bouncing in and out of the eligible range, over and over again.

Those who advocate the minimizing approach make several assumptions (Berger & Neuhaus, 1977; Kadushin, 1978). First, they see individual or family functioning as being on a continuum and assume that we can determine a critical point beyond which conditions are inadequate or maladaptive. Second, advocates of minimal intervention usually argue that we have limited resources for intervention but many people in need of services. Therefore, we can only guarantee minimum services to those beyond the critical point, for whom intervention is clearly needed. Finally, they argue that while we do not know how to optimize development, we do know how to remedy dysfunction. When these four points are put together, they justify a human services safety net to catch individuals who fall out of acceptable social and economic patterns.

In contrast to this, the optimization position advocates efforts to maximize an individual's or a family's potential to achieve the best possible outcome. While advocates of optimization agree that resources are limited, they argue that these resources are well-spent in pursuing optimal functioning for all families rather than targeting specific problems when they occur. (This implies a prevention approach that we will discuss later in more detail.) Those who favor an optimizing approach believe that we *do* know enough to intervene to facilitate development in some ways and that a positive approach will have greater long-term payoffs than a minimizing approach. Thus, for example, they may argue for expanding protective services to ever wider domains of family relations rather than limiting coverage to the families exhibiting life-threatening abuse.

The philosophy of optimization motivated enactment of Public Law 94-192, the Education for All Handicapped Children Act of 1975. This federal law called for integrating handicapped children into settings as nearly like those of nonhandicapped children as possible. Thus, for instance, it provides that handicapped children be allowed to live in homes or homelike environments instead of institutions, attend regular school classrooms for as many activities as possible, have access to public transportation and buildings, and have the recreational experiences that other children have, such as field trips, sports, and the like. This is an example of optimizing the handicapped child's experience in order to produce the best possible quality of life and the best possible developmental outcome for the child.

This minimization–optimization distinction is insufficient by itself. We also need to consider whether the service addresses the whole child or whole family rather than just one narrow aspect or problem. Services that deal with only one aspect of the client's life are called categorical. For instance, an agency that arranges foster placements for abused children takes a categorical approach to child abuse. Another agency may provide emergency day care, accompanied by counseling to the abusing parent and abused child, and social services required to reduce the family stresses that may have contributed to the abuse. A preschool intervention program may seek only to optimize cognitive development, or it may seek to increase general social and intellectual competence of children or families. The latter agency in each example is taking a more comprehensive or generic view of the client's situation. In other words, a comprehensive service approach takes into account several influential systems in the client's life. The intervention may focus on multiple aspects of the individual, as in a comprehensive health program that considers both mental and physical well-being. We can also consider systems on several ecological levels, as in a child abuse prevention program that incorporates individual counseling, family social services, and a community awareness campaign. While many (e.g., Kadushin, 1978) argue that comprehensive approaches are too costly to be feasible, others believe that categorical problem-oriented service delivery tends to fragment people's lives. Think of the family which must go to one office for food stamps, another office for infant food supplements, and yet another office to arrange for meals on wheels. The categorical approach can also lead to inefficient duplication of services and removing people from service rosters if they no longer meet the categorical requirements, but are still in need. The sum of the family's problems may put them in real need while no single problem does. A categorical approach also leads to focusing on problems outside the context of total family functioning. Comprehensive approaches to services are often unrealistic because of fiscal restraints, and most social service agencies make efforts to refer their clients to all necessary services. However, having an understanding of how mesosystems affect individual development may help us avoid fragmentation of clients' needs.

Another dimension of service delivery to consider is *when* services will be delivered: that is, whether they prevent or remediate problems. The goal of preventive programs is to reduce the incidence of a problem (the number of new occurrences) or even to promote positive outcomes. Remediation, on the other hand, seeks to fix problem behavior or characteristics. Prevention can aim at reducing negative events or facilitating desirable ones. The preventive–remedial dimension of service delivery can be distinguished from the optimizing–minimizing dimension on the basis that the first has to do with the *timing* of intervention, while the latter is related to the *goals* of intervention. Using another example, one of the debates in the study of child abuse is whether to prevent abuse by attacking the known risk factors (a preventive and minimizing approach) or by building up the positive styles of family life thought to be incompatible with maltreatment (a preventive and optimizing approach).

Many examples of prevention come from the field of public health: innoculation against disease, introducing fluoride in drinking water, sanitary control of water and food, educational campaigns to encourage physical fitness or discourage smoking. In the area of social services, it is more difficult to specify what is necessary to prevent negative outcomes. Causes of physical illness are often easier to define and eliminate than causes of poverty, instability, or family disruption. This is one reason why many people opt for remedial approaches to social services.

Staulcup (1980) has described two models of preventive intervention. The first involves external control of individual behavior. For instance, laws are passed to prevent speeding on the highway or smoking in public places. These are measures taken in the name of public welfare and enforced through the state's police power and citizen initiative. Internal control models, on the other hand, provide individuals with information to guide their decisions and to encourage them to act in a manner which will have positive outcomes. For instance, parent-education courses teach parents how to establish positive relationships with their children and public-education campaigns educate adolescents about the dangers of drug use. But the responsibility to implement the knowledge, in each case, rests on the individual.

Because of the difficulties involved in specifying desirable outcomes in social welfare, as well as in defining the methods for achieving these outcomes, most service delivery relies upon a remedial model. Where prevention is the goal, it is most often what Caplan and others call secondary prevention. Secondary prevention occurs when one has identified a group of high-risk people and seeks to prevent that high-risk status from being translated into occurrence of the problem itself. This is distinguished from primary prevention (preventing the problem by preventing the conditions that produce risk) and tertiary prevention (preventing the problem from recurring). Thus, delivering treatment to a parent who has abused a child is remedial, or tertiary prevention. Identifying families at risk for abuse and offering them services to reduce this risk is secondary prevention. Promoting nonviolent and emotionally supportive child rearing is considered primary prevention for child abuse.

The remedial and preventive approaches have very different implications for how, when, and to whom we deliver services. The remedial approach is typically applied on a case-by-case basis. Intervention occurs when a problem arises. Often this leads us to cure symptoms rather than causes. For instance, we treat poverty-stricken individuals by offering individual solutions (welfare) rather than seeking societal changes that will eliminate poverty (Ryan, 1976). This remedial perspective views the client as incapable of solving his or her own problems. Thus, the state is justified in assuming the role of surrogate caregiver because the family cannot adequately care for itself. This view sees social problems as the result of individual failures, rather than social misdirection. As we will see in the historical development of the human services, these orientations have their basis in the sociopolitical climate of our society.

Preventive models can also offer solutions based on attempts to change individuals. This is especially true when problems in development can be prevented by educating the public or providing adaptive behavioral skills. By taking the preventive focus over a remedial approach, however, we are more likely to seek the responsibility for family disruption in larger social forces over which individuals have little control. These forces affect everyone, not just the relatively few who fall victim to them. Promoting individual welfare becomes a legitimate concern of the state in order to help individuals gather resources that may otherwise be unequally distributed (Moroney, 1980). Because a strategy of optimizing outcomes also requires looking into the future, preventive approaches and optimizing approaches often, but not always, join hands in intervention. One example of this is found in innoculation programs for childhood disease. Innoculations prevent illness and promote good health.

The debate over where we put our money is crucial to the debate between advocates of remedial and preventive intervention. Proponents of remedial approaches argue that because we have limited funds we must treat the most serious cases first (and the advocates of minimal intervention would add "only"). This does not leave any room for prevention. Besides, they argue, why spend money on unproven preventive strategies when we know what works in crises?

Those who argue for prevention counter with the proposition that funds invested in prevention will reduce or eliminate the vast expenditures incurred in intervening after the fact and are thus more cost-effective. If we strengthen teeth—or families—now, we will not have to clean up dental—or social—decay later. A related point of view argues that if we remove obstacles to effective and powerful family functioning, families will provide services that otherwise the state would have to provide. It is more costly for the state to provide these services than for the family to do so. We will examine these concepts in greater detail later in this chapter.

Unfortunately, the limitation of financial and staff resources means that we cannot always provide a service to all. In the event of limited resources, we must take two steps: 1) define the population most likely to suffer from the problem; 2) evaluate the net gain to be achieved from the intervention. This second task can be approached in two ways. The first is cost-benefit analysis: measuring the estimated benefits of the intervention in comparison to its costs. For instance, suppose the cost of arresting, trying, and incarcerating criminals for future offenses, if they are not rehabilitated, is estimated at $2,000,000, and a program to rehabilitate prison inmates costs $1,000,000. Thus, the rehabilitation program has a cost–benefit ratio of 2:1—it would cost half as much in the long run to intervene than to not rehabilitate inmates.

The second way to assess the economic feasibility of intervention is to look at its *cost-effectiveness* in comparison to other means of achieving the same end. For instance, suppose we want to reduce the rate of juvenile delinquency in our community. Three approaches have been proposed, all with equal likelihood for success; that is, each will reduce juvenile delinquency among the youth who participate in it by the same amount.

| Approach | Cost |
|---|---|
| 1. A community center for all young people, with meeting rooms and recreational equipment. | $500,000 |
| 2. A psychiatric therapy program unit serving twenty troubled youth. | $200,000 |
| 3. A program coordinated between schools and churches to provide after-school athletics and community service employment. | $100,000 |

The last option would be most likely to be chosen since it is the least costly as well as the one that would reach a large number of adolescents. It has the additional advantage of working from agencies and resources that are already available.

In choosing between preventive and remedial approaches, the economic feasibility of a program along with its short- and long-term consequences must be considered. We must also consider who will be most likely to benefit from the intervention. Our inability to predict who will develop a particular problem often limits the usefulness of prevention. Although we would often prefer to advocate the preventive approach, the optimal means of husbanding our resources to meet the most pressing needs of the target population may require a remedial approach. This is especially true when successful treatment methods have been developed, but the effectiveness of preventive approaches is not yet clear, as would be the case in our example if the success of each program is undemonstrated.

Another dimension of service delivery relates to one's view of the roles of client and provider. The medical or corrective model views the client as having something wrong that a professional intervener can fix with his or her skills. This model has also been labeled an "illness" or "pathology" model since the client needs an expert "cure." For instance, an individual seeking psychotherapy because of a personal problem is "cured" by the psychiatrist, social worker, or psychologist who helps the person overcome the problem. This approach empowers the helper and casts the client as being incapable of solving her or his own problem. This model can also be applied to families. Some professionals view families as causes of their client's problems or as impediments to the delivery of services. An example of this is found in theories attributing schizophrenia to unhealthy family dynamics.

In the collaborative model, on the other hand, the client and professional share resources and competence (Moroney, 1980). The helper may have some skills that the client lacks in defining problems, resolving conflicts, or locating services, but there is no assumption that the client is helpless. The helper assists in defining the client's needs and assists the client in identifying and locating the resources or support systems that can fill those needs. The distinction between counseling (clients) and therapy (patients) reflects the important distinction between a situation where two parties have nearly equal status and share resources versus a situation where a competent, resource-rich party helps an incompetent, resource-impoverished party. Self-help groups for abusive parents, such as Parents Anonymous, contrast with psychotherapy on this dimension.

There are situations where each model, the corrective or the collaborative, is appropriate. In certain families, where a coercive style of family interaction has developed, the most fruitful solution may be to teach the parents and children to interact with each other in a positive manner. In other words, the corrective model would replace inappropriate behaviors with acceptable ones. In a single-parent family, where the parent feels isolated and unable to cope with child-rearing difficulties, bringing the parent together with a support group of other single parents and providing relief from child-care responsibilities may solve the problem. In some families, both corrective and collaborative approaches may be necessary to reduce the family's stress. For instance, a physical therapist can work with a handicapped child and train the parent to take over the treatment. These viewpoints have a major influence on how the professional interacts with clients.

One final concept relevant to human-service delivery that we will consider here is enhancement. Enhancing interventions aim to increase competence in dealing with future life events by using knowledge and skills to solve problems. During a major personal event such as acquiring a new job, for instance, an enhancing intervention would help the individual to marshal resources and skills developed from previous transitional experiences. Enhancing interventions pinpoint skills needed to pass critical life events adaptively and ensure that the individual learns these skills so that they will be available in similar future situations (Danish, Smyer, & Nowak, 1980). For example, one might teach teenagers techniques for nonviolent conflict resolution as the basis for improving future conjugal and parent-child relationships (Garbarino & Jacobson, 1978).

Any human-service program must consider several issues. First, we need to define the desired outcomes. Second, we need to define the steps to achieve these outcomes. This may involve changing individual characteristics or inter-personal behavior (microsystem), providing resources or creating support systems (meso- and exosystem), or even advocating social change (exo- and macrosystem). Third, we have to decide at which of these levels we can intervene most effectively. The history of human services reveals these issues in action, and shows how the United States has emphasized categorical and remedial approaches.

## The History of the Human Services

Several philosophical and political trends have contributed to the development of helping services in the United States. As we shall see, economic concerns have motivated our desire to help as frequently as has humanitarian inspiration. In the long run, the former may be more persuasive than the latter. Our hope, of course, is that these two interests will be congruent rather than discrepant.

Historically, families have provided many of the resources we now consider the domain of social services. A rural subsistence economy provided the means for most families to provide for themselves. When a family could not support itself, relatives usually helped out. Orphans and the elderly were absorbed into the extended family and community. When an extended family network was not available, neighbors, church congregations, or charitable groups stepped in. In other words, "social services" were provided by the family's informal support systems.

During the early 1800s both government and voluntary agencies began providing services to children and families. Two major social changes provided impetus to this rise of *formal* services. The growth of the cities, as a consequence of industrialization, created larger numbers of families who suffered from poverty and disruption of their life-styles. Cut off from many traditional sources of social support, they faced the multiple pressures of urban life, factory work, and adaptation to a new culture. All three contributed to family disorganization. Informal helping networks were disrupted by increased geographical mobility of families, leaving many children and adults isolated without traditional sources of assistance. Loss of cohesive primary groups also weakened previously powerful mechanisms of informal social control. Formal social services were devised and supported to counteract these effects.

Charitable care for families stemmed from a humanitarian desire to care for the unfortunate. Social agencies also intervened in an effort to reduce the likelihood that indigent children would become delinquent or a permanent social burden. Two types of services developed from this goal. Institutional care for children developed out of the philosophy that the government has the right to intervene when the family does not or cannot properly support children or monitor their behavior. In addition, as industries sought to expand their work forces, greater numbers of women began to work outside the home; day-care nurseries were established to meet the child-care needs of working mothers. Thus, nurturance and control were themes that arose early in the history of human services and remain issues to this day, particularly in the United States.

The second major impetus for child and family services derived from the goal of universal education. Once again, economic forces underlay social reform. Education became widespread in an effort to prepare people for productive roles in industry and to integrate immigrant populations (Greer, 1972). Public education also removed children from the labor market and provided daytime supervision for them. Both of these activities improved employment opportunities for parents, especially mothers. Compulsory education also had a socializing effect on immigrant children, teaching them how to be "good Americans." Social reformers saw the schools as a means for providing the literate public required to run a democratic country. Today, some see this as a humanitarian enterprise. Others see it as a kind of conspiracy to downplay ethnic diversity and control deviants through a process of homogenization.

The social philosophy of the 1800s and the early 1900s contained two opposing trends that help illuminate the control-nurturance issue. The first is represented by the doctrine of Social Darwinism: social philosophers broadened concepts of biological evolution to justify a view of society being ruled by the principle of "survival of the fittest." That is, those who are not able to fend for themselves will drop out, and those who are more skilled, competent, and fit will succeed in providing for their own needs. This philosophy supported an attitude of "hands off" or *laissez-faire* toward social problems. It also fit well with the American tradition of individualism and pulling oneself up "by the bootstraps."

On the other hand, American ideals include an emphasis on equality that extends to economic as well as political rights. The struggle to implement this value tells much of the American story. Despite the rhetoric and the real progress our society has made toward offering equal opportunity, major inequalities remain. Equality is supposed to go hand in hand with opportunity, although differences in outcome are a natural consequence of differences in individual capacity to capitalize on opportunity. Social reformers have sought ways to provide materials and skills that will equalize the opportunities of the less fortunate. These efforts have met with only limited success.

Levine and Levine (1970), in their provocative history of the helping services, showed that the orientation of the helping services fluctuates with the political mood of society. Thus, when the climate is conservative, the majority emphasize social order. Social problems are treated as failures of the individual rather than as qualities of society. When society enters a reformist period, people are more likely to seek solutions to social problems by changing social structures and institutions. During the late 1800s, the Depression years (1930s), and the Decade of the Great Society (1960s), concerned groups attempted to institute progressive social change. During the intervening periods, the climate was more conservative, and a focus on changing individuals predominated.

## Charity

Social services had their beginnings in the voluntary, charitable organizations that began to flourish in the late nineteenth century. These charities typically had a neighborhood base and emphasized meeting the survival needs of families through employment rather than alms (Kahn, 1976). Levine and Levine (1970) provided examples of settlement-house workers who lived in poor neighborhoods and got to know the problems of the families surrounding them. They would visit and care for the elderly and ill, give their sewing or laundry to a widow who had no means of support, or facilitate support arrangements between families. Church charities operated in a similar manner—identifying the needs of the local congregation.

Originally, social services were delivered to remediate problems or correct deficiencies. At the turn of the century, social workers began to recognize the value of preventive intervention (Ford, 1974). The first White House Conference on Children was a meeting of social workers concerned with the care of dependent children (Proceedings of the Conference on the Care of Dependent Children, 1909). They asserted that the public should take responsibility not only for children who were potentially delinquent, but also for children who were simply unfortunate. The conference participants concluded that a solid home life was the basis for character development. They recommended that income supports be given to parents

of worthy character, suffering from temporary misfortune, and children of reasonably efficient and deserving mothers who are without the support of the normal breadwinner . . . such aid being given as may be necessary to maintain suitable homes . . . (p. 17).

Their recommendations set the precedent for the later Aid to Dependent Children programs. By 1935 Title V of the Social Security Act created Child Welfare Services and Aid to Dependent Children programs (now Aid to Families with Dependent Children) in every state.

In the 1930s and 1940s, as social service became a "profession," service agents moved out of the neighborhoods into centrally located bureaucracies. These agencies continued to deal with the same sorts of problems: meeting the needs of dependent children and adults, employment referrals, adjustment of probationers and parolees, placing the mentally disabled. With the rise in popularity of psychotherapy, professional expertise became valued; expert diagnosis and treatment of problems were demanded.

After World War II, delinquency became a major concern of social service professionals. Delinquency was linked to "multiproblem families," a small number (6–8 percent) of families who consumed over half the social services provided in urban areas. These problems brought case workers back to the neighborhood in intensive efforts to gain insight into delinquency and other social problems of the slum. The street worker of the 1950s developed into the "grass roots" organizer of the 1960s. Thus, the delivery of social services had two emphases: a vast bureaucracy of impersonal services whose delivery depended on needs determined by experts, and local outreach movements that emphasized community representation, control, and action. (For a more detailed presentation of this development, see Kahn, 1976.)

## The Safety Net

The notion that we have a social responsibility to meet the needs of the underprivileged has traditionally been paired with the idea that we can step in when we believe that a child is being improperly cared for. The traditional model of service delivery has been remedial, minimal, and corrective. If a family needs help to meet its physical needs, service agents may define the parent as inadequate to guide or socialize children. The state's responsibility to guard the welfare of children implies a right to judge parents' skills.

In the United States, many believe that autonomy and independence are signs of maturity and mental health, but that dependency is a sign of failure and illness in the individual. These standards are projected to the family as well. Thus, much of our service system seems based on the premise that parents are solely responsible for raising their children, and any problems that might develop result from insufficient parental guidance and caring. This view postulates the healthy, mature family, like the mature individual, as a self-sufficient, autonomous entity. It sees any manifestation of dependency, such as the use of problem-oriented human services, as an admission of failure or at least a sign of illness. This is especially true for the poor. Low-income families are still stigmatized by the antiquated philosophy of Social Darwinism; we are quick to label these parents as inadequate. However, current thinking about service delivery is shifting to focus on supporting family functions rather than correcting parental failure. One of the results of the "grass roots" efforts of the 1960s was the increasing emphasis on a supportive or collaborative role for professionals in working with families. This means taking a developmental perspective, identifying what families need in order to function successfully (Ford, 1974).

Kahn (1976; Kamerman & Kahn, 1976) has described a system of "personal social services" that has grown up beside the traditional case-work services for the needy. The personal social services include those supports all of us may need, regardless of income: support in socialization and development of children and adults through such programs as day care or family planning; counseling and guidance (including family problems, substance abuse, and other crises); community mental health programs such as self-help and support groups; programs guaranteeing basic life support to allow handicapped, elderly, or other incapacitated individuals to continue living in the community; and information, referral, and integration services. These services have blossomed in the past two or three decades, but they have not been well integrated with the large social-service system which focuses on case services for the needy. There is no doubt that these services are sought by all community members, not only those below a particular income level. Their expansion demonstrates that many people need and use the personal social services. However, there is much debate over whether the personal social services should be viewed as "public social utilities" to be provided to all citizens. The cost of doing so would be tremendous. Although some argue that families above a minimal income level should be able to purchase these services from the private sector, the uneven quality and availability of private services may make this unrealistic (Keniston, 1977). Kamerman and Kahn (1976) propose that we offer the personal social services to all, with clients' fees assessed on a sliding scale according to their ability to pay. Others, as we will see later in this chapter, are attempting to foster these services informally by promoting the informal helping networks that exist within communities.

We have discussed the historical development of the helping services as a result of political and philosophical influences. Now we can classify the contemporary domains of human services. These domains may be expressed in terms of five principles for promoting and maintaining the well-being of children and the integrity of families: 1) Public education is a right of all citizens; 2) Health care and sanitation are essential preventive interventions; 3) Housing is a basic right; 4) Full employment is a primary social and economic goal; 5) Some sort of financial and resource support should be provided to those who are deprived through misfortune. When coupled with formal and informal social supports (i.e., psychologically supportive and enhancing personal networks of friends, neighbors, relatives, and professionals), these domains make up a comprehensive range of human services.

## Issues in Human Service Delivery

We believe that optimizing the development of children and families is a valid goal of the human services. But what do we mean by "optimizing development," and how do we go about it? To answer this question, we must build upon the concepts of development, opportunity, and risk presented in earlier chapters.

We believe society can sponsor intervention to improve the lives of children because we believe that we have some ideas about how children grow and that we can specify some preferred outcomes for children. We believe that the joint concepts of risk and opportunity help us specify what children need and what they cannot tolerate.

### Developmental Influences

The human services have traditionally focused on negative influences. However, if we want to optimize development, we cannot ignore the events that present important enhancing experiences to children as they grow. We need to increase, if not ensure, the likelihood of experiencing these events. Optimization requires specification of our developmental goals for children. What are some of these goals?

1. That they develop a positive and accurate self-concept.
2. That they become socially and intellectually competent.
3. That they grow into adults capable of providing for their own material needs.
4. That they provide emotional support to others and receive it in return.
5. That they learn the skills necessary to meet the needs of *their* children and families.

Together, these goals provide a capsule description of healthy socialization to adulthood (Garbarino & Gilliam, 1980). In Chapter 3, we discussed some of the factors that can promote these outcomes. We also pointed out some characteristics of the child's ecology that detract from her or his ability to grow and thrive. We know a great deal about what is *bad* for children. Our knowledge of what specifically is *good* for children is more limited. This lack of knowledge may exist precisely because children are flexible and adaptable and can thrive in diverse settings. In all this, we must remember, however, that children also need challenges in order to grow and develop well. In our search for ways to protect children from harm, we must be sure we do not deprive them of the challenges that induce growth. As always, and in nearly all things, moderation is the key. The risk of negative outcomes for children in difficult situations is reduced if they have adequate social and personal resources (Rutter, 1979).

In planning, delivering, and evaluating the effects of human services, we can consider three influences on human development (Baltes & Danish, 1979). One set of influences comes from the typical, age-related experiences of most children. The quality and consistency of parental care during infancy, for example, have important effects on children. Entering school has major impact on most 5- or 6-year-olds.

A second set of influences may only affect children of a particular historical period. As we saw in Chapter 3, the Depression of the 1930s had great impact on children growing up during those years through its dramatic impact on family resources and stresses (Elder, 1974). World War II did also in terms of the father absence it produced (Elder, 1980). The more subtle effects of post-war affluence and suburbanization on the socialization of youth are another example (Wynne, 1977). These events affect large groups of individuals in similar ways. And, they may affect children of different ages in different ways.

A third category of developmental influence contains those events that are more individual and unusual; that is, they are not the common experiences of most children. These events, like historical influences, can be positive or negative. Some examples of negative events that have impact on the child's development include accident or illness, loss or incapacity of a parent, and loss of income through unemployment. Positive events include improvement in previously unhealthy circumstances and resolution of a family conflict. As we shall see shortly, both positive and negative events can present developmentally enhancing challenges if they occur in a supportive context.

We know that a buildup of stress factors in a child's life generally bodes ill for the child's development (Rutter, 1979). The risk to the child and to the parents is greater when illness, unemployment, separation, and conflict come together. Of course some families and individuals cope better than others. Indeed, skills for handling or coping with events are a primary resource in dealing with stress affecting family members (Burgess, Garbarino, & Gilstrap, in press). Overall, however, families and individuals can grow from dealing with stress if they experience it as a challenge. While the details of this idea are not worked out well in existing research, it seems that children and parents will experience stress as a challenge if their primary social and psychological resources are strong. Thus, as we saw in Chapter 3, couples with strong marriages pulled together and produced stronger families when hit with the income loss produced by the Depression. Weak marriages were associated with nonproductive psychological crises for family members. Likewise, hospitalized children need not suffer serious psychological disturbances if parents remain with them, even if more than one hospitalization is required (Rutter, 1979). In our efforts to protect and enhance development, we should be careful to concentrate on maintaining basic social and psychological resources and not inappropriately seek to insulate the child from growth-inducing challenges.

This message finds expression in the following words found taped to a wall at a summer camp some years ago:

Have you only learned lessons from those who admired you and were tender with
you and stood aside for you?
Have you not learned great lessons from those who reject you and brace themselves
against you or who treat you with contempt or dispute the passage with you?

Challenge within a larger context of support is a positive influence, particularly
if we take a life-course perspective. Jones (1965) and others have reported, for
example, that youths who experience the stress of being either an early maturing
female or a late maturing male in adolescence show signs of disruption during
adolescence but in adulthood demonstrate signs of greater sensitivity, insight,
flexibility, and humor.

Characteristics of the child contribute to his or her development. A positive,
happy, responsive temperament may encourage significant others (parents, siblings, teachers) in a child's life to be supportive. A negativisitic, irritable, or
apathetic temperament may alienate these same significant others. The child
may be more or less adept at coping with disadvantages, more or less vulnerable
to stress. These characteristics of the child are not always malleable. Our growing
understanding of the role of the abused child in eliciting his or her own abuse
demonstrates this (Kadushin & Martin, 1981). Besides abused children, some
premature infants and handicapped children also appear to have characteristics
that make them more difficult to care for. These characteristics can serve as
cues for identifying care givers who may need greater than average support in
order to care for their child.

## Family Effectiveness

Family and outside factors that influence the child's development have figured
prominently in this book. Where one system is weak, others may meet the
needs of a child for emotional support or for feelings of self-esteem. For instance,
a child whose family microsystem is not emotionally supportive may receive
positive feedback from teachers rather than from parents. This process of systems
compensating for one another is vital. However, in some instances, the family
or individual is not lacking resources but instead has inappropriate means of
coping or adapting. Consider the support system of a street corner gang that
rewards members for vandalism, the teaching of a boy who guides his younger
brother in the arts of shoplifting, or the coercive interactions of the families of
aggressive boys (Patterson, 1979). Research with coercive families has shown
that it is possible to replace coercive interactions with positive ones through
programs of modeling and feedback (Burgess, Anderson, & Schellenbach, 1980;
Patterson, 1979). The Homebuilders program, described later in this chapter,
provides another example of skill training (either to build lacking skills or
replace inappropriate interactive styles) as a form of intervention.

Even in the most negative circumstances, we can find ways to strengthen the supports that guide the child's development by meeting basic needs. Meeting these needs sometimes requires direct intervention to supply the family with resources. In the most unfortunate situations, it requires placing the child away from the family in an alternative environment, with the hope that services may pave the way for successfully reuniting the family at an early, opportune moment. But in most circumstances, our role should be indirect. After all, the family, not the social service system, provides the primary context for human development. The overwhelming majority of children grow up within the confines of a family (Bane, 1976). A healthy family meets its basic responsibility to bear and rear prosocial children successfully.

What are some of the ways in which families fulfill their obligations to society? In brief, an effective family is one that provides:

1. A stable setting for childbearing.
2. A stable setting for child rearing.
3. A setting that reinforces pro-social behavior and the development of competence and positive self-regard.
4. A setting that provides intimacy and sexual satisfaction.
5. A setting that serves as an economic unit—for consumption and income transfers (and for production to some extent).

These functions are rooted in the evolutionary history and contemporary purposes of families (Garbarino, 1981a). Three of these obligations focus on the child's development. We give the family primary responsibility for fostering the development of children, yet often we interfere with the family's ability to do so.

We believe that the notion that each family functions as a totally independent unit is in error. This notion exacts serious human costs, and we should reassess it. Specifically, the social isolation fostered within a privacy-seeking ideology can constrict the necessary functioning of kinship, neighborhood, and institutional feedback loops, rendering them inoperative (cf., Bronfenbrenner, 1975). Support systems function on the premise of exchange between members of both tangible (e.g., child care) and intangible (emotional support in a crisis) items. When individuals are hesitant to offer support, they are less likely to receive it (Unger & Powell, 1980). We are presently faced with the task of reducing the negative aspects of family privacy without incurring unacceptable costs to freedom and individuality. We are trying to have our cake and eat it too, some would say. One way to discover some strategies for accomplishing this difficult balancing act is to look at how other cultures have dealt with the problem.

Korbin (1977) reviewed cross-cultural studies of family life. She pinpointed several factors that enhance the abilities of parents to provide a supportive emotional environment for their children. The availability of multiple care givers relieves stress on the primary care giver and provides multiple role models for the child. Multiple care givers serve as sources for additional positive relationships in case the parents cannot adequately meet the child's emotional needs. The primary care giver needs not only occasional relief from caretaking responsibilities ("babysitting"), but access as well to career opportunities and support systems outside the home. Furthermore, care givers need information about child development and behavior that can be obtained through contact with others who have reared children. Thus, both child and parent can profit from having other adults intimately involved in child rearing. In our society, where families have become isolated from traditional primary groups, we need to promote new social networks that will provide child rearing relief and support. Studies of high- and low-risk neighborhoods (Garbarino & Sherman, 1980; see Chapter 7) may offer clues to the key factors we need to emphasize in building these networks.

This discussion may appear to have taken us far afield from the subject of the human services. But the first "service" we can provide to families is to recognize that optimizing the child's development is their responsibility. This does not mean that families have to do this alone. Supporting parental competence should be a major function of informal and formal support systems. This was and still is the motivation and rationale for Head Start and related programs.

## The Family as a Social Service

Moroney (1980) argues that the family is a social service. Taking this unorthodox view can shed some light on the proper relation of informal and formal helping. Families meet some of the basic needs of individuals and, thus, promote their well-being. Families also care for the majority of the dependent members of our society (children, the elderly, the handicapped). In the first part of this chapter, we described several dimensions of service delivery. Moroney has applied these dimensions to professionals' views of families. In some cases, the family is considered part of the client's problem. This is very common with the mentally ill. Families are perceived as obstructing the professional's ability to treat the patient and may even be accused of contributing to the cause of pathology. From another point of view, family members are only considered as a resource to the client. No thought is given to the needs of other family members. A third perspective casts the family as extenders of professionals. They carry out professionally supervised treatments. The final perspective characterizes the family as the primary care giver. Professionals exist to provide the services families need to carry out this role. From this perspective, families may need resources that professionals have, either to provide care to a member with special needs or to relieve stresses associated with the demands this care places on them.

If we view families as both responsible for rearing children and as *capable* of doing so when they have access to appropriate community supports, then the last perspective on service delivery is the one we must adopt. This means that our role as professionals is not primarily one of treating pathology but rather that of supporting, relieving, or assisting. These are not simply semantic differences; they reflect a basically different approach. They require that we redefine our professional roles away from a stance as "experts" toward one as "facilitators and intermediaries" (Moroney, 1980, p. 155). These differences have very real implications for where, when, and how we choose to intervene. In the next section, we will offer some examples of programs that are trying to support families.

Redefining our professional roles as supporters of families means that we have to reconsider not only what constitutes services to families but what the most appropriate targets of intervention are. Recognizing the family's role as the principal nurturer of children means that we take the focus off children and put the spotlight on *families*. Rather than focusing on developing institutions for housing handicapped children, for example, we should develop supports such as respite care, visiting homemakers, and parent-support groups for families with handicapped children. Many of these same services would reduce the necessity to remove most abused children completely from their homes. These services relieve some of the strains of constantly caring for a special child, and they allow the family to continue functioning as the child's primary care giver.

Most families do not encounter problems as severe as having a handicapped child. But most families can benefit from supportive interaction with other individuals and groups who offer support in times of crisis, when they need information or need simply to overcome everyday problems in living. While the network of personal social services described previously is one way of filling this need, fostering informal support systems is equally important.

There are other important targets of intervention beyond the family, however. Each of us is influenced by multiple levels of systems interacting with each other. Because of these interactions, an intervention on one level can have impact on all ecological levels. In addition, how we choose to intervene reflects where we think the problem lies and what our goals and values are. We have stressed family-centered interventions because the family provides the primary context for the development of young children, but one can intervene on the exo- and macrosystem levels as well.

Intervention in the exosystem means structuring community organizations to meet families' needs for support. It can mean making the world of work more consonant with the needs of parents. It can also mean enhancing the stability and cohesiveness of neighborhoods. These changes require structuring our social values and policies to reflect the value of children.

Supporting families in meeting the developmental needs of children is not something that can be done by entering the picture only when a problem arises.

If our goal is to facilitate the best possible outcome for children, we have to lay the groundwork beginning before the child is born by making available to families the skills and resources they will require. A preventive approach is indispensable to optimizing child development. A full range of formal and informal support services is necessary to minimize the negative effects of family disruption.

When you put it all together, you begin to see a picture of what the complete community looks like with respect to human services. It is worth our time to briefly outline such a community. It has a sustainable economic base. Its primary economy is stable and sound, not subject to wild fluctuations that disrupt families. It has a system of comprehensive maternal and child health care. It has a strong system for providing substitute and alternative child care for families who need it—including infant day care and after-school care for children of elementary school age. It has a strong network of home-based services to support families in crisis and prevent placement of children in foster care. It provides for all families an active health-visitor program that is available when children of working parents are home sick from school. It has employer policies that facilitate flex-time and part-time work arrangements. It has generic social service providers assigned on a permanent basis to specific geographic areas, such as neighborhoods, who are charged with working as consultants to social networks and natural helpers. It has a school system that emphasizes basic skills and social competence. It has a network of individuals within agencies willing and able to work with families having trouble with their offspring's adolescence. A secure and family-oriented runaway shelter system is also part of such a network.

Is this an unrealistic utopian dream? Or, is it a realistic conception of our goals in this world? We think it can be achieved if we incorporate some basic principles about the relationship between the formal and informal human services. The keys are integration and appropriate scale, fitting professional and lay helpers together in manageable tasks and organizations. Can we do it? Abe Kaplan is said to have remarked: "An optimist believes this is the best of all possible worlds. . . . . A pessimist is afraid he's right." We need to make a better world and, thus, disprove both the optimist and the pessimist.

## Programs that Support Children: Case Studies

In this section, we return to elaborate on the concepts presented in the first part of the chapter by describing several human-service programs. Rather than present a practice capsule in this chapter, we present several examples of programs. We begin with an example of how services should *not* be delivered. We begin with foster care. The foster child care system has been lambasted frequently; unfortunately it appears that most of the criticism is deserved. The goals of foster care and protective child services are often in direct conflict with the outcomes they achieve.

There are no accurate national statistics available on the number of children in foster care. A survey conducted by the Children's Defense Fund (see Research Capsule) estimated that in 1975 more than 448,000 children were in out-of-home placement supervised by social welfare agencies. A more conservative estimate using Department of Health, Education, and Welfare data from 1972 reported 319,848 children in foster care, 78 percent of these in foster family homes (Wiltse, 1978).

Foster care provides *temporary* care when the child cannot be cared for in his or her own home, even with supplementary or supportive services (Kadushin, 1980). This happens most often in cases of illness of the primary care giver, death of a parent, divorce or desertion, inadequate financial support, abuse or neglect, or child behavior problems or handicaps with which the parent cannot deal.

The goals of foster care have been delineated by the Child Welfare League of America in their *Standards for Foster Family Services* (Wiltse, 1978). These goals include:

1. To maintain and enhance parental functioning to the fullest extent.
2. To provide the type of care and services best suited to each child's needs and development.
3. To minimize and counteract hazards to the child's emotional health inherent in separation from his or her own family and the conditions leading to it.
4. To facilitate the child's becoming part of the foster family.
5. To make possible continuity of relationship by preventing unnecessary changes.
6. To protect the child from harmful experiences.
7. To bring about the child's ultimate return to his natural family . . . or . . . develop an alternative plan that provides a child with continuity of care (Wiltse, 1978, pp. 63–64).

Unfortunately, for many foster children, these goals are often not met. Goal No. 1 intends to prevent placement of the child in foster care, to begin with, yet once social service agencies intervene in family problems, separation of the child is often the only recourse of the agency. The serious multiple problems of families and the inadequate resources of agency personnel to cope with these problems make unlikely such creative options as relief day care, homemaker service, counseling, and environmental supports. This same lack of alternative solutions reduces the probability that children will return to their homes. The Children's Defense Fund survey (1978) found that 51 percent of foster children had been out of their homes for more than two years, and this exceeds the common sense meaning of "temporary."

On the other hand, there is little attempt to provide permanent placement for the child outside of his biological family, thereby violating Goals Nos. 2, 3, 4, 5, *and* 7. There is no reasonable vehicle for terminating parental custody, making permanent adoption impossible. Foster parents are admonished not to form attachments to their wards since the arrangement is temporary; in some places, policy demands that children be moved periodically so that these attachments do not form. The lack of continuity for children in foster care has led some (e.g., Goldstein, Freud, & Solnit, 1979; Wald, 1980) to advocate swift and permanent termination of legal custody of the biological parent as soon as the child is placed outside the home.

These problems have come to light in the past decade and reforms are being tested. As we will see with the description of the Lower East Side Family Union, foster care is one social service area in which prevention can have a high benefit-to-cost ratio. However, the legal issues and personal tragedies involved in foster care create many controversies that are not easily resolved.

In spite of the bleak national picture for foster care, there are some agencies that are striving to reduce the problems of extended placement and family dissolution. An excellent example is the Lower East Side Family Union (LESFU) in New York City. LESFU serves a mixed ethnic community, one of the poorest in the city. When LESFU was begun with a grant from a private foundation, area residents were characterized by a history of family disruption over generations. Social services were fragmented, with numerous agencies often offering duplicate services to families. Of particular concern to social welfare agencies was the very high rate of foster placement in the city with tremendous costs to the public ($280 million in 1977). The goals of LESFU are to support and strengthen families threatened with disruption and to avoid the intervention of the juvenile justice and child welfare systems, since contact with these agencies often leads to placement of children outside the home. The project seeks to place children within the community when placement is necessary.

LESFU acts as a coordinator of services by connecting clients with the agencies who will best meet their needs. After several meetings with family members, the Family Union workers draw up contracts stating the family's, agencies', and LESFU's responsibilities in meeting the family's goals. An example of this is provided by Dunu (1979). The case involved an alcoholic mother who had been illegally excluded from welfare. She was without housing for herself and her youngest child. Five other children were in foster care, and the youngest son needed regular medical care for sickle cell anemia. The agreements made involved the following:

1. She was to enroll in a treatment program for alcoholism.
2. She had to make permanent plans for her children in foster care.
3. She had to keep all appointments and cooperate with agencies.

4. The hospital agreed to schedule all appointments conveniently.
5. The foster care agency agreed to accept a temporary placement for the youngest child contingent on the mother's finding housing.
6. LESFU agreed to oversee and coordinate the efforts of all agencies involved in providing housing, health care, and welfare payments.

In addition to social workers, LESFU also employs a cadre of homemakers who teach home management, child care, and parenting skills. They can fill in during an emergency and may prevent the break up of a family. LESFU also has a community development team that deals with broader issues of housing, employment, and so on.

LESFU appears to be an effective, preventive program reducing family disruption. In 1977 it served 420 families, 193 of whom were at risk of family breakdowns. During that year only 11 of these families required foster placement. While the duration of foster placement in New York City averages six years, no LESFU child has been placed for more than 18 months. The economic savings are tremendous—the per-family cost of $1,500 a year is much less than it would cost to put the 1,000 or so children of these families in foster care. Foster care for the same children would cost $5,000 to $30,000 per child/year (Dunu, 1979; "New York City Agency Keeps Families Together," 1980).

Homebuilders (Haapala & Kinney, 1979) is another program that deals with families in crisis. The program is based on two assumptions: first, that no family is "hopeless," and second, that "families are trying, in their own homespun, beautiful, error-filled ways, to make things work" (Haapala & Kinney, 1979, p. 254).

Staff are trained in communication skills and behavior change techniques as well as therapeutic skills. They enter the home of a family in a time of crisis—when regular agencies have given up. Each team member represents the position of one family member in negotiations designed to air grievances and reach agreements over steps to a solution.

The families that Homebuilders typically serve are threatened with family disruption because of foster placement of the children or psychiatric placement of an adult. In the first three years of the program, 86 percent of the families served were still intact one year after intake.

The main purpose of Homebuilders is to enable family members to work together to solve problems. They accomplish this by serving as a "negotiating" team and by teaching family members skills that will enable them to resolve interpersonal conflicts peacefully. However, Homebuilders staff members also help to contact and coordinate the social services the family needs.

While both Homebuilders and LESFU aim to keep families together, they represent opposite poles on several of the dimensions of service delivery discussed earlier in the chapter. Homebuilders is a remedial program. In fact, Haapala and Kinney (1979) state that Homebuilders prefers to serve a family in crisis, since this family will be more receptive to new ideas and behaviors. While LESFU certainly encounters many families in crisis, its intent is to avoid this situation by coordinating the delivery of services before the family enters a crisis stage. LESFU tends to be more comprehensive in service orientation. Homebuilders, while coordinating all necessary services, focuses on interpersonal conflict resolution as a first step to dealing with more global family problems. Both programs adopt the collaborative or supportive model of professional service. Homebuilders is especially strong in this regard, stating that every family has the capacity to resolve its problems, if it has the required skills and resources.

The next program we will describe blends formal and informal support systems in an attempt to strengthen an already existing system of child-care support (in Portland, Oregon). The family day-care network described by Collins and her colleagues (Collins, 1979; Collins & Pancoast, 1976; Collins & Watson, 1976; Pancoast, 1980) has become a model for supporting networks of "natural helpers" in the community. A natural helper is someone who has many connections to others in the community. Many turn to her for advice because she is well-informed and knows who can do what and how to get it. They are often individuals who have the energy, time, or special interpersonal skills needed to help or to bring people together.

The program developed by Collins and her colleagues places the professional in a consulting and supporting role with the natural helper. In some cases, information provided by the natural helper can identify families in need of formal intervention. However, the emphasis is on giving the natural helper support in acting on her or his instincts to help. The process of locating and assisting natural helpers was described in the practice capsule in Chapter 7.

The network consultation model is the ultimate in the collaborative role for the professional. The target of the intervention is not a particular family, but a neighborhood or social network. By locating the strong links in the network—the natural helpers—and by strengthening their role, the network is strengthened. Collins and her colleagues have applied this model to several problems (e.g., discharged mental patients, child abuse). In the case of family day care, the goal was to develop a network of neighbors and friends who could provide informal child care along the lines of an extended family (Collins, 1979). Natural helpers were identified by inquiring around the community about who offered child care. People who had contact with children and with a wide range of community members (the school secretary, public health nurse, church staff) were asked, as well as working mothers (waitresses, grocery clerks). Once a list of several names was established, day-care neighbors (natural helpers with special knowledge of day-care resources) were contacted and recruited. The relationship between day-care neighbor and professional consultant was formed with the goal of ensuring the best possible care for children. The consultant and natural helper worked together to match families in need of child care with day-care providers who best served their needs. As the consultant-helper relationships became firmly established, other agencies and individuals turned to the day-care team for referrals and suggestions on successful delivery techniques.

Finally, we will briefly describe two programs that offer seemingly simple preventive solutions to potentially serious problems. A newspaper clipping in the Dayton, Ohio, *Daily News* ("Denver Apartment Block Pioneers 1-Parent Style," 1979) illustrates one form of service delivery to a highly stressed group. The Warren United Methodist Church owns the apartment building and it rents to single parents at subsidized rates. There is a day-care center in the building, and a full-time staff helps the residents obtain needed social services. Besides relieving the living problems many single parents face, the community provides healthy role models for children. One parent said, "It makes a difference [to the children] to know that, despite what they read or see on TV, a whole lot of families are living in one-parent families. . . . They learn you're not 'weird' because you don't have a father or you don't have a mother."

The last program we will review is one of many examples of support groups established informally to help families overcome stress or gain information related to a transient or permanent condition. Parents Without Partners, Alcoholics Anonymous, Childbirth Education Association parent groups, or groups for parents of a mentally retarded child, are all examples of support groups. These groups can fulfill several functions: mutual support, self-help therapy, education, or advocacy for supportive policies. The Widow to Widow Program is an exemplary self-help organization in which already widowed women contact new widows and offer support while these women establish their new roles. The program is sponsored by several community-service and religious organizations that lend credibility to the value of the first contact by the widow care givers. The care givers share experiences, listen to concerns, and help the recipients make new social contacts. As the recipients learn to live as widows, some become care givers themselves (Silverman, 1976).

In each of the programs described, formal support systems acted to create or enhance natural helping networks. These programs have two great advantages: they are cost-effective, and they avoid disrupting natural-support structures. They demand that professionals adopt a collaborative role in supporting family functions.

## Integrating Formal and Informal Supports

To support and protect families and professionals, we must lose ourselves in the social landscape, blend in with the human terrain, and become part of the natural social systems of families and communities. At present, far too much of what we call the human-service system sticks out above the natural social horizon or is out of harmony with the social scene it seeks to aid. What can we do to blend into the social landscape and, in so doing, find the power to do the good that we seek? We have a series of suggestions, all of which are deceptively simple. We say deceptively simple, because each requires diligent, intelligent, sensitive, and loving action by each of us who is committed to improving the quality of life for children. With this in mind, here are our thoughts on what we need to do.

## Recognizing the Limits of Professionalism

Recognize the limits of professional intervention. Just as our economy depends upon private initiative and hard work to keep it going, the bulk of human services are delivered to families by the "free enterprise system of helping"—by friends, neighbors, and relatives. We forget this, at our peril. At best, we will overlook a great potential resource. At worst, we will disrupt the bread-and-butter services to children that these informal support systems and natural helping networks provide. What does this imply for our behavior? Two things are paramount: consultation and advocacy.

## Consultation

Become consultants to informal family-support systems and natural-helping networks (Collins & Pancoast, 1976). One of the greatest obstacles is the idea that "we" need to help "them." We recall a conversation with a woman from Western Europe who had been through a program that combined nursing with social-work training. She now served families in a well-defined area of a city. We wondered if her clients thought of her as a social worker or as a nurse and so asked her, "When you are visiting a family, how do they refer to you?" (thinking this would reveal how the clients perceived her professional role). She looked a bit surprised and responded, "Why, they call me Elizabeth!" By becoming an accepted part of the social environment, she had become a powerful consultant to the informal family support systems and natural helping networks. We believe the most pressing task we face is to strive for this kind of relationship.

## Advocacy

Become advocates of the parent–child relationship in the community power structure. This means seeking funds for formal services, of course, but it means much more. It means getting hospitals to adopt "family-centered" childbirth as the norm. It means making sure that the needs of children for safe, convenient places to play have a high priority with zoning boards and other government agencies. It means ensuring that residential development fosters and maintains the integrity of neighborhoods rather than destroying it. It means getting public officials to become models of how to serve the interests of children. All these things help provide a climate where caring for families is a "natural" phenomenon. We use the term "child-centered" to mean a community where the obstacles to being an effective family are removed and are replaced by a web of forces encouraging parents and children to become effective families. Such a community is the necessary foundation for specific efforts to help individual children and parents become better family members.

## Using Existing Social Resources

To help children and parents become better families we need intervention programs that *use the target's own strength to make things happen*. To do this we must avoid grand schemes, elaborate projects, expensive technology, and artificial programs, in favor of "appropriate social technology" (Rogers & Shoemaker, 1971). We need to develop and advance efforts that are *effective* (much of what we do is not of proven effectiveness); *inexpensive* (the high-cost demonstration program provides useful information, but we also need programs that can be done on a shoestring budget—i.e., in the *real* world); *locally relevant* (local responsibility is an essential complement to natural leadership, for we are a nation of thousands of communities when it comes to children and families); *flexible* (we need models that can be readily adapted to local conditions—be they Indian reservations or immigrant ghettos); *sustainable* (programs should not require or consume scarce resources, such as expert professional time or special funding); *simple* (they must be described in sufficient detail to be replicated by an "ordinary" user—you cannot empower people to help themselves if they cannot understand the directions on the label); *compatible* (whatever we propose must build upon—even if *away* from—existing values, past experiences and presently perceived needs). All this is a tall order, but it is the only order that will do the job. It does require a social policy climate that supports and encourages families, however. We deal with the nature and character of such a climate in our next chapter.

## RESEARCH CAPSULE

The Children's Defense Fund (CDF) is a national advocacy organization seeking to develop policies and practices that are beneficial to children. One arm of the organization conducts research on practices and programs that potentially cause mistreatment of children. One such study was conducted in 1975, when CDF looked at the status of foster care in this country. They considered:

1. Public and family responsibility for children.
2. How the child's need for a family is supported or ignored.
3. What practices and policies may be harmful to children.
4. How to define governmental responsibility to children in foster care.
5. What can be done to improve the situation of children in foster care, including information, programs, legislation, and advocacy.

(Researchers conduct surveys to discover the current incidence or distribution of a variable. Surveys can also assess the relationships between variables, as in surveys to measure party affiliation and voting patterns. The survey conducted by CDF is of the first type.)

To collect the data, CDF surveyed the status of children in foster care in 140 counties throughout the country. They studied seven representative states in depth. Finally, they surveyed all 50 states to learn about placement of children in institutions outside their home states.

Large-scale surveys, such as those done at the national level, cannot reach all members of a population because of the costs involved. Instead, sophisticated techniques for selecting representative samples from the population of interest have been developed. For instance, in the CDF study, since it was not possible to survey all counties and states in the United States, the sample selected represented a range in population, geographic location, and urban/rural balance. Such samples, if chosen correctly (by using the appropriate criteria for selection) can provide very accurate information that can be generalized to the entire population.

Here are some of CDF's findings:

1. Placement of children outside the home usually occurs without consideration of less drastic alternatives such as day-care or homemaker services. These alternative supports do not exist in most communities.
2. Placement with a relative is rarely considered, and many states do not pay for foster care with a relative.
3. Only one-half of the counties surveyed specifically encouraged visitation by parents. CDF estimated that 10,000 children are placed out of their own states, making regular contact with their families virtually impossible.
4. 52 percent of children in foster care had been out of their homes for two years or more; 18 percent had changed placements more than three times.
5. Monitoring of children in out-of-home placements is very poor. In the counties surveyed, welfare officials could not give information for one-half of the children on their ages or how long they had been in foster care.
6. Legal statutes are poorly defined; none of the seven states required reunification efforts. Only South Carolina included efforts to ensure permanent placement for a child, and no state gave priority to relatives or foster parents as potential adoptive parents.

In analyzing the results of the study, we have to keep in mind that CDF is an advocacy organization with a particular point of view to put forward. Still, this study is significant because of its interstate comparisons. Other attempts to make comparisons using the data collected by each state have been difficult to interpret because each state uses different data-collection techniques. Because record keeping in many states has been poor, the CDF study is one of the first to provide documentation for the criticisms of foster care in the United States. Of course, the quality of the foster-care system varies from place to place, but CDF's findings paint a grim overall picture.

CDF advocates the development of alternative services to avoid placement of children outside their families. However, there has been very little research conducted on the effectiveness of these programs. Programs such as LESFU and Homebuilders (see text) are a step in this direction. LESFU especially seems to provide a model for effective services that can avoid family disruption.

# FOR FURTHER READING

Caplan, G., & Killilea, M. (Eds.) *Support systems and mutual help.* New York: Grune and Stratton, 1976, 325 pp.

This volume provides a number of examples of the development of informal mutual-help groups as well as presentations of the theoretical concepts behind this form of intervention. Going beyond social work, the contributors to the book represent fields as diverse as literature, administration, and religion.

Garbarino, J., Stocking, S. H., & Associates. *Protecting children from abuse and neglect.* San Francisco: Jossey-Bass, 1980, 222 pp.

This book, oriented to practitioners and policymakers, discusses ways in which family support systems can be strengthened in order to prevent child abuse and neglect. It extends the mutual-help framework offered by Caplan and his colleagues by incorporating the ecological systems perspective. Contributions include discussions of the neighborhood, preventive services, and integration of formal and informal supports.

Goldstein, J., Freud, A., & Solnit, A. *Beyond the best interests of the child.* New York: The Free Press, 1973, 203 pp. and *Before the best interests of the child.* New York: The Free Press, 1979, 288 pp.

These two volumes represent a proposal by a lawyer and two psychoanalysts for the modification of our current child-custody system to support the needs of children. They apply psychoanalytic theory to child-custody decisions and advocate making permanent placement for children as soon as possible. Their view of the state's active role in decision making contrasts with Moroney's and has been heavily debated. The first volume lays out general principles; the second develops their implications for such situations as divorce, neglect, and foster care.

Kamerman, S., & Kahn, A. *Social services in the United States: Policies and programs.* Philadelphia: Temple University Press, 1976, 561 pp.

This is one of the most complete resources available on social services in the United States. It reviews the "state of the art" of several different services as well as pinpointing problems of service delivery. Chapters on child care, children's institutions, services for the aged, and family planning include discussions of the legislative framework for service provision, program descriptions, and research and evaluation. The final chapter develops the concept of the "personal social services."

Levine, M., & Levine, A. *A social history of the helping services.* New York: Appleton-Century-Crofts, 1970, 315 pp.

Levine and Levine review the development of community social services with special attention to the political and ideological influences which have led to reform. In chapters discussing the settlement-house movement and the development of the juvenile judicial system, among other topics, they portray the individuals involved in the development of services as well as the political and social events that influenced these developments. A very stimulating and thought-provoking book.

Moroney, R. M. *The family and the state: Considerations for social policy.* New York: Longman, 1976, and *Families, social services, and social policy: The issue of shared responsibility.* U.S. Department of Health and Human Services, DHHS Publ. No. (ADM) 80-846, 1980 (monograph), 214 pp.

Pointing out that social programs often act to supplant rather than support the family as primary care giver for its dependent members, Moroney offers a model of shared responsibility to guide family–state relationships in this area. He examines many of our cultural assumptions regarding the responsibilities families fulfill for the state and, based on a study in Britain, also examines whether social policies support family's functions or supplant them with formal social services. The monograph is based on the book and focuses specifically on these policies as they apply to handicapped children and the elderly.

# QUESTIONS FOR THOUGHT

1. Make up an ideal program for one of the following problems:
   - child abuse
   - juvenile delinquency
   - fetal alcohol syndrome (see Chapter 5)

   Mention some of the goals of the program, who the target population would be, and types of services provided. What might be some of the problems you would encounter in implementing your program?

2. In the program you designed for question No. 1, did you incorporate informal support systems? Why or why not? If you did not do so previously, redesign the program to incorporate informal support systems.

3. The ecological approach to human development suggests that prevention cannot be achieved only at the individual level. Describe a program designed to reduce stress in single parent families that takes into account the ecology of the family. How would you need to intervene on each ecosystem level?

4. One dimension of service delivery described in this chapter reflected the role of the professional. At one extreme, we find the corrective approach in which the professional is an expert who "fixes" the problem. At the other extreme is the collaborator who supports the client by providing the skills or information necessary for the client to solve the problem. Contrast these two approaches, applying them to the problem of unmanageable child behavior. What might be the parent's role in each approach?

5. Moroney called the family a "social service." What did he mean by this? Give an example of a service provided by an agency that could be provided by a family with appropriate supports. Examine the program you designed in questions Nos. 1 and 2. Are there services offered by agencies in your program that the family could assume? Revise your program to incorporate these changes.

6. The program examples offered in this chapter illustrated ways in which formal and informal support systems can work together. Give two advantages of developing informal social support networks as opposed to formal services as an approach to intervention. Name two instances in which formal services would be more appropriate than informal.

# Chapter 9

All systems of society must operate effectively together to make it possible for children to develop adequately. . . . . All systems of society must operate together effectively if families are to establish and maintain a climate that supports the continuing growth and development of both children and adults . . . What is needed is better policy-making that includes awareness of the needs of families as dynamic inter-action units linked to all the social systems. These more powerful systems need to protect and support the family as a complex unit rather than demanding that families be strained and fragmented in an attempt to cope with an inadequately organized and only partially adequate society. These systems, moreover, . . . need to be updated, modified, and coordinated through enlightened public policies, planning, and programs if society and its families are to weather the stresses of the years ahead . . . And persons concerned about the well-being of society and its families need to add to their skills some knowledge of the public social policy processes so that they can affect the political and other governmental processes that both create public policy and put it into operation.

(Chilman, 1973, p. 578.)

In Chapter 9, we explore many "systems of society" that influence the well-being of children and their families and some of the diverse factors that direct policy decision making and successful program implementation. As policy practitioners, we need to know about cultural values, political climates, and economics. We need a feel for school systems and service agencies, as well as student and client characteristics. It is most important to realize that "policy" is not some amorphous entity engineered by unknowns in distant places. Policy is everybody's business and everyone has an impact by way of his or her everyday actions. We will supply a conceptual primer and some practical tools for participating more actively in the policy arena.

# Social Policy, Children, and Their Families

We consider ourselves a nation that cares about children and their families. Yet policies and practices at every level in our society seem to reveal subtle biases against families. At the federal level, for example, we find a "marriage tax" that makes it more costly for people to live as married couples than to cohabit out of wedlock; a welfare system that contributes to family dissolution (Bahr, 1979); and a military system characterized by high rates of marital dissolution, child and spouse abuse, and alcoholism among its members and their families. Is our government antifamily? Is it antichild? With the federal government playing such a large role in shaping the social environment for children and families, we need to know.

Practices that undermine our country's families and children are not restricted to the federal government, of course. For instance, the adversarial nature of our courts and legal system in divorce proceedings maximizes the family-disrupting issues at hand, rather than negotiating ways to protect the family's integrity (Spanier & Anderson, 1979). Custody suits are well-known for pitting parent against parent and "her" family against "his" family, with the fate of the child decided by outsiders. The award-winning film *Kramer vs. Kramer* made this clear to the public as nothing else had before. Is American family law antifamily?

What about agencies of local government? Changes in zoning ordinances have caused tight-knit neighborhoods to dissolve by disrupting the traditional patterns of residential and commercial balance that provided stability. Neighborhood redevelopment programs have left people strangers on their own blocks. School boards have decided to close down smaller, more personalized neighborhood schools in favor of larger schools that seem more cost-efficient. Can it be that the boards and commissions of our local governments are antifamily and antichild?

What about the private sector? Corporate policies that require executives and middle managers to relocate in order to advance into desired positions are disruptive of all-important family support networks. Furthermore, these new positions often increase already long working hours, shorten weekends and vacations, and make travel more frequent for persons already too often away from their families. Blue-collar workers face their own set of dilemmas. Mandatory overtime, swing-shift and split-shift hours, and a clock-in/clock-out (hourly as opposed to salaried) pay standard limit this group's time with spouses and children. These practices are doubly stressful for single parents who must choose between income and doctor's appointments, school conferences, and little league games. Are business and industry also participating in a nationwide effort to disrupt the lives of children and their families?

Consider the policies and practices of our human service agencies. Rather than working to restore children to their families, foster-care agencies often act to prevent their reunion (Children's Defense Fund, 1978). Child protective services may interfere in parent–child relations in an arbitrary manner because they do not understand or accept ethnic and cultural traditions that differ from their own or because of social class bias (Katz, 1971). Some local agencies administering the Aid to Families with Dependent Children program use criteria in making decisions about food, clothing, and housing that disrupt the informal social networks that are so vital to the poor (deLone, 1979). Could our human service agencies be antifamily, too?

## Is Our Society Antifamily?

Is ours a culture and a nation that is at its roots antifamily and antichild? Our answer is NO; it is not. But the policies and practices cited above, and many others besides, make it more difficult for families to stay together, to take care of their members, and to build satisfying lives that contribute to a satisfying society. These policies limit access to economic resources and social supports. They reduce the range of choices available to family members, and limit their freedom to control their own lives and the development of their children. They displace the family as the unit with primary responsibility for the destiny of children and their parents. These policies and practices take their toll on our families and our children.

We do not believe that our country, governments, courts, businesses, industries, and human service agencies have instituted policies deliberately to undermine family unity and effectiveness. The policies and practices of these institutions certainly were not *intended* to have family-threatening effects. Their purpose was to address specific problems, often seeming to be quite unrelated to families, with effective and cost-efficient solutions. In most cases, in fact, the potential family impact was not even considered when the policy decisions were enacted. And therein lies the problem. *In most instances, the potential impact of proposed actions or policies on families was not even considered* (Johnson, 1978).

We think that the impact of social policies and practices on families should always be a primary consideration for this nation's institutions and decision makers. Creating and maintaining a sociocultural climate that actively supports children and their families requires purposeful, informed, and persistent efforts by many people at all levels of decision making in our society. We all can be part of that process, each in our own way.

Our purpose in this chapter is not to create social policy or political action experts. Rather, our intention here is to increase appreciation for the policy arena, increase consciousness about the effect of policies on both personal life and professional endeavors, and enhance the savvy necessary for making a positive impact on the social environment of children and families by affecting social policies. We intend to do this by:

1. Demonstrating how powerful policy can be in shaping the day-to-day lives of both professionals and family members.
2. Heightening sensitivity to implicit values and assumptions about families and children that are reflected in policy decisions.
3. Increasing awareness of the diversity of social policies that affect families.
4. Identifying and expanding on the policy implications of some child-centered practices discussed in earlier chapters.
5. Increasing awareness of how much, and in how many ways, individuals who make a personal commitment to the well-being of children and their families can affect family-related social policies.

To do this, we will utilize Bronfenbrenner's ecological model as an organizing framework. In Chapters 2 and 3 we used this perspective to discuss risk and opportunity. This time we will employ it to describe both the multiple sources of child- and family-related policies and the multiple points of impact that are of concern to children and families. First, however, we need to clarify what we mean by "policy" and to present the ideas and concepts that figure prominently in the discussion that follows.

# What Is Policy?

For our purposes, a policy is a statement or a set of statements intended to guide decisions, activities, or efforts that generally describe either desired (or undesired) outcomes and/or desired (or undesired) methods of achieving them. We should point out some implications of this definition. Policies can address either the ends of an endeavor ("It is our policy to see that every child gets an adequate education") or the means that are used ("Parents will be fully involved in the development of educational plans for their learning-disabled child"). In describing ends, policies can be either positive ("95 percent of all children will be immunized") or negative, expressing something bad to be avoided ("Vandalism in the neighborhood will not be allowed to rise above 1980 levels"). In discussing means, policies can either *pre*scribe what must be done ("Expectant couples must be told of their option for a family-centered birth experience") or *pro*scribe what must not be done ("Caseworkers may not ask personal questions that do not pertain directly to the welfare of the child"). Finally, policies—as we are referring to them—are explicit and deliberately chosen and bear some relation to institutional power and authority.

Policies, then, are principles that guide activities. They are more than personal opinion, although they may flow from the personal opinions of decision makers. They operate in every realm of society and vary widely in their specificity, from agreements on higher-order values ("We affirm a national policy of doing good for children") to specific policies that govern administrative practices ("It is our policy not to allow children under 12 years of age beyond the front desk"), internal family policies ("No one eats until Mom is served"), personal policies adopted in everyday life ("I make it a policy to offer my professional services at no charge to those who cannot afford to pay for them"), and to every point in between. Policies come in many forms and under many labels, including cultural norms, laws, regulations, judicial decisions, executive orders, administrative practices, and tradition ("We've always done it this way"). Policies also affect every level of society and every system in the social ecology of the child.

We find policies important to children and their families in the private sector (business and industry) as well as in the public sector (government) and at the neighborhood and community levels as well as at the state and national levels. These include economic, health, employment, housing, banking, transportation, consumer protection, environmental regulation, criminal justice, recreation, and military policies, to name but a few (National Academy of Sciences, 1976). "Social policy" is a broader term encompassing everything from a cultural consensus to a particular business policy. "Public policy," on the other hand, typically refers to social policies that are enacted by government agencies. Public policies are enforceable by the police and judicial powers of the state.

Having exposed the pervasiveness and many guises of policy, we now move on to a systematic discussion of social policies affecting children and their families. From our perspective, social policies are part of the ecology of child development. They arise from—and are shaped by—systems at each level of the family's social ecology, and they exert influence on the multiple systems that surround the developing child. In the next section of this chapter, we outline the role of ideological, cultural, and institutional macrosystems in providing the values and norms that shape policy. Following that, we discuss children and their microsystems and mesosystems as intended targets of many social policies and as unintended targets of many others. In the final section of this ecological view of child- and family-related social policies, we consider the broad spectrum of exosystems where cultural values translate into social policies and then are implemented, ultimately to affect the micro- and mesosystems of children.

## Ideological, Cultural, and Institutional Roots of Policy: The Macrosystem

Social policies are rooted in the macrosystem. Notions of desired and undesired ends, acceptable and unacceptable means, and of who has responsibility and priority flow from the shared belief systems of a society. These belief systems are the blueprints of a society—its rules and general game plan—both a source and a reflection of its cultural consensus on "the way things should be." From these systems arise the policies and other mechanisms by which a culture enforces and reinforces its fundamental ideology. It is these shared beliefs and assumptions and the mechanisms enforcing them that give consistency to the aims and actions of the many systems within a culture and distinguish cultures with differing ideological roots. That these beliefs and assumptions often are implicit rather than explicit does not make them any less influential. In fact, implicit, or unstated assumptions, may be some of the most influential. Child development specialist Laura Dittmann said it well:

> Although these cultural assumptions are used as guiding principles because they have always been a part of our daily lives, we may not recognize our belief in them because they may not have been put into words. One such assumption is that hard work produces success. Another is that successful people are good people (and, by implication, that those who fail are weak or of doubtful moral fiber). Probably most of us believe that the rights of the individual supersede those of the state, except in times of war. Many other unspoken beliefs of this nature not only determine what we can accept or endorse on each of the other levels, but also influence our leaders and spokesmen (Dittmann, 1979, p. 196).

The first part of this section presents some central ideological and value issues that have important implications for American families. The second part addresses societal institutions that are organized around major cultural values. Following that, we discuss some of the implications of the United States' pluralistic culture for family-related social policies and also the relationship of some current family-related social policies to our ideology of pluralism.

## Ideological Systems and Family-Related Values

Some cultural values pertain directly to the family. One of the important ideological issues for any culture, for example, is the fundamental relationship between the individual family and the larger society. Are families the creation of the state or is the state the creation of families? People who assume that the answer is self-evident—in either direction—may not be sensitive to the assumptions they carry with them. Like the fish who was asked to describe water and could not because he had nothing with which to compare it, these people need to look at the alternatives.

The Soviet Union views the family as an entity defined by the state and designed to serve the needs of the state (Makarenko, 1954). Children in a Soviet family are held in trust for society; parenthood is the job of correctly preparing citizens who will serve the state. The Soviet government seeks to dictate expected socialization and child-rearing practices in the form of a "regime" for child rearing (Bronfenbrenner, 1970). China similarly translates its concern for children and their families into totalitarian control of social relations (Kessen, 1975). In contrast, United States ideology holds that power and control reside initially with individuals, and hence with families, and that families create the state's authority so it may employ collective resources to achieve goals that families desire but cannot achieve by acting individually.

Another of our culture's strong family-first values holds that the family is a private matter and not an appropriate arena for public intervention, unless the circumstances are so critical that they warrant violating the privacy norm. On the one hand, this firm belief in family privacy offers important protection for families and is consonant with the idea that the state is responsible to families rather than the other way around. On the other hand, as we have seen in earlier chapters, allegiance to privacy as a value may keep critical conditions from being identified in some families. Furthermore, delaying intervention until a serious disruption occurs reduces significantly both the range of feasible options and the chances of their being effective.

Returning to the statement by Laura Dittmann, we find yet another set of beliefs with important implications for families. If one assumes that hard work produces success and those who fail are weak or otherwise undeserving, it then follows that being poor or troubled means being inadequate, and that a family's problems reflect that family's deficiencies. The assumption that troubled families are inadequate often accompanies the assumption that troubled families are not able to make good choices for themselves. We see this attitude frequently in policies that take the right of choice making away from a family and give it to some "wise" outsider, such as a social caseworker or family court investigator.

In addition to cultural values *about* the family, there are cultural beliefs transmitted *through* the family. Families are expected to instill in their offspring the culture's fundamental values concerning religion, education, citizenship, personal conduct, and many other areas. As we pointed out in Chapter 4, some people say that the role of families in some of these areas is decreasing, that it is being usurped by other systems in society. Others say that families are being overloaded with responsibilities that other social systems have cast off during the rapid growth of our society. Unfortunately, both groups may be correct. Society is placing increasing demands on families at the very time that formerly supportive social systems may be weakening or receding.

There also are many cultural values pertaining to nonfamily issues that have repercussions for families. Significant among these is the American commitment to the individual. This commitment undergirds our many safeguards on individual rights and liberties, and the protection guaranteed to individuals has frequently extended to their families as well. However, this focus on the individual at times operates at the expense of families. Attending only to the handicapped child and not to the entire family, for example, leads to policies that encourage institutionalization rather than home care with appropriate supports for the family. Focusing on just the juvenile offender results in intervention strategies almost certain to ignore the family crisis that may have precipitated the offense.

A final ideological issue relevant to American families is the accommodation of interdependence in a society that values independence. Extension of this insistence on independence from the individual level to the family sphere has produced the image of the family as a self-sustaining unit that is expected to take care of itself and succeed or fail on its own. This expectation of self-sufficiency, like other macrosystem values we have discussed, becomes evident in social policy and practice. The goal of independence, however, ignores the many direct and critical ties between the family and its social ecology. These ties affect the family's supplies of economic and social resources and the range of options available in the environment. They thereby affect the family's ability to attain self-sufficiency and to carry out its other tasks effectively. The *goal* of independence, in other words, ignores the *fact* of interdependence—the mutual dependency of American families and the social systems of their environment.

A cross-cultural perspective shows us that some cultures have positive conceptions of interdependence and place high value on people's reliance upon one another. In Japan, a major goal of psychotherapy is to restore the positive experience of interdependence. Other cultures, such as in Denmark (Wagner, 1978) and Sweden (Myrdal, 1968), have established family policies that explicitly recognize the notion of group interdependence. They emphasize the concept that "we're all in this together," while we seem to say "every man (woman and child) for himself!"

## Cultural Norms and Institutional Systems

Societal values and ideologies translate into cultural norms and institutions. A social "institution" is a system of roles and practices structured in accordance with a cluster of related values. In fact, a good way to identify or discover what is valued by a culture is to examine its institutions and what is considered normal behavior. A societal institution includes mechanisms for regulating behavior with the intention of assuring that roles and practices in the society continue to adhere to fundamental cultural values (Kenkel, 1960). Institutions, thus, are comprised of organizing ideologies, the normative behavior prescribed by such ideologies, and regulatory mechanisms for producing compliance. In most cultures, value clusters related to government, law, education, the family, and other social matters are institutionalized through norms and sanctions and are important macrosystem influences in the ecology of human development. These cultural institutions set the boundaries and rules within which many specific exosystems operate.

The institution of "the family" in the United States is like other institutions. At its core is a cluster of shared values about what families should and should not be and do, and norms about expected roles and actions that are derived from those values. Mechanisms for ensuring that actual practice corresponds to societal values and norms include family law and the family court system, and the informal but potent influence of social pressure exerted by neighbors, kin, and friends. Underlying values, prescribed norms, and regulating mechanisms pertaining to "the family" all have undergone gradual adjustments to adapt to changing historical, economic, and social circumstances. Divorce is no longer anathema to the family institution in this country—for most subgroups, at least. Active parenting is becoming an expected part of fatherhood as well as motherhood. Laws governing child custody are changing to reflect shared parental responsibility and involvement.

As we saw in Chapter 4, it is important to distinguish between the family institution, which is an abstraction, and any particular family or collection of families, which is not an abstraction at all but a group of very real people. While the institution may be quite influential in shaping the actions of individual families, the collective decisions of individual families, in turn, shape the characteristics of the family institution. "The American family" is getting smaller, for instance, because thousands of individual couples have opted for a family size that is, on the average, smaller than the average family size chosen by their parents. Social change proceeds through the collective actions of individuals, even when it is in response to macrosystem forces such as technological change.

The choice to have fewer children, while it does not conform to the cultural norms of earlier generations, in no way reflects disloyalty to the basic institution of the family (Blake, 1979). Neither, necessarily, does a choice that does not subscribe to current normative expectations. "The mother of an illegitimate child, for example, may agree with other Americans that children should be born and reared within a family. A bachelor may accept the notion of marriage as a basic societal good" (Kenkel, 1960, p. 192). In fact, the strong cultural loyalty to the family institution in this country probably makes it more able to accommodate a variety of family differences than if cultural commitment were weak and any stress threatened its collapse.

There are, then, two active sides to the interaction between families and the family institution, each influencing the other. Which side of the interaction is given primacy is in itself an important ideological issue for any society. It determines, for instance, how people evaluate a particular family being different from the culture's norm. If priority is given to the institution, if adherence is valued over individualism, if the family is the creation of the state, then the family will be labeled "deviant," and social mechanisms will work to eliminate the aberration. On the other hand, if primacy is given to the individual family, if we value family autonomy over social uniformity, if the state is the creation of the family, then we will see the family as "variant"—different, but not necessarily less accepted—and social mechanisms will adapt to the family rather than requiring that the family adapt to them. This is a fundamental aspect of pluralism.

## Pluralism in the Macrosystem: Toward an Appreciation of Cultural Diversity

Discussions of "the family institution" often give the impression that there is a single set of culturally endorsed norms regulating family form and function in this country. Many cultures, such as the Japanese, where people are generally homogeneous with respect to ethnic background, religion, social history, and cultural heritage, and also those cultures with totalitarian forms of government, do tend to have monolithic family institutions. America, however, is a culture of cultures, and little is more characteristic of Americans than their diversity.

Saul Alinsky, who described himself as an American Radical, opened his book *Reveille for Radicals* with a powerful description of the diversity of Americans. He described their geography as being "from Back Bay Boston to the Bottoms of Kansas City . . . to the sharecroppers of Arkansas," their religion as including "followers of all the major religions on the face of the earth," their origins as being ". . . the people of the world. They have come from all corners of the earth." "The people of America are . . . creating a new bridge of mankind *in between* the past of narrow nationalistic chauvinism and the horizon of a new mankind—a people of the world. Their face is the face of the future" (Alinsky, 1969, p. 7).

That our people come from so many places means that there is literally a world of variation in the values and norms active in the American culture. And probably nowhere is that accepted variation of beliefs and practices, that American pluralism, reflected more clearly or more significantly than in the families of America. "The American family" is, in fact, a collection of families that are as remarkable for their diversity as they are for the intensity of the loyalty they inspire. To evaluate all families against the unitary norms of any one culture is both to miss the richness and strength represented in this variety and to expect individual families to adapt their own lives to patterns that may not be adaptive for them—that is, to give the institution primacy over the individuality of families.

Our cultural respect for pluralism in family life is highly compatible with other fundamental values in our culture, such as independence, freedom of choice, and assured rights for minorities. "The concept of pluralism suggests that people know what they want and what they need. It contrasts with the principle that someone else knows best" (Demone, 1978, p. 17). "Pluralism rests on the conservative ideal of toleration, of a policy of live and let live, that may come to characterize the pluralistic society in which no group is powerful enough to prevail" (Livingston & Thompson, 1971, pp. 126–127).

Pluralism in the American family institution is a fact, and respect for pluralism is an American value. Pluralism, in other words, is a macrosystem characteristic in the ecology of human development in this country. For our children, it is a characteristic that offers much opportunity. It means that society should protect them and their parents from being labeled "deviant" or "weak" because of cultural differences. It offers those who provide child and family services an opportunity to build on unique cultural strengths for more effective service delivery. And, it provides our children with the chance to encounter and develop an appreciation for the diversity and adaptability that characterize the human family.

Unfortunately, when the values of our culture's macrosystem are translated into the practices of various exosystems, this respect for cultural pluralism frequently gets lost. Policies, regulations, court decisions, and other exosystem actions are based on various assumptions about how families "ought" to be. If these assumptions are unitary ("families should be *this* way") rather than pluralistic ("families can be *many* ways"), then the effect of these policies and other exosystem decisions will probably be not to help families but to punish diversity. And *that* is un-American.

## Social Policies and Children

The previous section looked at the ideological and institutional roots of social policies related to children and at the implications of these macrosystem factors for the way our culture regards its families. If the macrosystem furnishes the ideological roots of policy, the exosystems bring policies into being. We are concerned with social policies because they affect, in important ways, the quality of the child's social ecology and the ability of those who care for children to meet the children's essential developmental needs. To be sure that we do not lose sight of our central concern, we begin this section with a brief review of the fundamental needs of children. We then focus on three groups of exosystems responsible for social policies affecting children and discuss the impact of various policies on the child's social ecology.

## The Issue is Children

It is a common assumption that the arena of child-related social policies is limited to policies dealing directly with children and their families. The ecological framework used throughout this text, however, reminds us that children are affected by a large number of forces in their environments. Considering the direct ways in which social policies affect children and their families is a start, but it is not enough. We also must consider the impact of policy on schools, on neighborhoods, on other of the child's microsystems, on important mesosystems that incorporate those microsystems, and on exosystems that the child never encounters directly but that have weighty influence on the child's growth and development. When guided by an ecological perspective, we are aware of the importance of considering not only the effects of social policies targeted directly at children (e.g., immunization laws) but also the indirect effects that ripple out from efforts aimed at targets other than children and families, such as highway systems, farm subsidies, and milk price supports. We see that social policies affecting children encompass an enormous range of social and economic issues. These forces do much to maximize or undermine the sociocultural opportunities available to children and to minimize or compound sociocultural risks to child development.

Our ecological perspective thus sends us in many directions to search for sources and impacts of government- and private-sector policies. The focus of our concern, however, is children and how social policies of all types respond to their essential needs. Throughout this book we have discussed various expressions of children's needs for physical, emotional, and social nurturance assured by enduring, positive, and reciprocal relationships with a developmentally appropriate number of adults in different roles. These needs are either met or not met by the microsystems of childhood. If the composition and activities of a child's microsystems are characterized by pro-child qualities, then opportunities for optimal growth and development are present. If microsystems are socially or economically impoverished so that these needs cannot be met adequately, then the child is at risk and development is threatened.

The single most important microenvironment for children is their families. If the policies that guide actions by both public and private endeavors are to be truly and actively pro-child, then policy makers must consider carefully the potential effects of their decisions on the parents' ability to provide for their children's physical needs and to maintain the enduring, supportive relationships that are necessary for emotional and social well-being. There are other important microsystems for children, such as the school and the neighborhood. To foster an environment that is rich in support for child development, policies should positively affect the stability, social density, adult–child ratio, and other child-related attributes of these social systems.

Public and private sector social policies are important to children, not only because they affect children's microsystems, but also because they affect the mesosystems or linkages between those microsystems as well. It is important to a child's development that mesosystems be characterized by multiple, diverse, and stable connections, and by complementary values. Policies that support strong mesosystems with these characteristics represent opportunities for children. Those that weaken connections between microsystems place children at risk.

Having summarized those attributes of a child's micro- and mesosystems that pro-child policies must consider and protect, we turn now to the exosystems in the child's environment. These are the agencies, organizations, and settings affecting the family's social environment. Our discussion considers three subgroups of policy decision makers: governmental, legal/judicial, and private sector. Although we address them separately, we do not mean to imply that they should function in isolation from each other. Indeed, a little coordination among exosystems could go a long way toward meeting children's needs.

## Governmental Exosystems

Let us begin this discussion with a surprise quiz. How many of these alphabet agencies can you identify: NIH, NIMH, NICHD, DHHS, AFDC, GAO, OMB, HSMHA, ADAMHA, OCD, HRA, FDA, and PHS? And the list could go on. These all are abbreviations for some of the hundreds of federal agencies that have some programmatic concern for children and families. Within this federal alphabet avalanche, for child placement services alone "there are at least 34 federal programs administered by six different federal agencies that directly impact on the lives of children at risk of removal or placement. Within HEW (DHHS) alone, there are five different offices and numerous divisions with responsibility for these programs" (Children's Defense Fund, 1978, p. 9). Keep in mind that these are only federal agencies. Not mentioned, but very influential, are governmental bodies at the state, county, city, and other levels.

Usually we think of legislators as the creators of governmental policy and public administrators as the implementers of those policies. Much legislation, however, is written with a "broad brush," and in developing the implementing regulations and protocols, the program administrators in the bureaucracy become powerful policymakers in their own right.

The federal government now is involved in every social welfare category, and all levels of government are involved in a staggering array of social programs (Lynn, 1980). We can trace the impetus for our present reliance (some would say over-reliance) on the federal government at least back to 1935 and the creation of the Social Security Act. This "safety net," devised in reaction to the Great Depression of the 1930s, evolved to the point where "by 1978, states and localities were eligible for approximately 270 different human service grants" (Light, 1972, p. 2). The 1970s took the Social Security System to the brink of fiscal disaster as the system was broadened to include a very wide range of safety net programs without commensurate increases in its fiscal foundation. As this book is being written, a new administration in Washington is initiating cuts in the system's scope.

Several approaches might be taken to assist families more effectively while shifting the focus from federal to local initiatives. These include decentralizing community services, fostering the development of informal helping networks, and (most importantly) encouraging coordination of these separate, but related, resources.

Community-based agencies and organizations have the potential to form an important mesosystem support network. This was a theme in Chapter 8 and here we will recover some of this ground but with a different slant. Community service agencies have traditionally dealt with individual family problems in a discrete, case-by-case manner focused on intrafamilial troubles—an approach that has not kept up with family needs. The ever-rising caseloads of most agencies are testimony to this failure. The traditional approach is too narrow and neglects the importance of community and neighborhood supports. An increase in services based "close to home" can contribute much to the child's ecological niche. The quality of mesosystem connections is enhanced by congruence between the value systems of helper and helpee. Being closer to problems can help attune workers to ethnic and other indigenous values. Coordinating service agencies at the local level can add important new linkages to the child's mesosystems.

The child's ecology improves still further by the inclusion of diverse connections through informal networks. New models for service delivery rely more upon approaches that attempt to harness informal community strengths on behalf of families (Garbarino, Stocking & Associates, 1980). Although it is a far cry from model to program, the promise is there. Self-help groups (e.g., Parents Anonymous) are good examples of the power of supportive groups, in this instance with an emphasis on the professional helper (Lieber & Baker, 1977). We are reminded of the ways in which other groups in our nation's history have dealt with the problems of oppressive environments. In discussing "Ethnic Enterprise in America," Light (1972) detailed the occurrence of informal welfare systems among immigrant Chinese and Japanese peoples. For example, these groups developed systems of "rotating credit associations" to help finance new business enterprises for group members who could not get regular bank loans. Other immigrant groups have had similar support systems that included finance and job hunting assistance, English classes, and other means of fostering a feeling of community belonging and support. We can build on these traditions in programs for promoting family and community well-being in today's social scene. For example, a *Washington Post Magazine* article (March 29, 1981) dealing with food-stamp program cutbacks described a local "food bank" that aids people in need of food by providing emergency supplies. This particular food bank is housed in a local church basement and is an informal, volunteer-staffed program relying on private donations.

Schools provide another microsystem for the child, and the school–home mesosystem is a very important influence on development (Garbarino, 1981b). Neighborhood schools have long been the traditional means of meeting the educational needs of children in American communities. They naturally lend themselves to school–home and school–neighborhood mesosystems. Thus, policies that undermine neighborhood schools can have a negative effect on these mesosystems, whatever else they may accomplish. Busing to achieve racial integration may have this as one of its liabilities, whatever its benefits in other areas.

Local boards that govern schools must be careful to support the school–home and school–neighborhood mesosystem. Involving parents in school programs, providing home visits by school personnel, and increasing recognition of the rights of parents in matters related to the education of their children can enhance the school–home relationship. The school–neighborhood mesosystem can be strengthened in many ways also. Schools can allow local volunteer groups to use their educational facilities. These groups are often thwarted in their attempts to organize and contribute, simply because they have few resources. Schools can involve students and staff in neighborhood-related projects to the mutual benefit of all and otherwise improve a waning public image that many schools are experiencing. Schools are perhaps the most pervasive institutional outposts in contact with America's children and we should utilize this valuable resource.

Local governments figure prominently in discussions of decentralized services and informal supports. This will become even more obvious as states and localities engage in new forms of budget battling under the new federal block grant program in which federally collected dollars go directly to the states for disbursement. Not only is there less money to go around, but allocation rules have been changed. Cities, towns, and neighborhoods will be required to fight even harder than before to maintain acceptable levels of funding. Human services, no doubt one of the hardest hit categories, need to plan for alternative, cost-effective approaches before legislators force unacceptable plans on them.

## The Legal/Judicial System

Besides the legislative and administrative branches of government described above, there is the judicial branch, and its appendage, the legal or court system. Judicial decisions can have both direct and indirect effects on families. Court decisions to remove a child, for instance, affect one particular family, while judicial mandates about family life in general affect the institution of the family. Both sometimes result from the same "landmark" or "precedent-setting" case. "The judicial decision to intrude into a family, in the main, rests on legal standards formulated by a legislature and interpreted by courts. From a governmental perspective, state intervention is meant to be a response to parental failure" (Katz, 1971, p. 56).

The issue of child custody is a good case in point because it is an example that can relate our earlier discussions about ideology and values to an actual practice situation, the removal of children from their homes (as we discussed it in Chapter 8). Goldstein, Freud, and Solnit (1973, 1979) have been among the leaders in redefining the issues involved in child custody. They base their arguments on what they call the "least detrimental alternative" model. Essentially, they argue that a family's "integrity" should be safeguarded at all costs by raising the threshold for state-sponsored intervention to the highest possible level.

A major problem with their model is that it precludes early interventive or preventive involvement with families to avoid family breakup. The least detrimental alternative model results in intervention being legitimized only at the point of quite serious family trouble (Garbarino et al., 1982). As Maybanks and Bryce (1979) pointed out, "The distinctive skills in child welfare are those developed in the placement of children; and the distinctive body of knowledge is that pertaining to separation of the child from his family" (p. 17). This is not enough!

Legislative mandates and particular court decisions can have a tremendous impact on children and their families. This impact can be quite positive if the decision makers consider the implications of their actions for children. For example, the Children's Defense Fund (CDF Reports, 1981) gives us an encouraging note about a piece of legislation proposed in 1980. The Adoption Assistance and Child Welfare Act of 1980 (P.L. 96-272) sought to remedy, at least in statute, many of the troubles described in Chapter 8. The legislation sought to require a closer family-to-placed-child relationship. Workers and agencies would be encouraged to place children close to parents so that visits would be possible. More important would be several regulations to reduce the length of residential treatment, formulate plans for the child's future, and focus on family–child reunity. However, the institution of a block grant system for allocation of public funds has the potential to reduce the positive gains of this legislation through lack of fiscal support.

## The Private Sector

Much of our discussion has centered on issues in public policy—that is, policy in the form of enforceable legal mandate. But the private sector also is an important source of social policy. The previously mentioned impact of business's "move to move up" policy, along with our generally transient society, has done much to disrupt naturally occurring forms of support networks. Probably the greatest of these is the extended family, under considerable strain in today's America. People often do not settle down in the place where they grew up or elsewhere near to their family. And the "next best thing to being there" (the telephone company's cheerful ad for its long-distance service) is still *not* being there. Threatening to add to the disruptive forces are recommendations from a national advisory committee (see Chapter 7) to induce, even coerce, movement away from old neighborhoods, if they happen to be located in failing Northeastern industrial centers, in order to provide a workforce for rapidly developing areas of our nation in the Sun Belt. Although we are not suggesting that the committee intended to break up networks of kin and kith, nor denying that their hopes for revitalizing the economy are positively conceived, we do believe that they have not given adequate consideration to the quite predictable impact of these policies on extended support networks of families and to the potential consequences for children and the quality of social life in the affected areas.

The private sector (business and industry) can do much to support families. It can plan initiatives to humanize the work situation: for example, by reducing mandatory overtime that causes parental fatigue, thereby returning a more satisfied parent to a child's microsystem. Private concerns can be more aware of the parental responsibilities of employees and consider family-related needs in fringe benefits and company activities.

Another way in which the private sector can make contributions to the well-being of families is to become active in supporting community-based family programs. Landrum Bolling, Chairman of the Council on Foundations, has written that:

> The strengthening of private initiatives to serve human needs ought to be *one* national objective around which all political factions could unite [to] support those voluntary, nonprofit, nongovernmental institutions, agencies, and programs that care for the needy, promote community well-being, and enrich all our lives (1980, p. 1).

We see this supportive responsibility naturally extending to private business and industry. We agree with Alfred Claassen's (1980) depiction of social problems as "investment opportunities." That is, "capital disposed in a specified fashion over a given period of time will effect a greater contribution to the value of the net output of a set of social actors than will its employment in any known alternative pattern" (p. 529).

A good example of such private sector action is an insurance company's investment in a community-based program to prevent juvenile delinquency. There are obvious benefits to the community from a successful program of this sort. Beyond these, the company could accrue considerable benefit by a reduction in delinquent acts and a consequent reduction in insurance claims. It would seem that private sector investment in healthy families and safe communities can coexist with—if not complement—the free enterprise concern for profit.

## An Integrated Approach

Until now our discussion has taken us *from* various policy sources *to* their respective costs or benefits for children and families. However, as policy practitioners, we may be more interested in how to identify an appropriate source of policy after being confronted with a particular problem. Here we see the point about multiple influences shaping a specific issue being well illustrated.

Consider the problem of "latchkey children" who come home to empty houses after school because their adult caretakers are still at work. With increasing numbers of single parent households and economic conditions requiring both parents in two-parent families to work, more and more children are in this situation. At the same time, many households lack extended networks of family and highly involved neighbors to watch out for children who are on their own. Alternative policies, initiated by both the public and private sectors, could and should come to the aid of children and their caretakers. Government could support parents remaining at home to do the important job of child rearing and support the enforcement of child-support payments. The public sector could supply supports and incentives (e.g., tax write-offs) for after-school care programs. Businesses could institute on-site day care or assorted alternative scheduling programs (e.g., flex-time, or job sharing). Voluntary organizations could staff after-school co-ops. This should help assure the consistent care and supervision of school-age children, and support for day care could function in a similar manner for very young children.

The coordination of policy decisions is important for at least two reasons. First, policies frequently work against one another. Second, there is rarely a single clear solution to problems that trouble children and their families. Each level of policy intervention contributes to the overall goal of providing the care that children require. In the latchkey example, some potential solutions would enable increases in the amount of time that children and parents spend together. This would enhance the opportunity for reciprocal parent–child relationships. Other approaches focus more on supplying sufficient other adults to care for the children while parents are absent, thereby, increasing the quality and density of a child's network. Still others are primarily concerned with relieving the financial burdens that can drain an otherwise enthusiastic parent. All of these contribute to a positive approach to supporting children by supporting their care givers. Indeed, it is becoming an adage in the child and family services field that to support children, we must be willing to support their parents (Emlen, 1977).

## Social Policy and Family Support: It's Everybody's Business

In the first two sections of this chapter, we have considered some macrosystem and exosystem effects on social policies that affect children and their families. There is another level at which social policies are influenced, and that is the individual level. A personal commitment to supporting families and caring about children in everyday life can be expressed in both professional and personal efforts. It may involve attention not only to specific children and families, but also to the social and economic environment of families and their networks. A personal commitment to the quality of life of our children may include, therefore, efforts to influence social policies in pro-child directions. We conclude with this topic.

In this section of the chapter, we discuss strategies that individuals use to influence policy-making processes. By this we are not suggesting that human services professionals cast aside their chosen professions to become full-time political activists. Rather, we are recognizing that the roots of environmental risks to children often lie in social policies, and meeting the developmental needs of children may require policy-level adjustments in priorities and practices. In this respect, there is ample opportunity for all of us to make a difference in the lives of children and their families.

Children need concerned adults to become their advocates on both a personal and a political level. As Steiner and Milius (1976) pointed out, children do not vote, contribute to candidates, or lobby. "As political actors, children are useless and dependent. If children are to be either advantaged or simply protected, other groups must speak on their behalf" (p. 143). These groups are made up of committed individuals, and the level of intervention is not always the Congress of the United States. Demonstrating concern for children can involve helping an abused teenager find appropriate services and working on behalf of a needed school bond, as well as expressing disapproval of a proposed piece of legislation.

In both our professional and our personal lives, we should be alert to policies and practices that weaken supports for families and increase risks to children, and we should act as agents of change in those situations. Harold Demone (1978) described the change-agent role in human services reform as "part art form, part science, part experience, and part luck" (p. 8). He describes several types of "change agentry," of which three are most important to us here: the *lobbyist,* the *advocate,* and the *citizen participant.*

Lobbying is simply the act of letting one's views be known to elected representatives charged with policy decision making. As Demone put it:

> Fundamentally, the goal of the game is to enhance one's interest and failing that, to protect that interest. The interest may be personal, organizational, or an extended network. It may be self-centered or humanitarian, special interest or public interest. Often one lobbyist's special interest is another's public interest, and vice versa. Although one can lobby all sorts of organizations, it is commonly perceived as an activity directed at a public official or body (p. 17).

Related to the more formalized, rule- or law-governed lobbying tactic is the role of the advocate. "Advocacy has classical origins as an essential component of the practice of law. Similarly, the physician advocate speaks for his patient. Social workers have traditionally intervened on behalf of their clients, as architects do for their clients. Most, perhaps all, client-serving professions would define representation of their clients as a time-honored task" (Demone, 1978, p. 31).

Jane Knitzer favors the adoption of an advocacy role for community psychologists. She stated that:

> The term advocacy has become an integral part of the vocabulary of social-change agents. Advocacy refers to interventions designed to reduce or eliminate barriers within institutions or systems that result in the inequitable treatment of individuals or classes of individuals, the denial of needed services and resources, or the undermining of the individual's capacity for healthy development and self-determination. The target for change in advocacy is not the individual, but the policies and practices of the institution with which individuals must daily interact—the schools, the courts, the welfare bureaucracies, the hospitals; the local, state, and federal laws that shape so much of what happens in these institutions; the political decision-making process at all levels of government by which priorities and fiscal policies are determined; the administrative regulations that interpret laws and political mandates; and the practices and ideologies of professionals that get in the way of responsive help, particularly to those of a different culture or ethnic background (1980, p. 293).

The purposes and levels of advocacy and lobbying are similar. The distinction is usually thought of in terms of structure. That is, lobbying activity is regulated by law, whereas advocacy is not so structured. Also, lobbying is typically a class-action event (i.e., directing change for a group), while advocacy can be either class- or case-action directed (Knitzer, 1980). A good example of case advocacy is the "guardian ad litem," who may be appointed by the court in child abuse and neglect cases (see Fraser, 1977). In effect, the guardian ad litem offers independent representation for the abused or neglected child to advocate for his or her rights and best interest in court battles.

The last change-agent role—the citizen participant—is perhaps the most direct. Rather than working to influence policymakers, citizen participants become policymakers themselves, representing the needs of their own neighborhoods and communities on boards, commissions, and advisory councils of all types. Under the leadership of former HEW Secretary David Mathews, for example, the Department of Health, Education and Welfare (now Health and Human Services) set a goal of increasing public interaction and citizen involvement in its activities. At the peak of this effort, approximately 90 HEW programs called for citizen participation (Demone, 1978). At the local level, citizen participation can be an important force for change in human services agencies and hospitals, schools, zoning commissions, economic development departments, transportation authorities, and numerous other community policy bodies. Such grass-roots participation is a most effective means for people to get the services they need. It is the cornerstone of the family policy for the Good Society.

# RESEARCH CAPSULE

One of the foundations of policy research is the compilation of basic data on needs. Much of this research appears in local, state, and federal reports. We report here some examples focusing on the state of Texas:

In 1978, one in every nine children in the United States was living in Texas (Texas Department of Community Affairs, 1974, 1978, p. 147). In 1974 and 1978, the Texas Department of Community Affairs published 46 *things you need to know about Texas children: The darker side of childhood* and 78 *things you need to know about Texas Children: Still the darker side of childhood.* Together, these companion reports represent a commitment by Texas to gather policy-relevant information on children and their families residing in the state. The earlier publication focused on children ages 0–6, the later report was expanded to cover children 0–18 years of age. Data were collected from a wide variety of sources including: The U.S. Census Bureau, The Office of Early Child Development, several independent research centers and studies, and assorted Texas agencies with analogs in most other states.

These volumes are useful in many ways to those interested in the children of any locale. First, the variables identified and investigated form a "children's policy checklist" of sorts. Persons wishing to gather information about children as a first step in policy development or change can use this checklist of important indicators to decide what information to collect. Second, the volumes identify a multitude of information sources. Knowing where to locate existing information facilitates timely policy data collection. The sources used by the Texas staff may suggest potential sources in your area. Third, much of the data is reduced to county level units of analysis, and sometimes even lower levels. This is an imperative but often elusive level of analysis for those interested in addressing problem issues at the local level. Lastly, the potential implications drawn from these findings illustrate the powerful impact that the right kind of information can have in persuading decision makers that change is in order. A few examples of facts and sources directly from the reports follow:

Environment:

406,076 children live in the four most economically depressed regions of Texas (*Texas Fact Book 1978*, Bureau of Business Research, University of Texas, Austin).

Family:

40 percent of all Texas mothers with children under six are in the labor force—and 54 percent of all Texas mothers of school-age children (*1975 Handbook of Women Working*, U.S. Department of Labor).

Health:

24 Texas counties had no medical doctor in 1975—190 Texas counties had no obstetrician-gynecologist (*U.S. Fact Book*, 1978).

Nutrition:

75,000 Texas preschoolers eat no breakfast (*Texas Household Survey of Families with Children Under Six*, 1973).

Handicaps:

3,960 Texas handicapped children were found who had not been in school or who needed additional services (Project Child Find of the Special Education Department).

Education:

In a study of 1,252 children convicted of offenses in Texas, only 4.6 percent were at the proper grade level. ("What the Safe School Study Means to You," *American Educator*, July 1978).

Troubled Youth:

An estimated 15,624 Texas children will run away from home this year (1978). 13,774 runaways were arrested in 1977—3 out of 5 were females (Department of Public Safety, Uniform Crime Reporting Bureau).

Child Care:

An estimated 30,900 Texas children under six may be left to care for themselves while their parents work (*Texas Household Survey of Families with Children Under Six*, 1973).

Hidden Children:

Confirmed cases of child abuse and neglect in Texas tripled in three years—from 3,764 in 1974 to 14,685 in 1977 (Texas Department of Human Resources, Social Services Management System).

Contact: Early Childhood Development Division

Texas Department of Community Affairs

P.O. Box 13166 Capital Station

Austin, Texas 78711

---

# PRACTICE CAPSULE

During the 1970s, the Columbia University School of Social Work conducted a cross-national study of social services in Canada, France, Israel, Poland, the United Kingdom, the United States, West Germany, and Yugoslavia. The purposes of the study were not only to compare the various social service systems, but also to analyze ways in which political, economic, social, and cultural factors in each nation influenced those systems and their service-delivery mechanisms. One facet of the study focused on service provisions for early identification and intervention into child abuse and neglect. Thus, this study provided an excellent examination of *how* social policy affects professional practice.

One finding of the study was that different nations had different perceptions of how large the child maltreatment problem was and whether it was a distinct problem or part of a broader set of child development issues. Poland, for instance, reported the incidence of child abuse to be small, while in Yugoslavia it was viewed as part of the general problem of "predelinquency." Other nations saw the problem as being greater. Canada, the United Kingdom, and the United States were making efforts to define and distinguish among types and levels of abuse and neglect, while France, Israel, and West Germany were reluctant to distinguish abuse as a focus of concern separate from the problem of child maltreatment.

The United States, at the time of the study, was beginning to develop case identification strategies that often called for additions to existing social service mechanisms. In France, Israel, Poland, and the United Kingdom, on the other hand, case identification was being incorporated into existing universal maternal and child health programs that see all children from infancy on. Whether the nation's program included visiting health workers, as in the United Kingdom, or a network of low-cost clinics, as in Israel, these countries already had mechanisms for encountering all children at regular intervals. Case finding thus entailed alerting existing systems and personnel to look for signs of maltreatment or for situations that put children at risk for abuse or neglect, rather than initiating new systems for this purpose. Thus, a nation's need for a specific child-abuse identification policy differed significantly on the basis of the broader state of family policy. This tells us to keep the total policy context in mind whenever we consider specific policies.

# FOR FURTHER READING

Advisory Committee on Child Development. *Toward a national policy for children and families.* Washington, D.C.: National Academy of Sciences, 1976, 133 pages.

Data on families and children are reviewed with particular attention to economic resources, health care, child care and special services, government programs, and modes of service delivery. Future research recommendations emphasize naturalistic studies, program evaluation, impact analysis, and the development of social indicators on children—all important methods for policy interventionists.

Berger, P. L., & Neuhaus, R. J. *To empower people: The role of mediating structures in public policy.* Washington, D.C.: American Enterprise Institute for Public Policy Research, 1977, 45 pp.

This is a short, concise, and handy document. The authors have an easily read style. Issues in the welfare state are discussed in terms of institutions that mediate between individuals and the society-at-large (i.e., family, neighborhood, church, and voluntary associations). It emphasizes pluralism, people's strengths, and alternative policy strategies.

Gaylin, W., Glasser, I., Marcus, S., & Rothman, D., *Doing good: The limits of benevolence.* New York: Pantheon, 1978, 171 pp.

This thought-provoking set of essays examines both the appropriateness and the effectiveness of paternalism as a model for the relationship between society and its dependent members. The final essay offers an agenda for social policy based on an amended model.

Kamerman, S. B., & Kahn, A. J. (Eds.) *Family policy: Government and families in fourteen countries.* New York: Columbia University Press, 1978, 522 pp.

Policies and practices of various European nations relative to children, the elderly, women, and families are described by the contributors to this volume. It provides an interesting contrast to United States policies and programs. Content and style vary among contributors.

Keniston, K. The Carnegie Council on Children. *All our children: The American family under pressure.* New York: Harcourt Brace Jovanovich, 1977, 255 pp.

The Council investigates from a broad perspective the changing social contexts within which American families live. A great volume of data is harnessed to demonstrate the pressures of contemporary family life, and recommendations for remedy are made. These solutions are not limited to the typical services, which are also discussed, but include radical suggestions such as guaranteed income levels, changes in laws related to children and families, and other interventions aimed at altering societal institutions.

Rice, R. M. *American family policy: Content and context.* New York: Family Service Association of America, 1977, 159 pp.

This readable book has become a primer in family policy discussions. After documenting many of the ways in which families are vulnerable to societal pressures, Rice reviews several approaches to development of a family policy for the U.S. and outlines overarching values that should be supported by such a policy.

Steiner, G. Y., & Milius, P. H. *The children's cause.* Washington, D.C.: The Brookings Institution, 1976, 265 pp.

Tracing the history of children's defense movements, the authors illustrate the politicization and institutionalization of child development policy. Values are investigated, specific agencies are described from inception to demise, and the influence of the political environment is discussed. The text also reviews policy strategies, discussing dilemmas in certain types of programming and the politics of comprehensive policymaking.

# QUESTIONS FOR THOUGHT

1. Although respect for diversity in family forms is an American value, many policies and practices reflect an assumption that families consist of a husband who is employed, a wife who stays home, children, and no others. What are some of the consequences (positive and/or negative) of these practices for other family forms (e.g., two-earner, single-parent, childless, three generation)? Consider, for instance, tax policies, family health insurance coverage and benefits, and social security provisions.

2. The apartment is dirty, the kids are dirty, and they obviously do not get enough to eat, but their mother never leaves them unattended, and there is much affection among them. Should the state intervene on behalf of these children? If so, what form should the intervention take? What values and assumptions about children, families, and the role of the state are reflected in your answers?

3. What recent economic or employment trend, legislative enactment, court ruling, business or consumer protection decision, or other social policy action can you think of that will affect children and families? Was the intention of the policy to influence family life? How does it influence families? Are the results likely to be beneficial or harmful?

4. Conflicts often arise in policy decisions (e.g., between needs of children and needs of parents, between costs and allocations, and between the promise of a policy and its practical implication). Identify the probable origins of these conflicts. Explain how this identification exercise can aid in resolving these problems.

5. How is a policy different from a practice? Is there overlap? What are the problems of a patchwork approach to policy? What are some barriers to a comprehensive approach?

6. Traditional approaches to family troubles emphasize remedial, individual interventions. List alternatives that the human ecological model might suggest as legitimate types of intervention. (See Chapter 8.) Now, what would a policy practitioner do to influence decisions that would encourage and support these innovations?

7. In Norway and Sweden, fathers are offered paid paternity leaves following the birth of each child. Should paternity leaves be offered in the United States? Why or why not? If paternity leaves were available to American men, what do you think is the likelihood that they would be used to help provide child care?

# Chapter 10

The fundamental thing is for both decision makers and ordinary people to understand that the human lot cannot be trusted essentially to technologies, structures, legislations, and treaties—however indispensable this societal patrimony and its updating and revamping indeed are. There cannot be any salvation, unless people themselves change their values, mores, and behavior for the better—The question is, then, one of human quality, and how this can be improved. . . . This is the human revolution, which is more urgent than anything else if we are to control the other revolutions of our time and steer mankind towards a viable future.

(Peccei, 1977, p. xi)

Children always offer an opportunity for making the future better. Our physical resources may diminish, but our human ones will not. The quality of life for the next generation could be better than it was for past ones. To make the human quality of our children's lives better, we must understand children's needs and how to enhance elements in their lives to lead to a richer, more varied, more satisfying growing up both for them and their parents. This is what we will discover in "The Issue Is Human Quality."

# In Conclusion: The Issue Is Human Quality

## Childhood as the Eternal Frontier

The frontier is an important part of the American character and history. It stands for openness, independence, and equality among people. It also served as an important safety valve for defusing conflict in the established, populated areas of the East. The United States' Census Bureau declared the American Frontier closed in 1890 (Turner, 1894). And according to Turner, with its closing came a change in America, and the special American character was in jeopardy.

The frontier image is a powerful one. There is psychological and sociological truth in Turner's analysis, whatever its historical flaws and limitations. We are, in the 1980s, also at the end of a frontier. Just as the opportunities for western expansion were drying up at the turn of the century, we now find our frontier of cheap energy and unlimited, petroleum-based industrial growth similarly "closing." With the increasing emphasis on "the limits to growth" (e.g., Council on Environmental Quality, 1981), we need to find where our next frontier lies.

**232**

Where can we go to find open spaces to test and offer us the scope we need for our fullest human development? The exploration of outer space is a challenge open to only a few. The challenges of our material world—ecological, agricultural, and economic—are mainly to conserve. The personal and social frontiers, however, still offer challenges. Personal, spiritual, and social challenges come together in raising children. The opportunity is open to almost all, and it offers the awesome and wonderful task of breaking new ground, making the future. Childhood and child rearing are the new frontier.

Children, while they are not "unknown territory," always offer an opportunity to make the future better. They allow parents to reaffirm and rejuvenate their basic commitments to love, life, work, and play. Children allow them to say to the human race that they think well enough of the world and of people to bring new people into it, or to foster those already here. However, each new generation brings with it a challenge: How will the adults of their world make things "better for my kid than they were for me?" An impulse to better the human condition, while it is now tempered and toned down from bouncing nineteenth century optimism, is still a part of the human character. How shall we improve the quality of life for, and the human quality of, our children? Where do we stand now, and what can be done for the future? To answer these questions, we should look at the children, their characteristics and needs, and at the conditions of childhood.

When it comes to human resources, the most important basic measure is the welfare of children. A society that does not do well by its children abandons the quality of its future. Mary Ellen Burris, writing in 1979, presented this disturbing picture based on public opinion surveys:

> A happy marriage, an interesting job, and a job that contributes to the welfare of society—each of these factors *decreased* in the percentage of people naming them as ingredients of the good life. In contrast, these things *increased* in importance: a color TV, a lot of money, really nice clothes, a second color TV. And consider this: in late 1975, more people named children as an ingredient in the good life than a car; now it's just the reverse (*Behavior Today*, June 4, 1979).

Is this the beginning of an ugly future in which we turn our backs on children in favor of material comforts? For the best quality of life, we must focus our attention on children. In the long run, color TVs, cars, and nice clothes are a losing proposition when contrasted with children on *both* practical and moral grounds.

Why care for children in the first place? Because they are the future. The continuing of this good earth and whatever is good on it depends upon them. If children are to have first claim as our new frontier, then parents and the conditions of parenthood are of crucial importance. The condition of families is our first topic.

We begin with families because it is foolhardy to think of children apart from the conditions of life for their parents and guardians. Hansel and Gretel were left in the woods as they were because their family was starving and couldn't feed them. Scientists as well as story tellers affirm this. Arthur Emlen, an ally of children, put it: "If you care for children, then care for parents" (Emlen, 1977). "Parents" should be broadened, of course, to include all the care givers: grandparents, foster parents, child-care workers, etc.

Children reflect the quality of life for the adults in the society, for better or for worse. Child abuse reflects the worse. Commenting on domestic violence in the animal world, recall Desmond Morris' (1970) observation that adults typically respond to stress and pressure by taking out their frustrations on children:

> The viciousness with which children . . . . are subjected to persecution is a measure of the weight of dominant pressures imposed on their persecutors (Morris, 1970).

Complementing this observation is Rock's report (1978) that gorilla mothers who are socially impoverished (isolated from their peers) are prone to mistreat their infants. When they are restored to the simian community, however, these mothers perform adequately. Social impoverishment is equally destructive to human child rearing. Domestic violence among humans is also an indication of excessive stresses and strains (Straus, Gelles & Steinmetz, 1980). Abuse and neglect are associated with the family's isolation from friends, neighbors, and helpers (Garbarino, 1977a,b). The parents need love and support in order to be loving and supporting to their children. Their ability to be good parents is not solely their own doing—their society has a great say in what stresses and supports they will encounter.

For the thesis presented by Burris—that valuing things is taking the place of valuing children—there is the antithesis presented by public opinion polls that continue to show family life at the top of people's lists of what is important. Based on a recent survey of adults in the United States, Harris (1978) concludes that, "Clearly, the most satisfying part of life to many Americans today is family life. A substantial 92 percent of the public say this is very important to them. And 67 percent say they are very satisfied with the way their family life is going." Apparently most of us, despite flirtations with materialism, recognize that more luxury items are "the unreal objects of this world," as one Eastern philosopher puts it. The challenge in designing a better world for the future is to support and build on the truth that children are of paramount importance, not obscure it by overemphasizing and falsifying people's basic material needs.

There is a cultural struggle here. The things of real value that we have, and thus can offer to our children, are our time, our interest, and our attention— in short, our love and care. However, it must be a value of society as well as of the individual parent for that person to do the job well. We need to look at the adult's larger context—the society—for a moment.

## Society and the Good Life

Searching for the meaning of the "Good Life" has been *the* traditional philosophical issue. The search for the Good Life, while largely abandoned by contemporary philosophy, has been taken up by some within the social sciences. In its "soft" side, under the guidance of the gentle theorists Maslow and Rogers, modern psychology has sought to provide psychological answers to the eternal question: What is the good life? The *psychology* of self-actualization is an *ethic* of existential meaningfulness. There is, however, even within the "hard" side of psychology, a growing appreciation for the centrality of this most qualitative of issues. "Quality of life" is an important and growing research issue in its own right. To ask, What is the good life? is to pose the fundamental issue of psychological quality. It is to ask, What brings meaning to human experience? It is to ask, What makes reality a positive experience? Once this question is posed, it opens a whole new vista, or rather reopens it.

The issue of quality in a psychological context has new implications in the modern era. In the past, considerations of quality were intrinsically elitist. The material conditions of life did not permit a widespread concern with the quality of life. The promise (and premise) of the modern era has been its tantalizing prospect of making available adequate material conditions to permit quality of life to become a concern for the masses. Indeed, the whole body of utopian writing dating from the eighteenth century is built on the premise that technological improvements permit the dispersion of human quality (Garbarino & Garbarino, 1978). The trick is to build a society that can offer "the good life" in the long run. We call this "the sustainable society," and it requires technology to serve human needs in a humane way.

It is ironic that the same technology that offered the promise of the good life for all is now seen as the principal threat to that life in the future by making us hostages to an energy-intensive, unsustainable economy. Universal dispersion of the benefits of technology was (and still is) presumed to be the shortest route to widespread qualitative improvement in the human condition. This ideology permeated even to the creation of statistical indicators for measuring the day-to-day life and future of societies. As Campbell (1976) has noted, as early as 1798, Sir John Sinclair described statistics in the following language when he introduced them in his *Statistical Account of Scotland:* "The idea I annex to the term (statistics) is an inquiry into the state of the country, for the purpose of ascertaining the quantum of happiness."

As is often the case, the fullest picture of reality comes not from social science, but from fiction, where the rough edges of incomplete factual information can be smoothed by the visionary imagination. Some of the best thoughts on the sustainable society in which quality predominates over quantitative concerns come from the utopian novelists. Austin Tappan Wright's *Islandia* (1942) presents such a totally sustainable society, one in which the pursuit of human quality is totally preeminent over concerns with quantity. The productive and social unit in Islandia is the small family farm, handed down through generations. Family members make extended visits to other farms and meet annually for their only political event, a congress of landowners. Islandians have no contact with other countries and little "modern technology." They are educated in one-room schoolhouses and have one university. Individual work pace and family integrity are valued over speed and production. Formal social services are nonexistent. Informal helping networks provide routine help to individuals and families faced with acute problems. *Islandia* presents an alternative to all the superficial trappings of what we consider modern society. But, it allows for universal dispersion of quality through social organization and enough material technology to permit the dignity of economic adequacy to all. The two characters in the excerpt below are discussing how Islandia would change were it to become "modern" in the sense of the term understood by John, the contemporary American.

DORN:   Why should I change?

JOHN:   Progress!

DORN:   Speed, is that progress? Anyhow, why progress? Why not enjoy what one has? Men have never exhausted present pleasures.

JOHN:   With us, progress means giving pleasures to those who haven't got them.

DORN:   But doesn't progress create the very situation it seeks to cure—always changing the social adjustment so that someone is squeezed out? Decide on an indispensible minimum. See that everyone gets that, and until everyone has it, don't let anyone have any more. Don't let anyone ever have any more until they have cultivated fully what they have.

JOHN:   To be unhappy is a sign we aren't stagnating.

DORN:   Nor are we. "Happy" wasn't the right word. We are quite as unhappy as you are. Things are too beautiful; those we love die; it hurts to grow old or be sick. Progress won't change any of these things, except that medicine will mitigate the last. We cultivate medicine, and we are quite as far along as you are there. Railroads and all that merely stir up a puddle, putting nothing new in and taking nothing out. (Wright, 1942, pp. 84–85).

The essential issues of human experience are direct, simple, universal, and unchanging: the parents' mating, childbearing, and child rearing, is repeated by the children's puberty, adulthood, and once again mating. Wright's *Islandia* envisions a society in which technology is *selected* to permit a style of life in which those fundamental human concerns are the principal agenda for the human community, unencumbered by false issues of social change and social development. Wright's vision of "what matters" for quality in human life is paralleled in the "scientific study of human experience." Psychology merges with ethics.

In a paper entitled "Subjective Measures of Well-Being" (1976), Campbell reviewed the limitations of modern, objective measures of human society. He noted their fundamental falseness because they cannot attend to the subjective experience of reality, the ultimate criterion for judging meaning. Campbell built on the findings from national surveys, showing that during the period between 1957 and 1972, when most of the economic and social indicators were moving rapidly upward, the proportion of the American population who described themselves as "very happy" declined steadily, and that this decline was most apparent among the part of the population that was most affluent. Affluence alone is not enough. It must be accompanied by social meaning. When people living in those states (primarily in the Southeast) that have the lowest "objective quality of life" (measured by socioeconomic development) were asked about the subjective quality of their life, they reported more positive experiences than did their counterparts in the more affluent "developed" states. We should be wary of simple economic solutions to human problems. Campbell concludes that we need indicators of personal well-being to complement conventional social indicators.

These subjective measures would, in large part, tell us how things stand between children and their parents. Rather than being the simple accumulation of characteristics, human development is the process by which an individual constructs a picture of the world and acquires the tools to live in and with that picture. Bronfenbrenner (1979) defines development as:

> . . . the person's evolving conception of the ecological environment, and his relation to it, as well as the person's growing capacity to discover, sustain, or alter its properties (p. 9).

This concept of development will figure prominently in efforts to understand how the future of a sustainable society depends upon the quality of life it offers to children. *Although children develop abstractions, they do not develop in response to abstractions.* They are a genuine reflection of the actual quality of life as it is directly experienced. Compared to adults, children are much less liable to delusion, to being drawn away from the basics of life quality. But just what are "the basics," the fundamental determinants of quality for the subjective human organism? Campbell concludes that the basics are "the presence or absence of those various forms of interpersonal exchange that provide psychological support to people" (Campbell, 1976, p. 122).

Those interpersonal supports are just the things that provide a positive influence on human development, as Bronfenbrenner defines the term. They both enlarge the capacity of the developing human to utilize the environment, and provide the raw material that humans need to fashion a satisfying existence. The need for interpersonal support is the fundamental human need; satisfaction of that need is the foundation of social quality. Campbell was concerned with this fundamental need in adults, but when we consider the world of children, we recognize that the same interpersonal factors dominate.

For the child to flourish, the parent must have access to the social riches of family or family surrogates, kin and kith. Just as child and family are inseparable, both in interests and in functions, so family and community are wedded by a functional connection. Unless a society assures that parents have the means to rear children, it will be faced with an unfortunate mixture of unhappy parents and inadequately prepared children. Both are a direct threat to the goal of quality in the human experience.

It is reassuring to know that the fundamental needs of children and adults are relatively simple and basically unchanging. It is a challenge to meet both those needs simultaneously. To do so for the masses of the population—resulting in a quantum leap in happiness—is still further a challenge to the skill of society's social engineers, managers, politicians, and individual citizens. The task is not an easy one, and it demands a more precise examination of the conditions favoring an intensive social investment by parents in children without psychological bankruptcy to those adults. To that task our attention next turns.

## Poverty and Affluence

Although the economic needs of children are actually quite limited, we know that poverty is bad for children and adults alike. Severe economic stress is a fact of life for at least 15 percent of American children and their parents. We know poverty is bad for children because it undermines their health and well-being (National Academy of Sciences, 1976), unless they have compensatory social resources. It subjects them to damaging stresses, both directly by placing them in threatening situations and indirectly by undermining the ability of their parents to give what children rightfully deserve—finely attuned and affectionate responsiveness. Severe economic deprivation robs families of the social necessities of life; it leads to social impoverishment. Social impoverishment is the principal direct threat to human development. A socially rich child is better off developmentally than a socially impoverished one, even if the latter is materially wealthy.

The promise of modernity is to release families from the burden of poverty. The reality of poverty as a destructive social and psychological force is undeniable.

Margaret Sanger, a leader in the American family planning movement, gave this account of her work with mothers living on the Lower East Side of Manhattan during the early 1900s:

> Each time I returned to this district, which was becoming a recurrent nightmare, I used to hear that Mrs. Cohen "had been carried to a hospital, but had never come back," or that Mrs. Kelly "had sent the children to a neighbor and had put her head into the gas oven." Day after day such tales were poured into my ears—a baby born dead, great relief—the death of an older child, sorrow but again relief of a sort—the story told a thousand times of death from abortion, children going into institutions. I shudder with horror as I listened to the details and studied the reasons back of them—destitution linked with excessive child-bearing. The waste of life seemed senseless. One by one worried, sad, pensive and aging faces marshalled themselves before me in my dreams, sometimes appealingly, sometimes accusingly. (Sanger, 1938, p. 89)

When life is so impoverished that children are a burden, they tend to impoverish further rather than to enrich the quality of life. In our efforts to design a sustainable society centering on the labor-intensive nature of child rearing, we must avoid naive sentimentality about "the good old days." This parallels issues in the economic and technological spheres (Schumacher, 1973). Child rearing is fundamentally a labor-intensive rather than a capital-intensive enterprise. That is, it requires a person's time even more than money. Therein lies the challenge and the hope for a sustainable society.

Just how labor-intensive *must* child rearing be? This is an important issue. Can we substitute money for time and still get well-developed children? Children learn the world they experience and then seek to live in that world. A sustainable society must be composed of people who have constructed an internal reality based on human rather than material values. If material investment is substituted for psychological and social investment in the rearing of children, the only outcome can be a materialism incompatible with a sustainable society. The essence of development is the child's conception of the world and his or her ability to "discover, sustain, or alter its properties" (Bronfenbrenner, 1979, p. 9).

A sustainable society requires people who will direct their developing competence towards cultivating renewable, nonpolluting resources. Chief among these "clean" resources is social intercourse. Campbell found that social interchange, set in the context of enduring relationships, is the primary reliable source of meaning and satisfaction in the human experience. This bodes well for designing a sustainable society. Such a society is compatible with "human nature," if that society is built on labor-intensive enterprises that generate and sustain a comfortable social web, surrounding, dignifying, and supporting the individual human being. Children and child rearing must stand at the heart of such a web. They are the most reliable "occasion" for knitting people together in mutually satisfying, socially productive work and developmentally enhancing play. They are the perfect vehicle for organizing a sustainable society. What we need to do (and it is no small task) is to work out the implications of this principle for every aspect of our economic, political, and social life.

The temptation to use material investment as a substitute for psychological investment is real. The Soviet Union tried creating boarding schools to provide "disadvantaged" children with high-quality, professional child care. It abandoned this compensatory intervention program when they discovered that "you can't pay a woman to do what a mother will do for free" (Bronfenbrenner, 1979). We would add, that the same is true of fathers—they are not for sale. Material investment seems an easy way out of making the necessary labor-intensive investment, but it is ineffective at best and developmentally damaging at worst. Surveys in the 1950s showed that high on the list of reasons given for purchasing televisions was "to bring the family back together" (Garbarino, 1975b). The actual result, of course, was physical togetherness but psychological apartness, parallel rather than interactive social experience.

A reservoir of support for child rearing and family life exists, but its potential effects are often blunted by the tantalizing proposition that parents can have their cake and eat it too, invest in their children and do their own thing as well. Unless their "thing" is child rearing or they find someone else whose "thing" it is (the English nanny and Chinese granny come to mind), children may suffer a lack of attention and involvement with others. To do this thing well, parents need a social environment that cares for them as they care for their children. The issue is not simply working mothers or day care, but a social environment that supports parents—fathers and mothers—in meeting all their parental, occupational, and spiritual needs.

In discussing material versus social/psychological investment in child rearing, we must return to the concept of support systems raised in earlier chapters. Support systems provide *both* nurturance and feedback. They provide the individual with warmth and security in addition to guidance and direction. The protective function is particularly important for effective parenthood and nontraumatic childhood.

Support systems are the staff of life in child rearing. Indeed, the principal factor mediating between the parent–child relationship and the larger society is precisely the family's network of support systems. The richness, diversity, and strength of these support systems contribute to their effectiveness in providing nurturance and feedback to parent–child relationships. This richness is one of the principal environmental determinants of the child's developmental robustness. In this respect, the good life for families resembles the political good life for communities: Social pluralism both protects society from dangerous excesses and provides diverse and enriching experiences by combining consensus and diversity (Garbarino & Bronfenbrenner, 1976b).

While most of the public debate concerning the fate of children centers around the "decline of the American family," the issue actually lies outside the family, in the family's relation to the community. Understanding this relationship is necessary for looking at the state and future of American families. The principal threat of the modern world to the psychological quality of life is the weakening of traditional sources of social pluralism. Social pluralism is a wide range of people and groups surrounding the family which, although they may differ in some attitudes and values, share a basic commitment to the family in whatever form it takes. Without support systems, the parent–child relationship is thrown into jeopardy, and it is this jeopardy that is commonly referred to as "the decline of the American family." Lack of support systems is "social impoverishment."

Social impoverishment springs from a variety of factors. Among these are geographic mobility, instrumental interpersonal relationships, and the erosion of stable neighborhoods. Though it has its positive side (financial security, for example), geographic mobility strains and often breaks the functional relationships that underlie support systems. While modern communications permit support systems to function over long distances, as in the case of the weekly transcontinental phone call to grandparents, such geographically dispersed social networks cannot have the same day-to-day significance as more concentrated, localized ones. Perhaps equally threatening, however, is the fact that geographic mobility may produce an adaptive cultural response in which short-term, immediate relationships become desirable in place of the more long-term interpersonally invested relationships that require daily contact over an extended period. Geographic mobility may make it more difficult for children and parents to have a common history with those in their current support system and to have shared experiences that build trust, understanding, and the motivation needed to provide nurturance and feedback. Interpersonal relationships may become more instrumental. Such relationships are inconsistent with genuine support systems in which validating the intrinsic worth of the person is the essential element.

The notion of "designing a sustainable society" presupposes that we can make alternative arrangements even though we cannot recapture what was good about the past. The promise of modern life was to relieve the physical burdens of the past, and thus permit social enrichment to grow in the context of material adequacy. Will it? It all depends upon whether or not we can shape a cultural consensus on the new social frontier. Our goal in this book has been to help define that new social frontier in terms of childhood and meeting the needs of children. In that frontier, we will find the very social and cultural agenda that will also deliver *adults* from spiritual and material crisis.

It may seem to be a contradiction in terms, but we think there is a need for "applied utopian thinking" to meet the social challenges before us. We say this because so many of our problems seem to call forth extremes of thinking—

either so concrete they never get beyond noses on faces, or so visionary they don't help people see how we might get from the proverbial here to there. We need a kind of middle range vision to guide us. As we have stated before in this book, we think children and child rearing *can* provide the necessary focus— if we are willing to see it.

## Making the Social Investment in Children

Just where do we stand on the matter of psychosocial investment in children? What are the prospects for the future? The evidence is mixed and often ambiguous. The challenging intellectual task of sorting out this evidence is complicated by the fact that experts often go well beyond their data to reflect their hunches, their bias, their fears, and even their political aspirations. Issues of family and children were the leading edge for political ideologies and social activism in the 1970s (Featherstone, 1979). This complicates the task before us because it demands that we separate enduring patterns of change and development from transitory politicized "events."

There is a deeply rooted tension—one might even say conflict—in American life about children. We hold ourselves up as a child-oriented society, but we consistently place ourselves at odds with the needs of children. We do so because of a kind of cultural poison (Zigler, 1976). As *Time* magazine put it "those who detect a pervasive, low-grade child aversion in the United States find it swarming in the air like pollen" (Morrow, 1979, p. 42). Politically, children are losers (Featherstone, 1979; Zigler, 1976). When the crunch comes in matters of budget and priorities, children lose out to the economic interests of adults and corporations. The issue is really one of investment: Where do we place that which we value? We think that several important points can be made on this score.

First, most Americans retain a fundamental and unwavering commitment to parenthood, despite the declining birth rate (Glick, 1979). In an extensive review of childlessness in the United States, Judith Blake (1979) reported the results of a nationwide survey of adults dealing with the advantages and disadvantages of childlessness. She found that adults will not be priced out of the parenthood market by the high economic costs of childbearing and child rearing, although they will decrease the number of children. People do value children for their intrinsic worth, and this affirmation is our bedrock for the future (Blake, 1979).

On balance, it seems clear that having and caring for children is a primary investment that is still being made and will continue to be made in the future. Smaller families are still families and tend to be good families at that (Lieberman, 1970). This fundamental commitment to having a child or children saves us from one side of the problem. It does not, however, guarantee the future. The quality of life (that is, the quality of children) in the future is by no means assured simply by the fact of their being born. The issue of enduring, appropriate, and necessary psychological and social investment remains. The thrust toward self-gratification may be incompatible with parenthood. Some data we cited earlier (Chapter 3) suggest this is a real problem and bear repeating.

A study by Bahr (1978) offers us a rare opportunity to compare adolescents' views of their parents in the same community over a 50-year span. It should come as no surprise that teenagers value fathers who spend time with them. Having enough time with one's father is a continuing and pervasive issue. In 1924, 64 percent of the females and 62 percent of the males felt that the most desirable attribute in the father is the fact that he spends time with his children. In 1977, these figures had risen to 71 percent and 64 percent respectively. This change is small and reflects the unchanging nature of father-adolescent relations. What is of real interest, however, is a significant change occurring in how much adolescents value their mothers spending time with them. In 1924, 34 percent of the boys and 41 percent of the girls placed a premium on having their mothers spend time with them. By 1971, the percentages had risen to 58 percent and 66 percent. This may reflect the gradual departure of mothers from the day-to-day lives of their adolescents over a 50-year period; a period that corresponds directly with the tremendous increase in mothers working outside the home. Mothers and fathers have become more alike in their day-to-day relations with children, we suspect. These data complement others collected by Bronfenbrenner (1979) and his colleagues that show a continuing decline in the amount of active time spent by parents with their children and link this decrease to a variety of disturbing trends, including impaired social functioning, alienation, and even profound unhappiness.

What makes people happy? For most adults, happiness lies in what Erikson (1963) called the issue of one's relation to the future, that of "generativity versus stagnation." Happiness lies in psychological and social investment in the future, for the quality of the future. Investment in children, either directly as a parent or indirectly as one who makes the world a better place for children, is important for happiness and shows a generally healthy world view. How well does our society do, and how well can it do in the future, in making this investment a productive one, a happy one? The answer will be found in the neighborhood and institutional lives of adults.

## Neighborhoods and the Institutional Life of the Community

Whether or not the intrinsic value of children will triumph over their cost depends in some measure on how supportive the family's neighborhood is. The quality of neighborhoods as contexts for family life has become a significant issue for students of community and human development. Although attractive in principle, "neighborhood" has proven very difficult to define in operational, specific terms as we reported in Chapter 7. Perhaps one of the best statements of what a good neighborhood is comes from Kromkowski (1976), when he says that:

> A neighborhood's character is determined by a host of factors, but most significantly by the kinds of relationships that neighbors have with each other. . . . A healthy neighborhood has some sort of cultural and institutional network which manifests itself in pride in the neighborhood, care of homes, security for children, and respect for each other (p. 228).

When stated this way, the significance of neighborhoods as support systems for families is clear and indisputable. A strong and supportive neighborhood can make the task of parenthood easier and more rewarding.

Economically and demographically, similar settings can present very different social environments, and the quality of life for parents and children can be likewise affected. In a recent study (Garbarino & Sherman, 1980, as discussed in Chapter 7), two neighborhoods were selected on the basis of their economic and demographic similarity and their child maltreatment rates. While well-matched economically and demographically, one area was particularly high-risk for children while the other was proportionally at lower risk. The rate of child maltreatment differed by a factor of five. When these two settings were examined, expert informants ranging from elementary school principals to mailcarriers saw the low-risk area as a healthy neighborhood and the high-risk area as a socially sick environment. Samples of families drawn from each neighborhood were interviewed. The families identified very different patterns of stresses and supports, different patterns in the use and source of help, differences in the size and quality of family social networks, differences in the use of formal support systems, and differences in parental evaluation of the neighborhood as a setting in which to raise children. Also, parents in the high-risk neighborhood reported high levels of stress in their day-to-day lives, and a general pattern of social impoverishment. High-risk neighborhoods are areas in which neighbors do not help each other, where there is suspicion about contact between parents and children, and in which the norms and behavior increase family weakness. We do not know exactly how this applies to rural areas, but the available evidence suggests social isolation is a threat in the rural environments as well (Rosenberg & Repucci, 1981).

Creating and maintaining strong neighborhoods for families is one of the principal challenges in designing a sustainable society. All the elements of quantitative growth work against neighborhoods. Mobility is a threat. Use of motorized transportation permits bedroom communities, undermines walking, and works against neighborhoods. Restrictive rezoning that produces residential ghettos works against neighborhoods because a functioning neighborhood requires some commercial activity. Within cities, strong neighborhoods resemble strong small towns (see Chapter 7). Will the seemingly inexorable trends toward the destruction of neighborhoods be permitted to continue? The answer will come in public decisions concerning rezoning and mass transportation. The quality of life for children is determined in large part by progress in the institutional (exosystem) life of the community.

The design and delivery of human services, the nature of adult work, and the structure and function of educational institutions all have a significant effect on the quality of life for children. Human services are delivered formally through a variety of public and semipublic institutions. How well can these formal support systems be integrated and balanced with the informal support systems, the "private enterprise system" of human services that offers most help on a day-to-day basis? As Chapter 8 showed, models for integrating formal and informal support systems are being developed, and in fact, are already in place in some communities (Garbarino, Stocking & Associates, 1980).

In the world of work, the concern is whether the role of parent will be sufficiently recognized. The entrance of large numbers of mothers of young children into the work force has made us keenly aware of the need to balance the relationship between work and home. The issue of working mothers has not been resolved satisfactorily—both their needs and the children's needs must be met. Providing adequate and developmentally enhancing day care for preschool children is an unsettled and highly charged issue. Our solutions to these dilemmas will have a bearing on the quality of life for children and, in fact, on the quality of children—their ability to be happy, productive adults—for life. When the world of work forces an adult, male *or* female, to choose between being a good parent and a good worker, children suffer and ultimately, the future is impoverished. As we move toward designing a sustainable society, we must keep in mind the need to establish norms about the world of work that will reduce its intrusion into family life. As we saw in Chapter 2, a well-adjusted person is distinguished by the ability both to work and to love. A high-quality society will arrange itself so that people can do justice to both. We find a parallel process at work in the schools.

Children's primary "work" is play, but most of their formal work takes place in school. Research on school size suggests that large schools (enrollments greater than 600 in grades 9–12) tend to become psychologically unsustainable (Garbarino, 1980d). Large schools discourage participation, create elitism, encourage staff inflexibility, and most insidiously, alienate those students who are already academically marginal (Barker & Gump, 1964). As of the 1970s, most youth in the United States were enrolled in big schools. Historical data on school size chronicle the decline of quality of life for children in this, their primary institutional setting. In this area perhaps more than any other, we have seen an unthinking policy of growth undermine and destroy socially desirable settings (small schools) in deference to goals of quantitative progress. The assumption that big schools mean power and opportunity directly parallels the notion that an unlimited policy of growth means progress. However, depersonalization and a reduction of social pluralism in the child's experience are alarming consequences of large schools. Bigger means, paradoxically, *less* social diversity for the individual student. Although school size nearly tripled from 1950 to 1980 (Garbarino, 1980d), the data suggest that a reverse of this trend is possible, particularly with shrinking enrollments. Just as escalating energy costs have given pragmatic impetus to "walking neighborhoods," these same forces will increasingly demonstrate the cost effectiveness of small schools. Such schools can now be technology-intensive to permit a resource-ladened environment: both academically rich *and* character-building (Garbarino, 1981b). Even where physically separate, small schools are not feasible, several small, complete schools can share the same facility.

Family, neighborhood, and the institutional life of the community are always in flux. Economic and demographic conditions may shift the direction of their influence, sometimes favoring supportive environments, sometimes undermining them, but the constant issue in all three areas is the stance taken by social policy.

A cross-national survey of public policy and public services for families concluded that the United States is relatively lax in providing for families and their support systems. The study conducted by Kahn and Kamerman (1975) found that in many respects: "The rhetoric in the United States proclaims the value and sanctity of children in family life; reality is something else. We provide nothing like the child-care services or cash benefits to protect child and family life that the European countries do." Former director of the Office of Child Development Edward Zigler (1976) echoed Kamerman and Kahn's judgment: "We think we care more than our actions would say." The scene in Washington seems to pit the "truly needy" vs. the "truly greedy," with powerful special interests winning out.

Decisions in the future must take into account the needs of children (our future) and of their parents (our present). For example, can we give workers adequate time for family and still have profitable corporations? The answer, we believe, is "yes." It is the nature of ideology to permeate all aspects of everyone's daily life. Thus, whether or not we develop a suitable pro-child ideology will be revealed not in grand pronouncements or even in master legislation, but in the day-to-day decisions that affect and shape the lives of families. The central position of ideology returns us to the political debate about the future.

# Children and the Social Policy Debate

To recapitulate, social impoverishment is the denuding of the individual's environment of those relationships that function as support systems and that provide nurturance and feedback. Growth, defined by quantitative product only, leads to social impoverishment. If we permit the social impoverishment of parents' lives, we undermine the quality of life for children and thus the quality of our future. Material growth ideology undermines children by contributing to social impoverishment. It does so by destroying the social integrity of neighborhoods, by increasing the demographic and social homogeneity of neighborhoods, by devaluing parenthood, by overemphasizing the importance of material productivity as a criterion for personal value, by increasing the instrumentality of social relations, by divorcing work and home, by promoting large schools, and by fostering values that emphasize material gratification over social responsibility. The growth policy debate must come to terms with the possibility that conventional thinking—the quantitative product orientation—is not socially sustainable.

It is a great temptation to propose a nostalgic, "good old days" solution, but this is useful only for comparison. What did families need in the old days that they still need now? With our different world, how can we give them what they still need? As individual families struggle with this issue, institutions (schools, courts, businesses, labor unions, churches, etc.) can make a vital contribution; they will decide how successful most families will be. If institutions are dominated by a quantitative orientation to growth, then families will be swimming against a tide that, for most, will be irresistible. The future is a public policy issue. There are at least five areas in which productive action is possible. These topics reflect an intermingling of action and ideology, of cause and effect, of shaping events and shaping minds. To design a sustainable society we must make progress on each of the following fronts.

## Family Impact Analysis

A scientific basis for evaluating the impact of change—particularly economic growth—on families is rudimentary. Investment in this area of research and development is a high priority item on the agenda in designing a sustainable society (Johnson, 1978). We need to make progress in moving toward a kind of "social currency" that can be used to compute the costs and benefits to families of various policies and decisions (Giarini, 1980).

For work to proceed on the family impact analysis concept in earnest we need to make progress in developing some sort of "social currency" with which to evaluate the wisdom and costs of alternative social arrangements. The "beauty" of economics is that it has an irrefutably important, dependent variable with palpable face validity: goods and services to which dollar values are readily attached. This elegantly simple conception of reality allows the advance of economic theory and research. It enhances the value of economic theory and research. Moreover, it permits economists to participate in the formulation and implementation of social policy. It is true that the forecasting and prediction that economists offer are often misleading, if not simply wrong. More important than those errors, however, is the fact that we know when they are wrong and have a reasonably firm basis for evaluating the magnitude and consequences of those errors—in terms of wholesale and retail price indices, GNP, unemployment rates, inflation rates, and all the other dollar-based paraphernalia of economic analysis.

It is true that economists have many faulty assumptions about social reality. The concept of "rational economic Man," for example, argues that all human behavior is governed by conscious, rational weighing of advantage. It is furthermore true that most economists do not have an adequate concept of the "hidden costs" of technology and the modern, energy-intensive, petroleum-based economy (Schumacher, 1973; Commoner, 1971). All this and more is true. But the strength of economics remains: It has a basic, dependent variable that provides coherence and a measure of conceptual order to its efforts. We find one of the best examples of the value of dollars as an organizing principle in the set of "budgets" published by the Department of Labor. For an economic environment such as the typical urban or suburban area, these budgets indicate the dollars needed for a family to function at several standards of living—what are termed "poverty," "low," "middle," and "high" income levels. These budgets provide an anchor point for socioeconomic analyses of all types (e.g., Garbarino, 1975a, 1980d). Based upon the availability of dollar resources to meet essential needs (food, clothing, housing, taxes) and make discretionary purchases (vacations, recreation, cultural resources), the standard budgets are a marvelous product of economic analysis, even if one disagrees with the specific dollar values at each level.

The budgets are important and insightful because they begin to recognize that the value of money is not primarily a matter of each additional dollar having the same impact as the previous one. That is, when using money as a factor in analyzing social phenomena, the key question is not simply, How much does one have?, but rather, What *kind* of life style can one purchase? The major phenomena are essentially qualitative. Is a family doomed to poverty? to struggle with no discretionary income? to a comfortable material existence? When applied to broader social analysis, the questions become these: What proportion of the population is comfortable? Are some groups confined to poverty while others are uniformly comfortable?

Simple analyses of average income do not answer these questions, for they do not address the essential issue of human behavior and development. The beauty of "dollars" as a unifying variable is that it can translate diverse items of interest (such as the multiple factors in the material conditions of life) into a single composite measure with validity and analytic power. The concept of dollars is, of course, limited in its application, since many vital social phenomena are not readily translatable. And that limitation brings us to the need for a social equivalent to "dollars."

Students of human development do not as yet have an equivalent to "dollars" as an organizing concept for research and theory. Research focuses on the documentation of statistically reliable differences. These differences are usually hard to relate to one another for purposes of combination or comparison. There is no underlying "currency" into which we can translate variables for purposes of integrating analyses. Does human development research and theory have a direct analog to GNP? to poverty? to price indices? to inflation rates? Is there a basis for the delineation of model social "budgets" to establish different standards of living in the noneconomic spheres?

The answer, of course, is no. But the need is quite real. One of the big tasks facing social science in the coming decades is to make progress on such a social currency. This will reform economics as well (Giarini, 1980). We believe the development of competence is a natural focus for such progress. A rich environment is one that succeeds in socializing competent children while maintaining a high quality environment.

## Neighborhoods as Units for Analysis and Planning

Local governments and corporate leaders need to become aware of the importance of thinking of neighborhoods—not simply of individuals and communities—as units of analysis. Data collection policies of the U.S. Census Bureau are already being changed to reflect this orientation, and in many ways adequate data are a precondition for intelligent policy. Growth policies must consider how they affect existing neighborhoods as well as how socially sustainable new residential developments will be (National Commission on Neighborhoods, 1979). Without such a conception at the heart of planning and zoning decisions, neighborhoods are doomed to be eroded and new "developments" will not be neighborhoods.

## Education of the Public

People should be educated about the importance of families in the social structure. The allure of materialism is great, but there are reservoirs of support for the primacy of family-related "payoffs" manifest in public opinion polls (cf., Harris, 1978). There is support for family life and there is recognition that family stability is a precondition for meaningful existence. We need public articulation of how personal and institutional decisions can tap these resources and respect the values they reflect. We need to resolve the conflict between home and work.

## Linking Professionals and Natural Helping Networks

Natural helping networks provide effective "human services" as well as substantial psychic payoffs (see also Chapter 8). A socially sustainable society requires that we reduce the exclusiveness of professionalized institutions. Also, it requires that we not build up budgetary expectations that are a constant economic drain and a periodic political liability. Instead, we should encourage greater sharing of helping functions with natural helping networks (Froland et al., 1979) and demystify psychological services.

## Age Integration

We need to decrease age segregation in our society. One goal is bringing adults into contact with youth in the context of purposeful, goal-directed activities and projects that encourage cooperation (Sherif, 1958). A second is to reward peer groups for pursuing prosocial goals. Coleman (1974) has noted our failure to make use of peer groups as a positive force in children's lives. Coleman's proposal for varsity athletics is one way to approach this (Coleman, 1961). A third is to promote cross-age tutoring (Gartner, Kohler and Riessman, 1971) and residential integration on the basis of age (VanVliet, in press).

# In Praise of Children

A sustainable society, one that is ecologically sound, should have children as its focal point because they are labor-intensive. Children benefit from a "small is beautiful" philosophy. Producing smaller, rather than larger schools is one concrete step that can serve as a focal point for efforts to enhance the psychological and social circumstances of childhood, and thus generally enrich the quality of human life. Directing institutional practice and policy toward families is imperative. This includes everything from giving families priority in the logistics of travel to offering tax incentives for responsible parenthood. As we look for ways to shift recreational activities away from excessive energy/material consumption, children and their activities are appealing. Play is both developmentally important and socially enriching. Some have lost sight of this in their efforts to make children's play more professional, as in the proliferation of costly and equipment-dependent sports. Family hikes and other "primitive" activities provide ecologically sound and psychologically satisfying, as well as developmentally enhancing, alternatives to energy-consuming activities.

As pointed out earlier, since it is demonstrably true that the thing of greatest value we have to offer children is our time and interest, it is a pleasant coincidence that such an investment is also a precondition for an ecologically sound and sustainable future society. Will we come to terms with the eternal frontier, with childhood? Children tell us much about the adults who rear them. What story will we tell about ourselves through our children? Our faith in the species is reflected in our having them and in our treatment of them.

> The childhood shows the way
> as morning shows the day.
>
> John Milton, *Paradise Regained*

What will tomorrow bring?

---

# PRACTICE CAPSULE

Kanter, R. M. *Work and family in the United States: A critical review and Agenda for research and policy.* New York: Russell Sage Foundation, 1977.

In her 1977 volume, *Work and Family in the United States,* Rosabeth Moss Kanter explored theoretical and practical issues in the interactions of family systems and the work world. She cited a number of factors that are eliciting adjustments in those relationships, including the women's movement, the increase of women in the paid-labor force, the increasing numbers of single-parent families, changes in expectations regarding life styles, growing awareness of life-style options, and revaluing of family life by organizational professionals. In reviewing some of the research on family—work relationships, she noted findings linking the skill level of a person's job to health indices; continued employment and work satisfaction to high longevity; occupational level in an organization to type of stress experienced; socioeconomic status to type of mental illness experienced; and income and socioeconomic status to happiness.

In the conclusion of her book, Kanter out-

lined a number of social policy innovations to adjust the family—work place relationship more in favor of families. Her proposals for changes in the policies and practices of employers included:

1. Widespread adoption of flex-time (flexible working hours) systems in which workers, within specified limits, set their own hours.
2. Organizational change and job redesign— for instance, to increase job control, expand sense of personal efficacy and discourage "workaholic" executives.
3. Joint family and work-group meetings and workshops in which families of co-workers raise, explore, and work to resolve common problems.
4. Bringing children (and perhaps spouses) to work for shared time with workers.
5. Leaves and sabbaticals, including maternity and paternity leave and other brief career interruptions.
6. Worker's compensation for families of work victims and for white-collar worker disabilities such as heart attacks.
7. "Family responsibility statements" in which organizations document their concern for families, perhaps including a review of the

potential family impacts of organizational policies such as working hours, promotion practices, job control, and executive transfers.

---

# FOR FURTHER READING

Bronfenbrenner, U. *Two worlds of childhood: U.S. and U.S.S.R.* New York: Simon and Schuster, 1972; orig. Russell Sage Foundation, 1970, 190 pp. (Although this also appears after Chapter 2, it is worth mentioning again.)

Bronfenbrenner is concerned that "we are experiencing a breakdown in the process of making human beings human" (xv). He contrasts life in the Soviet Union (a highly collectivist society) with life in the individualist United States. The book is a modern classic.

Coomer, J. (Ed.). *Quest for a sustainable society.* New York: Pergamon Press, 1980, 253 pp.

This book contains the 1979 winners of the Mitchell Prize, awarded by the Woodlands Conference on Growth Policy. Each chapter describes strategies and tactics for building a more ecologically sane and sustainable society in which human quality is the primary motivation and rationale for institutional life.

Elgin, D. *Voluntary simplicity.* New York: William Morrow, 1981, 312 pp.

The subtitle of this book is, "Toward a way of life that is outwardly simple, inwardly rich." Elgin suggests ways to simplify material needs while fulfilling emotional, psychological, and spiritual needs. While not specifically a work on families, this book offers both theoretical and practical suggestions that would lead to a sounder environment for children and their care givers.

*The family of man.* New York: Museum of Modern Art, 1955, 192 pp.

This classic photo essay expresses the basic human themes of Chapter 10 with unparalleled clarity. If a picture can be worth a thousand words, these 503 pictures are an eloquent feast.

Garbarino, J. *Successful schools and competent students.* Lexington, Mass.: L Lexington Books, 1981, 170 pp.

This book applies the human-quality theme developed in Chapter 10 to schools and schooling. It is a case study of how to analyze from an ecological perspective the workings and failings of one sector of the social environment.

Peccei, A. *The human quality.* New York: Pergamon Press, 1977, 214 pp.

Peccei asserts "the human lot cannot be trusted essentially to technologies" (xi); he helped found the Club of Rome on this basis, and gives several practical examples (businesses and international agreements) of how the emphasis on human quality works. The problem of growth is a concern of Peccei's and the Club's; he outlines values and goals for policymakers. Peccei describes "six missions for mankind"—ways to preserve the quality of life in the world community. Peccei is a self-described "revolutionary humanist," and his concerns are global.

Zablocki, B. *The joyful community: An account of the Bruderhof.* Baltimore: Penguin, 1971, 362 pp.

A utopian description rather than a theoretical piece, this book shows the successes (and failures) of child rearing and parenthood in an intentional community. The Bruderhof is the oldest collective in America.

Bennett, J. W. *Hutterian Brethren: The agricultural economy and social organization of a communal people.* Stanford: Stanford University Press, 1967, 298 pp.
Also a detailed account of a working alternative to the standard American one-family/one-home system.

---

# QUESTIONS FOR THOUGHT

---

1.  Read the sections of Plato's *Republic* and B. F. Skinner's *Walden Two* that deal with child rearing and education. Do they advocate the same methods? The same goals?

2.  Is a child infinitely malleable? What are the constraints and the probabilities? Sociobiologists offer some ideas on this (see Caplan's edited collection, *The Sociobiology Debate,* New York: Harper and Row, 1978).

3.  "The tragedy of life is that we need other people." Explore this statement.

4.  What does "labor-intensive" mean? Create a child rearing scenario with this idea in mind.

5.  Why are children important? Are they only important to their parents? How does the community define and exhibit its responsibility for children?

6.  What elements in our society point toward a positive valuing of children? What ones to a negative valuing?

7.  What are the essentials of happiness? (Bertrand Russell thought they were good health, good work, and good friends, in that order.) Where do children fit in?

# Afterword: What Does It Mean To Be Human?

We have come a long way in this text. We have wrestled with a broad range of issues in applied human development, and that is a major accomplishment for student and author alike. But we cannot end without posing one fundamental question that has lurked beneath the surface of our discussion, never fully surfacing. We have left this question unspoken for two reasons. First, our primary task was to examine the nuts and bolts of applied human development: the role of the professional helper in the social environment of children and families. Second, this unspoken question goes beyond the conventional scope of professional development and social science research. These are reasons enough to put off this question, but they do not justify ending our discussion without raising it, and so we ask: *What does it mean to be human?* In this section, we will consider this most fundamental of questions for the student of behavior and development. In so doing, we will raise some philosophical and theological matters with which each of us should wrestle as we seek to recognize and fulfill our roles as professionals and our destinies as people.

## Who Are We? How Do We Know? Should We Be So Sure?

Who are we? Where do we come from? How did we get here? Where are we going? These are the fundamental and eternal questions of human existence, yet we rarely find time for them in social service and social science discussions. Notice that these questions use the collective pronoun "we" instead of the singular "I." This may seem strange because as Americans we are accustomed to thinking of ourselves first as individuals, and only secondarily as part of a group. But our individualistic emphasis may obscure some of the most important truths about human existence. To understand individuals, we must understand the groups from which they come. To know who we are as individuals, we must know where we fit into the human community. This even applies to genetics, where the sum of a group's genes (its gene pool) is its biological legacy. To know where we are going, we must understand where our people have been. We can understand individual characteristics only when we can place those characteristics in the context of the larger human community in which they develop.

When a baby is born there is a rush to see who it looks like. "Your nose, but my eyes!" "Uncle George's chin!" "His brother's ears." Children are the currency of kinship. They are what bind the generations together.

When we scrutinize old photos of ourselves, we look to find some evidence of our current self in that younger stranger frozen in time. Many adopted children search endlessly in their adult lives to discover their "true roots," meaning their biological origins. When we see teenagers struggling with pimples, we remember. When we hear the old people tell stories about the "way it was," we seek some way to connect ourselves to that past. When a person struggles to avoid becoming what her or his parents were, we can sympathize. Human life is as much the past as it is the present and the future.

Who cannot be moved by the excitement of discovering one's ancestors? Who is not enriched by uncovering the connections of kinship? After searching through old and faded archives in a small Scottish parish church and tracking down the kindly rector, Anne Garbarino received a suggestion that she search among the gravestones for a relative who had been dead for some two hundred years. The search was rewarded. The moment was magnificent. Equally so was the expression on her paternal grandmother's face when she saw pictures of the gravestones and the records from the parish church. This feeling of wholeness and connection with the past through one's family is central to the human experience.

When we see a young child struggling to master a skill we now possess, we are made aware of the enormous growth and change that takes place in the everyday life of our fellow human beings. What parents do not share the unbounded glee of their infant child's accomplishments! Ah, to be able to turn over! To sit unaided! To crawl! To stand unassisted! And, miracle of miracles, to walk! We all can appreciate these wonders, but the special bond between parent and child goes further. To be a parent is to have a special feeling of responsibility for a special being. The Russian novelist Leo Tolstoy captured the parental perspective in his epic *War and Peace*.

> The universal experience of the ages, showing that children grow from the cradle to manhood, did not exist for the Countess. The growth of her son had been for her at every stage as extraordinary as though millions and millions of men had not already developed in the same way. Just as twenty years before it had seemed unbelievable that the little creature lying under her heart would ever cry, nurse at the breast, or talk, so now she could not believe that this same little creature could be that strange brave officer, that paragon of sons and men, which, judging by his letter he now was (Tolstoy, pp. 291–292).

The study of human development is literally a science of miracles. The baby is created out of near nothingness, built from minute specks of human matter. From two people comes the potential for a third. From a tiny creature—capable only of the most primitive functions—comes a person capable of language, love, thought, art, and science. From infant organism to cultured person, human development is a series of miracles, one after another.

And then there are the painful challenges arising from the growth process gone awry. The human condition also contains the potential for hate, disfigurement, violence, greed, and evil. We cannot ignore the stagnation of a biologically healthy brain by a harsh and depriving environment. We cannot avoid seeing the pain in broken relationships or in personal decline (e.g., despair, depression, frustration, violence) that replaces growth with deterioration in an uncaring environment (a sociocultural risk factor). What does it all mean?

*What does it mean to be human?* Ask a fish to describe water. Like the fish, we *experience* our existence and are hard-pressed to know what that existence is like in contrast to other, alternative existences. But unlike the fish, *we* can try to answer the question. And try we must. For the human service professional, who must deal with the limits of humanness on a day-to-day basis, the question cannot long remain unasked, if not unanswered. The profoundly retarded, the senile, the psychotic, the terminally comatose, all these force us to ask, "What does it mean to be human?" For those of us who choose the role of professional helper, it certainly means to choose to do what we can do to make the world a better place for children and families. To do this, we must know what will not be accepted in the name of political expediency and economic self-interest. Writing in the fourth century B.C., the Chinese philosopher Mericius said it well when he said that people:

> ". . . must be decided on what they will not do, and then they are able to act with vigor in what they ought to do." (Book IV, 2:8)

We must act on our beliefs and our feelings with compassion and with vigor.

> The only thing necessary for the triumph of evil is for good men to do nothing
> (Edmund Burke)

To be fully human is to decide.

When does life begin? Is abortion "murder," or is it an acceptable medical procedure on behalf of the mother? When does life end? Is it murder to cease treating a permanently comatose accident victim, a terminally ill elder, a grotesquely deformed neonate? What does it mean to be a person? How can we decide the appropriate point at which individual interests should be subordinate to group interests, at which living should be subordinate to life? Can science tell us?

Consider the classic case of the Elephant Man, John Merrick. What does science contribute to our understanding of this character made famous by a film and a Broadway play? Merrick, living in the 1880s, in England, was victim of a severe case of neurofibromatosis in which his entire body was misshapen and covered with large discolored tumors. That grotesque body hid his beautiful spirit and fine mind, and he had to struggle daily to achieve recognition of his very personhood. In analyzing Merrick and his life, Ashley Montague offered the following conclusion:

> Merrick bore with courage and dignity the hideous deformities and other ills with which he was afflicted. The nightmare existence he had led during the greater part of his life, he put behind him. He never complained or spoke unkindly of those who had maltreated him. His suffering, like a cleansing fire, seems to have brought him nearer to that human condition in which all the nonessentials of life having fallen away, only the essential goodness of man remained. (Montague, 1979, p. 78).

His physician and friend, John Treves, said of Merrick:

> As a specimen of humanity, Merrick was ignorable and repulsive; but the spirit of Merrick, if it could be seen in the form of the living, would assume the figure of an upstanding and heroic man, smooth browed and clean of limb, with eyes that flashed undaunted courage. (cited in Montague, 1979, p. 37)

What does it mean to be human? What does it take to be a person? Intelligence? Language? Soul? We can easily get out of our scientific depth here, but we cannot avoid at least asking. Recent research on primates and dolphins forces the issue. A monkey can now communicate with a person via sign language and symbolic computerized machinery. Dolphin language is being subjected to sophisticated analyses. Some say that if the intelligence of the planet's organisms was viewed as a landscape, we would readily acknowledge two peaks towering above the hills and plains below. On one would be the

*Homo sapiens;* on the other, the dolphin. Likewise, recent developments in the study of language and thought among the apes lead Carl Sagan to ask how far chimpanzees will have to go in demonstrating their abilities to reason, feel, and communicate before we define killing one as murder, before missionaries will seek to convert them.

And, after visiting a lab in which chimps were kept imprisoned in their cages, Sagan wondered:

> If they are "only" animals, if they are beasts which abstract not, then my comparison is a piece of sentimental foolishness . . . but I think it is certainly worthwhile to raise the question: Why, exactly, all over the civilized world, in virtually every major city, are apes in prison? (Sagan, 1977, p. 120–121)

This is no new issue, of course. One of the first items on humankind's agenda has always been to ask, Who are we? and Where do we stand in the world? Classical philosophy arose in part as an attempt to wrestle with the very question before us: What does it mean to be human? We, of the late twentieth century, have a particularly hard time of it because science has debunked many of our most cherished myths. Darwin's theory of evolution put us into the animal lineup as what Desmond Morris so aptly called "the naked ape" (1972). Sigmund Freud undermined the very rationality to which we have appealed for a sense of superiority. Science seems to put us in our place, and it's not surprising that many people feel uncomfortable, if not actually resentfully angry, about what that place appears to be. We are left to make a place for ourselves, to make peace with the world. It is fundamentally human to search for the Good. But to seek the Good as we do is to turn away from The Bad. And so, as professionals, as social scientists, and as people, we need to consider the perennial and inescapable problem of Good and Evil. We close our discussion with this issue and hope that raising it will be a stimulus to professional and personal growth and development.

Does evil exist? Certainly we would all agree that terrible things occur in our world. Can we infer the existence of evil from our observations of the day-to-day world, just as we infer the existence of gravity? Both are all but inescapable conclusions, so long as we don't torture common language to escape them. While evil may be a theoretical or hypothetical idea, it is no less real for being such. Developments in the emerging field of sociobiology even suggest genetic mechanisms for both good and evil, altruism and selfishness. There are ample grounds for presuming the existence of evil in human behavior. The practical corollary is that the harmful conditions in which many people exist (sometimes just barely), are themselves evil.

This concern about the nature of being human, and the conception of good and evil, is alien to most of what we call social science. However, there is a kind of shadow government, a counterforce to the dominant view, that has questioned the moral limitations of social science since its inception. This view is most naturally represented by those people who seek to combine, in one person, the secular (nonreligious) rationality of modern social analysis and the transcendent moral commitment of religion. Reinhold Niebuhr, twentieth-century American theologian and social critic, was such a notable person. Neibuhr's injunction was to do good with our eyes open.

> The children of light must be armed with the wisdom of the children of darkness but remain free from their malice. They must know the power of self-interest in human society without giving it moral justification. They must have this wisdom in order that they may beguile, deflect, harness, and restrain self-interest, individual and collective, for the sake of the community. (Niebuhr, 1944, p. 41).

Can we ignore good and evil in social policy and practice? Can we ignore the conflicts inherent in setting priorities among values, in ordering our principles? Should the proper foundation for social policy and practice include a set of principles designed to enhance good and suppress evil? As Niebuhr points out, our characteristic scientific philosophy results in an idealism that may not be suited to the real world.

> Whenever modern idealists are confronted with the divisive and corrosive effects of man's self-love, they look for some immediate cause of this perennial tendency, usually in some specific form of social organization. One school holds that men would be good if only political institutions would not corrupt them; another believes that they would be good if the prior evil of a faulty economic organization could be eliminated. Or another school thinks of this evil as no more than ignorance, and therefore waits for a more perfect educational process to redeem man from his partial and particular loyalties. But no school asks how it is that an essentially good man could have produced corrupting and tyrannical political organizations or exploiting economic organizations, or fanatical and superstitious religious organization. (Niebuhr, 1944, p. 17)

We face this problem as well when we attempt to deal with issues in human services. Where do social problems such as child abuse, rape, and economic exploitation come from? In what way are they a manifestation of evil? In what way are they a corruption of goodness? What are our prospects for dealing with them if we rely only on education and persuasion, while ignoring social control and conversion? Can we develop a legitimately scientific stance toward good and evil in the world? What *does* it mean to be human? What will we make of this opportunity that we all share to answer this question in the way we live our lives?

# Bibliography

Action for Children's Television News. Fall, 1976, 6(1).

Aiello, J. R. Children, crowding, and control: Effects of environmental stress on social behavior. In J. F. Wohlwill & W. van Vliet (Eds.), *Habitats for children: The impact of density*. New York: Academic Press, in press.

Ainsworth, M. D. S. The development of infant—mother attachment. In B. M. Caldwell & H. N. Ricciuti (Eds.), *Review of child development research*, Vol. 3. Chicago: University of Chicago Press, 1973.

Ainsworth, M. D. S., & Bell, S. M. Mother—infant interaction and the development of competence. In K. J. Connelly & J. S. Bruner (Eds.), *The growth of competence*. New York: Academic Press, 1974.

Albee, G. *Politics, power, prevention and social change*. In G. Gerbner, C. Ross, & E. Zigler (Eds.), *Child abuse: An agenda for action*. New York: Oxford University Press, 1980.

Aldous, J., & Hill, R. Breaking the poverty cycle: Strategic points for intervention. *Social Work*, 1969, *14*, 3—12.

Aldrich, R. The influences of man-built environment on children and youth. In W. Michelson, S. Levine, & E. Michelson (Eds.), *The child in the city*. Toronto: University of Toronto Press, 1979.

**261**

Alinsky, S. D. *Reveille for radicals.* New York: Vintage Books, 1969.

Almond, G., & Verba, S. *The civic culture: Political attitudes and democracy in five nations.* Princeton, N.J.: Princeton University Press, 1965.

American Medical Association. *Statement on parent and newborn interaction.* Chicago, IL, 1977.

Anderson, R. E., & Carter, I. *Human behavior in the social environment: A social systems approach* (2nd ed.). New York: Aldine, 1978.

Aries, P. *Centuries of childhood.* London: Jonathan Cape, 1962.

Bahr, H. Change in family life in Middletown: 1924–1977. Paper presented at the Annual Meeting of the American Sociological Association, Chicago, IL, August, 1978.

Bahr, S. J. The effects of welfare on marital stability and remarriage. *Journal of Marriage and the Family,* 1979, *41*(3), 553–560.

Bailey, A. A wartime childhood (part I). *New Yorker,* January 19, 1981.

Baldwin, W. H. Adolescent pregnancy and childbearing: Growing concern for Americans. *Population Bulletin,* 1976, *31*(2).

Baltes, P., & Danish, S. Intervention in life-span development and aging: Issues and concepts. In R. R. Turner & H. W. Reese (Eds.), *Life-span developmental psychology: Intervention.* New York: Academic Press, 1979.

Bane, M. J. *Here to stay: American families in the twentieth century.* New York: Basic Books, 1976.

Barash, D. P. *Sociobiology and behavior.* Elsevier: New York, 1977.

Barker, R., & Gump, P. *Big school, small school.* Stanford, CA: Stanford University Press, 1964.

Barker, R. G. & Schoggen, P. *Qualities of community life: Methods of measuring environment and behavior applied to an American and an English town.* San Francisco: Jossey-Bass, 1973.

Bateson, G. *Steps to an ecology of mind.* New York: Chandler, 1972.

Baumrind, D. A dialectical materialist's perspective on knowing social reality. *New Directions in Child Development,* 1979, *2,* 61–82.

Baumrind, D. New directions in socialization research. *American Psychologist,* 1980, *35,* 639–652.

Baumrind, D., & Block, A. E. Socialization practices associated with dimensions of competence in pre-school boys and girls. *Child Development,* 1967, *38,* 291–327.

Beckwith, L. Caregiver–infant interaction as a focus for therapeutic intervention with human infants. In Walsh & Greenough (Eds.), *Environments as therapy for brain dysfunction.* New York: Plenum, 1976.

Bell, R. Q. A reinterpretation of the direction of effects in studies of socialization. *Psychological Review,* 1968, *75,* 81–95.

Bell, R. Q. Contributions of human infants to caregiving and social interaction. In M. Lewis & L. A. Rosenbaum (Eds.), *The effect of the infant on its caregivers.* New York, John Wiley & Sons, 1974.

Belsky, J. Early human experience: A family perspective. *Developmental Psychology,* 1981 *17,* 3–23.

Belsky, J., & Benn, J. Beyond bonding: A family-centered approach to enhancing early parent–infant relations. Chapter to appear in the proceedings of the Sixth Annual Vermont Conference for the Primary Prevention of Psychopathology. Hanover, NH: New England Press, in press.

Belsky, J., & Steinberg, L. The effects of day care: A critical review. *Child Development*, 1978, *49*, 929–949.

Benedict, R., Continuities and discontinuities in cultural conditioning, *Psychiatry*, 1938, *1*, 161–167.

Berger, P. L., & Neuhaus, R. J. *To empower the people: The role of mediating structures in public policy*. Washington, DC: American Enterprise Institute for Policy Research, 1977.

Bernard, J. The good-provider role. *American Psychologist*, 1981, *36*, 1–13.

Berry, W. *The unsettling of America*. San Francisco: Sierra Club, 1977.

Bettelheim, B. Untying the family. In E. Douvan, H. Weingarten, & J. Scheiber (Eds.), *American families*. Dubuque, IA: Kendall and Hunt, 1980.

Biehler, R. F. *Child development: An introduction* (2nd ed.). Boston: Houghton-Mifflin Co., 1981.

Bing, E. Lamaze childbirth among the Amish people. *Birth and the Family Journal*, 1975, *2*, 39–42.

Blake, J. Is zero preferred? American attitudes toward childlessness in the 1970's. *Journal of Marriage and the Family*, 1979, *41*, 245–265.

Blehar, M. C. Families and public policy. In E. Corfman (Ed.), *Families today: A research sampler on families and children*. Washington, DC: U.S. Government Printing Office, DHEW Publication No. ADM 79-815, 1979.

Block, C. R., & Block, R. L. The effect of support of the husband and obstetrician on pain perception and control in childbirth. *Birth and the Family Journal*, 1975, *2*, 43–47.

Block, C. R., Norr, K. L., Meyering, S., Norr, J. L., & Charles, A. G. Husband gatekeeping in childbirth. *Family Relations*, 1981 *30*, 197–204.

Bogue, D., & Bogue, E. *Essays in human ecology*. Chicago: University of Chicago, 1976.

Bolling, L. R. For the strengthening of private and volunteer services. *Foundation News*, 1980, *21*(6), 1.

Bolton, F. G., Jr. *The pregnant adolescent: Problems of premature parenthood*. Beverly Hills, CA: Sage Publications, 1980.

Booth, A. Quality of children's family interaction in relation to residential type and household crowding. In J. F. Wohlwill & W. van Vliet (Eds.), *Habitats for children: The impact of density*. New York: Academic Press, in press.

Brackbill, Y. Extinction of the smiling response in infants as a function of reinforcement schedule. *Child Development*, 1958, *86*, 3–80.

Brackbill, Y. Obstetrical medication study. *Science*, 1979, *205*, 447–448.

Brazelton, T. B. Parental perceptions of infant manipulations: Effects on parents of inclusion in our research. In V. L. Smeriglio, *Newborns and parents*. Hillsdale, NJ: Lawrence Erlbaum Associates, 1981.

Brazelton, T. B., Koslowski, B., & Main, M. The origins of reciprocity: The early mother–infant interaction. In M. Lewis & L. A. Rosenblum (Eds.), *The effects of the infant on its caregiver*. New York: John Wiley & Sons, 1974.

Brim, O. G. Macro-structural influences on child development and the need for childhood social indicators. *American Journal of Orthopsychiatry*, 1975, *45*, 516–524.

Brim, O. G., Jr., & Kagan, J. (Eds.). *Constancy and change in human development*. Cambridge, MA: Harvard University Press, 1980.

Bronfenbrenner, U. *Two worlds of childhood*. New York: Russell Sage Foundation, 1970.

Bronfenbrenner, U. Developmental research, public policy, and the ecology of childhood. *Child Development*, 1974, *45*, 1–5.

Bronfenbrenner, U. The origins of alienation. In U. Bronfenbrenner and M. Mahoney (Eds.), *Influences on human development.* Hinsdale, IL: Dryden Press, 1975.

Bronfenbrenner, U. *The ecology of human development: Experiments by nature and design.* Cambridge, MA: Harvard University Press, 1979.

Bronfenbrenner, U. & Crouter, A. Work and family through time and space. In S. B. Kamerman and C. D. Hayes (Eds.), *Families that work: Children in a changing environment of work, family, and community.* National Academy of Sciences, 1982.

Bronfenbrenner, U., & Crouter, A. C. Research models in field studies of human development. In P. Mussen (Ed.), *The handbook of child psychology,* in press.

Bronfenbrenner, U., & Mahoney, M. The structure and verification of hypotheses. In U. Bronfenbrenner & M. Mahoney (Eds.), *Influences on human development.* Hinsdale, IL: Dryden Press, 1975.

Bronowski, J. *Science and human values.* New York: Harper & Row, 1965.

Bruner, J. S. *The process of education.* Cambridge, MA: Harvard University Press, 1960.

Burgess, R. L. Relationships in marriage and the family. In S. Duck & R. Gilmour (Eds.), *Personal relationships.* London: Academic Press, Inc., 1980.

Burgess, R. L., Anderson, E. A., & Schellenbach, C. J. A social interactional approach to the study of abusive families. In J. P. Vincent (Ed.), *Advances in family interaction, assessment and theory: An annual compilation of research* (Vol. 2). Greenwich, CT: JAI Press, 1980.

Burgess, R. L. & Conger, R. Family interaction patterns in abusive, neglectful and normal families. *Child Development,* 1978, *49,* 163–173.

Burgess, R. L., Garbarino, J., & Gilstrap, B. Violence to the family. In E. Callahan & K. McCluskey (Eds.), *Life-span developmental psychology: Non-normative life events.* New York: Academic Press, in press.

Burris, M. E. Food marketing institute: State of the industry. Presentation made in American Marketing Institute Conference, Dallas, Texas, May 7, 1979, *Behavior Today* (June 4, 1979).

Butnarescu, G. F., Tillotson, D. M., Villarreal, P. P. *Perinatal nursing* (Vol. 2). *Reproductive Risk.* New York: John Wiley & Sons, 1980.

Caine, L. *Widow: The personal crisis of a widow in America.* New York: William Morrow, 1974.

Campbell, A. Subjective measures of well being. *American Psychologist,* 1976, *31,* 117–124.

Campbell, A., Converse, P. E., & Rodgers, W. *The quality of American life: Perceptions, evaluations and satisfactions.* New York: Russell Sage Foundation, 1976.

Campbell, D. T. On the conflicts between biological and social evolution and between psychology and moral tradition. *American Psychologist,* 1975, *30,* 1103–1126.

Caplan, G. *Support systems and community mental health.* New York: Behavioral Publications, 1974.

Cherlin, A. *Marriage, divorce, remarriage. Changing patterns in the postwar United States.* Cambridge, MA: Harvard University Press, 1981.

Children's Defense Fund. *Children out of school in America.* Washington, DC: Washington Research Project, Inc., 1974.

Children's Defense Fund. *Children without homes: An examination of public responsibility to children in out-of-home care.* Washington, DC: Children's Defense Fund, 1978.

Children's Defense Fund. *CDF Reports,* 1981, *3,* No. 9, September, 1ff.

Chilman, C. S. Public social policy and families in the 1970's. *Social Casework,* 1973, *54,* 575–585.

Chilman, C. S. *Adolescent sexuality in a changing American society: Social and psychological perspectives.* Washington, D.C.: U.S. Department of Health, Education, and Welfare, 1980.

Chodorow, N. *The reproduction of mothering: Psychoanalysis and the sociology of gender.* Berkeley, CA: University of California Press, 1978.

Claassen, A. The policy perspective: Social problems as investment opportunities. *Social Problems,* 1980, 27 (5), 526–539.

Clark, A. L. Historical perspectives. In A. L. Clark & D. D. Affonso (Eds.), *Childbearing: A nursing perspective* (2nd ed.). Philadelphia: F. A. Davis Co., 1979.

Clausen, J. A. Family structure, socialization, and personality. In L. W. Hoffman & M. L. Hoffman (Eds.), *Review of child development research.* Vol. 2. New York: Russell Sage, 1966.

Clemente, F., & Sauer, W. J. Life satisfaction in the United States. *Social Forces,* 1976, 54, 621–631.

Cleveland, H., & Wilson, T. *Human growth: An essay on growth, values, and the quality of life.* Aspen, CO: Institute for Humanistic Studies, 1978.

Coleman, J. S., *The adolescent society: The social life of the teenager and its impact on education,* Glencoe, IL: Free Press, 1961.

Coleman, J. S. *Youth: Transition to adulthood.* Chicago, IL: University of Chicago Press, 1974.

Coleman, J. S. *Equality of educational opportunity.* Washington, DC: U.S. Government Printing Office, 1966.

Coles, R. *Children of crisis: Privileged ones.* Boston: Little, Brown, 1978.

Collins, A. The establishment and maintenance of a family day care network. In S. Maybanks & M. Bryce (Eds.), *Home-based services for children and families: Policy, practice, and research.* Springfield, IL: C. C. Thomas, 1979.

Collins A., & Pancoast, D. *Natural helping networks.* Washington, DC: National Association of Social Workers, 1976.

Collins, A., & Watson, E. *Family day care.* Boston: Beacon Press, 1976.

Collins, A. H. Helping neighbors intervene in cases of maltreatment. In J. Garbarino, S. H. Stocking and Associates, *Protecting children from abuse and neglect.* San Francisco: Jossey-Bass, 1980.

Colman, R. A. D., & Colman, L. L. *Pregnancy: The psychological experience.* New York: Herder & Herder, 1971.

Commoner, B. *The closing circle: Nature, man and technology.* New York: Alfred P. Knopf, 1971.

Cooper, B., & Gath, D. Psychiatric illness, maladjustment, and juvenile delinquency: An ecological study in a London borough. *Psychological Medicine,* 1977, 7, 465–474.

Coopersmith, S. *The antecedents of self-esteem.* San Francisco: Freeman, 1967.

Council on Environmental Quality, "Global Future: Time to Act," Washington, DC: U.S. Department of State, 1981.

Crain, R. Why academic research fails to be useful. *School Review,* 1976, 84, 337–351.

Daly, H. E. *Toward a steady-state economy.* San Francisco: W. H. Freeman Co., 1973.

Danish, S., Smyer, M., & Nowak, C. Developmental intervention: Enhancing life-event processes. In P. B. Baltes & O. G. Brim, Jr. (Eds.), *Life-span development and behavior* (Vol. 3). New York: Academic Press, 1980.

Danziger, S. The medical context of childbearing: A study of social control in doctor-patient interaction. *Social Science and Medicine,* 1979a.

Danziger, S. On doctor watching: Fieldwork in medical settings. *Urban Life,* 1979b, 7(4).

Degler, C. N. *At odds.* London: Oxford University Press, 1980.

deLone, R. *Small futures: Children, inequality, and the limits of liberal reform.* New York: Harcourt Brace Jovanovich, 1979.

Demone, H. W. Stimulating human services reform. Washington, DC: U.S. Government Printing Office, DHEW Publication No. OS-76-130, 1978. (Also, *Human Services Monograph Series,* No. 8, June, 1978.)

Denver apartment block pioneers 1-parent style. Dayton, OH, *Daily News,* December 24, 1979.

Devereux, E. *A critique of ecological psychology.* Paper presented at the Conference on Research Perspectives in the Ecology of Human Development, Cornell University, Ithaca, NY, August, 1977.

Dittmann, L. Affecting social policy in community and nation. *Childhood Education,* 1979, February/March, 194–199.

Doering, S. G., & Entwisle, D. R. Preparation during pregnancy and ability to cope with labor and delivery. *American Journal of Orthopsychiatry,* 1975, 45(5), 825–837.

Douvan, E., & Adelson, J. *The adolescent experience.* New York: Wiley & Sons, 1966.

Dreeben, R. *On what is learned in school.* Reading, MA: Addison-Wesley Publishing Company, 1968.

Dunu, M. The Lower East Side Family Union: Assuring community services for minority families. In S. Maybanks and M. Bryce (Eds.), *Home-based services for children and families: Policy, practice, and research.* Springfield, IL: C. C. Thomas, 1979.

Duvall, E. M. *Family development.* Philadelphia: J. B. Lippincott, 1975.

Eells, L. The good life: Smaller is better. *Nebraska Annual Social Indicators Survey* (NASIS-80 #11), 1981.

Ehrlich, P. Diversity and steady state. In J. C. Coomer (Ed.), *Quest for a sustainable society.* New York: Pergamon Press, 1981.

Elder, G. H. *Children of the great depression.* Chicago: University of Chicago Press, 1974.

Elder, G. H., Adolescence in historical perspective. In J. Adelson (Ed.), *Handbook of Adolescent Psychology,* New York: John Wiley and Sons, 1980.

Elder, G. H., & Rockwell, R. *The life course and human development: An ecological perspective.* Unpublished paper. Boys Town, NE: Boys Town Center for the Study of Youth Development, 1977.

El Sherif, C., McGrath, G., & Smyrski, J. T. Coaching the coach. *Journal of Obstetrical and Gynecological Nursing,* March–April, 1979, 87–89.

Emlen, A. *If you care about children, then care about parents.* Address to the Tennessee Association for Young Children, Nashville, TN, November, 1977.

Erikson, E. *Childhood and society* (2nd ed.). New York: Norton, 1963.

Erikson, E. *Identity: Youth and crisis.* New York: Norton, 1968.

Erikson, K. T. *Everything in its path: Destruction of community in the Buffalo Creek flood.* New York: Simon and Schuster, 1976.

Eron, L. D. Prescription for reduction of aggression. *American Psychologist,* 1980, 35, 244–252.

Featherstone, J. Family matters. *Harvard Educational Review,* 1979, 49, 20–56.

Federal Bureau of Investigation. *Uniform crime reports for the U.S., 1977.* Washington, DC: U.S. Government Printing Office, 1978.

Federal Bureau of Investigation. *Uniform crime reports for the U.S., 1979.* Washington, DC: U.S. Government Printing Office, 1980.

Fein, R. A. Men's entrance to parenthood. *The Family Coordinator,* 1976, *25,* 341–348.

Feiring, C., & Lewis, M. The child as a member of the family system. *Behavioral Science,* 1978, *23,* 225–233.

Finkelhor, D. *Sexually victimized children.* New York: The Free Press, 1979.

Ford, D. Mental health and human development: An analysis of a dilemma. In D. Harshbarger and R. Maley (Eds.), *Behavior analysis and systems analysis: An integrative approach to mental health programs.* Kalamazoo, MI: Behaviordelia, 1974.

Foss, B. M. (Ed.). *Determinants of infant behavior.* London: Methuen, 1965.

Fraiberg, S. Parallel and divergent patterns in blind and sighted infants. *Psychoanalytic Study of the Child,* 1968, *23,* 264–299.

Fraiberg, S. Blind infants and their mothers: An examination of the sign system. In M. Lewis & L. Rosenblum (Eds.), *Origins of behavior* (Vol. 1). New York: John Wiley & Sons, 1973.

Franzier, A., & Lisonbee, L. K. Adolescent concerns with physique. *School Review,* 1950, *58,* 397–405.

Fraser, B. G. Independent representation for the abused and neglected child: The guardian ad litem. *California Western Law Review,* 1976–77, *13*(1), 16–45.

Freedman, D. *Human infancy: an evolutionary perspective.* Hillsdale, NJ: Lawrence Erlbaum Associates, 1974.

Freud, A., & Dann, S. An experiment in group upbringing. In *The psychoanalytic study of the child* (Vol. 6). New York: International Universities, 1951, 127–168.

Friedman, R. Child abuse: A review of the psychosocial research. In Herner & Co. (Eds.), *Four perspectives on the status of child abuse and neglect research.* Washington, DC: National Center on Child Abuse and Neglect, 1976.

Froland, C., Pancoast, D., Chapman, N., & Kimboko, P. Networking: What's it all about. *Caring,* 1979, *5*(3), 1–10.

Furby, L. Sharing: decisions and moral judgments about letting others use one's possessions. *Psychological Reports,* 1978, *43,* 595–609.

Furstenberg, F. *Unplanned parenthood: The social consequences of teenage childbearing.* New York: The Free Press, 1976.

Galle, O., Gove, W., & McPherson, J. Population density and pathology: What are the relationships for man? *Science,* 1972, *176,* 23–30.

Garbarino, J. *Religion and democracy.* Unpublished thesis, St. Lawrence University, Canton, NY, 1968.

Garbarino, J. The meaning and implications of school success. *The Educational Forum,* 1975a, *40,* 157–168.

Garbarino, J. A note on television viewing. In U. Bronfenbrenner and M. Mahoney (Eds.), *Influences on human development.* Hinsdale, IL: Dryden Press, 1975b.

Garbarino, J. A preliminary study of some ecological correlates of child abuse: The impact of socioeconomic stress on mothers. *Child Development,* 1976, *47,* 178–185.

Garbarino, J. The human ecology of child maltreatment: A conceptual model for research. *Journal of Marriage and the Family,* 1977a, *39,* 721–736.

Garbarino, J. The price of privacy: An analysis of the social dynamics of child abuse. *Child Welfare,* 1977b, *56,* 565–575.

Garbarino, J. Child abuse: What resources for meeting the problem? *Vital Issues,* 1978a, *28*(2).

Garbarino, J. The elusive "crime" of emotional abuse. *Child Abuse and Neglect,* 1978b, *2,* 89–100.

Garbarino, J. Changing hospital childbirth practices: A developmental perspective on prevention of child maltreatment. *American Journal of Orthopsychiatry,* 1980a, *50,* 588–597.

Garbarino, J. Defining emotional maltreatment: The message is the meaning. *Journal of Psychiatric Treatment and Evaluation,* 1980b, *2,* 105–110.

Garbarino, J. Latchkey children: Getting the short end of the stick? *Vital Issues,* 1980c, *30*(3).

Garbarino, J. Some thoughts on school size and its effects on adolescent development. *Journal of Youth and Adolescence,* 1980d, *9,* 19–31.

Garbarino, J. The child as an organism: Implications for family structure. Paper presented to the International Symposium on "The Child and the City." International Pediatric Society and the Japanese National Institute for Research Advancement, Tokyo, Japan, March 26, 1981a.

Garbarino, J. *Successful schools and competent students.* Lexington, MA: Lexington Books, 1981b.

Garbarino, J. The issue is human quality: In praise of children. In J. Coomer (Ed.), *The quest for a sustainable society.* New York: Pergamon Press, 1981c.

Garbarino, J. Habitats for children: An ecological perspective. In J. F. Wohlwill & W. van Vliet (Eds.), *Habitats for children: The impact of density.* New York: Academic Press, in press.

Garbarino, J., & Bronfenbrenner, U. *Research on parent–child relations and social policy: Who needs whom?* Paper presented at the Symposium on Parent–Child Relations: Theoretical, Methodological and Practical Implications. University of Trier, Trier, West Germany, May, 1976a.

Garbarino, J., & Bronfenbrenner, U. The socialization of moral judgment and behavior in cross-cultural perspective. In T. Lickona (Ed.), *Moral development and behavior.* New York: Holt, Rinehart, & Winston, 1976b.

Garbarino, J., & Crouter, A. C. Defining the community context of parent–child relations. *Child Development,* 1978, *49,* 604–616.

Garbarino, J. & Ebata, A. Ethnic and cultural differences in child maltreatment. Paper presented at the conference on Research Issues in Prevention sponsored by the National Committee for the Prevention of Child Abuse and the Johnson Foundation, Wingspread, Racine, WI, June, 1981.

Garbarino, J., Gaboury, M. T., Long, F., Grandjean, P., & Asp, E. Who owns the children: An ecological perspective on public policy affecting children. *Child and Youth Services Review,* 1982, *5*(1/2), (Spring/Summer), 41–61.

Garbarino, J., & Garbarino, A. Where are the children in Utopia? Paper presented at the Second National Conference on International Communities, Omaha, NE, October 17, 1978.

Garbarino, J., & Gilliam, G. *Understanding abusive families.* Lexington, MA: Lexington Books, 1980.

Garbarino, J., and Jacobson, N. Youth-helping-youth as a resource in meeting the problem of child maltreatment, *Child Welfare,* 1978, *57,* 505–512.

Garbarino, J., & Plantz, M. C. *Urban environments and urban children.* ERIC/CUE Urban

Diversity Series, #69. New York: ERIC Clearinghouse on Urban Education, 1980.

Garbarino, J., & Sherman, D. High-risk neighborhoods and high-risk families: The human ecology of child maltreatment. *Child Development,* 1980, *51,* 188–198.

Garbarino, J., Stocking, S. H., & Associates. *Protecting children from abuse and neglect: Developing and maintaining effective support systems for families.* San Francisco: Jossey-Bass Publishers, 1980.

Gardner, H. *Developmental psychology: An introduction.* Boston: Little, Brown, 1978.

Gartner, A., Kohler, M., and Riessman, F. *Children Teach Children,* New York: Harper and Row, 1971.

Gearing, J. Facilitating the birth process and father–child bonding. *The Counseling Psychologist,* 1978, 7(4), 53–56.

Germain, C. Space: An ecological variable in social work practice. *Social Casework,* 1978, *59,* 515–522.

Getzels, J. W. Socialization and education: A note on discontinuities. *Teacher's College Record,* 1974, 76, 218–225.

Giarini, O. *Dialogue on wealth and welfare.* New York: Pergamon Press, 1980.

Gil, D. *Violence against children: Physical child abuse in the United States.* Cambridge, MA: Harvard University Press, 1970.

Gilligan, C. *In a different voice.* Cambridge, MA: Harvard University Press, 1982.

Ginsberg, H. & Opper, S. *Piaget's theory of intellectual development.* Englewood Cliffs, NJ: Prentice-Hall, 1969.

Glick, P. *The future of the American family.* Washington, DC: U.S. Government Printing Office, 1979.

Gold, M. *Status forces in delinquent boys.* Ann Arbor, MI: University of Michigan, 1963.

Goldberg, S. Social competence in infancy: A model of parent–infant interaction. *Merrill–Palmer Quarterly,* 1977, *23,* 164–177.

Goldberg, S. Premature birth: Consequences for the parent–infant relationships. *American Scientist,* 1979, *67,* 214–219.

Goldstein, J., Freud, A., & Solnit, A. J. *Beyond the best interests of the child.* New York: The Free Press, 1973.

Goldstein, J., Freud, A., & Solnit, A. J. *Before the best interests of the child.* New York: The Free Press, 1979.

Gottlieb, B. The role of individual and social support in preventing child maltreatment. In J. Garbarino, S. H. Stocking, & Associates, *Protecting children from abuse and neglect.* San Francisco: Jossey-Bass, 1980.

Gray, J., Cutler, C., Dean, J., & Kempe, C. H. Prediction and prevention of child abuse and neglect. *Child Abuse and Neglect,* 1977, *1,* 45–58.

Greenberg, M., & Morris, N. Engrossment: The newborn's impact upon the father. *American Journal of Orthopsychiatry,* 1974, *44,* 520–531.

Greenberg, M., Rosenberg, I., & Lind, J. First mothers rooming-in with their newborns: Its impact upon the mother. *American Journal of Orthopsychiatry,* 1973, *43*(5), 783–789.

Greer, C. *The great school legend.* New York: Viking Press, 1972.

Grobstein, R. Innovations in the premature nursery: A survey of parental visiting and related practices. Presentation to a round table on Maternal Attachment and Mothering Disorders, Sausalito, CA, October, 1974.

Grossman, F. K., Winickoff, S. A., & Eichler, L. S. Psychological sequelae of caesarean delivery. Paper presented at the International Conference on Infant Studies, New Haven, CT, April, 1980.

Gruber, A. R. *Children in foster care: Destitute, neglected, betrayed.* New York: Human Services Press, 1978.

Gump, P., & Adelberg, B. Urbanism from the perspective of ecological psychologists. *Environment and Behavior,* 1978, *10,* 171–191.

Gurry, D. L. Child abuse: Thoughts on doctors, nurses and prevention. *Child Abuse and Neglect,* 1977, *1,* 435–443.

Haapala, D., & Kinney, J. Homebuilders' approach to the training of in-home therapists. In S. Maybanks & M. Bryce (Eds.), *Home-based services for children and families: Policy, practice, and research.* Springfield, IL: C. C. Thomas, 1979.

Hagestad, G. O. Problems and promises in the social psychology of intergenerational relations. In R. Fogel, E. Hatfield, S. Kiesler, & J. March (Eds.), *Stability and change in the family.* New York: Academic Press, 1981b.

Hagestad, G. O. Personal communication, 1981a.

Haire, D. The cultural warping of childbirth. *Environmental Child Health,* 1973, *19,* 171–191.

Hales, D. J., Lozoff, B., Sosa, R., & Kennell, J. H. Defining the limits of the maternal sensitive period. *Developmental Medicine and Child Neurology,* 1977, *19,* 454–461.

Harris, L. Importance and satisfaction with factors in life. *The Harris Survey,* November 23, 1978.

Hartup, W. W. Perspectives on child and family interaction: Past, present, and future. In R. M. Lerner & G. B. Spanier (Eds.), *Child influences on marital and family interaction.* New York: Academic Press, 1978.

Harvey, M. Home births. *Boston Sunday Globe* (New England magazine), October 16, 1977, 10–60.

Havighurst, R. J. *Growing up in River City.* New York: John Wiley & Sons, 1962.

Hawley, A. *Human ecology: A theory of community structure.* New York: Ronald Press, 1950.

Helfer, R. E. Developmental deficits which limit interpersonal skill. In C. H. Kempe & R. E. Helfer (Eds.), *The battered child.* Chicago: University of Chicago Press, 1980.

Heller, P. L., & Quesada, G. Rural familism: An interregional analysis. *Rural Sociology,* 1977, *42,* 220–240.

Hempel, C. G. *Philosophy of natural science.* Englewood Cliffs, NJ: Prentice-Hall, 1966.

Hennepin County. *Family study project.* Unpublished program materials. Minneapolis, MN, 1979.

Henry, J. *Pathways to madness.* New York: Random House, 1973.

Hermes, P. H. WD medical update: Crib death. *Woman's Day,* February 10, 1981, 14–16.

Hersh, S., & Levin, K. How love begins between parent and child. *Children Today,* 1978, *1*(2), 2–6, 47.

Hetherington, E. M., Cox, M., & Cox, R. The aftermath of divorce. In J. H. Stevens, Jr. & M. Matthews (Eds.), *Mother-child father-child relationships.* Washington, DC: National Association for the Education of Young Children, 1978.

Hetherington, E. M., & Parke, R. D. *Child psychology: A contemporary viewpoint* (2nd ed.). New York: McGraw-Hill, 1979.

Hillery, G. A., Jr. Definitions of community: Areas of agreement. *Rural Sociology*, 1955, 20, 111–123.

House, J. S. *Work stress and social support*. Reading, MA: Addison-Wesley, 1981.

Howard, J. *Families*. New York: Simon & Schuster, 1978.

Howells, J. G. Childbirth is a family experience. In J. G. Howells (Ed.), *Modern perspectives in psycho-obstetrics*. New York: Brunner/Mazel, 1972.

Huessy, H. R. Tactics and targets in the rural setting. In S. E. Golann & C. Eisdorfer (Eds.), *Handbook of community of mental health*. New York: Appleton-Century-Crofts, 1972.

Hughey, M., McElin, T., Young, F., & Young, T. Maternal and fetal outcomes of Lamaze-prepared patients. *Obstetrics and Gynecology*, 1978, 51, 643–647.

Hutt, C. Sex differences in human development. *Human Development*, 1972, 15, 153–170.

Iber, F. L. Fetal alcohol syndrome. *Nutrition Today*, September/October, 1980, 4–11.

Jacobs, J. *The death and life of great American cities*. New York: Random House, 1961.

Janson, C. G. Factorial social ecology: An attempt at summary and evaluation. *Annual Review of Sociology*, 1980, 6, 433–456.

Jencks, C. *Inequality: A reassessment of the effect of family and schooling in America*. New York: Basic Books, 1972.

Johnson, S. Interim report of the family impact seminar. Washington, DC: George Washington University, 1978.

Jones, M. C. Psychological correlates of somatic development. *Child Development*, 1965, 36, 899–911.

Kadushin, A. Child welfare strategy in the coming years: An overview. In *Child welfare strategy in the coming years*. USDHEW 78-30158, 1978.

Kadushin, A. *Child welfare services*. New York: Macmillan, 1980.

Kadushin, A., & Martin, J. A. *Child abuse: An interactional event*. New York: Columbia University Press, 1981.

Kahn, A. Service delivery at the neighborhood level: Experience, theory, and fads. *Social Service Review*, 1976, 50, 23–56.

Kahn, A., & Kamerman, S. *Not for the poor alone: European social services*. Philadelphia: Temple University Press, 1975.

Kamerman, S. B. Eight countries: Cross-national perspectives on child abuse and neglect. *Children Today*, 1975, 4(3), 34–37.

Kamerman, S. B., & Kahn, A. J. *Social services in the United States: Policies and programs*. Philadelphia: Temple University Press, 1976.

Kanter, R. M. *Work and family in the United States: A critical review and agenda for research and policy*. New York: Russell Sage Foundation, 1977.

Kantor, D., & Lehr, W. *Inside the family*. San Francisco: Jossey-Bass, 1975.

Katz, S. *When parents fail: The law's response to family breakdown*. Boston: Beacon Press, 1971.

Kaye, E. *The family guide to children's television*. New York: Pantheon Books, 1974.

Keller, S. *The urban neighborhood: A sociological perspective*. New York: Random House, 1968.

Keller, S. Does the family have a future? *Journal of Comparative Family Studies*, 1971, 2, 1–14.

Kelly, J. The last days of Poletown. *Time*, 1981, 117, 29.

Kempe, R. S., & Kempe, C. H. *Child abuse*. Cambridge, MA: Harvard University Press, 1978.

Keniston, K. Youth: A new stage of life. In T. J. Cottle, *The Prospect of Youth*, Boston: Little, Brown, 1972.

Keniston, K. *All our children: The American family under pressure*. New York: Harcourt Brace Jovanovich, 1977.

Kenkel, W. F. *The family in perspective*. New York: Appleton-Century-Crofts, 1960.

Kennell, J., Voos, D., & Klaus, M. Parent–infant bonding. In R. Helfer & C. H. Kempe (Eds.), *Child abuse and neglect: The family and the community*. Cambridge, MA: Ballinger, 1976.

Kennell, J. H., Jerauld, R., Wolfe, H., Chesler, D., Kreger, N. C., McAlpine, W., Steffa, M., & Klaus, M. H. Maternal behavior one year after early and extended post-partum contact. *Developmental Medicine and Child Neurology*, 1974, *16*, 172–179.

Kessen, W. (Ed.) *Childhood in China*. New Haven, CT: Yale University Press, 1975.

Kessner, D. M., Singer, J., Kalk, C. E., & Schlesinger, E. R. *Infant death: An analysis by maternal risk and health care*. Washington: Institute of Medicine, 1973.

Klaus, M., Jerauld, K., Kreger, N., McAlpine, W., Steffa, M., & Kennell, Jr. Maternal attachment—importance of the first postpartum days. *New England Journal of Medicine*, 1972, *286*, 460–463.

Klaus, M., & Kennell, J. *Maternal–infant bonding*. Saint Louis, MO: C. V. Mosby, 1976.

Knitzer, J. Advocacy and community psychology. In M. S. Gibbs, J. R. Lachenmeyer & J. Sigal (Eds.), *Community psychology: Theoretical and empirical approaches*. New York: Garner Press, 1980.

Kogan, L., Smith, J., & Jenkins, S. Ecological validity of indicator data as predictors of survey findings. *Journal of Social Service Research*, 1977, *1*, 117–132.

Kohn, M. L. *Class and conformity: A study in values* (2nd ed.). Chicago: University of Chicago Press, 1977.

Konner, M. J. Relations among infants and juveniles in comparative perspective. In M. Lewis & L. Rosenblum (Eds.), *Friendship and peer relations*. New York: Wiley, 1976.

Konopka, G. *The adolescent girl in conflict*. Englewood Cliffs, NJ: Prentice-Hall, 1966.

Kopp, C., & Krakow, J. (Eds.) *The child: Development in social context*. Boston: Addison-Wesley, 1982.

Kopp, C. B. & Parmelee, A. H. Prenatal and perinatal influences on infant behavior. In J. D. Osofsky (Ed.), *Handbook of Infancy*. New York: John Wiley & Sons, 1979.

Korbin, J. Changing family roles and structures: Impact on child abuse and neglect?— A cross-cultural perspective. Paper presented at the Second Annual National Conference on Child Abuse and Neglect, Houston, April, 1977.

Korbin, J. *Very few cases: Child abuse in the People's Republic of China*. In J. Korbin (Ed.), *Cross cultural perspectives on child abuse*. Berkeley, CA: University of California Press, 1982.

Kowinski, W. Suburbia: End of the golden age. *New York Times Magazine*. March 16, 1980, 16ff.

Kromkowski, J. *Neighborhood deterioration and juvenile crime*. (U.S. Department of Commerce,

National Technical Information Service, PB-260 473), The South Bend Urban Observatory, Indiana, August, 1976.

Lamb, M. E. *The role of the father in child development.* New York: John Wiley & Sons, 1976.

Lamb, M. E. The role of the father: An overview. In M. E. Lamb (Ed.), *The role of the father in child development.* New York: John Wiley & Sons, 1977a.

Lamb, M. E. Father–infant and mother–infant interaction in the first year of life. *Child Development,* 1977b, *48,* 167–181.

Lamb, M. E. Infant social cognition and "second order" effects. *Infant Behavior and Development,* 1978, *1*(1), 1–10.

Lander, B. *Towards an understanding of juvenile delinquency: A study of 8,464 cases of juvenile delinquency in Baltimore.* New York: Columbia University Press, 1954.

Lang, R. *The birth book.* Felton, CA: New Genesis Press, 1972.

Lasch, C. *The culture of narcissism: American life in an age of diminishing expectations.* New York: Norton, 1978.

Leboyer, F. *Birth without violence.* New York: Alfred A. Knopf, 1975.

LeFrancois, G. R. *Of children* (3rd ed.). Belmont, CA: Wadsworth Publishing Company, 1980.

Leidermann, P. H., & Seashore, M. J. *Mother–infant neonatal separation: Some delayed consequences.* Ciba Foundation Symposium 33, Parent–Infant Interaction, Amsterdam, ASP, 1975, 213–239.

Lerner, R., & Spanier, G. B. (Eds.) *Child influences on marital and family interaction.* New York: Academic Press, 1978.

Levine, J. *Day care and the public schools.* Newton, MA: Education Development Center, 1976.

Levine, M., & Levine, A. *A social history of helping services: Clinic, court, school and community.* New York: Appleton-Century-Crofts, 1970.

Levy, J. M., & McGee, R. K. Childbirth as crisis: A test of Janis' theory of communication and stress resolution. *Journal of Personality and Social Psychology,* 1975, *31*(1), 171–179.

Lewis, J. M., Beavers, W. R., Gossett, J. T., & Phillips, V. A. *No single thread: Psychological health in family systems.* New York: Brunner/Mazel, 1976.

Lewis, M., & Weinraub, M. The father's role in the child's social network. In M. E. Lamb (Ed.), *The role of the father in child development.* New York: John Wiley & Sons, 1976.

Lieber, L., & Baker, J. Parents anonymous and self-help treatment for child abusing parents: A review and an evaluation. *Child Abuse and Neglect,* 1977, *1,* 133–148.

Lieberman, E. J. Reserving a womb: Case for the small family. *American Journal of Public Health,* 1970, *60,* 87–92.

Liebert, R. M., Neal, J. M., & Davidson, E. S. *The early window: Effects of TV on children and youth.* New York: Pergamon Press, 1973.

Light, I. N. *Ethnic enterprise in America: Business and welfare among Chinese, Japanese and Blacks.* Berkeley, CA: University of California Press, 1972.

Livingston, J. C., & Thompson, R. G. *The consent of the governed.* New York: Macmillan, 1971.

Lynn, D. *The father: His role in child development.* Monterey, CA: Brooks/Cole, 1974.

Lynn, L. *The state and human services: Organizational change in a political context.* Cambridge, MA: M.I.T. Press, 1980.

Maccoby, E. (Ed.) *The development of sex differences.* Stanford, CA: Stanford University Press, 1966.

Maccoby, E., & Jacklin, C. *The psychology of sex differences.* Stanford, CA: Stanford University Press, 1974.

Maccoby, E. & Jacklin, C. Sex differences in agression: a rejoinder and reprise. *Child Development,* 1980, *51,* 964–980.

Maccoby, E., Johnson, J. P., & Church, R. M. Community integration and the social control of juvenile delinquency. *Journal of Social Issues,* 1958, *14,* 38–51.

Macfarlane, A. *The psychology of childbirth.* Cambridge, MA: Harvard University Press, 1977.

MacIntyre, S. The management of childbirth: A review of sociological research issues. *Social Science and Medicine,* 1977, *11,* 477–484.

Makarenko, A. S. *A book for parents.* Moscow, USSR: Foreign Languages Publishing House, 1954 (American edition).

Makarenko, A. S. *The collective family.* New York: Doubleday, 1967.

Matas, L., Arend, R. A., & Sroufe, L. A. Continuity of adaptation in the second year: The relationship between quality of attachment and later competence. *Child Development,* 1978, *49,* 547–556.

Maybanks, S., & Bryce, M. *Home-based services to children and families: Policy, practice, research.* Springfield, IL: C. C. Thomas Publishers, 1979.

McBroom, P. Partners in the dance of life. *Today:* (the Inquirer Magazine). *Philadelphia Inquirer,* January 18, 1981, 12–22.

McCall, R. B., & Stocking, S. H. *A summary of research about the effects of divorce on families.* Boys Town, Nebraska: The Boys Town Center for the Study of Youth Development, Spring, 1980.

McClelland, D. C. Testing for competence rather than for "intelligence." *American Psychologist,* 1973, *28,* 1–14.

McClelland, D. C. *Power: The inner experience.* New York: Irvington Publishing Company, 1975.

Mead, G. H. *Mind, self and society.* Chicago: University of Chicago Press, 1934.

Mead, M. *Sex and temperament in three savage tribes.* New York: William Morrow, 1935.

Mead, M. *Cultural patterns and technical change.* New York: New American Library, 1955.

Mead, M. *Sex and temperament in three primitive societies* (3d ed.). New York: William Morrow, 1963.

Mead, M. Neighbourhoods and human needs. *Ekistics,* 1966, *21,* 124–126.

Mead, M. Marriage in two step. In E. Douvan and Associates, *American families.* Dubuque, IA: Kendall/Hunt Publishers, 1980.

Mead, M., & Heyman, K. *Family.* New York: Macmillan, 1965.

Michelson, W., & Roberts, E. Children and the urban physical environment. In W. Michelson, S. Levine, & A. Spina (Eds.), *The child in the city.* Toronto: University of Toronto Press, 1979.

Mills, C. W. *The sociological imagination.* New York: Oxford University Press, 1975.

Mitchell, R. Some social implications of high density housing. *American Sociological Review,* 1971, *36,* 18–29.

Money, J., & Ehrhardt, A. *Man and woman, boy and girl.* Baltimore: Johns Hopkins University Press, 1972.

Montague, A. *The elephant man: A study in human dignity*. New York: E. P. Dutton, 1979.

Moroney, R. *The family and the state: Considerations for social policy*. New York: Longmans, 1976.

Moroney, R. *Families, social services, and social policy: The issue of shared responsibility*. Washington, D.C.: Government Printing Office, DHHS Publication No. ADM 80-846, 1980.

Morris, D. *The human zoo*. New York: Dell, 1970.

Morris, D. *The naked ape*, New York: Dell, 1972.

Morrow, L. Wondering if children are really necessary. *Time*, March 5, 1979, p. 42ff.

Munroe, R. L., & Munroe, R. H. *Cross-cultural human development*. Monterey, CA: Brooks/Cole Publishing Company, 1975.

Mussen, P., Conger, J., & Kagan, J. *Child development and personality*. New York: Harper & Row, 1974.

Myrdal, A. *Nation and family: The Swedish experiment in democratic family and population policy*. Cambridge, MA: M.I.T. Press, 1968.

National Academy of Sciences. *Toward a national policy for child and families*. Washington, DC: U.S. Government Printing Office, 1976.

National Association of Attorneys General. *Legal issues in foster care*. Raleigh, NC: Committee on the Office of Attorneys General, 1976.

National Commission on Neighborhoods. *Final report of the commission*. Washington, DC: U.S. Government Printing Office, 1979.

New York City Agency keeps families together. *Children's Defense Fund Reports*, 1980, 2(6), 6–7.

Newman, D. and Associates. Cross-cultural psychology's challenges to our ideas of children and development. *American Psychologist*, 1979, 34, 827–833.

Newman, W. M. *American pluralism*. New York: Harper & Row, 1973.

Newson, J., & Newson, E. *Seven years old in the urban environment*. London: Allen & Unwin, 1972.

Newton, N. Cross-cultural perspectives. In A. L. Clark & D. D. Affonso (Eds.), *Childbearing: A nursing perspective* (2nd ed.). Philadelphia: F. A. Davis Co., 1979.

Niebuhr, R. *The children of light and the children of darkness*. New York: Charles Scribner's Sons, 1960.

Norwood, C. *At highest risk: Environmental hazards to young and unborn children*. New York: McGraw-Hill Book Company, 1980.

Nuttal, R. Coping with catastrophe: Family adjustments to natural disasters Paper presented at Groves Conference on Marriage and the Family, Gatlinburg, TN, May 31, 1980.

Oakley, A. A case of maternity: Paradigms of women as maternity cases. *Signs: Journal of Women in Culture and Society*, 1979, 4, 607–631.

O'Connor, S., Vietze, P., Hopkins, J., & Altemeir, W. Postpartum extended maternal–infant contact: Subsequent mothering and child health. *Sociological Pediatric Research*, 1977 (Abstract).

Offer, D. *The psychological world of the teenager*. New York: Basic Books, 1969.

Ogburn, W. F. *Social change*. New York: B. W. Huebsch, 1922.

O'Hara, R. The roots of career. *Elementary Journal*, 1962, 62, 277–280.

Olds, D. Improving formal services for mothers and children. In J. Garbarino, S. H.

Stocking, & Associates, *Protecting children from abuse and neglect.* San Francisco: Jossey-Bass, 1980.

Olds, D. Selected prenatal outcomes in the pilot study of the Prenatal-Early Infancy Project. Papers presented at the annual meeting of the American Public Health Association, Detroit, October, 1980.

Olds, D., Tatelbaum, R., Chamberlin, S., & Roberts, S. *The prenatal-early infancy project.* Elmira, NY: Comprehensive Interdisciplinary Developmental Services, 1980.

Ooms, T. Teenage pregnancy and family impact: New perspectives on policy. Preliminary Report. Family Impact Seminar, The George Washington University, Institute for Educational Leadership, June, 1979.

Otto, S. E. ICEA: The challenges of childbirth education . . . yesterday, now and tomorrow. *Mother's Manual,* January–February, 1978, 36–38.

Pancoast, D. L. Finding and enlisting neighbors to support families. In J. Garbarino, S. H. Stocking & Associates, *Protecting children from abuse and neglect: Developing and maintaining effective support systems for families.* San Francisco: Jossey-Bass, 1980.

Parke, R. Father-infant interaction. In M. H. Klaus, T. Leger, & M. A. Trause (Eds.), *Maternal attachment and morthering disorders: A round table.* 1974.

Parke, R. D. Perspectives on father–infant interaction. In J. D. Osofsky (Ed.), *Handbook of infant development.* New York: John Wiley, 1979.

Parke, R., & Collmer, C. W. Child abuse: An interdisciplinary analysis. In E. M. Hetherington (Ed.), *Review of child development research* (Vol. 5). Chicago: University of Chicago Press, 1975.

Parke, R. D., & O'Leary, S. E. Father–mother–infant interaction in the newborn period: Some findings, some observations and some unresolved issues. In K. Riegel & J. Meacham (Eds.), *The developing individual in a changing world.* (Vol. 2). *Social and environmental issues.* The Hague: Mouton, 1975.

Parke, R. D., & Sawin, D. B. The father's role in infancy: A reevaluation. *The Family Coordinator,* 1976, *25,* 365–371.

Parsons, T. The kinship system of the contemporary United States. In T. Parsons, *Essays in Sociological Theory.* New York: The Free Press, 1949.

Parsons, T., & Bales, R. *Family, socialization and interaction process.* New York: The Free Press, 1955.

Parsons, T., Bales, R., & Shils, E. *Working papers in the theory of action.* Glencoe, IL: Free Press, 1955.

Patterson, G. R. A performance theory for coercive family interaction. In R. B. Cairns (Ed.), *The analysis of social interactions: Methods, issues, and illustrations.* Hillsdale, NJ: Lawrence Erlbaum Associates, 1979.

Peccei, A. *The human quality,* Oxford, England: Pergamon Press, 1977.

Pedersen, F. A., & Robson, K. S. Father participation in infancy. *American Journal of Orthopsychiatry,* 1969, 466–472.

Pedersen, F., Zaslow, M., Cain, R., & Anderson, B. Cesarean childbirth: The importance of a family perspective. Paper presented at the International Conference on Infant Studies, New Haven, CT, April, 1980.

Peters, D. L. Social science and social policy and the care of young children. *Journal of Applied Developmental Psychology,* 1980, *1,* 7–27.

Peters, D. L., & Benn, J. L. Day care: Support for the family. *Dimensions,* 1980, *9,* 78–82.

Peterson, G. H., Mehl, L. E., & Leiderman, P. H. The role of some birth-related variables in father attachment. *American Journal of Orthopsychiatry*, 1979, *49*, 330–337.

Photiadis, J. D. Rural southern Appalachia and mass society. In J. D. Photiadis & H. K. Schwarzweller (Eds.), *Change in rural Appalachia: Implications for action programs*. Philadelphia: University of Pennsylvania Press, 1970.

Piaget, J. [*The origins of intelligence in children.*] Trans. M. Cook, New York: International Universities Press, 1952.

Piaget, J. *Six psychological studies*. New York: Vintage Books, 1967.

Polansky, N. Analysis of research on child neglect: The social work viewpoint. In Herner and Company (Eds.), *Four perspectives on the status of child abuse and neglect research*. Washington, D.C.: National Center on Child Abuse and Neglect, 1976.

Proceedings of the Conference on the Care of Dependent Children, Washington, D.C., January 25–26, 1909, pp. 17–18.

Ramsey, P. G. Ownership behaviors in young childrens' social interactions. Paper presented at the annual meeting of the American Psychological Association (Division 7), Montreal, September, 1980.

Rappaport, J. *Community psychology: Values, research, action*. New York: Holt, Rinehart & Winston, 1977.

Rebelsky, F., & Hanks, C. Fathers' verbal interaction with infants in the first three months of life. *Child Development*, 1971, *24*, 63–68.

Reiger, N. I. Changing concepts in treating children in a state mental hospital. *International Journal of Child Psychotherapy*, 1972, *1*(4), 89–114.

Rein, M. *Social science and public policy*. Middlesex, England: Penguin Books Ltd., 1976.

Reiss, I. *Family systems in America* (3d ed.). New York: Holt, Rinehart & Winston, 1980.

Ricciuti, H. Fear and development of social attachments in the first years of life. In N. Lewis & L. A. Rosenblum (Eds.), *The origins of human behavior: Fear*. New York: John Wiley & Sons, 1974.

Ricciuti, H. Effects of infant day care experience on behavior and development: Research and implications for social policy. In *Policy issues in day care: Summaries of 21 papers*. Washington, D.C.: Office of the Secretary for Planning and Evaluation, 1977.

Richardson, R. Using family age grading to predict parental behavior in abusive, neglectful, and normal families. Unpublished master's thesis, The Pennsylvania State University, 1981.

Robinson, N. M., Robinson, H. B., Darling, M. A., & Holm, G. *A world of children: Daycare and preschool institutions*. Monterey, CA: Brooks/Cole Publishing Co., 1979.

Rock, M. Gorilla mothers need some help from their friends. *Smithsonian*, 1978, *9*(4), 58–63.

Rockwell, R. Personal communication, 1978.

Rodes, T., & Moore, J. *National child care consumer study: American consumer attitudes and opinions on child care*. Arlington, VA: Kappa Systems, Inc., 1975.

Rogers, E. M., & Shoemaker, F. F. *Communication of innovations: A cross-cultural approach*. New York: The Free Press, 1971.

Rohner, R. *They love me, they love me not*. New Haven, CT: Human Relations Area Files Press, 1975.

Rohner, R., & Nielsen, C. *Parental acceptance and rejection: A review of research and theory.* New Haven, CT: Human Relations Area Files Press, 1978.

Rollins, B., & Cannon, K. Marital satisfaction over the family life cycle: A reevaluation. *Journal of Marriage and the Family* 1974, *36,* 271–282.

Rollins, B., & Feldman, H. Marital satisfaction over the family life cycle. *Journal of Marriage and the Family,* 1970, *32,* 20–28.

Rosen, M. G. (chairman) Cesarean childbirth. *National Institute of Health Consensus Development Conference Summary,* 1980, *3*(6).

Rosenberg, B., & Sutton-Smith, B. *Sex and identity.* New York: Holt, Rinehart & Winston, 1972.

Rosenberg, M. S., & Reppucci, D. Child Abuse: A Review With Special Focus on an Ecological Approach in Rural Communities. In T. Melton (Ed.), *Rural Psychology,* in press.

Rosenfeld, A. A., & Newberger, E. H. Compassion vs. control: Conceptual and practical pitfalls in the broadened definition of child abuse. *Journal of the American Medical Association,* 1977, *237,* 2086–2088.

Rossi, A. Transition to parenthood. *Journal of Marriage and the Family,* 1968, 26–39.

Rotenberg, M. Alienating-individualism and reciprocal-individualism: A cross-cultural conceptualization. *Journal of Humanistic Psychology,* 1977, *17,* 3–17.

Rutter, M. Maternal deprivation, 1972–1978: New findings, new concepts, new approaches. *Child Development,* 1979, *50,* 283–305.

Ryan, W. *Blaming the victim.* New York: Vintage Press, 1976.

Sagan, C. *The dragons of Eden: Speculations of the evolution of human intelligence.* New York: Random House, 1977.

Sale, K. *Human scale.* New York: Coward, McCann, & Geoghegan, 1980.

Sameroff, A. J., & Chandler, M. J. Reproductive risk and the continuum of care-taking casualty. In F. Horowitz, M. Hetherington, S. Scarr-Salapatek & G. Siegel (Eds.), *Review of Child Development Research,* Vol. 4. Chicago: University of Chicago Press, 1975.

Sanger, M. *Margaret Sanger: An autobiography.* New York: W. W. Norton, Co., 1938.

Sarason, S. B., Carroll, C., Maton, K., Cohen, S., & Lorentz, E. *Human services and resource networks.* San Francisco: Jossey-Bass, 1977.

Satir, V. *Peoplemaking.* Palo Alto, CA: Science & Behavior Books, 1972.

Sattin, D., & Miller, J. The ecology of child abuse. *American Journal of Orthopsychiatry,* 1971, *41,* 675–678.

Sawin, D. B., & Parke, R. D. Fathers' affectionate stimulation and caregiving behaviors with newborn infants. *The Family Coordinator,* 1979, *28*(4), 509–513.

Schoggen, P., & Schoggen, M. Exploratory behavior and density. In J. F. Wohlwill & W. van Vliet (Eds.), *Habitats for children: The impact of density.* New York: Academic Press, in press.

Schorr, A. The child and the community. In W. Michelson, S. Levine, & E. Michelson (Eds.), *The child in the city.* Toronto: University of Toronto Press, 1979.

Schumacher, E. F. *Small is beautiful: Economics as if people mattered.* New York: Harper & Row, 1973.

Schwarzweller, H. K. Social change and the individual in rural Appalachia. In J. D. Photiadis & H. K. Schwarzweller (Eds.), *Change in rural Appalachia: Implications for action programs.* Philadelphia: University of Pennsylvania Press, 1970.

Seashore, M. J. Mother–infant separation: Outcome assessment. In V. L. Smeriglio (Ed.),

*Newborns and parents: Parent–infant contact and newborn sensory stimulation.* Hillsdale, NJ: Lawrence Erlbaum Associates, 1981.

Segal, J., & Yahraes, H. *A child's journey.* New York: McGraw-Hill, 1978.

Shapiro, W. The cost of cutting food stamps. *The Washington Post Magazine,* March 29, 1981.

Shaw, C. R., & McKay, H. D. *Juvenile delinquency and urban areas.* Chicago: University of Chicago Press, 1942.

Shaw, C. R., Zorbaugh, F. M., McKay, H. D., & Cottrell, L. S., Jr. *Delinquency areas.* Chicago: University of Chicago Press, 1929.

Shelton, L. G., & Gladstone, T. Childbearing in adolescence. Paper presented at the American Orthopsychiatric Association, Washington, DC, April, 1979.

Sherif, M. Superordinate Goals in the Reduction of Intergroup Conflict. *American Journal of Sociology,* 1958, *63,* 349–356.

Sherif, M., & Sherif, C. *Reference groups.* New York: Harper & Row, 1964.

Shevky, E., & Bell, W. *Social area analysis.* Stanford: Stanford University Press, 1955.

Shirer, W. L. *The rise and fall of the third reich: A history of Nazi Germany.* New York: Simon & Schuster, 1960.

Short, J. F., Jr. Juvenile delinquency: The sociocultural context. In L. W. Hoffman and M. L. Hoffman (Eds.), *Review of child development research,* Vol. 2. New York: Russell Sage Foundation, 1966.

Sibbison, V. The influence of maternal role perception of attitudes toward and utilization of early child care services. The Pennsylvania State University: Center for Human Services Development, PDCSP Tech. Report 10, 1972.

Silverman, P. R. The widow as a caregiver in a program of preventive intervention with other widows. In G. Caplan & M. Killilea (Eds.), *Support systems and mutual help.* New York: Grune & Stratton, 1976.

Sinclair, Sir J. A statistical account of Scotland 1798. See Campbell, Subjective areas of well-being. *American Psychologist,* 1976, *31,* 117–124.

Slater, P. E. Toward a dualistic theory of identification. *Merrill-Palmer Quarterly,* 1961, 7 pp. 113–126.

Slater, P. E. *The pursuit of loneliness: American culture at the breaking point.* Boston: Beacon Press, 1970.

Smith, C. J. Residential neighborhoods as humane environments. *Environment and Planning,* 1976, *8,* 311–326.

Smith, E. Issues in child custody. In J. S. Mearing & Associates, *Working for children: Ethical issues beyond professional guidelines.* San Francisco: Jossey-Bass, 1978.

Snyder, D. J. The high-risk mother viewed in relation to a holistic model of the childbearing experience. *Journal of Obstetrical and Gynecological Nursing,* May–June, 1979, 164–170.

Solnit, A. J., & Provence, S. Vulnerability and risk in early childhood. In J. D. Osofsky (Ed.), *Handbook of infant development.* New York: John Wiley & Sons, 1979.

Spanier, G. B. The family: Alive but not well. *Wilson Quarterly.* Washington: Smithsonian Institute, 1980.

Spanier, G. B., & Anderson, E. A. The impact of the legal system on adjustment to marital separation. *Journal of Marriage and the Family,* 1979, *41,* 605–613.

Spanier, G. B., Lewis, R. A., & Cole, C. L. Marital adjustment over the family life cycle: The issue of curvilinearity. *Journal of Marriage and the Family,* 1975, *37.*

Spitz, R. A. Hospitalism: An inquiry into the genesis of psychiatric conditions in early childhood. In A. Freud, et al. (Eds.), *The psychoanalytic study of the child* (Vol. 1). New York: International Universities Press, 1945.

Sroufe, L. A. Attachment and the roots of competence. *Human Nature,* October, 1978.

Staats, M., & Staats, S. Looking up: A child's view of the adult world. *Quest,* 2(6), 1978.

Staulcup, H. J. Primary prevention in social welfare: Practice, education, and research. Unpublished manuscript, National Committee for Prevention of Child Abuse, 1980.

Steinberg, L., Catalano, R., & Dooley, D. Economic antecedents of child abuse and neglect. *Child Development,* 1981, *52,* 975–985.

Steinberg, L. D., & Hill, J. P. Patterns of family interaction as a function of age, the onset of puberty, and formal thinking. *Developmental Psychology,* 1978, *14,* 683–684.

Steinberg, L. D., & Hill, J. P. Family interaction patterns during early adolescence. In R. Muuss (Ed.), *Adolescent behavior and society: A book of readings* (3d ed.), 1980.

Steiner, G. Y., & Milius, P. H. *The children's cause.* Washington, DC: The Brookings Institution, 1976.

Stern, D. A micro-analysis of mother–infant interaction. *Journal of the American Academy of Child Psychiatry,* 1971, *10,* 501–517.

Stern, D. Mother and infant at play: The dyadic interaction involving facial, vocal, and gaze behaviors. In M. Lewis & L. Rosenblum (Eds.), *Origins of Behavior,* Vol. 1. New York: John Wiley & Sons, 1973.

Stinnett, N., Chesser, B., & DeFrain, J. *Building family strengths: Blueprints for action.* Lincoln, NE: University of Nebraska Press, 1979.

Straus, M., Gelles, R., & Steinmetz, S. *Behind closed doors.* New York: Doubleday, 1980.

Terkel, S. *Hard times.* New York: Parthenon, 1963.

Texas Department of Community Affairs. *46 things you need to know about Texas children: The darker side of childhood,* 1974.

Texas Department of Community Affairs. *78 things you need to know about Texas children: Still the darker side of childhood,* 1978.

Theodorson, G. A. *Studies in human ecology.* Evanston, IL: Harper and Row, 1961.

Thomas, W. I., & Thomas, D. S. *The child in America.* New York: Alfred P. Knopf, 1928.

Tietjen, A. Formal and informal support systems: A cross-cultural perspective. In J. Garbarino & S. H. Stocking & Associates, *Protecting children from abuse and neglect.* San Francisco: Jossey-Bass, 1980.

Toennies, F. *Community and society.* (Trans. Charles Loomis.) East Lansing, MI: Michigan State University Press, 1957.

Toffler, A. *Future shock.* New York: Bantam Books, 1970.

Tolstoy, L. *War and Peace.* London: John C. Winston Co., 1949, orig. 1865–1869.

Trivers, R. L. Parent–offspring conflict. *American Zoologist,* 1974, *14,* 249–264.

Tucker, M. J. The child as beginning and end: Fifteenth and sixteenth century English childhood. In L. de Mause, *The history of childhood.* New York: The Psychohistory Press, 1974.

Tulkin, S. R. An analysis of the concept of cultural deprivation. *Developmental Psychology,* 1972, *6,* 326–339.

Turner, F. J. *The frontier in American history.* New York: Holt, Rinehart & Winston, 1965 orig. 1897.

Udry, J. R. *The social context of marriage* (2nd ed.). Philadelphia: J. B. Lippincott, 1974.

Unco. *National child care consumer study.* Washington, DC: U.S. Department of Health, Education, and Welfare, 1975.

Unger, D. G., & Powell, D. R. Supporting families under stress: The role of social networks. *Family Relations,* 1980, *29,* 566–574.

U.S. Bureau of the Census. *Daytime care of children,* Current Population Reports, Population Characteristics Series P-20, No. 298. Washington, DC: U.S. Bureau of the Census, October, 1976.

U.S. Bureau of the Census. *Divorce, child custody and child support,* by R. Sanders & G. B. Spanier, Current Population Reports Series P-23, No. 84, 1979.

U.S. Bureau of the Census. *Current population reports: Population characteristics,* 1980a.

U.S. Bureau of the Census. *Current population reports: American family and living arrangements,* 1980b.

U.S. Bureau of the Census. *1980 census of population and housing,* Advance Reports, Florida (PHC80-V-11), Rhode Island (PHC80-V-41). Washington, DC: U.S. Bureau of the Census, 1981.

U.S. Bureau of Labor Statistics. *State, county, and selected city employment and unemployment: January–December, 1979.* Washington, DC: U.S. Bureau of Labor Statistics, April, 1980.

U.S. Department of Commerce, Bureau of the Census. *Population profile of the United States: 1978, population characteristics* (Current Population Reports, Series P-20, No. 336). Washington, DC: U.S. Government Printing Office, April 1979.

U.S. National Center for Health Statistics. *Vital statistics of the United States, 1977,* Vol. 2—Mortality, Part B. Hyattsville, MD: Public Health Service, 1980.

Urban, H., & Vondracek, F. Delivery of human intervention services: Past, present, and future. In S. R. Goldberg and F. Deutsch (Eds.), *Life-span individual and family development.* Monterey, CA: Brooks/Cole Publishing Co., Inc., 1977.

van den Berghe, P. *Human family systems: an evolutionary view.* New York: Elsevier, 1979.

Vandenburg, S. G., & Hakstian, A. R. Cultural influences on cognition: A reanalysis of Vernon's data. *International Journal of Psychology,* 1978, *13,* 251–279.

VanEs, J. C., & Brown, J. E. The rural–urban variable once more: Some individual level observations. *Rural Sociology,* 1974, *39,* 373–391.

van Vliet, W. The role of housing type, household density, and neighborhood density in peer interaction and social adjustment. In J. F. Wohlwill & W. van Vliet (Eds.), *Habitats for children: The impact of density.* New York: Academic Press, in press.

Vasaly, S. M. *Foster care in five states: A synthesis and analysis of studies from Arizona, California, Iowa, Massachusetts, and Vermont.* Washington, DC: Social Research Group, George Washington University, 1976.

Vygotsky, L. S. *Thought and language.* Cambridge, MA: MIT Press, 1962.

Wachs, T. D., Uzgiris, I. C., & Hunt, J. McV. Cognitive development in infants of different age levels and from different environmental backgrounds: An exploratory investigation. *Merrill-Palmer Quarterly,* 1971, *17,* 283–317.

Wagner, M. *Denmark's national family guidance program: A preventive mental health program for children and families.* Washington, DC: U.S. Government Printing Office, DHEW Publication No. ADM 77-512, 1978.

Wald, M. S. Thinking about public policy toward abuse and neglect of children: A review of *Before the best interests of the child. Michigan Law Review,* 1980, 78(5), 645–693.

Warren, D., & Warren, R. *The neighborhood organizer's handbook.* Notre Dame, IN: University of Notre Dame Press, 1977.

Warren, R. L. *The community in America* (2nd ed.). Chicago: Rand-McNally, 1973.

Warren, S. The relocation of Ozawkie, Kansas. Unpublished manuscript, University of Kansas, 1968.

Weatherly, D. Self-perceived rate of physical maturation and personality in late adolescence. *Child Development,* 1963, *35,* 1197–1210.

Weisner, T. S., & Gallimore, R. My brother's keeper: Child and sibling caretaking. *Current Anthropology,* 1977, *18,* 169–190.

Weissman, M., & Paykel, E. *The depressed woman.* Chicago: University of Chicago Press, 1974.

Wertz, R., & Wertz, D. *Lying in: A history of childbirth in America.* New York: The Free Press, 1977.

White, R. Motivation reconsidered: The concept of competence. *Psychological Review,* 1959, *66,* 297–333.

Williams, R. M. Why children should draw: The surprising link between art and learning. *Saturday Review,* September 3, 1977, 11–16.

Wiltse, K. T. Current issues and new directions in foster care. In *Child welfare strategy in the coming years.* Washington, DC: DHEW Publ. No. (OHDS) 78-30158, 1978.

Winch, R. *The modern family.* New York: Holt, Rinehart & Winston, 1965.

Wohlwill, J. F. Residential density as a variable in child-development research. In J. Wohlwill & W. van Vliet (Eds.), *Habitats for children: The impact of density.* New York: Academic Press, in press.

Wright, A. T. *Islandia.* New York: Holt, Rinehart & Winston, 1958; orig. 1942.

Wynne, E. Privacy and socialization to adulthood. Paper presented at the meeting of the American Educational Research Association, Washington, DC, March, 1975.

Wynne, E. Adolescent alienation and social policy. *Teachers College Record,* 1976, *78,* 33–39.

Wynne, E. A. *Growing up suburban.* Austin: University of Texas Press, 1977.

Yang, R. K. Maternal attitudes during pregnancy and medication during labor and delivery: Methodological considerations. In V. L. Smeriglio (Ed.), *Newborns and parents.* Hillsdale, NJ: Lawrence Erlbaum Associates, 1981.

Zajonc, R. B. & Markus, G. B. Birth order and intellectual development. *Psychological Review,* 1975, *82,* 74–78.

Zigler, E. The unmet needs of America's children. *Children Today,* 1976, May–June, 39–42.

Zimmerman, C. C. *Family and civilization.* New York: Harper & Row, 1947.

Zuspan, F. P., Quilligan, E. J., Iams, J. D., & Geijn, H. P. HICHD concensus development task force report: Predictions of intrapartum fetal distress—the role of electronic fetal monitoring. *The Journal of Pediatrics,* 1979, *95,* 1026–1030.

# Subject Index

# Author Index

## DATE DUE